OST

OST

Letters, Memoirs and Stories from Ostarbeiter in *Nazi Germany*

Memorial International

Alena Kozlova, Nikolai Mikhailov,
Irina Ostrovskaya and Irina Scherbakova

Translated from the Russian by Georgia Thomson

GRANTA

Granta Publications, 12 Addison Avenue, London, W11 4QR
First published in Great Britain by Granta Books 2021

Original Russian edition, *Знак не сотрется, судьбы остарбайтеров в письмах, воспоминаниях и устных рассказах*, first published in 2016 by Memorial International (Международный Мемориал) of Karetny Ryad 5/10, 127006, Moscow, Russia

Published by arrangement with ELKOST Intl. Literary Agency.

Unless otherwises stated, all images and captions provided by Memorial International (Международный Мемориал), Moscow. Captions translated by Georgia Thomson.

A CIP catalogue record for this book is available from the British Library

9 8 7 6 5 4 3 2 1

ISBN 978 1 78378 527 8
eISBN 978 1 78378 529 2

Typeset by Avon DataSet Ltd, Arden Court, Alcester, Warwickshire B49 6HN
Printed and bound in Italy by Legoprint

www.granta.com

Contents

Index of Place Names

The names of settlements and administrative divisions, and references to settlements belonging to particular administrative divisions, are as they were in 1941. Where mentioned, divisions into districts and regions refer to the delineations that existed in the RSFSR, Ukrainian Soviet Socialist Republic and Belarusian Soviet Socialist Republic.

Where semicolons appear in the list below, the translator has added current geographical information (accurate at the time of printing) after the semicolon to reflect some of the changes that have occurred since 1941.

A

Albertstadt, Germany
Altendorf, Austria
Altengrabow, Germany
Angermünde, Germany
Angerwiese, Germany; today Krasnoye Selo, Kaliningrad
Apolda, Germany
Arkhangelskoye village, Ordzhonikidze region, Soviet Union; today Russia
Arnswalde, Germany; today Choszczno, Poland
Artern, Germany
Augsburg, Germany

B

Bad Freienwalde, Germany
Bad Rappenau, Germany
Baranovichy, Brest region, Soviet Union; today Belarus
Barth, Germany
Berlin, Germany
Birkenhof, Germany
Bitterfeld, Germany
Bochum, Germay
Bogen, Germany
Bolkhov, Oryol region, Soviet Union; today Russia
Brandenburg, Germany
Braunau am Inn, Austria
Bremen, Germany
Breslau, Germany; today Wrocław, Poland
Brest region, Soviet Union; today Belarus
Bryansk, Soviet Union; today Russia
Bryansk region, Soviet Union; today Russia
Buiskoye, Poltava region, Soviet Union; today Ukraine
Bürstadt, Germany
Büttelborn, Germany

C

Chemnitz, Germany
Cherkessk, Cherkessk Autonomous Region, Soviet Union; today Russia
Chernigov region, Soviet Union; today Ukraine

Cloppenburg, Germany
Cologne, Germany
Cuxhaven, Germany

D

Danzig, Germany; today Gdańsk, Poland
Darmstadt, Germany
Dashkovichy, Brest region, Soviet Union; today Belarus
Delitzsch, Germany
Delmenhorst, Germany
Dessau, Germany
Dnepropetrovsk, Soviet Union; today Dnipro, Ukraine
Dnepropetrovsk region, Soviet Union; today Ukraine
Dornbirn, Austria
Dörverden, Germany
Dramburg, Germany
Dresden, Germany
Driesen, Germany; today Drezdenko, Poland
Dubovichy, Chernigov region, Soviet Union; today Ukraine
Duisburg, Germany
Düsseldorf, Germany
Dyatkovo, Bryansk region, Soviet Union; today Russia
Dzhankoy, Crimean ASSR

E

Eilenburg, Germany
Eisenberg, Germany
Eltville, Germany
Engerau, Germany; today Petržalka, Slovakia
Enns, Austria
Erfurt, Germany
Eschwege, Germany
Essen, Germany

F

Fallersleben, Germany
Feldkirch, Austria
Frankfurt am Main, Germany
Frankfurt an der Oder, Germany
Freiburg im Breisgau, Germany
Freising, Germany
Fürstenberg, Germany

G

Gablonz, Germany; today Jablonec nad Nisou, Czech Republic
Gaivoron, Kirovograd region, Soviet Union; today Ukraine
Garmisch-Partenkirchen, Germany
Gatchina, Leningrad region, Soviet Union; today Russia
Gelsenkirchen, Germany
Genichesk, Kherson region, Soviet Union; today Ukraine
Genthin, Germany
Gladbeck, Germany
Gomel region, Soviet Union; today Belarus
Gorlovka, Stalin region, Soviet Union; today Donetsk region, Ukraine
Gotenhafen, Germany
Göttingen, Germany
Greifenberg, Germany
Griva, Kalinin region, Soviet Union; today Tver region, Russia

H

Hagen, Germany
Haichur, Zaporozhye region, Soviet Union; today Ukraine
Halberstadt, Germany
Halle, Germany
Hamburg, Germany
Hanover, Germany
Herbede, Germany
Hermsdorf, Germany
Hildesheim, Germany
Hinterweiler, Germany
Hirschberg, Germany
Hof (on Saale), Germany
Holzwickede, Germany

I

Isakovtsy, Kamenets Podolsk region, Soviet Union; today Khmelnytsky region, Ukraine

K

Kalinin region, Soviet Union; today Tver region, Russia
Kaluga, Soviet Union; today Russia
Kamen, Germany
Kamenets Podolsk, Soviet Union; today Ukraine
Kamenets Podolsk region, Soviet Union; today Khmelnytsky region, Ukraine
Kassel, Germany
Kempten, Germany
Kerch, Crimean ASSR
Kharkov, Soviet Union; today Ukraine
Kharkov region, Soviet Union; today Ukraine
Kherson, Soviet Union; today Ukraine
Kherson region, Soviet Union; today Ukraine
Khuralevo, Gomel region, Soviet Union; today Belarus
Kiev, Soviet Union; today Ukraine
Kiev region, Soviet Union; today Ukraine
Kirovograd, Soviet Union; today Kropyvnytskyi, Ukraine
Kirovograd region, Soviet Union; today Ukraine
Kitaigorod, Kamenets-Podolsk region, Soviet Union; today Khmelnytsky region, Ukraine
Klagenfurt, Austria
Kleve, Germany
Köflach, Austria
Königsberg, Germany; today Kaliningrad, Russia
Könnern, Germany
Kornwestheim, Germany
Korvinovka, Zhytomyr region, Soviet Union; today Ukraine
Krasnoye Selo, Leningrad region, Soviet Union; today Russia
Krefeld, Germany
Krolevets, Sumy region, Soviet Union; today Ukraine
Kronstorf, Austria
Kryski, Chernigov region, Soviet Union; today Ukraine
Kryukovo, Kursk region, Soviet Union; today Russia
Kursk, Soviet Union; today Russia
Kursk region, Soviet Union; today Russia
Kuteynikovo, Rostov region, Soviet Union; today Russia
Kyslychuvatoye, Dnepropetrovsk region, Soviet Union; today Ukraine

L

Lackenbach, Austria
Lanzendorf, Austria
Lauta, Germany
Lauterecken, Germany
Leipzig, Germany
Leningrad, Soviet Union; today St Petersburg, Russia
Leningrad region, Soviet Union; today Russia
Libau, Germany; today Liepāja, Latvia
Linz, Austria
Lippersdorf, Germany
Loburg, Germany
Lower Silesia, Free State of Prussia; today Poland
Lozovoy hamlet, Zaporozhye region, Soviet Union; today Ukraine
Ludwigsdorf, Germany
Ludwigshafen, Germany
Lüneburg, Germany
Lvov; today Ukraine
Lyuban, Leningrad region, Soviet Union; today Russia
Lyublin, Poland

M
Magdeburg, Germany
Mainz, Germany
Mannheim, Germany
Mariupol, Stalin region, Soviet Union; today Donetsk region, Ukraine
Mecklenburg, Germany
Merefa, Kharkov region, Soviet Union; today Ukraine
Merfeld, Germany
Metz, France
Minsk, Soviet Union; today Belarus
Mittelwalde, Germany – today Międzylesie, Poland
Mogilev region, Soviet Union; today Belarus
Möllersdorf, Austria
Moscow, Soviet Union; today Russia
Mühlhausen, Germany
Muksha-Borishkovetskaya, Kamenets-Podolsk region, Soviet Union; today Khmelnytsky region, Ukraine

N
Neheim-Hüsten, Germany
Neudietendorf, Germany
Neumarkt, Germany
Neustadt, Germany
Nikolayev region, Soviet Union; today Ukraine
Nikolayevka, Sumy region, Soviet Union; today Ukraine
Nindorf, Germany
Nizhyn, Chernigov region, Soviet Union; today Ukraine
Nordhausen, Germany
Nördlingen, Germany
Novgorod region, Soviet Union; today Russia
Novgorod-Volynsky, Zhytomyr region, Soviet Union; today Ukraine
Novocherkassk, Rostov region, Soviet union; today Russia
Novoduginskaya, Smolensk region, Soviet Union; today Russia
Novorossiysk, Krasnodar Krai, Soviet Union; today Russia
Novoselka, Kharkov region, Soviet Union; today Ukraine
Novoukrainka, Kirovograd region, Soviet Union; today Ukraine
Nuremberg, Germany

O
Oberhausen, Germany
Odessa, Soviet Union; today Ukraine
Odessa region, Soviet Union; today Ukraine
Offenberg, Germany
Ordzhonikidze Krai; today Stavropol Krai, Russia
Ortelsburg, Germany; today Szczytno, Poland
Osnabrück, Germany
Osovets, Gomel region, Soviet Union; today Belarus
Oryol, Soviet Union; today Russia
Oryol region, Soviet Union; today Russia

P
Paris, France
Peine, Germany
Peremyshl, Poland
Perevalochnoye, Chernigov region, Soviet Union; today Ukraine
Pirmasens, Germany
Platkower Loose, Germany
Poltava, Soviet Union; today Ukraine
Poltava region, Soviet Union; today Ukraine
Poznań, Poland
Prignitz, Germany
Proskurov, Kamenets Podolsk region, Soviet Union; today Khmelnytsky region, Ukraine
Pskov region, Soviet Union; today Russia

Pukhovichy, Gomel region, Soviet Union; today Belarus
Pustoshka, Pskov region, Soviet Union; today Russia

R

Rangsdorf, Germany
Red Partisan kolkhoz, Saratov region, Soviet Union; today Russia
Remscheid, Germany
Rochlitz, Germany
Romanovo, Zhytomyr region, Soviet Union; today Ukraine
Rostock, Germany
Rostov region, Soviet Union; today Russia
Rostov-on-Don, Soviet Union; today Russia
Rovensky region, Soviet Union; today Ukraine
Rudo, Pskov region, Soviet Union; today Russia
Rügen, Germany
Rzhev, Kalinin region, Soviet Union; today Tver region, Russia

S

Saalfeld, Germany
Sabovka, Stalin region, Soviet Union; today Donetsk region, Ukraine
Salzwedel, Germany
Saratov, Soviet Union; today Russia
Saratov region, Soviet Union; today Russia
Schlochau, Germany; now Poland
Schöneberg, Germany
Schwarz (Saale), Germany
Schwerin, Germany
Schwerte, Germany
Seebach, Germany
Seletskoye, Dnepropetrovsk region, Soviet Union; today Ukraine
Senftenberg, Germany
Sevastopol, Crimean ASSR
Shterovka, Voroshilovgrad region, Soviet Union; today Lugansk region, Ukraine
Siegen, Germany
Simferopol, Crimean ASSR
Singen, Germany
Skotovataya, Stalin region, Soviet Union; today Donetsk region, Ukraine
Smolensk region, Soviet Union; today Russia
Soelden, Austria
Soltau, Germany
Sömmerda, Germany
Spremberg, Germany
Stadthagen, Germany
Stalin region, Soviet Union; today Donetsk region, Ukraine
Stalingrad, Soviet Union; today Volgograd, Russia
Stalino, Soviet Union; today Donetsk, Ukraine
Starodub, Bryansk region, Soviet Union; today Russia
Stettin, Germany; today Szczecin, Poland
Steyerberg, Germany
Storkow, Germany
Stuttgart, Germany
Suhl, Germany
Sumy region, Soviet Union; today Ukraine

T

Taganrog, Rostov region, Soviet Union; today Russia
Tempelburg, Germany; today Czaplinek, Poland
Tessin, Germany; today Cieszyn, Poland
Tharau, Germany; today Vladimirovo, Kaliningrad region, Russia
Tolochyn, Vitebsk region, Soviet Union; today Belarus
Tuttlingen, Germany

V
Velbert, Germany
Vienna, Austria
Vinnytsia region, Soviet Union; today Ukraine
Vitebsk region, Soviet Union; today Belarus
Voitsberg, Austria
Volyn region, Soviet Union; today Ukraine
Voroshilovgrad, Soviet Union; today Lugansk, Ukraine
Voroshilovgrad region, Soviet Union; today Lugansk region, Ukraine
Vyazhishche village, Pskov region, Soviet Union; today Russia
Vyazma, Smolensk region, Soviet Union; today Russia

W
Waldheim, Germany
Wedel, Germany
Weimar, Germany
Weinbergen, Germany
Weinstadt, Germany
Wels, Austria
Wiesen, Austria
Wilhelmshaven, Germany
Winterdorf, Austria
Winterlingen, Germany
Wissen, Germany
Witten, Germany
Wittenburg, Germany
Wuppertal, Germany

Z
Zagan, Germany; today Poland
Zaporozhye, Soviet Union; today Ukraine
Zaporozhye region, Soviet Union; today Ukraine
Zasluchnoe, Kamenets Podolsk region, Soviet Union; today Khmelnytsky region, Ukraine
Zenkov, Poltava region, Soviet Union; today Ukraine
Zhytomyr, Soviet Union; today Ukraine
Zhytomyr region, Soviet Union; today Ukraine
Zolotonosha, Poltava region, Soviet Union; today Ukraine
Zwickau, Germany

Foreword

Painful Memories

The patch will be ripped off
Memories will fade
And you will forget me
(from *Ostarbeiter* folklore)

OST: An Untold History of Nazi Germany's Forced Labour Camps is neither a historical research project nor a collection of archival material. It is a mosaic, pieced together from an immensely varied source of collective memory. The memories belong to the former 'eastern workers', the approximately 3.2 million Soviet citizens* deported during the Second World War and forced to work for the Third Reich. In Germany they were referred to as *Ostarbeiter* (singular and plural), but this word only began to appear in Russian print in the 1990s, replacing other long-standing and problematic alternatives such as 'repatriates'.

This literary mosaic has been assembled from a medley of sources, including interviews, memoirs, documents, letters and photographs – all of which have been collected and stored in the archives of the international history and human rights organisation Memorial. The history of this particular archive is typical of many of those founded in the early 1990s. In 1989, members of the Green parliamentary party of the German Bundestag identified the *Ostarbeiter* as 'forgotten victims' of the war. As such, they reasoned, Germany had an obligation to compensate the millions of Eastern Europeans who had carried out forced labour. The questions that these deputies

* This figure has been obtained from documents found in historical archives.

raised in their letters to Andrei Dmitrievich Sakharov, the chairman of the then recently established Memorial, highlighted just how little was known about the fate of these eastern workers. How many had there been? How many were currently living in former Soviet states? What had happened to them? Was it true that many had ended up in Stalin's labour camps? What was their current status?

These questions demanded answers, and it became clear that somebody needed to draw society's attention to the fate of the *Ostarbeiter.* In April 1990, the newspaper *Nedelya* (the Sunday supplement to the newspaper *Izvestiya*) published a short and somewhat vaguely worded article concerning the *Ostarbeiter*, from which it was possible to draw the erroneous conclusion that all those who had formerly worked in Germany were soon to receive a special pension, and that Memorial was to assist in the process. The article was reprinted in hundreds of regional newspapers and shortly afterwards correspondence began pouring in from former *Ostarbeiter*, with sacks of post landing on the table in the tiny room where Memorial was operating at that time. In just a few weeks Memorial received more than four hundred thousand letters. Knowing very little at that time about the eastern workers (being as yet unaware of the true statistics), this huge number of letters was not only unexpected but also truly astonishing.

It seemed inconceivable that, despite the huge number of surviving witnesses, these stories and recollections had never entered the public realm. But there was a reason for this protracted silence: the lives and fate of the eastern workers had never been written into either Stalin's, or Brezhnev's, official Soviet narrative of the Great Patriotic War. The *Ostarbeiter* served only as an unwelcome reminder that, as a result of the terrible blunders and misconduct of the Soviet military commanders, and above all Stalin, by autumn 1941 more than sixty million Soviet citizens were living in territory occupied by Germany and its allies. Just a few months later, the mass deportation of young Soviet men and women began, as the Third Reich sought to boost its dwindling workforce. Later, during the Nuremberg trials, the use of slave labour on a mass scale was to become an important charge in the allegations of 'Crimes Against Humanity' levelled at Nazi leaders.

When they finally returned home, however, the eastern workers were not given status as victims of the Nazi regime. Instead, the government chose to ignore the inconvenient truth that they had been deported to work in Germany against their will. Accordingly, the language of Soviet bureaucracy dubbed all *Ostarbeiter* 'repatriates'; a nondescript label that said nothing of all that they had endured during the war.

Before they could return home to the Soviet Union, *Ostarbeiter* were required to pass through 'filtration camps', where they were 'screened' and subjected to prejudiced interrogations at the hands of the NKVD, who zealously undertook to root out and expose all 'traitors'. The slightest suspicion that someone had collaborated with the Germans was enough to charge them with 'betrayal of the Motherland' and sentence them to a spell in the Gulag. After liberation, many *Ostarbeiter* were sent to join so-called 'work battalions', which rebuilt mines and hydroelectric plants that had been damaged during the war, or carried out other heavy manual labour such as felling timber.

Repatriates were not permitted to settle in Moscow, Leningrad (St Petersburg) or Kiev, even if these cities had been their homes before the war. Those who were allowed to return home spent many years being denied admission to various institutions and undergoing repeated interrogations by the secret police, simply to obtain an official passport (rather than just a written document confirming that they had passed through the filtration process). Right up until Stalin's death in 1953 it was widely held that all *Ostarbeiter* were 'dubious' characters with 'bad résumés', and as such many were kept under the clandestine surveillance of the secret police for years. The 'repatriate' label often proved to be an insurmountable barrier to further education and study, and even the most humble of formal careers was generally off-limits to anybody who had been in Germany during the war. In their letters to Memorial, many *Ostarbeiter* revealed that they had spent most of their lives avoiding making any mention of their war years in Germany.

After Stalin's death, the situation improved a little, and surveillance was lifted from most former *Ostarbeiter.* But even in the post-Stalin years, they were mentioned far less than Soviet prisoners of war or victims of the Nazi concentration camps. Between 1960 and 1970, as books and films on the subject began to emerge, society started to develop a picture, albeit an oversimplified one, of prisoners of the Third Reich. They were almost always members of the Resistance, imprisoned behind barbed wire, dressed in striped clothes and wearing wooden clogs . . . But *Ostarbeiter* did not fit into this construct. They had worked in factories and on farms, or as nannies for German families and, as a result, their experience was a 'grey area'. They formed part of an incongruous picture of daily life in Germany during the war, about which very little was known.

The role and place of *Ostarbeiter* in the established memory of the war was undefined; they were neither victims, nor war veterans, and as such they were simply treated as bystanders. Ultimately, the years that they had spent in Germany counted for nothing, both in terms of professional development, and in relation to their country's struggle during the war. On Victory Day, when *Ostarbeiter* ought to have been celebrating their liberation, they felt like outsiders. There was no place for them at the parades, where war veterans, decorated with medals, walked alongside their children and grandchildren or were invited to give speeches to schoolchildren. Likewise, journalists were never sent to record their stories, and the distinct lack of creative writing or investigative historical journalism during the Soviet period meant that there was no medium through which *Ostarbeiter* could make their voices heard. The exception, when it came, appeared in the form of an autobiographical novel by Vitaly Syomin called *The OST Breast Badge*, which was published in the early 1970s after a long battle with censorship.

It wasn't until the early 1990s that *Ostarbeiter* finally felt able to talk openly about their past, and the letters they sent to Memorial were, in many cases, their very first steps towards disclosure. Most of these letters contained only the most rudimentary snippets of biographical information; when the individual had been deported, for example, or where in Germany they had been sent. Sometimes the letters would be accompanied by a note bearing words such as: 'I have no other documents. Only my memory.' This came as no surprise. As a rule, during the filtration process, all German documents confirming that an individual had spent time in Germany were destroyed. Moreover, even after the war, holding on to any such documents was risky. As a result, almost all evidence connected with time spent in Germany was disposed of, either by *Ostarbeiter* or by their frightened relatives.

Despite the risk, some did hold on to a few pieces of physical evidence from their time in the Third Reich, often secreting their past away in an inconspicuous drawer or box somewhere. That said, barely one in ten of the letters received by Memorial was accompanied by any sort of document. These, when they did appear, ranged from summonses for deportation from the occupying forces, typed in faded print on scraps of paper, to neatly written German work identity cards complete with photographs and fingerprints. There were also work passes for factories and workshops, medical documents issued to those who had suffered injuries or fallen ill, and a variety of other pieces of written evidence. Very occasionally an OST badge would be found slipped inside an envelope, its white letters printed onto a square-cut piece of blue cloth. These badges were compulsory for all 'eastern workers' to wear pinned to their clothes while in Germany.

There were also photographs depicting life in Germany, almost always taken by Germans. These snapshots were mainly used for official documents such as identification papers or work cards. The photos provide a clear indication of the photographer's attitude towards the *Ostarbeiter*, many of whom are photographed with an identification placard hung around their necks and an OST badge pinned to their chest. To the Germans behind the lens, here were people who had been stripped of their individuality and reduced to mere numbers.

Group photographs of *Ostarbeiter* at work or outside the barracks where they lived were also fairly common. Either consciously or unconsciously, the Germans taking these photos were attempting to normalise the presence of 'eastern workers' in Germany. 'Here you see people going about their jobs as usual', they seem to say . . . 'and there are people wearing OST badges working here too. Here you can see where they live; here they are going for walks; here they are working for German families, looking after the children. Their employers are kindly towards them – look, you can see for yourselves in the photos.'

Among the photographs received, there were some, particularly of the young women, that showed their subjects looking surprisingly cheerful. At first glance, this appears to contradict the accounts of hunger and hardship in Germany. But it is important to remember that the experiences of *Ostarbeiter* varied enormously for they all lived very different lives. It goes without saying that working in a mine or munitions factory was quite unlike working in domestic service or as a nanny for a German family. It is also important to remember that these photos were often taken in a studio, after an *Ostarbeiter* had saved up enough Reichsmarks from their paltry wage, and were intended as presents for friends or family or, most importantly, as mementos. As a result, the girls tried to look their very best, styling their hair and donning their best clothes. They usually attempted to hide their OST badges in an effort to reclaim their individuality and dignity. The postcards they sent home often depicted views of the cities in which their work camps were located and at times the beautiful pictures would conceal a darker truth exposed by the text on the reverse. One postcard sent from an *Ostarbeiter* reads:

> Dear Zinochka, this sequence of photos shows the village where I am living . . . the right-hand one shows the former monastery, which is now the Russian camp. This is where I live. It looks very pretty from the outside, but life on the inside isn't great.

This book contains letters and postcards that are now stored in Memorial's archive. Unbeknown to many, *Ostarbeiter* were permitted to exchange letters with their families and friends, and they could also correspond with friends living within the Third Reich.

It is these short letters and postcards (some of which were censored) rather than the staged photographs that provide a true insight into the harsh realities of their daily lives. One postcard reads:

> We work 12-hour shifts. We take over at 6 p.m. and work until 6 a.m., and then in the morning the day shift takes over, and they work until 6 p.m. We are fed three times a day. In the morning we get coffee and 150g bread, at lunch we have soup and 150g bread, and in the evening, just soup.

The value of these letters is not limited to the wealth of information they provide on the lives of *Ostarbeiter.* Crucially, they also shed light on the emotional state of those who penned them, illustrating just how overwhelming the despair at being separated from loved ones could be. The teenagers deported from the countryside, who constituted the vast majority of those sent to Germany, often voiced their despair in mournful laments:

> Think of me Mama, even just once on a Tuesday, and meanwhile I will think of you forty times a day.

> I am living in a foreign country; where my world has lost all light and meaning.

> Bitter tears spill down my cheeks. Once I have had a good cry, my heart feels lighter for a while, and I can return once again to my frightening life.

> And no matter where I find myself, no matter where I go, I cannot find a corner to call home. Whether I am doing the washing or the mending, I remember my dear and beloved Mama.

> If we are never to meet again, if fate is to be cruel to us, then let my name and handwriting serve as a memento. (1943)

Ostarbeiter also recorded songs and poems, not only in letters, but also in exercise books that they often carried with them. Many recalled that this helped to alleviate the grief. Some also kept diaries, although Memorial's archive contains only one such example: a diary in the form of a notebook that belonged to seventeen-year-old Zhenya Kisselkova, who kept a record of her experiences following her deportation from Belarus. Between 1942 and 1943 she assiduously described each day of her life, noting down details such as what time she got up, what she ate, where she worked, what was ailing her and who had punished her that day. In these brief notes, this young country girl conveys not only the monotony of life as a captive in a German work camp, but also a pervading sense of hopelessness that remains unparalleled in similar accounts of the past, even decades later.

Ultimately, however, it was neither diaries, nor letters, nor memoirs that proved to be the primary source of information for this book. The vast majority of *Ostarbeiter* had not grown up amid a culture of writing and therefore very few kept written memoirs of their time in Germany. As a result this book is based predominantly on oral interviews with former *Ostarbeiter*, almost two hundred of which have been documented and archived by Memorial since the early 1990s.

Of course, the oral evidence that was gathered represents only a tiny drop of what was once a vast ocean of collective *Ostarbeiter* memory. It became apparent, as Memorial began collecting the information, that it was going to be a race against the clock, as by the time interviews began many *Ostarbeiter* had already passed away. It was felt that their written recollections would also paint a picture, albeit one that was far from complete. Ultimately, this book is their portrait of the past, painted as they remember it.

Struggling back through the memories was sometimes extremely difficult. The majority of those interviewed had been sent to Germany between the ages of sixteen and eighteen. They had possessed little to no life experience, having seen almost nothing of the world outside the small towns or villages where they had grown up. Some had not even completed seven years of schooling by the time the war broke out, so describing all that they had lived through during these years was sometimes far from easy. Much depended on whether they had succeeded in furthering their education after the war. As a result, the language of the interviewees varied enormously; some spoke in an eloquent and erudite manner about their experiences, while the speech of others was less refined. Some of the interviews were conducted in Ukrainian or Belarusian, or indeed a confusing blend of languages, and this too came with its own set of challenges.

At times *Ostarbeiter* would share complete stories, the threads of which tied neatly together, while at other times the interviewer's questions would be met with truncated answers. Some were able to dredge up reams of particularities and minutiae from the depths of their memories, while others struggled to conjure up even a vague outline of events. There were occasions when people spoke of what they had experienced with an extraordinary openness, as though their answers were flowing out as a visceral response. Others reduced their recollections to stereotypical sketches in a bid to bypass all the memories that were painful and tragic.

Sometimes the stories were tangled and hard to follow. In most cases this was because many *Ostarbeiter* had spent time in more than one place in Germany; they might have been transferred from one factory to another, or sent from a farm or family to work in a manufacturing plant. Many were unable to recall the exact name of the village or town where they had been sent, particularly since few of them were able to speak German. It became clear that a knowledge of German and a desire to remember both geographical names and German words had a distinct bearing on a person's ability to recall, and therefore to reflect on their work there. So deeply rooted was the language of their experience that German words, relics of a former life, would spill out, automatically. *Appell*; *Holzpantoffeln*; *Kantine*; *Lagerführer*,* were just some of those regularly heard.

The task of pulling all these stories together into one cohesive unit of collective memory was far from simple. The book has been

* Roll call; wooden clogs; canteen; camp commandant.

separated into key life events – life before the war, the outbreak of war, the arrival of the Germans, deportation, work in the Third Reich, liberation and, finally, return to the Motherland – but at times, it was difficult to identify and extract even these common denominators. Working with memories presented a number of challenges for both the narrator and the listener. Not only did both parties have to grapple with the discord and disunity of the tangled recollections, but there were also difficulties associated with the *Ostarbeiter* being so young at the time of their deportation.

Interestingly, many of the young men and women sent to the front were the same age, or only fractionally older than the *Ostarbeiter*. And yet, many of these people carried vivid memories of the war with them all their lives. Although these memories too were often defined by tragedy, society considered them to be mementos of a heroic chapter of the past; something to be proud of, rather than concealed. As a result, such memories were often embellished or even mythologised. The reverse mechanism came into play where *Ostarbeiter* were concerned, driven by two key elements of trauma: fear and guilt. These emotions had a profound impact upon their recollections.

As the interviews were conducted, it soon became apparent that for many *Ostarbeiter*, fear had been a constant in their lives. For some, it had begun in early childhood, when the repression* of a parent or family member resulted in them being made a pariah at school or among their fellow Young Pioneers.† Later, during the occupation years, there was fear of the German invaders and their ruthless police forces. For many, this was accompanied by the dread of deportation to Germany, which in turn led to the relentless fear of assault, concentration camps and bombing raids. After liberation, if

* Translator's note: Political repression is the use of political violence carried out by state bodies (in this case in the USSR) against individuals and certain groups of people as a means of perpetuating a regime. Repression in the USSR took various forms, with methods of punishment including arrest, torture, incarceration in prisons and labour camps, exile and deportation.

† Translator's note: The Vladimir Lenin All-Union Pioneer Organisation (often abbreviated to Young Pioneers) was a Communist mass youth organisation in the Soviet Union for children aged nine to fifteen. It existed from 1922 until 1991.

people succeeded in returning home, they were confronted with accusations of having betrayed their Motherland. Many were afraid to admit, even to those closest to them, that they had been forced to 'work for the enemy' and that they (particularly those who had worked on farms or looked after the children in German families) had lived and eaten far better than they had back home. Fear induced silence. The *Ostarbeiter* felt unable to admit, for example, that not all the Germans they had encountered had been 'Fascist monsters'. On the contrary, some had treated them with kindness. What was more, the *Ostarbeiter* could recognise that there was a dissonance between much of what they had seen and experienced in Germany and the messages touted by Soviet propaganda. It often transpired that the more complicated a person's experience, and the harder it was to marry with black and white Soviet clichés, the greater the fear of sharing their story.

During Soviet times it was not uncommon for people to conceal facts about their past or to sever themselves entirely from family roots. But *Ostarbeiter* were saddled with the extra burden of maintaining their silence for tens of years. They had been obliged to develop two versions of their personal histories: one in Germany and another after their return to the Soviet Union. Later, in the 1990s, they were to bring forward a third version.

Another important factor influencing the memories of *Ostarbeiter* was guilt. There was an underlying, but at times distinct, sense that they had somehow been to blame for their deportation to Germany. Naturally not everyone spoke directly about this sense of guilt, but in almost every individual's account it is possible to detect a desire to justify and explain why it was they were unable to avoid deportation, why they didn't join the Partisans, why they didn't die, or why they didn't join the Resistance.

> You must understand that it is very difficult to banish these thoughts from one's mind. They convinced me that I was guilty, and I live with the guilt to this day. No, I cannot wrap my head around the possibility that I am not guilty. I am guilty in some way. And so I live with this guilt. (Yevgenia Savranskaya)

Today, it is difficult to pinpoint exactly when this feeling of guilt began to pervade the consciousness of the *Ostarbeiter.* Was it while they were still in Germany, during the closing stages of the war? Or was it later – post-liberation – a product of the atmosphere of mistrust that had settled around the 'repatriates'? This was an atmosphere rooted in Soviet propaganda stereotypes, and it had been formed and fostered by the Soviet state, which benefited from making certain members of its population feel responsible for their fate. Prisoners of war, *Ostarbeiter*, soldiers who had been surrounded by the enemy, and even those who simply had the misfortune to live in territory occupied by the German army, were instilled with a sense of culpability. By pointing the finger at these people the state could shrug off any responsibility for the fate they had suffered and justify its suspicion and cruelty towards them.

Many found it extremely difficult to discuss their past. Time and again, those conducting the interviews looked on as people wrestled with old grievances and reopened old wounds. However, guilt and fear were not the only emotions suppressing the voices of these men and women – the humiliation they had suffered in Germany was also playing a part. *Ostarbeiter* found it difficult to discuss the degrading treatment that they had endured, even with those closest to them. There had been many such incidents, not least being 'sold' at the labour market, where their teeth and muscles had been prodded and inspected, and being forced to wear badges bearing the letters OST. Almost each and every *Ostarbeiter* had experienced the sting of abasement and humiliation.

Not only did they remember the hunger, forced labour and beatings for the rest of their lives but they also recalled the slaps in the face and insults such as 'Russian pig' that streamed constantly from the mouths of the Germans. Even more acute was the hurt women felt at being called 'German prostitutes' by their own people when they returned home to the Soviet Union. Galina Agranovskaya said: 'I'm not sure that I can tell you everything in a coherent manner. After all, it's been fifty years now, and you forget the pain and hunger. But you never forget the fear and humiliation.'

The *Ostarbeiter* were left to come to terms with the fear, hurt and trauma on their own. They never stopped to consider that these emotions would only be dispelled when society committed the simple act of acknowledging all that they had suffered, and the injustices that had been done to them. It wasn't until the 1990s that this idea became conceivable for the first time. One of the thousands of letters received by Memorial contained the following line: *Are there really people out there who have not forgotten us?*

It was only around this time that *Ostarbeiter* finally began to open up about all they had gone through. Articles began to appear in publications, exhibitions were organised, and the German government announced its intention to compensate them for their forced labour during the war.

However, after an initial flare of interest into the stories of the former *Ostarbeiter*, in recent years interest has waned. Of course, this is partly due to the fact that many of the last survivors of the deportations have now passed away. However, equally significant is the way anything tragic, complex or contradictory is today being dispelled from society's collective war memory. The *Ostarbeiter*, who effectively became victims of two separate dictatorships, are finding once again that they do not fit comfortably into today's glossy and simplified image of the Second World War victory. Even at the time of writing, there are still no permanent exhibitions or scientific research centres in Russia preserving the rapidly vanishing memory of the 'eastern workers'. This book aims to serve as a reminder of the fate of these people and to act as a repository of their memories.

PART 1

Before Deportation to Germany

A Peacetime Childhood

The childhood and adolescent memories harboured by the *Ostarbeiter* of their lives before the war were often vague and confused. Some attached no significance whatsoever to their pre-war experience, sharing only the most rudimentary details. They would tell us where they were born, where they studied and when they left school, and then swiftly steer the conversation on to what they considered to be 'more important matters': notably, the outbreak of war.

The war and the time they spent in Germany were, to them, their most significant and momentous experiences. It was these events that they considered to be the defining features of their lives – the rest in their eyes was of little import. When asked about the particulars of their lives before the war they would say: 'Why talk about that?' and 'Who needs to know about such things?' So complete was the schism caused by their deportation to Germany that the childhood memories of many were simply erased, to be supplanted by later episodes. And yet, in many ways, it was the pre-war years that defined their attitudes towards their subsequent experiences in Germany.

'There was nothing to wear'

When the Second World War broke out most of the *Ostarbeiter* we spoke to had been between the ages of fifteen and seventeen. A large majority were living in small towns and villages in the southern regions of Russia and Ukraine, often members of large peasant families. Their lives were typical of country dwellers of the late 1930s: they lived in small wattle-and-daub houses, or *mazanka*, often with thatched roofs and earth floors. Collectivisation policies had left them with precious little – perhaps a cow or a pig if they were lucky, or else a couple of sheep, a few chickens and a vegetable patch.

One of the men we spoke to, Victor Shuldeshov, grew up in a small village (Kryukovo) in the Kursk region. He proudly recalled receiving presents from his uncle, a military instructor, as a young child:

> He helped us – he sent me a camera, a pocket watch and a good suit. At that time, I was the only person in the village with such things. And he bought a gramophone for us to share with my aunt's family. One month we would have it, and the next month it would be their turn.

Victor's experience was indeed remarkable – items such as cameras, watches and gramophones were considered luxuries even in the cities, so naturally they were almost unheard of in the villages and small rural communities of the Soviet Union.

For most families life was a constant struggle. Anna Odinokova, who lived in the Chernigov region before the war, has vivid memories of her childhood diet: 'I was one of five children . . . I wouldn't exactly say that we were well fed. In the mornings, we'd

A crowd gathered outside a grocery store in Kharkov in 1932–3. (Photographer: A. Vinerberger, from the collection of Cardinal Theodor Innitzer; Diocesan archives of Vienna)

be given potato before school, then we'd come home and have . . . potato, and in the evening . . . again, potato!'

The *Ostarbeiter* described the poverty of their childhood years as though it was simply a matter of course. Sergei Driga (from the Odessa region) recalled:

> Our poverty meant that I often missed school – I had to run two kilometres barefoot in the frost to get there. There was nothing to wear – no clothes, no shoes . . . [. . .] But if I got there, my teacher would take one look at my red feet and praise me for coming anyway.

Young Pioneers in the Ivanovo region, 1920s.

Life in the cities was difficult too, particularly if the father and breadwinner of a family had been arrested, as was the case for Galina Agranovskaya (Bryansk): 'I remember wondering how to hang myself at the age of just nine – I had dropped the bread in a puddle. I couldn't go home empty-handed – Granny was disabled, my father had been arrested, my brother was only little.'

'I remember the famine of 1933 well'

Those who grew up in the countryside had vivid recollections of the famine of 1932–3. Most of those we interviewed were between six and ten years of age at the time, and their first conscious memories were often characterised by an enduring sense of hunger. Anna Odinokova told us:

> I remember the famine of 1933 well. I went out to gather rotten potatoes in the spring. We had to put nettles and saltbush into the bread. It was a truly frightening year. [. . .] I was in my first year at school and my mother's sister invited me to have dinner with her family after lessons. Her husband was a foreman at the machine tractor station,* so they always had bread. [. . .] We would sit down to eat, but I couldn't get the food down. I remember sitting, tears running down my cheeks – I knew that everyone at home was starving, while I sat there, eating.

Domnikiya Skiba from Zasluchnoe, in the Kamenets-Podolsk region, recalled: 'Our people lay in their beds, swollen; they fell down and died right there in the streets.'

Others spoke of events that led up to the famine, of its causes, and the effects on the peasants of political decisions taken by the state. Pavel Mikhailov, from the Zaporozhye region, explained:

> The authorities took all of our grain reserves. They searched everywhere – even pierced our mattresses with pitchforks. Absolutely everything was taken, even a couple of kilos of beans that my mother had hidden away behind the icon. But there were six of us to somehow find a way to feed. My mother baked pumpkin for us – they didn't take the pumpkins. And when the black locust plants began to flower we dried out the blossoms and added them to milk to make a soup. It was lucky that we had a cow – that cow alone saved us.

* Translator's note: Machine tractor stations were state-owned rural agencies that supplied collective farms with agricultural machinery and skilled personnel to operate it.

Some also recalled hearing frightening rumours of cannibalism:

> What did we eat? Pickled beetroot and polenta. [. . .] But we didn't have such luxuries every day. I remember picking up apple cores that I found on the streets – if somebody hadn't eaten the whole apple, I would pick up the core, dust it off, and eat it. When I started my first year at school, Papa began to walk me there and back. Why? Because children were being taken, and eaten. (Neonila Rozhkova, Korvinovka, Zhytomyr region)

We were told of the cruelty and brutality that the terrible hunger brought out in people:

> I went to the market with my father one day. You could buy borscht there, as well as fried cabbage and small pieces of bread – just like in a stolovaya.* A young man grabbed a piece of my bread and scarpered. He was chased down and beaten. People ran over to watch. (Vera Dergachova, Stalin region)

Yevdokiya Verkholantseva (Pskov region) remembers: 'Mama resorted to begging – she took my sister and I along to beg too. Some people were kind; they invited us into their houses, gave us bread. Others set their dogs on us, complaining, "There are so many of you layabouts here!"'

People spoke too of the pain of losing their families: 'I had six sisters; they all died in 1932. All six of them starved to death in front of my mother's eyes.' (Ivan Zapirin, Kursk region.)

Many still wrestle with the pain of childhood memories of events that came to tragically alter the course of their lives. Galina Shalankova, who grew up in a small rural community in the Ordzhonikidze region, describes one such episode:

> My mother had three children left – my brother, my sister and I. The famine of 1933 was severe, terrifying; people were dying

* Translator's note: Inexpensive canteen-style restaurants, typical of the Soviet Union.

> in the streets. It's awful to remember, even now. My mother worked as a swineherd and we would go and gorge ourselves alongside the pigs at the trough – it actually wasn't bad. We went begging for food too. At some point our neighbours advised my mother to take us to an orphanage.
>
> 'Why are you struggling on like this?' they asked.
>
> So my mother put the question to us – I was nine and my brother was six years old at the time.
>
> 'Galya, Misha, would you like to go to the children's home?' she asked.
>
> 'Will they give us bread there?' we asked.
>
> 'They will,' she said.
>
> 'Well, then we'll go.'
>
> She took us by the hand and walked us to the station. 'I'm going to leave you here,' she said. 'You just need to walk up to a nice old man and say, "Please could you take us to the orphanage."' And so that's what we did.

Getting into an orphanage was often far from easy. They were usually reluctant to take in orphans whose parents worked on the collective farms (*kolkhoz*), as Anna Yermilova from the 'Red Partisan' kolkhoz in the Saratov region recalls:

Children from an orphanage queuing for the bathhouse, 1930s.

> I was eight years old when my mother died, and one of four children. My father had died sometime earlier. But the orphanage wouldn't take us. 'You're from the kolkhoz [collective farm],' they said. 'You're all one big family there – they can look after you.'
>
> A neighbour took us in. We lived with her, and the kolkhoz provided her with three kilograms of flour in return for our keep. But we were hungry as dogs. We had nothing to wear, nothing to put on our feet.

The fate of those who did manage to find a place in an orphanage hinged upon the human decency and morality of the people who ran the establishment. Aldona Volynskaya, who was taken in by a Ukrainian orphanage in 1938, remembers:

> We were hungry and thirsty, but when they doled out the food, even the little ones wouldn't eat it. Each bowl of soup was swimming with flies. But we ate it in the end. [. . .] This particular orphanage had been established to house children whose parents had died during the famine of 1933. We dreamed of food from morning until night . . . When we visited the nurse, she would rub some *zelenka** on our scabs and say, 'You really need to eat some meat.'

Children born into workers' families in small towns and cities often lived a little better, especially if the father received a worker's ration card. Even so, many types of food were luxuries far beyond their reach. Anna Gulyaeva, whose father was a railway worker, remembers falling very ill aged seven:

> I really wasn't well. I was weak, listless. And I was desperate for some butter. My father came to see me in Vyazma, where we were living at the time.
>
> 'What can I bring you, darling?' he asked.

* Malachite green or aniline green. A popular, bright green antiseptic in the USSR.

> 'Butter, butter!' I said. I begged him to get me some – I was absolutely desperate for it.

We did speak to several *Ostarbeiter* who had grown up in the cities, in families that were fairly comfortably off. They were often the children of engineers, military men, or members of the Communist Party, and their pre-war childhoods differed starkly from those of their less fortunate contemporaries. Antonina Serdyukova, the daughter of one of the engineers commissioned to build the Stalingrad Tractor Plant,` recalls that family members of the engineers were fed at an 'American-style canteen': 'We ate there for just pennies – practically for free. In 1933, when people were falling down in the streets, swollen and starving, we lived a life of plenty.'

Antonina's account is interesting, not only from the social perspective of inequality in 'the fairest workers' and peasants' state in the world' (a key Soviet propaganda myth of the time), but also in that it appears to show inequality as an accepted norm: injustice was simply seen as a fact of life.

Adults did not always show the same inclination to pity as their children when it came to those suffering from starvation. Igor Malitsky, the son of a military official, remembers seeing the starvation in Ukraine first-hand as a young boy. Until then, the privileged position enjoyed by his father had meant that the family had remained entirely remote from the tragedy unfurling around them. He remembers:

> We took a summer holiday to a resort reserved exclusively for military personnel. The canteen had big glass windows, and children and elderly people stood lining up outside, watching us eat. They stood there, clutching empty tin cans. I remember running around the canteen, collecting leftovers and putting them into their cans. I was severely scolded for doing so.

'My father was arrested'

The childhood years of *Ostarbeiter* before the outbreak of war played out against the backdrop of the most terrible years of Stalinist repression. Directly or indirectly, several became victims or witnesses of both the 'dekulakisation'* campaign of the early 1930s and the Great Terror of 1937–8. Perceptions of these campaigns of persecution varied from family to family but, in contrast to the prevailing myth that most of the Soviet Union's citizens were

Canteen pass for members of the Odessa Regional Executive Committee of the Petrograd Soviet (Ispolkom), 1930s. (From the collection of M. Poizner)

The family of the director of a division of the General Red Army headquarters on holiday in Crimea in the 1930s.

* Translator's note: The Soviet campaign of political repression (1929–32) carried out against kulaks (wealthy peasant farmers). The kulaks believed in private ownership and therefore resisted collectivisation policies. Stalin sought to 'liquidate [them] as a class' through mass deportations, executions and arrests.

Staff at a print works, Moscow, 1924.

oblivious to the tyranny being carried out around them, almost every person we spoke to was only too aware of it.

In 1937, Taissa Tolkachova was twelve years old and living in the city of Genichesk. She remembers:

> At school we had a little book containing portraits of leading Soviet figures entitled 'Comrade'. Our teacher would ask us to open it up on one page or another and then tell us to scribble out a portrait.
>
> 'This person is an enemy of the people,' she would say. 'Cross him out.'
>
> And then the next day, 'Cross out this portrait – he's an enemy of the people.'
>
> We would cross out another, and then another. One day my father came home and said to my mother, 'Have you heard? Our accountant has been arrested.'
>
> Next, word reached us that the priest who lived on our street had been taken. Then another person, and another . . . I heard my father lamenting, 'Oh what times we are living in. Everyone has become an enemy.'

> We began to worry. 'Oh Lord!' we thought. 'If they are taking people like the accountant, perhaps they will come for us too.' We lived with this terrible sense of unease.

Parents often tried to avoid talking about the repression in front of their children, but snippets of their hushed conversations were occasionally overheard: 'My father was very troubled by the arrests,' remembers Elizaveta Krestyantseva, whose father was a member of the military. 'He often spoke to my mother about it, and would usher us out of the room. "Off you go and play," he would say. He went to great lengths to ensure that we never listened in to their conversations.'

Despite their parents' best efforts to shield them from the truth, many children could sense the atmosphere of tension and disquiet. Worse still, several witnessed the arrest of their parents first-hand.

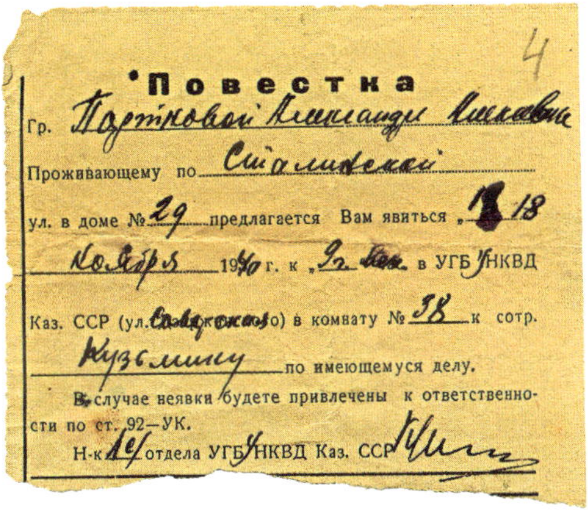

Повестка

Гр. [illegible]

Проживающему по [illegible]

ул. в доме № 29 предлагается Вам явиться „18"

[illegible] 19[illegible] г. к „[illegible]" в УГБ НКВД

Каз. ССР (ул. [illegible]) в комнату № 38 к сотр.

[illegible] по имеющемуся делу.

В случае неявки будете привлечены к ответственности по ст. 92—УК.

Н-к [illegible] отдела УГБ НКВД Каз. ССР [illegible]

A summons to the NKVD, 1940.

> I was thirteen years old. My father was in the military; he was a Captain 1st Rank and taught at the Baltic Fleet Technical School in Kronshtadt. On 23 February 1937, he was awarded a medal for his work, and on the 24th he was arrested. I woke up in the middle of the night to the sound of my mother crying. I pretended to be asleep, but I knew that my father had been arrested. (Lidia Dadzis, Leningrad region)

Galina Agranovskaya remembers the arrest of her father, the writer Fedor Kamanin:

> It was night. They carried out a search of our apartment. My Mama stood by the stove with her hands behind her back. She was pale, shivering. I huddled close to her and could feel her

> shaking. My grandmother sat on a chair in the corner. I was nine years old, and yet, somehow, I knew not to ask what had happened.

The sense of shame and injustice experienced by children who had to contend with a shift from being regarded as a 'good Soviet schoolchild' to becoming the stigmatised son or daughter of an 'enemy of the people' was profound. Indeed, for many, this time of their lives proved no less traumatic than their wartime experiences and, for this reason, it often proved to be one of the first tremors to shake their faith in the USSR. Was it really 'the most wonderful country in the world'?

Igor Malitsky (the same boy who had run around the holiday resort canteen gathering food to fill the cans of the starving people lined up outside) spoke of how his adolescent world was turned upside down by the arrest of his father:

> The hardest moment of my life, worse even than the time I spent in the concentration camp, was an event that occurred at school in 1940. All of the Pioneers were told to form a line, and I was called into the middle. Then the lead Pioneer said that the son of an enemy of the people could not wear the red tie [uniform of the Young Pioneers]. I don't know how I lived through it. Our school – No.30 – wasn't far from the Kharkov bridge; I ran there and threw myself off. Some people pulled me from the river and took me home. But I stopped going to school after that. My mother tried to persuade me otherwise.
>
> 'Darling,' she said, 'you need to prove to everyone that you are an honest boy, and the son of an honest man.'
>
> I swore that I would do just that.

Fate was also cruel to Aldona Volynskaya whose parents had relocated from Minsk to Moscow before her first birthday. Following the arrest of first her father, and then her mother, the eleven-year-old Aldona was sent to an orphanage. She remembers:

A meeting of Young Pioneers in the 'Lenin corner'*, Moscow, 1930s. (Photographer: I. Shagin. PhotoSoyuz Agency)

Mama put on a black dress, and left. That was it. Three days passed, and still there was no sign of her. My father had already been arrested by this time. I continued going to school, went out to pay the rent for our flat and played with the other little girls on Sretensky Boulevard. It was spring, and we were playing outside with a skipping rope when a neighbour ran up and told me that some people had arrived to see me. I found several people congregated in our room.

'Gather your belongings,' they said. 'You're going to stay with your grandmother.'

I remember wondering how I would get there when I didn't even know her address. And they hadn't asked me for her address either. I was taken into the next-door room, where our belongings were lying strewn about. They would only let me take children's things. I packed a book by Pushkin and one by Chekhov – big, grey volumes. And with that, they put me into the 'Emka' [GAZ-M1 model] and took me to the orphanage. It was 1938. I was taken into the hallway of the Danilovsky orphanage where they took my photograph, and my fingerprints.

* Translator's note: Also called 'the red corner', this was a dedicated space hung with portraits of Party and state leaders, propaganda posters and ideological art.

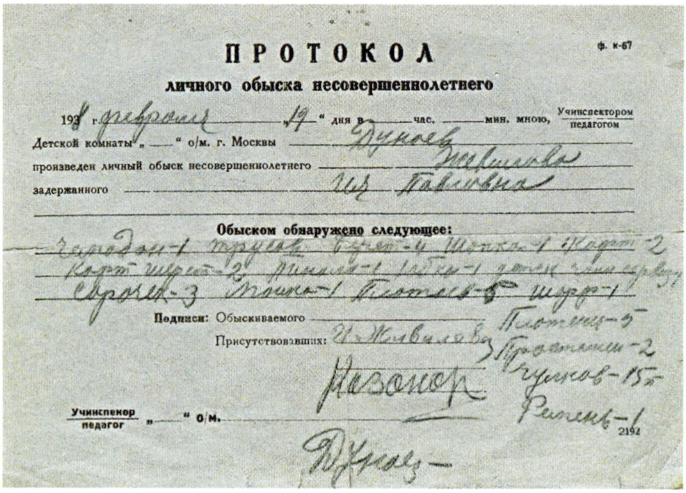

ПРОТОКОЛ ф. к-67

личного обыска несовершеннолетнего

193_ г. февраля 19 „__" дня в ___ час. ___ мин. мною, Учинспектором / педагогом

Детской комнаты „___" о/м. г. Москвы

произведен личный обыск несовершеннолетнего

задержанного

Обыском обнаружено следующее:

Подписи: Обыскиваемого

Присутствовавших:

Учинспектор / педагог „___" о/м.

A search record for a minor. Danilovsky NKVD orphanage, Moscow, 1938.

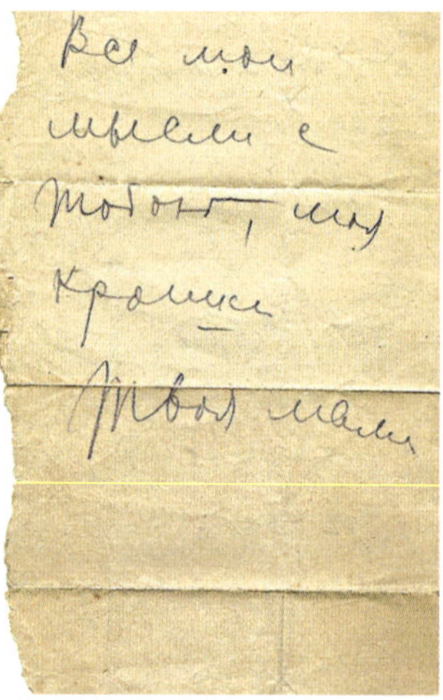

Все мои мысли с тобою, моя крошка

Твоя мама

A note left by a mother during her arrest, 1938. It reads: *All my thoughts are with you, my little one, Your Mama.* (From the Shulder-Nemchenko family archive)

Those who lived in the countryside also remember the Great Terror of 1937–8. Vladimir Shchebetyuk, the son of a kolkhoz engineer living in the small Ukrainian village of Isakivtsi, recalls: 'In 1937, I was in my fifth year of school. That year, many people from our community were repressed. First, my father was taken, then the postman. Next, the vet, the doctor, two of our teachers . . . they took them all – straight from their homes.'

Tatiana Zhelamskaya (Pskov region) remembers: 'My father's brother was the director of the kolkhoz. He was arrested during the "Great Purge" and disappeared for ever. Why was he arrested? A stack of peas rotted. They said it was sabotage.'

Antonina Ulanovskaya (Voroshilovgrad region) recalls a similar experience in 1938:

> People were talking in hushed voices down at the water pump.
>
> 'Vakhlai has been arrested,' somebody said. 'Is he a saboteur or a spy?'
>
> Surely he can't have been a spy, I remember thinking. He was a drunk! But he had got absolutely sozzled while we were all listening to Kalinin's report on the loudspeaker. Lots of people had gathered to listen to the speech, and he had walked up to the loudspeaker and slurred, 'What's he banging on about?'
>
> That was his act of sabotage. He was arrested that night and taken away. He had a wife and children – I was in the same class as his daughter, Lida, at school. But Vakhlai himself simply disappeared into thin air.

Children at an orphanage prepare for the 1st of May celebration parades, Ukraine, 1939.

Most of the stories we heard regarding arrests in the countryside were connected with the 'dekulakisation' campaign. While they are certainly no less tragic, for some reason these accounts tended not to be as emotionally charged as those related by the men and women living in the cities.

> My father died aged twenty-nine during the dekulakisation process. He was a Communist, and the authorities had given him a task. He was told to gather a certain number of people to form a kolkhoz. But my father happened to live in an area where nobody wanted to join one, or perhaps he just wasn't able to force anyone to do so. As a result, he was arrested along with the kulaks, and then shot. (Hanna Muzalyova, Kharkov region)

> I remember them coming to 'de-kulak' our area – we were evicted from our house and it was sold. We were left homeless, wandering about. My father was arrested and sent to work on the White Sea–Baltic Canal. (Grigory Kulbaka, Dnepropetrovsk region)

> My father was supporting six of us, as was our neighbour, Uncle Savva. They decided to club together to buy a cow and, in order to raise some money to clothe us, they slaughtered it and took it to the market to sell. When they got there, somebody discovered that the cow had recently calved. They were both arrested on the grounds that they had tried to conceal the calf from the government. (Anna Shtepa, Rostov region)

These stories of searches and arrests during the dekulakisation campaigns were sometimes described in a remarkably casual manner. There was a sense of resignation; an acceptance, particularly among those who grew up in the countryside, that this was just the way life was. It was not worth trying to understand. Perhaps this stands to reason. After all, the country dwellers of the Soviet Union bore the brunt of many of the state's violent campaigns.

Taking away the grain. Vyatka Governorate, 1930s.
(Photographer: A. Shishkin, PhotoSoyuz Agency)

Postcard, 1934.

As such, they often recounted personal experiences of violence as though they were accepted elements of everyday life, sometimes accompanying their accounts with no analysis whatsoever. Fedor Dudko's account of his father's arrest is a case in point (Kryski, Chernigov region):

> My father made a bit of a blunder. He worked at the distillery and had to transport barrels of spirit by horse and cart. One day the horse kicked out while on the ferry and a barrel fell into the water. My father got two years in a labour camp for that.

It is significant that all these years later, Fedor still considers a punishment of 'two years in a labour camp' to have been perfectly natural. 'My father made a bit of a blunder' is the extent of his analysis of the event.

The stories of those who lived in the countryside are punctuated with phrases that reveal a sense of hopelessness, an unprotesting acceptance of fate, and a feeling of submissive resignation before the state. Time and again, we heard sentences such as: 'There was nothing we could do'; 'Where could we have gone?'; 'There was no point in resisting.' Domnikiya Skiba (Kamenets-Podolsk region) remembers:

> They confiscated everything – our cow, both horses, the pig – and evicted us from our hut. They just threw us out onto the street! Why? Because we didn't want to join the kolkhoz. Where did we go? Well, what choice did we have? We joined the kolkhoz and all worked there.

If it was the case that some of the children growing up in the cities had been sheltered by their parents from some of the harsh realities of daily life, and thereby remained unaware of events unfolding

A barge carrying 'special resettlers' down the Togurskaya Ket river, near the settlement of Togur in the Tomsk region, 1930s. (From the archive of the Tomsk Memorial NKVD Prison Museum)

around them, this was absolutely not the case in the country. The dekulakisation affected everybody – fellow villagers, neighbours and relatives alike. Some were lucky; others were not. Some became victims of the campaign while others played an active part in it.

Victor Shuldeshov's father was head of the community council in their village in the Kursk region. He remembers: 'We lived in the house of a dispossessed kulak. He hadn't been deported – he still lived in our village. He built himself a little hut on the outskirts and lived there.'

Of course, children often interpreted the tragic events in their own particular way. Some saw deportation as an opportunity for adventure. Tatiana Zhelamskaya described her outlook on the events unfolding around her in the Pskov region: 'Our Papa was expelled from the kolkhoz a few times too, and plans were made to deport us. My sister and I couldn't wait to be deported – at least we would get to travel on a train!'

'But it was such a happy life!'

The stories from *Ostarbeiter* sharply contradict the myth, carefully curated over the next few decades, of a happy and carefree Soviet life

Line-up, 1934. (Photographer: E. Yevzerikhin. PhotoSoyuz Agency)

in the pre-war years. Some recall wrestling as youngsters with the paradox between the harsh realities of daily life and their firm belief in the righteousness of the Soviet regime. Nevertheless, it is clear from their accounts that in the years preceding the outbreak of war

Young Red Army pupils, 1936. (Photographer: E. Yevzerikhin. PhotoSoyuz Agency)

the vast majority were committed and faithful citizens of the Soviet state. They were all members of the first generation to be born and educated in the wake of the October 1917 Revolution and, as such, were instilled from the earliest moments of childhood with a firm belief in the Communist Party, in Stalin, in the invincibility of the Red Army, and in the fact that they lived in the best country in the world. Their minds displaced recollections of all the negative aspects of their childhood – poor clothes, poverty and starvation, to name but a few – replacing them with a carefully curated cache of the very brightest memories. They described the childhood events that they remembered most clearly: becoming a Pioneer, attending Pioneer camps, enjoying the wealth of different clubs they could choose to join.

Anna Odinokova (Chernigov region), remembers:

> Yes, we were short of food. But it was such a happy life! When I turned fourteen, I was invited to apply for the Komsomol.* 'You are a star-student,' I was told. 'You ought to set an example and apply for the Komsomol.' I ran the school newspaper you see, and I wrote poems. [. . .] Oh, how I remember the Pioneer camp – they really fed you well there. You'd be given a slice of fresh, white bread with butter, and coffee, as far as I recall. I've always had a terrible memory . . . was it coffee or cocoa they gave us? I can't remember. [. . .] Oh, I felt that I had gone to heaven.

Another of those we interviewed, Irina Sokolova, grew up in Moscow. She remembers:

> I was such an active member of the Komsomol. I believed wholeheartedly in the Soviet state and in the bright future it promised. I would go so far as to say that back then I considered

Children from the countryside with a banner reading 'Children of the Revolution! Prepare yourselves to continue and complete the work of Ilyich [Lenin]', 1933–4. (Photographer: M. Markov-Greenberg, PhotoSoyuz Agency)

* The All-Union Leninist Young Communist League was the Communist Party's youth organisation.

> it a calamity if I didn't get to see Stalin on the rostrum at the annual parade held on the first of May. When I walked out onto Red Square each year, I felt as though his eyes were on me alone.

Similarly, Anna Gulyaeva recalls:

> We never doubted that our politicians were doing the right thing. Following the annexation of Western Ukraine and Western Belarus [by the USSR in 1939], I remember singing in class: 'The old "Pan-Poland" is no more, the cunning witch has gone. Poland, you won't get your paws on our workers.'*

Vladimir Shchebetyuk, whose childhood was spent in the small Ukrainian border village of Isakovtsy, remembers:

> There was just one motor vehicle in our kolkhoz – a GAZ AA truck. We would put benches into the back of it on the May and October celebration days and then all of the primary

Pioneers learning about small petrol motors, 1930s. (Photographer: I. Shagin, PhotoSoyuz Agency)

* A ditty by Vasily Lebedev Kumach, written in 1939 in connection with the Red Army's 'liberation campaign' in Poland.

> school children would sit down on them. We were given little red flags to wave and as we drove along the border they told us to sing songs so that the Romanians could see just how well the children in the Soviet Union lived. The commander of the border guards came out to our field and told the women to wash and iron their headscarves well, because the Romanians and Poles were watching them. Nobody felt that this was all just for show – we considered it to be absolutely necessary – we were Soviets after all.

Of course, the authorities were keen to propagate a culture of vigilance and attentiveness. Taissa Tolkachova (Genichesk) explains:

> They asked us, as members of the Komsomol, to keep an eye out.
>
> 'The enemy has many disguises,' they said. 'It could take the form of an old man, or an old woman, so be vigilant!'
>
> On one occasion, we had been put on surveillance duty at the seaside – there were five of us: one boy and four girls. We heard a boat approaching and saw a figure walking up the beach towards us. We ran towards him shouting, 'Stop! Put your hands above your head!' The tall man duly raised his hands and I saw . . . my father! He had been fishing that night and we had caught him, so to speak! It's quite a funny anecdote!
>
> I later recounted the story of my mistake to the district committee of our Komsomol whereupon the secretary general said, 'Not to worry, you made a mistake this time. It happens.'

The collective statement that 'we all believed' espoused by many Soviet adolescents is slightly at odds with Nadezhda Izmalkova's assertion below that 'we all understood'. She describes her experience at school in Kiev:

> We all understood. When we wrote any sort of essay, we knew that we had to start it with the words 'Under the leadership of the Communist party and the human genius, Joseph Stalin . . .'. You had to use this sentence at both the beginning and the end

> of your essay. If not, you would be given a C. We understood this, and joked about it. We were children – we just accepted life as it was.

It is important to mention that often by the age of ten or eleven, having spent just four or five years in school, many of those we interviewed were the most educated members of their families.

At school in the late 1930s. (Photographer: M. Markov-Greenberg, PhotoSoyuz Agency)

Lessons at an orphanage in Saratov, 1939.

They were the first generation in the USSR to benefit from the system of compulsory primary school education that was introduced by the government in the 1920s. Compared with most of those around them, a youngster who had spent seven years at school was considered to be highly educated – their mothers could usually neither read nor write and their fathers might at best have received a general education at the parish school.

Schools sought to instil their pupils with a determinedly anti-religious spirit and, although few people actually took down the icons in their homes, it was usually only the elderly who went to church, if indeed there still was one in the vicinity. Children were usually christened but that was the extent of their religious introduction – parents understood that anything more could lead to 'unpleasantness' at school. Some of those we spoke to found religion later in their lives, having returned from Germany to discover that they had lost both family and loved ones. They remembered the destruction of the churches and icons, as well as the punishments meted out to supposedly guilty individuals.

A church converted into an anti-religious museum, Tyumen, 1930s. The sign above the entrance reads: *Religion is opium to the people.*

Regina Lavrovich's father was headmaster of a school in the Belarusian village of Osovets. She recalls that he played a part in the demolition of their church:

> The church was to be destroyed and a school built in its place. When the time came to demolish it though, somebody realised

that the bell needed to be taken down. But nobody wanted to do it.

Eventually some guy turned up. He crossed himself and said 'Well, my life is in God's hands' before climbing to the top of the church and taking the bell down.

In 1943 a bomb fell in our village – just one. And this very same man lost his hand in the explosion.

'That's for our church,' the villagers said.

My father died very young, in 1941 – perhaps he too was punished for his part in the destruction of the church.

It was impressed upon every Soviet citizen from earliest childhood that the USSR was the best country in the world. But in the 1930s, cracks were slowly beginning to appear, and with the outbreak of war people began to wonder whether this *beau idéal* of a common and unanimous ideological belief in their country truly was an honest reflection of reality.

Anti-religious alphabet book, 1933.

War

For many, war began unexpectedly. Varvara Khabarova (Zolotonosha) said: 'It never crossed our minds that there might be a war. To us, it came totally out of the blue.'

Others had seen it coming and witnessed the preparations first hand. Pavel Mikhailov lived in the Zaporozhye region and remembers that the newspapers wrote non-stop about the prospect of war. 'People were on edge,' he recalls. Likewise, seventeen-year-old Lidia Dadzis recalls that in Leningrad '[we] were all expecting war'.

Schools were particularly active in preparing the population for an enemy attack. The older schoolchildren – admittedly, mainly in the cities – were put through a 'Ready for Labour and Defence of the USSR' (GTO) programme. Many also earned their 'Voroshilov Sharpshooter' marksmanship badge and were enrolled on nursing courses or encouraged to join flying clubs (e.g. Grigory Kulbaka, Olga Smirnova, Maria Vitkevich and Vadim Novgorodov). It would be no exaggeration to say that Soviet culture in the pre-war years had been dominated by the theme of war; it had formed the subject of numerous books, films and popular songs. However, the looming threat of conflict was also used as justification for widespread repression: in order to defeat the foreign enemy, declared the authorities, it was first necessary to eliminate the internal enemy – namely, the fifth column of spies and traitors. Propaganda persistently declared the Red Army to be 'mightier than any other military force' and films such as *If War Comes Tomorrow* vowed that the enemy would be trounced on their own territory 'with little bloodshed and a mighty blow'.

Olga Golovina (Moscow), a prisoner of war, remembers:

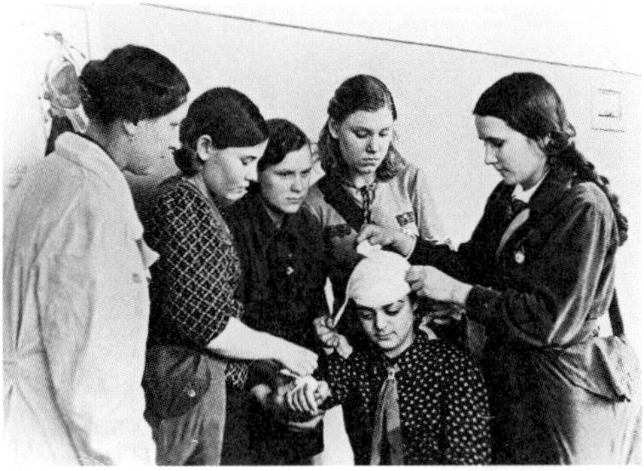

Children receiving military defence training at school, Moscow, 1939.

Pioneer Camp: practising drills in the event of a gas attack, 1930s. (Photographer: M. Markov-Greenberg. PhotoSoyuz Agency)

> We knew about war from our books, plays and radio broadcasts. How did we take the news? 'Oh, it won't last long,' we thought. We'll dispatch them in no time . . . we'll see them off! Nobody considered the Ribbentrop–Molotov Pact,* the war with Finland, the partition of Poland or the annexation of the Baltic countries, Western Ukraine and Belarus as indicators that this was to be a significant war. Most Soviet citizens had no idea who their principal enemy even was, let alone who they would be fighting.

Antonina Vladimirova (Cherkessk) said: 'We lived a peaceful, ordinary life. Nobody thought that the Germans would invade. It all happened so unexpectedly.'

* A non-aggression pact between the Soviet Union and Nazi Germany, signed in August 1939.

A propaganda poster entitled 'What Hitler Wants', Kuznetsky Most, Moscow, 1941. (Photographer: A. Ustinov, PhotoSoyuz Agency)

'I sat there listening to Molotov's* announcement'

All those we interviewed remembered 22 June 1941 as though it were yesterday. Time and again, they emphasised the sheer unexpectedness of the war. Some people's memories took on an idealistic tone, for this moment often marked the end of peaceful family life as they knew it.

Galina Agranovskaya remembers:

> It was a wonderful June day. [. . .] I had turned thirteen just one month earlier and my Papa had given me a book: *Gargantua and Pantagruel*. I remember my father working at his desk as I sat reading it on Granny's sofa, roaring with laughter. [. . .] Each

* Vyacheslav Molotov, a leading Bolshevik politician, was Soviet Minister of Foreign Affairs from 1939 to 1949 (and 1953 to 1956). Molotov was the prinicipal Soviet signatory of the Molotov–Ribbentrop Pact.

> time I did so, my father would raise his head and say, 'A little quieter please, sweetheart, I can't concentrate.'
>
> Just then our neighbour peered in through the open window and said, 'Fedor Georgievich! What are you sitting there writing for? The war has started!'

Galina's father was the journalist and author Fedor Kamanin, who had recently been released from prison and was soon to join the Partisans, for whom he would become editor of the Partisan newspaper in Bryansk. His family would later be deported to Germany.

That same summer, Valeria Fyodorova travelled from her home in Leningrad to her father's native home in Western Belarus. It was here that she had her first encounter with war:

> On Sunday night we woke to the hum of aeroplanes and the thunder of explosions. At first, we thought that it must be some sort of military training routine, but when the planes turned about, we saw the black crosses under their wings and understood that the Germans were bombing us and that the war had started. By Monday we saw the first refugees – women and children walking from the border, down the road from Brest to Minsk.

For most of those we interviewed, however, in June 1941 war had still seemed a long way off. Year 10 pupils celebrated leaving school as normal, as Nadezhda Bulava (Stalino) remembered: 'We had our school leavers' celebration on the evening of the 21st, and by the 22nd, we were at war.'

For these children, there was little sense that this was to be the end of life as they knew it. Vera Dergachova recalls:

> I finished school, received my leaving certificate and was preparing to enrol at the Medical Institute in Makhachkala. [. . .] I remember a friend asking, 'But Vera, haven't you heard that we're at war?'
>
> 'No,' I replied. 'What do you mean?'
>
> That was the first I had heard of any such news.

Taissa Tolkachova remembers:

> The morning of the 22nd was glorious; so quiet, peaceful and sunny. I was tidying up around the house. The radio was playing snippets of an operetta. [. . .] Suddenly the music stopped, the radio went quiet, and Molotov made an announcement about war.
>
> 'How terrible. War has begun,' my father said.
>
> But this meant nothing to me. I had no idea what war meant.

Antonina Serdyukova (Stalingrad) said:

> I graduated from music school in 1941 and we had our leavers' concert on 22 June. It was a beautiful morning – still and peaceful, with blazing sunshine. [. . .] My number was called and I walked up onto the stage, but before I could reach the piano, somebody pushed me aside from behind. A man walked out onto the stage.
>
> 'Comrades, we're at war!' he announced.
>
> I stood there, watching him silently. Then my teacher, Sergei Nikolaevich, took me by the hand and led me over to the piano.
>
> 'Play,' he said.
>
> I could hear people sobbing in the hall, the doors flew open, but he repeated 'Play' and I began to perform Brahms's Hungarian Dance No.1.

Anna Shtepa (Rostov) went to the hairdresser on 22 June 1941:

> I sat there, listening to Molotov's announcement on the radio. As soon as he had finished, I stood up to go.
>
> 'Surely you're not just going to leave?' the hairdresser asked in surprise.
>
> And with that, I sat back down and she carried on with my hairdo.

First day of Red Army enlistment, Moscow, 23 June 1941. (Photographer A. Ustinov, PhotoSoyuz Agency)

Muscovites listen to Molotov's announcement on the radio that Germany had attacked the USSR, 22 June 1941. (Photographer: I. Shagin, PhotoSoyuz Agency)

Not only do these accounts underscore the adolescent naivety of the young *Ostarbeiter*, but they also demonstrate their unanimous conviction that the war would be over in no time at all. They could not possibly have imagined what lay ahead, just around the corner.

'The films we saw in the cinema made it seem as though we had nothing to fear,' explains Anna Odinokova. Victor Zhabsky (Novocherkassk) also recalls the influence of the cinema:

> After all, we had been brought up to be patriots, hadn't we? [. . .] When we watched a film at the cinema and it showed

> one of our leaders – Stalin, Voroshilov,* Molotov or Budyonny† – everybody in the auditorium would get to their feet and applaud. And if you tried to remain seated, people would look at you, wondering whether you were going to stand.

According to Vera Sherenkova (Northern Caucasus): 'When they handed out our ration cards we said to each other, "We'll only have to make do like this for half a year or so, and then the war will be over."' This was the overriding mood with which people met the outbreak of war. Many hurried to sign up as volunteers, eager to have the chance to play their part in crushing the 'Fascists'.

Olga Smirnova (Lyuban, Leningrad region) said:

> The following morning my whole class gathered outside the military recruiting centre. We thought we'd be given new uniforms and assault rifles, and then march off to have a crack at the enemy. But there were so many people wanting to volunteer that we couldn't even get into the recruiting centre. They told us that they would invite us back when we were needed.

Maria Vitkevich (Krasnoye Selo, Leningrad region) remembered:

> I went straight to the District Committee on the Monday to volunteer for the front because I knew how to bandage. I wanted to be a doctor, you see. But they wouldn't take me – they said that I didn't have a Komsomol membership card. In fact, I later discovered that they only turned me down because they didn't trust me – I was the daughter of a kulak. I was assigned to trench digging instead.

---

* Kliment Voroshilov was appointed People's Commissar (Minister) for Defence in 1934 and later (1935) became a Marshal of the Soviet Union, the highest military rank in the state.

† Semyon Budyonny was a senior military figure and commander of the 1st Cavalry Army during the Russian Civil War. He was Marshal of the Soviet Union from 1935 to 1954 and awarded Hero of the Soviet Union three times.

Victor Zhabsky (Novocherkassk) said: 'There was a huge tide of patriotism in the early days. My friends and I dreamed of crushing Germany in three days or so, and then going on to Africa, where they had their colonies. We'd conquer those and so on . . .'

Parents rarely shared their children's optimism. Their experiences of the Russian Civil War and the years of hardship that had followed had taught them to prepare for the worst, and to stockpile supplies for survival. Taissa Tolkachova (Genichesk) remembers:

> Mama hurried back from the market and when she got home my father asked her whether she knew that the war had started.
>
> 'Oh good God!' she cried. 'Let's go and buy food supplies straight away . . . we'll bake crusts [. . .] Hurry, hurry, let's start stockpiling, we need to get everything ready.'
>
> My mother was such a scaredy-cat that she also insisted we dug a cellar.
>
> 'If they start bombing us, we won't stand a chance,' she said.
>
> So we got to work. We dug a huge, deep cellar.

The experienced adults knew exactly what they needed to stockpile. Nadezhda Kepet lived in the small village of Pukhovichy, in the Gomel region. She remembers: 'When the war broke out, Mama turned to me and said, "Darling, run to the shops and buy salt." I ran there and bought a full bag. I was almost trampled in the rush.'

The outbreak of war and the disastrous first few days of fighting had been so unexpected that people's faith in the veracity of official propaganda suddenly began to waver. For Regina Lavrovich, who lived in Belarus, the myth of the Soviet Union's impregnable borders was shattered overnight:

> It was the third day of war. My father received a summons, ordering him to report to the military recruitment office the following day. I remember it all so clearly; my parents stayed up all night. They lay there, talking, and my father said to my

mother (she told me this later): 'If I come back alive, I will tear up my Party membership card and we will get out of here – never again will I be a Communist.'

'It was awful . . .!'

The panic and chaos that followed the announcement of war were triggered by more than just a failure to anticipate its onset; the situation was undoubtedly exacerbated by the effects of the widespread system of repression carried out over the preceding years. Any Soviet workers or Party members who had managed to survive the Great Terror, or those who had benefited from promotions into positions that had been 'freed up', were often afraid to face up to the truth and take any degree of responsibility for their actions. Sergei Bogdanov (Rzhev) said:

> My mother worked as an accountant for the Rzhev Municipal Services Committee. As the German army neared Rzhev, the management called an organisation-wide workers' meeting. The workers were told that there was no way that the Germans would ever get anywhere near Rzhev, let alone capture the city. This they maintained, despite the fact that news trickling through from the front told a very different story. The next day, my mother went to work as usual, only to find that not one of the workers' managers who had spoken at the meeting, nor a single member of the city council, was in evidence. They had all abandoned Rzhev already; they knew it would fall to the Germans.

The victorious mood among the younger generation also began to fade rapidly. As Victor Zhabsky recalls, his conviction that a swift Soviet victory was a foregone conclusion began to waver as, one after another, Soviet cities fell to the Germans:

> We were still young – only fourteen years old – but somehow we understood the situation. Our courtyard was quite large, and the men in our building began to gather there to quietly

> discuss developments. We overheard some of their conversations: 'Kiev has been taken . . . how can it be . . . what on earth is going on?'
>
> And we listened and watched with our own eyes as regiments left for the front. We noticed that half of them didn't even have rifles.

Many witnessed the army retreating in panic. Sergei Bogdanov (Rzhev) recalls: 'I saw our woebegone troops on the run. Well, they weren't really troops – just desperate soldiers who had abandoned their weapons and were darting through the woods.'

The retreating Red Army soldiers were a pitiful sight, and they certainly didn't resemble the staunch defenders they had been made out to be. On the contrary, before long they were turning to the teenagers and their families for help, asking for food, medical assistance, or a place to hide from the Germans or the local police. Victor Shuldeshov lived in a small rural settlement in Russia's Kursk region. He described seeing Soviet soldiers fleeing the Germans:

> Do you know how they retreated? It was awful to watch! They just kept coming, these soldiers. They would fall down and just lie there – they didn't have the strength to stand. They came in droves of filthy, ragged men. They begged us for something to eat. Well, we gave them everything we had left.

Taissa Tolkachova describes how the city Komsomol committee in her hometown of Genichesk tried to gloss over the retreat of the soldiers by throwing a welcome party:

> We were assembled at school and told, 'Let's greet them with flowers!' We ran up to the column of troops [. . .] the soldiers were shabby, filthy, frightening. They tucked the little bouquets under their armpits and marched on, haggard, half-dead from exhaustion. Of course, flowers were the last thing on their mind.

People were shocked by the lies they were fed by those in charge. Many remember being urged not to succumb to panic by individuals who then hurriedly left in front of their very eyes. Larisa Shvidchenko (Rostov-on-Don) remembers:

> As ever, nobody told us the truth. But we could see for ourselves what was happening – the cannons were being towed away; the army was leaving.
>
> 'What's going on?' we asked the soldiers. 'Are you retreating?'
>
> 'No, we've just been redeployed,' came the reply.
>
> Why did they need to lie? Why did our own people lie to us?

Neonila Rozhkova lived in a rural village in the Zhytomyr region, where many Jewish families had settled. She recalls that the Jews began to leave as soon as the war started: 'But then the authorities announced that the Germans had been beaten back to such-and-such a distance. They encouraged the Jews to return home and take up their work again. All those who returned were shot.'

As the Germans penetrated further and further into Soviet territory, youngsters, both boys and girls, found themselves on the front line. They were put to work digging trenches, building anti-tank defences and caring for the wounded. The government attempted to muster some sort of defence, dispatching teenagers to face the advancing German troops. Many of those we interviewed remember this well. Vadim Novgorodov (Taganrog) told us of his experience:

> On the 10th or 12th October 1941, the town commander issued an order for everyone to come to the defence of Taganrog. We were to build fortifications.
>
> I picked up a shovel and a crowbar and went to the assembly point. Just as we finished digging a large anti-tank ditch, the commander drove up. 'Here you go,' he shouted, chucking something at us. 'Two bottles of petrol. Throw them at the German tanks when they arrive.' And then he drove off. [. . .] On 17 October, my Mama came running up to us. 'Put down

> your shovel,' she said, 'the German tanks are already rolling down Leninskaya Street.'

Vera Dergachova also remembered digging ditches:

> Well, there we were – we had already finished digging one great trench. The next morning we woke to be told that the enemy had changed direction, so we were to change the orientation of our anti-tank ditches too. [. . .] A few days later we awoke to find ourselves alone – there was no sign of anybody, not even our soldiers. It transpired that the Donbass region had been surrounded and our soldiers had scarpered, abandoning us in a bid to save themselves. [. . .] There was nobody to command us so we decided to head for home. But by the time I got back to my village the Germans were already there. They had beaten me to my own house.

First encounters with the horrors of war were indelibly etched in the memories of those we spoke to. Yevdokiya Verkholantseva lived in the Pskov region and though she worked in peat production she had also been taught to administer first aid. She shared one harrowing memory with us:

> They gave us bandages and explained what to do with them. I saw one of our soldiers lying wounded and ran up to him.
>
> 'Help me! Help me!' he was crying.
>
> I glanced at him and saw his intestines. I thought I was going to be sick. And I didn't help him, I didn't help him, oh, I didn't help him . . . I'm such a bitch [she cries]. And by the time I got up and ran away he was already dead.

An extract from the diary of Antonina Ulanovskaya (Shterovka, Voroshilovgrad region) reads:

> Suddenly, high up in the blue sky we saw a grey-black bomber. He circled around our little train station. Then the bombs

> began to fall from the plane as though somebody was scattering potatoes from a bucket. The bombs whistled horribly as they fell. Eeeeee-zhakh! We lay between the rows of corn, scared to death. Powerful explosions split the air, one after another. When the smoke cleared, we looked for our house with its dovecote on the roof. It was intact! Unable to believe our eyes, we ran home. Something caught our attention on the side of the road . . . I couldn't believe what I was seeing . . . it was a dirt-smeared human leg and foot.

Varvara Kramarenkova worked in a munitions factory in Sevastopol after leaving school. She remembers the night she fled the city ahead of the Germans:

> Just two or three days earlier, we had sent a telegram to Stalin saying that we would not give up Sevastopol. [. . .] We left during the night, crossing around the harbour under the Germans' very noses. As we walked, we heard voices calling out in the dark, 'Brothers, my dears, I'm still alive. Save me, I'm still young.'
>
> Another cried out, 'I'm crippled, I don't want to live any longer. Please just shoot me.'

Antonina Serdyukova lived in Stalingrad. She remembers:

> We sat in the basement. The bombing never stopped; debris whistled through the air. This lasted for three weeks. Whenever there was the slightest silence, we would crawl down to the Volga to fetch water. [. . .] The streets outside were a place of silent horror – the whole road down to the Volga was thick with bodies. [. . .] A bomb fell on our house during one of the last attacks – it landed in the next-door entrance. It went right into the building, killing everyone there. But our house was only buried in rubble, so we began to claw our way out. There was another family with us – a husband, wife and their two children – one was still a baby, just a few months old.

Красноармеец!

Жиды самые подлые, самые опасные грызуны подтачивающие основы нашего мира. Ты борешься за них, в бесчисленном количестве жертвуешь добром, здоровьем, жизнью, для того чтобы они и дальше могли об'едаться в тылу и набивать себе карманы.

Только когда последний жид будет изгнан из твоего отечества настанет мир.

Бей жидовское отродье!

Уничтожай этот бич человечества и ты этим закончишь войну!

Только так ты сможешь добиться лучшего будущего для твоей страны и счастья в твоей жизни.

Эта листовка действительна, как пропуск
Dieses Flugblatt gilt als Passierschein

ASd 095

An anti-Semitic German propaganda leaflet addressed to Red Army soldiers encouraging them to stop sacrificing their 'young, healthy' lives so that 'Jews can sit safely at home, lining their pockets'. It urges the soldiers to 'eleminate this scourge of mankind and, in doing so, end the war. (From the collection of M. Poizner)

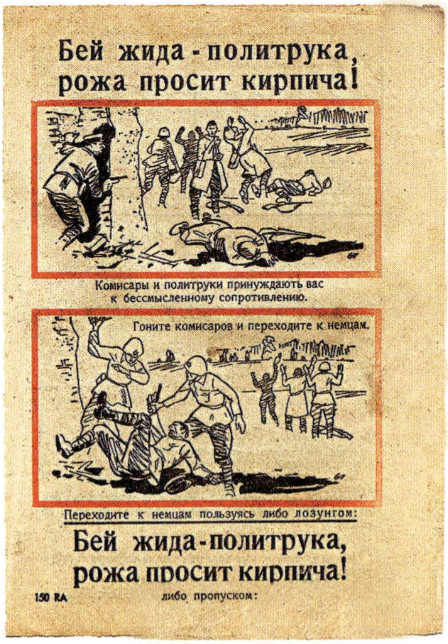

An anti-Semitic German propaganda leaflet calling on people to 'beat the Jews and political leaders with a brick' and 'join the Germans'. (From the collection of M. Poizner)

> The mother gave this little girl to me to hold, but she was no longer crying from hunger. She died right there in my arms.

'We didn't manage to evacuate in time'

Evacuation was a painful recurring theme in the stories recounted by the *Ostarbeiter* for, ultimately, failing to evacuate in time resulted in their deportation to Germany. The Germans advanced rapidly, and the evacuation of business enterprises, party members and the Soviet political elite was prioritised. Women, children and ordinary workers were often unable to leave and therefore stayed behind in occupied territory. We spoke to two individuals who were left behind in Taganrog. One was Nikolai Gulyaev:

> Papa worked in the factory. They detached all the machines from their foundations and loaded them into a lorry.
>
> 'Prepare to evacuate!' came the order.

> They were supposed to be taken to Novosibirsk. He worked until one o'clock in the afternoon, and then he returned home. But by 2 p.m. the Germans were already in Taganrog.

Another was Valentina Gridchina: 'My Mama worked at the military aviation factory as a typing clerk. She returned home one night and told us that we would be evacuating. She left me to wait with the packed bags. But we didn't manage to evacuate in time.'

It was not uncommon for a husband to be evacuated with his company, but for his wife and children to be left behind. Valentina Sekhina (Stalino) remembers:

> Papa was evacuated straight away – on the second day of the war. He was a Communist and the manager of a coke fuel plant. My mother and I were left behind – they were meant to evacuate us, but it never happened. There was no evacuation. We didn't get away in time. The Germans arrived.

Vadim Novgorodov remembers the haste with which the senior management departed from Taganrog. His mother worked as a cleaner at the Communist Party district committee in the city:

> Once they had occupied our city, the Germans ordered everyone to return to work as usual, so my mother was sent to tidy up the mess in the district committee office. When she entered the building, she was confronted with disorder and total chaos – record cards had been carelessly tossed everywhere.

The *Ostarbeiter* remembered that the mass looting of abandoned properties and shops began as soon as the local authorities had fled, and before the Germans had even arrived:

> We heard talk that there had been shooting in town, and that the shops were being looted. When our boys got there, they found that the shops had been completely emptied, and all they brought back were masses of buttons. They told us that there

> was nobody in town, neither Red Army soldiers, nor Whites, nor Germans, nor any of our own people. (Aldona Volynskaya, Novoukrainka, Kirovograd region)

Nadezhda Izmalkova (Kiev) said: 'By 18 September, Kiev was leaderless – all those in charge had left. People had already begun to smash windows and steal things. They took away anything they could carry – flour from the bakery, things from the shops.'

The theme of evacuation also came up in conversations with those who had lived in cities or villages with large Jewish populations. Several of those we spoke to inadvertently revealed anti-Semitic attitudes – we were told a number of times that 'the Jews managed to evacuate because they were rich' (Neonila Rozhkova; Nikolai Bogoslavets; Anna Odinokova; Nadezhda Izmalkova). They voiced an opinion that had been prevalent at the time, stating that the Jews themselves were responsible for the fate that befell them. 'They didn't leave in time, and that's why they died' was a view commonly espoused. Some shrugged off all responsibility for events that had occured in front of their very eyes.

However, we also heard many people speak with deep compassion and sorrow about the tragic fate of the Jews who did not manage to evacuate. Elena Markova (Stalin region) said:

> We were very close to one Jewish family in particular – there were two sisters, both doctors. I remember them from childhood – they were very good friends of both my mother and father. They were fairly elderly, even then. One sister, Tamara Samuilovna, taught me French. In the end, they decided to evacuate. [. . .] But it turned out that the Germans were already ahead of them, so they came back. By then, however, the Germans had arrived here too. They asked me to live with them so that, if the Germans came to their house, I could open the door. They thought that if a Russian girl opened the door the Germans would leave straight away. So I lived with them for a while. But, of course, eventually they were taken and killed. A great many of our Jewish friends were killed.

Valentina Gridchina spoke of her friends in Taganrog:

> A Jewish family lived next door – my mother was very close to them. The husband was evacuated, but Sara didn't want to go.
>
> 'I don't believe this twaddle on the radio,' she said.
>
> My mother told her to go, but Sara refused. She stayed behind with her daughter, who was younger than me – she hadn't yet started school. She was such a beautiful little girl, with wavy blonde hair.

Frida Palko (Starodub, Bryansk region) said:

> My grandmother, God rest her soul, wasn't to blame for the decision she made. She remembered the previous war with the Germans – they hadn't killed anyone; they had behaved like normal people. Nobody believed that there would be such savagery this time. So when the time came to evacuate, we didn't leave.

As a result, Frida's entire family died in the ghetto that the Germans created at Starodub.

Irina Vatman (Odessa) recalled: 'My grandparents refused to evacuate. "The Germans are cultured people," my grandfather said, "they invented the clock." They stayed behind in the city.'

While evacuation might have been an option for those living in industrial centres, it was usually completely off the cards for people living in the countryside or in small towns and cities. When we asked people how they came to be left behind in occupied territory, many said that they simply hadn't felt they needed to evacuate. Varvara Khabarova explained frankly: 'Party members, managers and NKVD officers all left. They knew that the Germans would execute them so they hightailed it out of there.'

Taissa Tolkachova (Genichesk) remembered:

> Who was evacuated? All those in charge – all the district commissioners, the city Party Committee (the Gorkom) members,

> the kolkhoz directors, Party workers and their families – they were all evacuated in vehicles. But nobody even asked us if we wanted to go – it was a matter that didn't concern us.

Many *Ostarbeiter* also explained that they stayed behind because they could not bring themselves to abandon their mothers to care for a brood of little brothers and sisters alone. Anna Odinokova remembers that her mother was worried for her and tried to persuade her to leave their village of Dubovichy: 'I was a girl – she knew what lay in store for me. She wanted to save me. But, crying bitter tears, I told her that I would stay anyway – there was no way I could leave her with four little ones.'

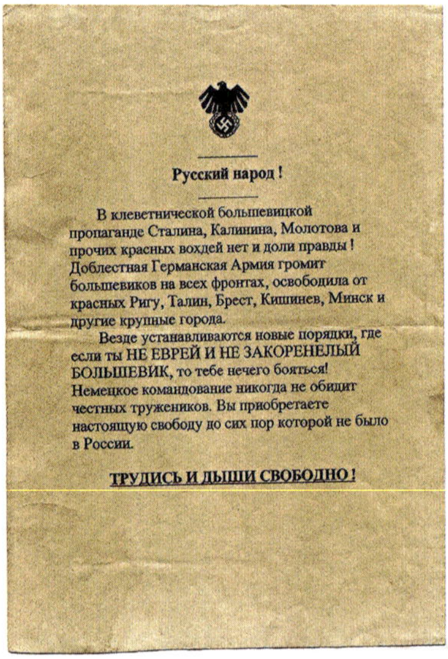

Русский народ !

В клеветнической большевицкой пропаганде Сталина, Калинина, Молотова и прочих красных вохдей нет и доли правды ! Доблестная Германская Армия громит большевиков на всех фронтах, освободила от красных Ригу, Талин, Брест, Кишинев, Минск и другие крупные города.

Везде устанавливаются новые порядки, где если ты НЕ ЕВРЕЙ И НЕ ЗАКОРЕНЕЛЫЙ БОЛЬШЕВИК, то тебе нечего бояться! Немецкое командование никогда не обидит честных тружеников. Вы приобретаете настоящую свободу до сих пор которой не было в России.

<u>ТРУДИСЬ И ДЫШИ СВОБОДНО !</u>

German propaganda leaflet (from the collection of M. Poizner).

Russian People!
There is not a shred of truth in the libellous propaganda of Stalin, Kalinin, Molotov and the other Red leaders. The valiant German Army is crushing the Bolsheviks on every front – Riga, Tallinn, Brest, Kishinev, Minsk and other large cities have already been liberated from the Reds.

A new order is being established everywhere, and unless you are A JEW OR AN INVETERATE BOLSHEVIK, you have nothing to fear! German command will never harm honest workers. You will enjoy true freedom, the like of which you never had in Russia.

KEEP WORKING AND BREATHE EASILY!

'And then we saw them – Germans!'

The Germans arrived, and all those who had been unable to evacuate in time were left behind in what was now occupied territory. Sergei Bogdanov (Rzhev) said:

> We didn't manage to get out ahead of the Germans, so we turned our carts around and headed back home. The Germans

> were riding motorcycles – they were quite an impressive sight, and a little frightening too. After all, the enemy is the enemy. We wondered what change they would bring, what sort of order they would impose. A few of the German soldiers at the front of the group immediately surrounded us, shouting, '*Oh! Partisanen!*'
>
> But then they saw that we had women and a fifteen-year-old lad with us. They lifted our clobber from the cart and shook it all out, but we had nothing with us except for a few blankets and a bag of grain that we had taken for the journey. [. . .] They let us go.

Lev Tokarev recalled:

> We knew that the Germans were already just outside Peterhof. But we hadn't seen any ourselves – not one! And then, suddenly, one morning the door opened and a German walked in. [. . .] He was holding a *kolotushka* – their type of hand grenade.
>
> 'Are there any Communists here?' he asked.
>
> 'None,' we replied.
>
> He looked around the room and then turned to my grandmother. '*Zucker*. Give me *zucker*,' he said.
>
> But my grandmother didn't understand.
>
> 'He's asking for sugar,' I said.
>
> 'You tell this monster that I have no sugar,' she bristled.
>
> This the German seemed to understand. Brandishing his grenade at her, he opened the cupboard and found a jar containing a few small chips of sugar. Opening it, he poured the sugar into his pocket, brandished his grenade at my grandma once again, and left. That's how I met my first German.

Neonila Rozhkova (Zhytomyr region) said:

> We were terribly frightened. We had heard that they were going to burn us all to death. When they arrived, there was no fight at all. We sat huddled in the cellar, unable to see what was

> going on outside. We were terrified – oh, they were going to burn us all to a crisp! We sat there and prayed. Then we heard somebody coming down the stairs. We counted the steps. This was it. We were going to be killed and set alight. An old man walked in – he was the owner of the house. He led us across the road [. . .] And then we saw them – Germans! They were coming down the road towards us, sleeves rolled up and getting closer all the time.
>
> 'Good day to you, Sirs,' we said to them.
>
> And they laughed out loud.

The Soviet population awaited the arrival of the occupying forces with considerable fear and trepidation. However, for the rural population who witnessed their arrival, first impressions were sometimes pleasantly surprising. They recalled that at least in the very early days the Germans behaved fairly peaceably towards them. Elizaveta Krestyantseva (Kirovograd) said: 'The first Germans to arrive didn't lay a finger upon us [. . .] And then the SS arrived in their black uniforms. They were the real killing squads.'

According to Fedor Apyonkin (Vitebsk region):

> At first they didn't come past us at all – I never even saw them. But we heard that they had arrived in the neighbouring village of Sokolyanka so a crowd of us gathered to go and see what all this talk of Germans was about. It was true – their cars were there. They had arrived, and were giving out pieces of sugar or chocolate to the children. I have to say, the people were sort of smiling as they looked on, myself included. I watched, and I couldn't quite comprehend it. There was a lot that I didn't fully comprehend.

Something that everyone remembers, however, was that the German soldiers demanded food and tried to get their hands on domestic livestock. Nikolai Bogoslavets (Zenkov, Poltava region) recalled:

> My first impression of the Germans was that they were healthy, well-fed men. They were well dressed and well armed. I was surprised that each soldier had his own standardised, polished wooden club. At first, I had no idea what they were for. It was only when I saw them in use that I understood. They would throw them on the ground where the chickens were pecking about, smashing their legs, and then carry them off. [. . .] They would come to our house without weapons – just with these clubs.

Anna Kirilenko (Rostov-on-Don) recalled encountering a German soldier looking for Partisans:

> The first time I saw a German [. . .] I was sitting in the courtyard when I saw a strapping red-haired man wearing shorts and carrying an automatic rifle crossing the courtyard in front of me. I froze. [. . .] A trench had been dug out in the courtyard. He walked up to it and unleashed a volley of bullets from side to side: du-du-du-du-du. He finished shooting, turned on his heel and left.

The women we spoke to, many of whom had been very young girls at the time of occupation, were extremely frightened that they would become victims of sexual violence. They spoke constantly of their mothers' insistence that they wrapped up in old rags and pulled their headscarves down low over their faces. Anna Gulyaeva (Novoduginskaya, Smolensk region) remembered: 'Mama was afraid. Whenever we went out, she would wrap us up in headscarves like old women and say, "Don't show your mugs." Well, that didn't stop them. Those sorts of things happened back then.'

Only one woman anonymously shared her experience of rape:

> I have never spoken of this to anyone. I was at home that day, lying on my bed. My neighbour, Lyonka, and sister Lyuba were also at home with me. Two Germans came in, carrying automatic rifles. They sent Lyonka and my sister out immediately, but kept

> me behind. And one German raped me. The other stood and watched the whole time. When they left, I went out into the street where the neighbours had gathered. One of them, Uncle Kolya, said, 'Raped you, did they?'
>
> 'Yes,' I replied.
>
> And that was that.

This account sounds detached and casual, as though the subject of conversation was something altogether different. Her reflection on the incident came only at the end of our conversation, when talk turned to her experiences in Germany. Following her deportation, she had been sent to work as a housemaid for an elderly German couple of whom she had only very fond memories. Referring back to her terrible experience during the occupation, she remarked, 'Where on earth did such heartless monsters come from? There were good people there [in Germany], but look what their children did.'

The contrast between the replete, cheerful, well-equipped German soldiers and their Soviet opponents was a worrying sight, for the surrounded Red Army soldiers and columns of Soviet prisoners of war conveyed an altogether different impression of the Soviet Union's military might than that touted by propaganda. Tatiana Zhelamskaya (Rudo, Pskov region) said: 'We lived near the main road and used to see them herding the prisoners of war – our soldiers – down it. We saw the poor things, with nothing but foot wraps on their feet. They were chased along with dogs.'

Zoya Yeliseeva's father was taken prisoner by the Germans. He had been conscripted into the Red Army a month before Dzhankoy, the Crimean city where he lived with his family, surrendered to the Germans. Zoya remembers that her neighbour rushed over to tell her that a prisoner convoy was marching past, and her father was among them:

> It was mid-November, cold, and very muddy – they were knee-deep in slushy mud. The entire convoy was made up of prisoners of war. The security guards escorting them were

shouting. [. . .] People were walking along beside the convoy. It was awful! We were searching, shouting. And then, we found him! I walked alongside him and he said, 'Quick, run home and fetch my coat and peaked cap – they're hanging up. Bring them back as fast as you can.'

I ran home, grabbed his coat and cap and ran back again. But the escort guards chased me away – they fired shots into the air. I ran forward, screaming 'Papa! Papa!' But he wasn't there. I thought they would open fire on us, but the crowd dispersed and I walked home in tears. A neighbour saw me and said, 'Don't cry, you fool. He's at home.'

It transpired that he had seized an opportune moment to run home.

Olga Smirnova saw Soviet prisoners of war on the outskirts of Leningrad: 'They had neither felt boots, nor sheepskin coats. They had wrapped their feet in newspaper, and then bound them with rags. They walked along: frostbitten, sick, ragged.'

We received many detailed descriptions of the way the occupying forces were met in various towns and villages. Some *Ostarbeiter* were incredulous and vocal in their condemnation of the considerable number of people who celebrated the arrival of the Germans. Nikolai Bogoslavets (Zenkov, Poltava region) recalled:

It was strange to see people in my hometown of Zenkov, people that I knew well, greeting the Germans with bread and salt. [. . .] Among them was an absolutely beautiful girl I knew. She had done very well at school. They gave her a loaf wrapped in a scarf and she stood before everyone wearing our national costume.

Frida Palko said:

The war had started on 22 June, and on 18 August the Germans arrived on their motorcycles. Many people welcomed their arrival. One of these guys – his name was Stukachko – lived on our lane. He took them bread and salt. He was thrilled that

> the Germans had arrived to liberate us from the Soviet regime. There were many people who shared his sentiments.

Many of those who greeted the Germans with bread and salt hoped that the new order would rid them of the Bolsheviks and the widely despised system of kolkhoz farms. These people were, however, in the minority. Most met the Germans with a strong sense of trepidation, albeit mixed with a little curiosity. Lyubov Shkulyova (Kirovograd) remembered:

> We lived with my grandmother on the outskirts of Kirovograd. Suddenly we heard people chattering – they were saying that the Germans had arrived. There was silence – the sound of gunfire had stopped. Then suddenly we heard that the Germans were already on Ovrazhna Street. The sound of a gramophone could be heard. 'How interesting,' I remember thinking. 'I must go and see what's going on.' The Germans had got hold of a gramophone somewhere – they had wound it up and put on some of our records. They stood there roaring with laughter.

Nadezhda Izmalkova (Kiev) said:

> I walked along and took it all in. Khreschatyk Street was packed with people. Everyone was walking about, holding flowers. Strapping young men sat atop tanks rolling down Khreschatyk Street and people scurried about, chatting, meeting friends. [. . .] I was astounded and ran home, horrified.
>
> 'My God! The Germans are in Kiev! What on earth are we going to do?' I cried. 'We're done for!'
>
> But nothing really happened. The Germans wandered about, and chatted with girls.

Irina Vatman (Odessa) recalled:

> You should have seen the Germans arriving in Odessa! The street was packed with people handing out salt and bread, and

celebrating. At last, order would be restored! Order was restored: a gallows was constructed in front of the fire tower and three people were hanged on it. One of them was my grandfather – the same man who had said that the Germans were 'cultured people'. That's how the occupation began.

Occupation

The *Ostarbeiter* we spoke to had spent varying lengths of time living in occupied territory. Although some were deported to the Third Reich as early as the autumn of 1941, most were not sent away until the following spring or summer when the mass deportations got underway. Others remained in the Soviet Union until as late as 1943. Each individual had a very different story to tell about life in occupied territory, and personal experiences varied hugely, in line with a number of factors including age, literacy and life experience. It was one thing to undergo occupation in a large city such as Kiev or Rostov, but for those living in the countryside or small villages life was very different. Moreover, stories recounted by Ukrainian villagers, for example, often differed starkly from those told to us by villagers in Belarus. The extent to which people came into contact with the occupiers also varied from place to place, and while some people barely laid eyes on a German invader, others were obliged to share their homes with not only German, but also Romanian and Hungarian soldiers. Ultimately, the distance a person lived from the front was a factor in their experience and much depended upon whether or not families could continue to live under their own roofs within occupied territory. If not, they became refugees.

As a result of this diversity of experience, the accounts by the *Ostarbeiter* paint a patchy and contradictory picture, full of gaps and things left unsaid. These inconsistencies are due, in part, to the fact that even the phrase 'life under the Germans' was effectively forbidden for many years. For a long time, all events that negated the 'great victory of the Soviet people' were carefully erased from the historical Soviet war narrative.

Accordingly, journalism, literature, cinema and textbooks

Identity card, Rovensky region, April 1942.

Identity card, Vitebsk region, July 1943.

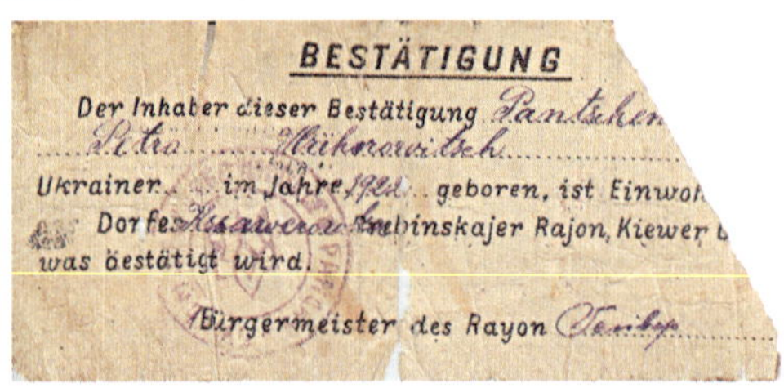

Identity card, Kiev region,1942.

presented a distorted and one-sided account of life under occupation, depicting only the savagery of the occupiers and the resistance of the Soviet people. Having lived through the years of suffering and fear, many witnesses, either purposefully or subconsciously, erased certain memories of the occupation from their minds. By mentally adjusting their personal experiences to fit within the parameters of the safe and the ordinary they avoided uncomfortable discussions about their past. As a result, we found the stories that breached the safety of this pattern of familiarity particularly fascinating, although they did demand a degree of openness from *Ostarbeiter* that many found difficult to provide. Those who had survived occupation and deportation as teenagers generally found these conversations easier because, as a rule, they were less likely to have been accused of collaborating with the Germans when they returned home. It was much harder for those who had been deported as adults, many of whom were obliged to spend years justifying themselves and explaining why they hadn't joined the Partisans or become members of the underground resistance movement. Tens of years later, some told us how they had coped in these difficult circumstances.

This was 'German order' now

Descriptions of life under occupation were almost always punctuated by references to 'German order', '*Ordnung*' and 'new order'.* This order almost always began with registration, followed by the institution of various controls over the local population.

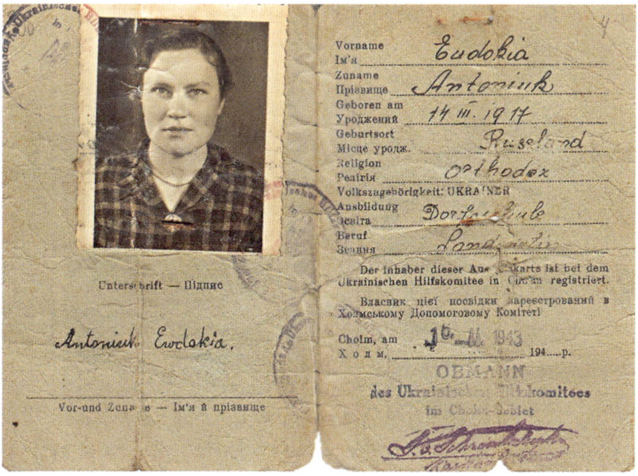

Identity card, Novgorod region, February, 1943.

---

* The concept of 'new order' was based on an order by Hitler on 17 June 1941 regarding 'civic governance in occupied eastern territories'. The Reich Ministry for the Occupied Eastern Territories was established under the leadership of Alfred Rosenberg. Letters were circulated stipulating that the police would register all citizens in their place of residence. People were expressly forbidden to leave their homes without written permission from the administrative body in their area – offices were established in the cities for this purpose. Rural areas were served by their military police commandants. Military commanders held positions of absolute authority in the regions and townships, and heads of *volost* (burgomasters) and elders were appointed to oversee the rural districts, towns and villages.

Nikolai Bogoslavets (Zenkov, Poltava region) remembered: 'A list was hung on the front door of every home. That way they could check whether somebody was living in the house who shouldn't be there. [. . .] This was the German way of doing things.'

Victor Zhabsky recounts: 'The first order that they issued was for all commissars, Communists and Jews to register with the police headquarters. They also announced that they would shoot a hundred people for every German killed. That was the choice. These were the sorts of menacing orders they imposed.'

'Order' was maintained with the help of the police and administrative officials recruited from the local population. The relationship between those who voluntarily or involuntarily assisted the Germans in the small towns and villages, and those who did not, was extremely difficult. This was particularly true of the villages, where everyone knew each other and there were close ties between neighbours and relatives who had attended school or worked together before the war. Many were shocked and confused by the behaviour of friends and relatives in the new circumstances.

> The Germans appointed a village elder and policemen from among our own villagers. Our elder was Vladimir Fedorovich Babenko – my brother-in-law. (Grigory Kulbaka, Dnepropetrovsk region)

> My friend and former classmate's father was appointed as an elder. He would arrive every morning to hand us an assignment sheet for work – the police headquarters gave them to him. (Anna Gulyaeva, Novoduginskaya, Smolensk region)

Those who joined the German police force were especially feared and hated, often more so than the Germans themselves.

> There were more policemen than were needed. Our people too – Russian '*Polizei*'. But they were lowlifes – the lowest of lowlifes. (Nadezhda Bulava, Stalino)

> I went into the village to exchange a few things. I had traded something for a fish, and had put it in my bag. A couple of guards were standing there – one German, and with him, a Russian policeman. And this Russian policeman grabbed the fish from me.
>
> '*Mutter krank*,' I said to the German, explaining that my mother was lying ill at home and I couldn't give them the fish (we had learned German at school). The German told the Russian policeman to give it back to me. (Lidia Beketova, Taganrog)

> The policeman was selected at a village gathering.* [. . .] They chose an energetic young man. What did the policeman do? He obeyed commands. The high commissioner would tell him to get some meat. And he would get it. Then he began to take the livestock – pigs, then calves and, finally, the cows. This is what the policeman did. Oh, and he sent people to work in Germany. He made no exceptions for anyone. (Pavel Mikhailov, Zaporozhye region)

The *Ostarbeiter* had particularly personal relationships with the village elders, the police and those who worked in the German command headquarters. After all, it was they who compiled the lists of people for deportation to Germany, and more often than not, the names on the lists were those who had come to be in the police's bad books (often over personal matters, such as having expressed sympathy for the Soviet state). Of course, the lists also included those who had been unable to buy their way off them.

The Germans had expected that people who were discontented or had grievances with the Soviet regime would voluntarily elect to work for them, and in many instances this proved to be the case. Anna Odinokova (Dubovichy, Chernigov region) remembers:

* It is likely that our interviewee may have confused the selection of the policeman with the selection of the village elder.

> The police were all our guys. First, they chose volunteers, but those who did not volunteer were forced. [. . .] Our policeman had recently been dispossessed [a kulak] and was unhappy with the Soviet regime. He was my sister's father-in-law [. . .] He had a son my age – we had studied in the same class at school. Do you know what he did? He kept his own son at home, and sent me to Germany! He sent me away from a sick mother and four little brothers and sisters. That's the kind of monster he was!

Like many of her friends, Aldona Volynskaya was sent to an orphanage following the arrest of both her parents. There, she heard of other children who had been betrayed by their communities. 'Your time has come,' they had been told. 'You must declare that you are the children of arrested parents.' Her parting comment that 'there were no such traitors' among her own community was a cutting indictment on those who turned against their own.

There were also individuals who played both sides, quickly adjusting their positions to suit first one group, then another. Aldona Volynskaya:

> The Komsomol organiser at our orphanage was Dasha Dankina – she was always the first to voice her disapproval of children whose parents had been repressed. When the Germans arrived [. . .] she became very pious; she once beat a few children for taking some pumpkin seeds into church. She became a real hypocrite. She also snitched on an old lady [Larisa Antonovna] who helped out at the orphanage. Larisa stayed with the children throughout the occupation, for which she was later accused of collaboration [. . .]
>
> . . . And when our soldiers arrived at the end of the war, this Dasha Dankina was given a job in the district committee office and spoke as a witness at the trial against Larisa Antonovna. Larisa was sentenced to fifteen years in a labour camp. She was very old, and truly was a remarkably kind woman. She did everything she could for the children; she never thought of herself [. . .] Of course, she never made it out of there.

Life under occupation was never black and white, and as such people learned that help often came from the least expected places. Galina Agranovskaya (Dyatkovo, Bryansk region):

> Papa joined the Partisans [. . .] We lived on a knife edge. If someone had informed on us, we would all have been killed. As it happens, we were saved by a member of the Polizei, who just happened to be the father of one of my mother's pupils. The boy was an awful little oaf, and a D-student to boot, but my mother would sit with him after classes and drag him from lesson to lesson at school. His father had been a policeman before the war, and when the Germans arrived he joined their police force.
>
> Anyway, one night he came and knocked on my mother's window and whispered to her that her name was on a list of people due to be shot. 'Vera Mikhailovna,' he said, 'be outside the school at five o'clock tomorrow morning. I am going to be calling out the names of people to be deported to Germany. There will be trucks waiting there. I have put your name on the list, but spelled your surname differently. Listen carefully and remember this surname: Khamakhina, not Kamanina, but Khamakhina.'

The following extract from a conversation with Zinaida Komissarova (Vyazhishche village, Pskov region) is a reminder that life was often more complex than it seemed, and people were regularly forced to make difficult choices:

> Our village elder was a member of the *volost*.* Fedoseev, he was called. He didn't have any arms. After the war there was a trial. I was required to give a witness statement and when asked whether it was true that my father had given bread to the Partisans and Fedoseev had known about this, I replied, 'Yes. He knew and he didn't inform on my father.' I declared this

* An administrative rural unit of self-government.

> in front of the court. I also spoke of how he had us deported to Germany. You see, though Fedoseev had given my father bread from the village store to provide to the Partisans, he had also forcibly deported us to Germany. He was sentenced to ten years – it could have been more if my father and I had not given evidence in his defence.

From our conversations, it was sometimes difficult to get a sense of how people really felt during the first few months of occupation. Some clearly wondered whether the German order would last long, while others questioned whether life as they knew it was over. Anna Gulyaeva remembers that the question of who would win the war was turned into a childhood game:

> The goatherd brought us two kids. We called one Ruslan and the other Fritz. I wonder who will win? we thought. Will our Soviet Union stand its ground or will the Germans win? We youngsters had heads on our shoulders too, you know. What do you think happened? Our Ruslan turned tail and Fritz stayed. The Germans lodging with us came over to watch. 'Oh! A kid! What's his name?' they asked.
>
> 'Fritz,' we replied.
>
> 'Oooh, Fritz!' they laughed.
>
> They found this so entertaining. They gave Fritz some pea soup – it was a lovely meaty one though, with spam. I would gladly have eaten it myself.

The Shtalin kolkhoz

It was almost impossible, even for the teenagers, to avoid carrying out the manual labour duties* imposed on those living in occupied territory. Nikolai Kireev (Bolkhov district, Oryol region) said:

---

* Labour duties were introduced on 5 August 1941, even before the mass deportations began. The *Arbeitsamt* (labour exchange) was established to count, organise and allocate the workforce to various tasks. In theory, only individuals aged between eighteen and forty-five were eligible for labour duties, but in reality teenagers were required to carry out necessary tasks too.

The population of an occupied city gathered outside the German labour exchange, 1941. (From the Russian State Documentary Film and Photography Archive, Krasnogorsk, Opis'.3, Delo.112, Sn.10)

A German propaganda poster entitled 'New Agrarian Order'. (From a publication by L. Belousov and A. Vatlin, *A Pass to Heaven*, Moscow, 2007)

> Our elder was a man called Kuzmich, the former secretary of the agricultural committee. He made an inventory of everyone's names and ages. One day he came to our house and told my mother, 'You've got full-grown children; they need to help the Germans.' [. . .] We had to make planking so the tanks could come through.

Anna Gulyaeva said:

> How old was I? About fifteen I think. Each morning we were given our work orders. Our felt boots were holey and we were barefoot inside them – we didn't have any stockings. We cleared the railway lines, cleaned the rails. The older people cut down trees – the woods had to be cleared back fifty metres from the railway. We worked, and they harried us. They forced us to clean the floors and do their washing too.

The population in the occupied territories was swiftly sent back to work, including the youngsters in the countryside, who continued to work on the kolkhoz farms just as they had done before the arrival of the Germans. During the winter months, these teenagers were put to work clearing the roads of snow. (Anna Gulyaeva spoke of this, as did Nadezhda Bulava, Anastasia Arkhipenko, Lidia Dadzis and others.) Hopes that the Germans would dissolve the kolkhoz farms soon faded.

Raissa Pervina, a university student in Moscow, was sent on a summer field trip to Belarus in June 1941. She was shocked by the poverty she saw in the kolkhoz villages, which was far beyond anything she could have imagined. The hatred with which the villagers spoke of the kolkhoz also astounded her:

> I was a good Komsomol member – I believed in the idea and was under the impression that everything was going well. But the terrible poverty I saw in Belarus really forced me to think. How could that happen when we had built socialism! [. . .] We walked through an occupied zone and somewhere around

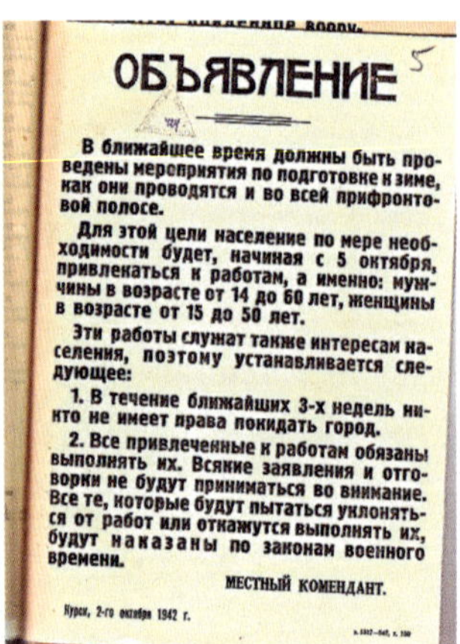

ОБЪЯВЛЕНИЕ

В ближайшее время должны быть проведены мероприятия по подготовке к зиме, как они проводятся и во всей прифронтовой полосе.

Для этой цели население по мере необходимости будет, начиная с 5 октября, привлекаться к работам, а именно: мужчины в возрасте от 14 до 60 лет, женщины в возрасте от 15 до 50 лет.

Эти работы служат также интересам населения, поэтому устанавливается следующее:

1. В течение ближайших 3-х недель никто не имеет права покидать город.

2. Все привлеченные к работам обязаны выполнять их. Всякие заявления и отговорки не будут приниматься во внимание. Все те, которые будут пытаться уклоняться от работ или откажутся выполнять их, будут наказаны по законам военного времени.

МЕСТНЫЙ КОМЕНДАНТ.

Курск, 2-го октября 1942 г.

Statement on labour duties, Kursk, 1942. (State Archive of the Russian Federation, Fond.7021, Opis'.29, Delo.1059, List.5)

Notice: In the coming days it will be necessary to carry out preparations for winter, as is the case in all areas of the combat zone.

To this end, as of 5th October the local population is to be summoned for work as and when required. This applies to: men between the ages of 14 and 60 and women between the ages of 15 and 50.

It is in the interest of the population that this work is carried out and therefore:

1. For the next three weeks, nobody is permitted to leave the city.

2. Anybody summoned for work is required to carry out their duties. No excuses or requests for exemption will be considered. Any person who refuses or attempts to shirk from these duties will be punished in accordance with wartime legislation.

Local Commandant

> Minsk I overheard a peasant saying, 'Thank God those days are over.' His was a view shared by many of the peasants.

The Germans, however, were in no rush to dissolve the kolkhoz farms.* Aldona Volynskaya described one comic consequence of the preservation of Soviet ways of life:

> A car pulled up on the road and a German got out.
>
> 'Where is the Shtalin kolkhoz?' he asked.
>
> It was called the Shtalin kolkhoz right until the end – they never closed the kolkhoz.

And so the peasants went on working, just as before. Domnikiya Skiba remarked: 'We even had the same kolkhoz director.'

Raissa Nefyodova (Ukrainka, Kirovograd region) remembered:

> In the winter we were all mobilised to clear the roads of snow for the Germans. And in the summer we worked in the fields at the kolkhoz. [. . .] We made bread. They forced us to harvest, thresh, take in the straw, weed the crops and bind the sheaves – we did all of that.

Nikolai Bogoslavets (Poltava region) said:

> They divided the kolkhoz into ten parts. Each tenth received one tenth of everything; cows, horses, kolkhoz property. We were forced to work just as we had before, but this time for the Germans. It was easier for the Germans to collect the taxes that way. The head of each tenth would collect from us and send it to the town council.

---

* On 16 February 1942, a new law was introduced in the occupied territories entitled 'On new agrarian order in liberated territories' and in June 1943 a declaration was made 'on the private ownership of land by peasants in Russian, Ukrainian and Belarussian territories liberated from the Bolsheviks'. These acts announced the dissolution of the kolkhoz farms and a return to peasants farming individual plots of land. The land was to be transferred to the ownership of the German Agricultural Directorate and be worked by the peasant communities under the management of the directorate.

The Germans implemented and enforced a strict regime. They established mutual dependence systems in the communities for the payment of both monetary taxes and taxes in kind. The entire community was held responsible if a family did not pay its taxes, or failed to pay the full amount owed. Private ownership of land was only permitted in cases where quotas of supplies were fulfilled.

German agrarian innovation was also met with varying levels of enthusiasm. According to Leonid Osipov (Khuralevo, Gomel region):

> I must say, by the way, that we lived better under the Germans than we did before the war. The Germans gave land to everybody – they counted how many families there were and divided the land accordingly. Some people got five hectares, some got seven, and some six. We had five hectares of land. We worked it and paid our taxes – mainly in potatoes. [. . .] We ran our own little farm with a cow and five pigs.

Leonid Osipov was the son of a Soviet kolkhoz worker and he has vivid memories of the famine of 1932–3 and the campaigns of collectivisation and dekulakisation that were carried out in the countryside. Other *Ostarbeiter* also remembered these horrors but Osipov was the only person we actually heard praise the agricultural system implemented by the Germans.

Valeria Fyodorova lived in the Brest region, which had only been incorporated into the USSR in 1939. She remembers that the Germans

> broke up all the peasant smallholdings that had been combined into the kolkhoz before the war. Everyone returned to their strip of land and the Germans demanded that taxes be paid, not only in marks, but also in various forms of farm produce. You could only kill a boar if you had permission from the authorities and, what's more, you had to give away half of the meat as well as the head and trotters.

Fedor Khmara (Poltava region) said: 'What did they do? They recorded exactly who owned what livestock and, when the time came, you had to hand it over. It was then up to you to muddle through without it.'

Below is a letter dated 25 August 1943 sent to Germany from the small rural community of Sabovka, in the Stalin region. The letter bears a censorship stamp on one side.

> Greetings, my darling daughter Nina. First of all, I want to let you know that everyone is alive and well and we hope that you are too and that God is being good to you. We were so happy to receive your second letter with your second set of news. We received it on 24/I-1943. I shall tell you our news. They gave us some land, including some for you. We have sown it all and are now waiting for the harvest. [. . .] We were so, so glad to receive your letter – please write more often. Warm greetings from your Papa, Mama, Marusya, Liza, Vitya, Ulyana, Prosya, Kolya, Shura and Grandma. They all send their very best wishes to you, our darling little daughter Nina. I'd better say goodbye. Please reply. Your dear Papa and Mama. Liza is at home with the kitchen maid. Papa, Mama.

A letter dated 22 December 1943, sent to Germany from the Kamenets-Podolsk region (translated from Ukrainian):

> Good day, my dear brother. I am sending you my ardent greetings and wish you all the best in your endeavours. We

> were so grateful to receive your long-awaited postcard dated 12/X-43 on 16/XII-43. At present we are all in the same state of health as we were when you left [. . .] We have enough bread to last us a little while yet. As for fats, we don't even think of them in this family of six – we have neither salted fat, poultry, nor milk. The clothing and shoe situation is even worse.
>
> . . . Just to buy a pair of shoes. . . you have to hand over 5 poods* of rye, and repairing your boots can cost anything up to 20 poods. I wrote to you about [some lines here were censored]. Our Papa was chosen as an elder, but he declined the role as we didn't think he needed to take it. It's war now, and work is hard. [. . .] I'm sure that you are reading the same news from the front in the papers – Korosten and Zhytomyr have gone the same way as Nikopol and Kerch. Goodbye.

Dress shoes in return for two beetroots

While people in the countryside still had the ability to feed themselves to an extent, this was not the case in the cities, where people soon felt the gnawing effects of famine. Those who lived in large towns and cities told us of the lengths to which they went in order to buy groceries – they sold their belongings at the market or travelled out into the countryside to exchange their possessions for food:

> The shops had been emptied by looters – there was nothing left, nothing to eat. There was no work either – it was a frightening state of affairs. After two months, people had eaten through their supplies, and hunger really set in. What could we do? Well, people traded their belongings. They went round the small villages, taking their clothes to swap for food. (Nadezhda Izmalkova, Kiev)

> My brother and I bought tobacco at the market. We rolled cigarettes at home and then took them to the factory to sell to

* Translator's note: A former Russian unit of measurement. 1 pood was equivalent to approximately 16kg.

the workers. We used this money to buy a few things. (Nikolai Gulyaev, Taganrog)

We started going to the exchange, to trade our clothes for food. I remember so clearly the day that I sold my mother's dress shoes, they were beautiful ones, for a round piece of *makukha*[*] and two beetroots. That's all I went home with. (Lidia Yerastova, Merefa, Kharkov region)

There was nothing to eat. [. . .] My friend and I loaded our belongings onto a sledge and went out to the village to exchange them for food. We asked to stay the night but nobody would let us!

'Get out of here,' they said. 'You'll find the police station over there.'

We found an empty barn teeming with mice and rats. Oh Lord, it was scary! We walked out into the steppe and discovered what was attracting all the mice – piles of wheat and oats. We shook them out and scooped up all the grain. (Anastasia Arkhipenko, Horlivka, Stalin region)

Reichsmarks introduced in the occupied territories. (From the collection of M. Poizner)

Below is a letter dated 17 July 1943, sent to Germany from Zhytomyr (translated from Ukrainian):

Greetings, Vasya. This is a letter from your family: Papa, Mama and your two brothers, Alyosha and Misha. First of all, I want to

* *Makukha* was made from the compressed husks of sunflower seeds, a by-product of sunflower oil production.

> tell you that we received your postcard dated 24/V. You asked about life at home. For now, all is well at home. [. . .] The only thing we have trouble with is clothing – you can't buy clothes anywhere, and they are very expensive. Vasya, if you are able to do so, then buy some clothes. Try as hard as you can to buy some, won't you? There is talk that you might be given some holiday leave. Nobody else went to Germany after you left – all your friends are still at home. We have so much to tell you, but nothing I can put in a letter. We look forward to your return, Vasya. The fortune-teller told us that you will be back soon. We miss you. Life here has worsened, but never mind, we'll get through these difficulties. Goodbye. Best wishes to you from all the family, Vasya.

A postcard dated 5 August 1942 sent to Germany from Simferopol:

> Greetings, my darling daughter Galichka! In these first lines of my postcard I hasten to tell you that I am alive and well, and hope that you are too. Yesterday, the third of August, I received your postcard, which I am hurrying to reply to. Darling Galichka, you wrote that I must go and see Ivan. I would go, but they won't give me a travel pass, and I'm frightened to go without one. If you can contact Ivan, then write and tell him to try to get me a pass and I will go as soon as he can come for me. [. . .] Every time I go out into the vegetable patch it makes me cry to think that I am alone here. Galichka, can you also write and tell me how you are clothed – have your shoes and dress got holes in them or are they OK? I also entreat you, for the second time, to send me your photograph – either glue it to a postcard or attach it with a small pin. And tell me how Dunya is too. I really want to know how you both are. Goodbye for now. I remain alive and well, your Mama. 5 August, present year. 'Hello from everyone, Tonya'. 'Hello from Lida'

Some details, often mentioned in passing, were truly awful. Varvara Kramarenkova (Sevastopol, Crimea) told us:

> We walked around the villages. Sometimes people would give you something, and sometimes you'd pick something up from the fields. The sea also came to our rescue – there were huge quantities of crabs and prawns because of all the corpses. We went out with a net and fished them off the bodies.

Daily life under occupation went on as before, albeit in a different or distorted form. In time, schools reopened, and some children managed to return to their studies. Albert Vaindel (Kerch, Crimea) said:

> When they took Kerch, the first thing that the Germans did was to reopen the school. We studied all the same subjects as before, except the constitution. They did tear out the pages in our history textbooks on the government, Stalin and such like. But apart from that, it was just the same as before.

Aldona Volynskaya (Kirovograd region) recalled:

> Little by little, we started going to school again. We'd heard that we would be beaten there, but there were no beatings at our school. [. . .] We had a German teacher who everybody in town called Schnapps. I remember that one day he took out a ten-rouble note with a picture of Lenin on it. 'Say "dog", say "dog" say "dog",' he demanded. Everybody went silent, nobody said it; we were all very frightened. Then he burst out laughing, and that was it. There were no consequences.

Those who had broken former taboos found such episodes engraved in their memories. Before the war, Pavel Kosushko was training to be an artist at a studio for Young Pioneers in Dnepropetrovsk. This club remained open throughout the occupation and Pavel relayed a story about his time there that he had never told anybody before:

> The Germans planted a 'Freedom Oak' in Chkalov Park and declared that day a celebration day. Among other events, they held an open exhibition of Dnepropetrovsk artists. I was ordered to produce a picture of the Führer for it. They gave me a piece of canvas designed for pastels. And I drew it. The exhibition was open to the public – Boris Mukhin's portrait of the Führer was on display at this same exhibition.*

Below is a postcard dated 20 May 1943 sent to a friend in Germany from Gaivoron (translated from Ukrainian):

> Greetings, Valechka. I'm sending you a second postcard and wishing you a good and happy life – but don't forget about your family. What should I tell you, Valya? Well, Nastasya married Pavel. Your Mama and father often come over to our house to talk about you. [. . .] Nina is always hosting parties, but I am always reminded of you when I hear the songs that you used to sing. Lyuba, Nina and Larisa Y. are leaving for Germany, but some people are still here, although I don't know how long for. Valya, if you are all right over there and the work isn't too hard, if you have food to eat, then don't feel homesick, because life isn't that rosy here. The young have been taken and those left behind are working their fingers to the bone. Anna K has married – I sent a photo of her and her husband – as has that woman Kozikha. I haven't received a photo from you though. Goodbye. My parents and sister say hello. Send me a photo. It's a shame that I don't have many postcards – I've run out of space to write. Goodbye. Lida

Concert halls and cinemas remained open in the cities. Lidia Dadzis (Gatchina, Leningrad region) recalled:

---

* Boris Ivanovich Mukhin (1912–85) was a portrait artist. After the war he was sentenced to seven years in a labour camp for drawing a picture of Hitler. He served his sentence at the Pechorlag where he worked as an artist. He was later rehabilitated.

> There was a Russian theatre near the Baltic railway station in the former Officers' Club. Pechkovsky* sang and the ballet choreographer was Dudko.† We watched classical concerts and listened to opera arias. I remember that one old man asked Pechkovsky to sing 'Shine, Shine, My Star' and the whole auditorium was reduced to tears. We also went to the cinema – it was only for Russians, and they showed undubbed German films.

Those who lived in the countryside often broke with the traditional idea of life under occupation. Young men and women would gather to sing and dance to the accordion, and sometimes they

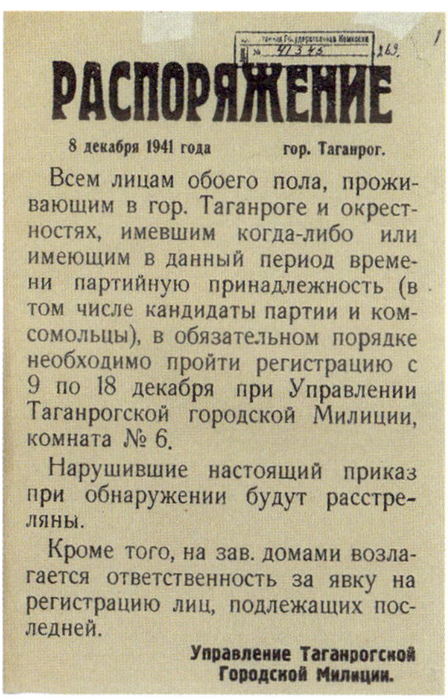

РАСПОРЯЖЕНИЕ

8 декабря 1941 года гор. Таганрог.

Всем лицам обоего пола, проживающим в гор. Таганроге и окрестностях, имевшим когда-либо или имеющим в данный период времени партийную принадлежность (в том числе кандидаты партии и комсомольцы), в обязательном порядке необходимо пройти регистрацию с 9 по 18 декабря при Управлении Таганрогской городской Милиции, комната № 6.

Нарушившие настоящий приказ при обнаружении будут расстреляны.

Кроме того, на зав. домами возлагается ответственность за явку на регистрацию лиц, подлежащих последней.

Управление Таганрогской Городской Милиции.

Order for compulsory registration of Communists and Komsomol members, Taganrog, 1941. (State Archive of the Russian Federation, Fond.7021, Opis'.148, Delo.63, List.1)

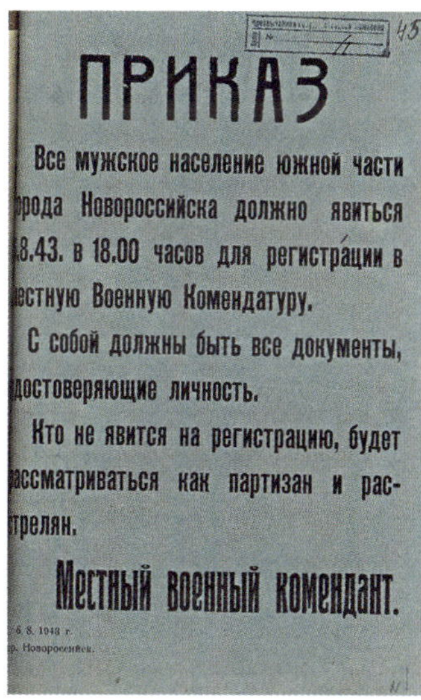

ПРИКАЗ

Все мужское население южной части рода Новороссийска должно явиться 8.43. в 18.00 часов для регистрации в естную Военную Комендатуру.

С собой должны быть все документы, достоверяющие личность.

Кто не явится на регистрацию, будет ассматриваться как партизан и расстрелян.

Местный военный комендант.

Order for compulsory registration of all male members of the population in the occupied city of Novorossiysk, 1943. (State Archive of the Russian Federation, Fond.7021, Opis'.148, Delo.63, List.45)

---

* Nikolai Konstantinovich Pechkovsky (1896–1966) was an opera singer and People's Artist of the Soviet Union who lived in occupied territory in 1941. After the war, he was sentenced to ten years in a labour camp for 'collaboration with the occupiers'.

† Mikhail Andreevich Dudko (1902–81) was a ballet dancer at the Kirov Leningrad Theatre of Opera and Ballet and a People's Artist of the Soviet Union. During the occupation the Germans appointed him head of the ballet troupe at the Gatchina theatre. He too was charged with 'collaboration with the occupiers' and sentenced to ten years in a labour camp. Both men were rehabilitated (a Soviet legal practice by which a person is cleared of the crimes previously attributed to them) after Stalin's death.

would be joined by young German soldiers of their own age. A few of the *Ostarbeiter* spoke, albeit sparingly, about such occasions. Pavel Mikhailov (Lozovoy hamlet, Zaporozhye region) said:

> We didn't have a curfew, and by the time we were sixteen or seventeen years old we began to go out in the evenings. We would take it in turns to host parties at our homes. The German soldiers guarding the railway would join us. It was as though life had almost returned to normal, and they befriended some of the girls.

Nadezhda Izmalkova openly admitted that in order to survive and find work, you needed to be able to speak German:

> A German language course opened in Kiev. [. . .] I attended for three months (you had to pay) and picked it up quickly – I could recite a few useful dialogues by heart. There was no method to the teaching, but I studied as hard as I could. I studied and studied, because I understood that if I couldn't speak the language, I would find the new situation very difficult.

A letter dated 20 July 1943 sent to Germany from Mariupol (translated from Ukrainian):

> A letter to our darling daughter Tanya, from her parents. We are sending you our heartfelt maternal and paternal greetings and wish you all the very best from life. Your brothers and sister, Vanya, Kolya and Katya, also send their greetings – they wish you happiness and hope to see you soon. Tanya, you say that we have not sent you any letters, and so you are upset with us, but we have written replies to every letter you sent. They don't accept letters in envelopes though. Life here is fine for now. I am working at the same place as before and Vanya is working with me. Mama has also been working for three months now. Kolya worked in the fields for two months, but yesterday he finished and came home. [. . .] You ask what we are harvesting.

> We grow all the same things as we did when you were here. We planted maize, potatoes and a few watermelons in the garden. But this garden isn't very substantial, and we haven't had much rain. And the quotas are due to increase on the 19th – it says so in the paper, but we still don't know what the new quotas will be. Goodbye, we're sending you a big kiss, your Mama and Papa. Tanya, don't worry about us, and look after yourself and your health while you're young.

It became clear that hunger had been a defining feature of life under occupation – countless people spoke of their struggle to find enough food to sustain themselves. The necessity of learning to survive also accelerated the transition from adolescence into adulthood as teenagers hurriedly adapted to their new circumstances.

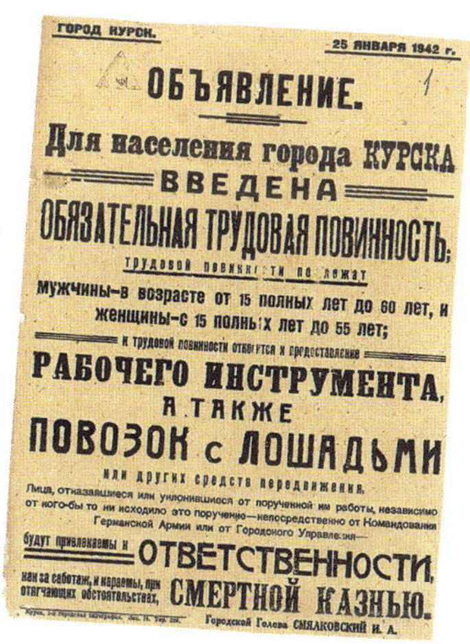

ГОРОД КУРСК. 25 ЯНВАРЯ 1942 г.

ОБЪЯВЛЕНИЕ.

Для населения города КУРСКА
ВВЕДЕНА
ОБЯЗАТЕЛЬНАЯ ТРУДОВАЯ ПОВИННОСТЬ;
трудовой повинности подлежат
мужчины–в возрасте от 15 полных лет до 60 лет, и
женщины–с 15 полных лет до 55 лет;
к трудовой повинности относится и предоставление
РАБОЧЕГО ИНСТРУМЕНТА,
А ТАКЖЕ
ПОВОЗОК с ЛОШАДЬМИ
или других средств передвижения.
Лица, отказавшиеся или уклонившиеся от порученной им работы, независимо от кого-бы то ни исходило это поручение—непосредственно от Командования Германской Армии или от Городского Управления—
будут привлекаемы к ОТВЕТСТВЕННОСТИ,
как за саботаж, и караемы, при отягчающих обстоятельствах, СМЕРТНОЙ КАЗНЬЮ.

Городской Голова СМЯКОВСКИЙ И. А.

A declaration on compulsory labour conscription for the population of Kursk, 1943. (State Archive of the Russian Federation. Fond.7021, Opis'.29, Delo.1059, List.1)

What kind of men are these Germans?

The *Ostarbeiter* spoke surprisingly candidly and objectively about their relationships with the Germans. The occupiers evoked in them a broad spectrum of feelings, ranging from fear and hatred to gratitude for assistance and, in some cases, even sympathy. They remembered friends and neighbours who had entered into liaisons with 'some German or other'. Such associations were mentioned casually and without judgement. Of course, unlike members of their own communities who joined the Germans, either as police or in roles such as village elders, many of the Germans mentioned in these stories were mere faceless embodiments of a disturbing enemy apparatus. There were some, however, whose features were described in great detail, particularly those who lived among the *Ostarbeiter*, sometimes within their very homes.

Vadim Novgorodov spoke of the German 'guests' staying in Taganrog:

> These soldiers were no more than *Gefreite*.* They were quite good-natured towards us, perhaps the more so because I could speak German to them and we were pretty much the same age. [. . .] I remember one lad was very unhappy – he was homesick and had terrible regrets about the war.

Maria Vitkevich (Krasnoye Selo, Leningrad region) said: 'We had a Commandant staying with us. [. . .] He brought us soap and bread, and asked us to do his laundry. He called my sister and I "Annchen" and "Mariechen".'†

Some feared the Hungarian soldiers more than the Germans. Nadezhda Izmalkova remembered: 'We hated the Hungarian soldiers, and they couldn't stand us. They were so cruel, the Hungarians. We were frightened of them. They would hit you. We never spoke to them.'

The situation at the front often had a direct impact upon the way the Germans treated the Soviet population. As defeat loomed, both those living under occupation and the *Ostarbeiter* labouring in Germany noticed a marked shift in the attitudes of their German occupiers and employers. Lidia Yerastova (Merefa, Kharkov region) said: 'We had Germans and Hungarians living in our flat. In 1943, the Germans were retreating and they brought my mother half a bag of flour, saying, "Mutti, this is for you."'

Nikolai Kireev (Bolkhov, Oryol region) remembers the aftermath of the Battle of Moscow during the winter of 1941:

---

* Translator's note: A rank equivalent to lance corporal

† Translator's note: German diminutives for the names Anna and Marie/Maria.

> The Germans all sat there, crying. '*Matka, Matka*,'* they sobbed – this was how they addressed the Russian women. They showed us photographs of their children and offered us schnapps. They did not think they would be leaving the snowy fields of Russia. They were only too aware of the situation.

Many remembered the Germans as ordinary men, and not the monsters they were purported to be. Nonetheless, demonstrations of humanity often served to highlight the other, very different realities of life under occupation, which could be rife with violence, cruelty and abuse.

As a consequence of Nazi propaganda calling for the extermination of 'Yids and Communists', no sooner had the occupying forces arrived in the Soviet Union than reprisals began against the Communists, Soviet workers and Jews who had not managed to evacuate in time. Fedor Apyonkin (Tolochyn, Vitebsk region):

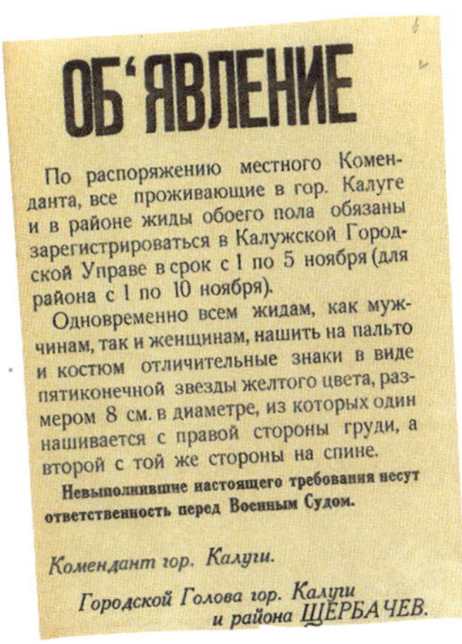

ОБ'ЯВЛЕНИЕ

По распоряжению местного Коменданта, все проживающие в гор. Калуге и в районе жиды обоего пола обязаны зарегистрироваться в Калужской Городской Управе в срок с 1 по 5 ноября (для района с 1 по 10 ноября).

Одновременно всем жидам, как мужчинам, так и женщинам, нашить на пальто и костюм отличительные знаки в виде пятиконечной звезды желтого цвета, размером 8 см. в диаметре, из которых один нашивается с правой стороны груди, а второй с той же стороны на спине.

Невыполнившие настоящего требования несут ответственность перед Военным Судом.

Комендант гор. Калуги.

Городской Голова гор. Калуги и района ЩЕРБАЧЕВ.

A mandate issued by the Commandant of Kaluga for the registration of Jews stipulating that they were required to wear the yellow star, Kaluga, 1941. (State Archive of the Russian Federation. Fond.7021, Opis'.148, Delo.156, List.6)

Eastern Ukraine, 1941. (*Vernichtungskrieg / Verbrechen der Wehrmacht 1941 bis 1944*, Hamburg 1997)

---

* Translator's note: *Matka* means 'mother' in both Polish and Czech. The soldiers may have picked up this word while fighting in Eastern Europe.

'As far as I remember, German leaflets depicted members of the Politburo as Jews, because, as they alleged, the Jews had started the war.'

German interrogations and capital punishment were often carried out by members of the local police force, so when the *Ostarbeiter* spoke of the SS and the Gestapo, they referred not only to the Germans but also to the members of their own communities who had joined the Germans as police.

Grigory Kulbaka (Dnepropetrovsk region): 'There were some Communists in our village. A German shot them straight away. My geography teacher, Ekaterina Fedorovna, was a member of the Party – they hanged her immediately.'

Vera Fedorchenko (Zhytomyr region) recalled:

> The Germans arrived and began to round up all the Party members. One was a teacher – an historian – and there were two others. They took them to a barn and beat them. They beat them black and blue for three days straight. And then they took them out into the woods and buried them alive.

Ghetto, Kaunas, 1941–2. (M. Berenbaum, *The World Must Know*: US Holocaust Memorial Museum, Washington 2006)

Anna Odinokova said:

> They [the Germans] took away the headmaster of our school [. . .] and interrogated him. They cut off his ears and threw his body into the park – they wouldn't allow anyone to bury him. He had been informed upon by the family of a dimwit-pupil who didn't do well at school and had been given bad grades. They told the Germans that the headmaster was a Communist.

Olga Zimnitskaya (Smolensk region) mentioned that:

> Before the war, my father worked as a forest ranger. [. . .] He and my elder brother joined the Partisans. And my mother was arrested as the wife of a Communist and Partisan. [. . .] She was interrogated by a man called Sedkin at the police station. He gripped her head between his boots and beat her with a rubber whip. She was as black as cast-iron afterwards; she couldn't walk, so they dragged her to a cell.

Vasily Kononenko (Nizhyn, Chernigov region) remembered:

> We had just woken up on the morning of 4 March when we heard a loud bang on the door. The police entered. 'Get dressed,' they said. 'The village elder has sent for you.'
>
> I already knew what this meant, because before this all the Communists, Komsomol members and activists had been taken. They had all been shot. [. . .] We were taken to Nizhyn prison. [. . .] Six people were shot, but we, the youngest five, were taken straight from the prison to Germany. This hadn't happened before – all those taken to the prison before had been executed. A message had been scratched deeply into the wall of our prison cell. It read: *All died on 2 February*.

Jews – to one side; non-Jews – to the other

It had been clear from the very outset of occupation that one group among the 'peaceable Soviet citizens' had been condemned to death. Members of the Jewish population were often betrayed by neighbours, and executed by members of the Polizei. Soviet propaganda subsequently preferred not to talk of this. The prevailing official line was that nobody had betrayed the Jews – all Soviet citizens were victims of the Nazi regime. Taissa Tolkachova (Genichesk) said:

> Yes, they went around the houses where the Jews lived. They chased them from their homes and formed columns of adults, children and the elderly – I saw it with my own eyes! Before the Germans had arrived, we had dug anti-tank ditches, but the Germans used them to bury the people they shot. I remember the family who lived next door to us hadn't managed to evacuate. They had little children and an elderly woman lived with them too – they were formed into a column and taken to the ditches. Of course, we heard the shots. For the most part, they were shot right there and then. It wasn't the Germans who buried them. No, it was our own members of the Polizei – they made a careless attempt to bury them.

To this day, the theme of participation by the local populace in reprisals against Jews remains extremely painful. We spoke to one man who lived in Lithuania during the occupation. He struggled anxiously to find the right words to assure us that the reality had been different: 'It has been said that Lithuanians somehow shot these . . . errrr . . . Yids. But as a matter of fact this was very rarely the case. I only met one person who had actually shot Jews.'

Most of those we spoke to found it very difficult to talk about the slaughter of their Jewish compatriots, many of whom were former classmates, neighbours or acquaintances, killed for no reason other than the fact that they were Jews. The *Ostarbeiter* we interviewed often played the agonising role of witnesses to terrible events that they were powerless to prevent. Regina Lavrovich (Osovets) recalled:

> A Jewish family lived next door to us. He was called Haim and she – Dvosya. We children were playing outside in the courtyard one day while Haim groomed one of the Germans'

> horses. Once he had finished, a German walked up to him, placed his pistol in his ear, and killed him.

Elizaveta Krestyantseva also remembered:

> We had our own home in Kirovograd. Well, we shared the building and courtyard with four other families – all of them Jews. They were very good people – doctors, lawyers and members of the intelligentsia. They were all shot. The caretaker of our building was a man called Roman who became a very committed member of the Polizei under the Germans. We lived next to a Moldavian naval officer and sea captain and his wife, Sonya, who was Jewish. They had two children – Tolya was seven and Garik was still very little – Sonya still carried him about. The Germans shot Sonya and Garik, but Tolya managed to escape to us. The caretaker saw him with us and called out to him. 'Tolya, Tolya, come with me,' he said, taking him away. He gave the little boy to the Germans, he told them that he was a Jew. It was awful! Awful! [. . .] And yet he had always been so polite, that caretaker.

All the Jewish children were taken from the Novoukrainka orphanage where Aldona Volynskaya lived, and shot. Decades later, she still voices her incredulity that someone within the orphanage could have given the police a list detailing the ethnicity of each child living there.

There were also accounts of people helping their Jewish friends and neighbours. Nadezhda Kepet (Pukhovichy) said:

> There was a ditch in our village where the Jews were buried once they had been shot. One night, a neighbour, Haya, ran to my Aunt Arina's house. She had managed to crawl out of the ditch and run away. She was covered in blood. Arina gave her a change of clothes and hid her. Later, somebody – I don't remember who – handed her over to the Partisans, and she survived.

Pavel Kosushko remembers trying to persuade his Jewish friend not to move into the ghetto in Dnepropetrovsk:

> She was such a wonderful, beautiful girl. I pleaded with her not to go – I told her to stay with us.
>
> 'We'll hide you. Stay. You're going to your death,' I told her.
>
> I begged her not to go. Then I went to the park, picked a bouquet of flowers, and took them to her. 'For God's sake, don't go,' I implored again.
>
> 'No. I can't stay, I'm going with my parents,' she replied.
>
> And so she went too. That beautiful girl. It was awful.

Nadezhda Izmalkova (Kiev) risked her life to hide her Jewish friend. She spoke of it as though it were nothing; a mere matter of course:

> I had a Jewish friend called Dora. We had been friends from the age of six and lived next door to each other. [. . .] She was in the army, and was taken prisoner. But she said that she was a non-Jewish Ukrainian, and the Germans believed her, and let her go. She came to our house and was afraid to come in. She stood there, tiny, in her greatcoat and cap – she wasn't very tall. [. . .] My mother saw her and understood immediately. 'Oh, Fenechka! Come here!' she said, quickly thinking up a name for her. She lived with us for a while after that. Now I'm amazed at what we did – how were we not afraid? After all, people knew her.

Nadezhda's recollections then took an almost comic turn, as she described persuading a German soldier to help fetch Dora's belongings from her old house:

> Her apartment had been closed up, but her wardrobe of clothes was inside. [. . .] I found some German to help us, so that we could fetch it without being stopped. [. . .] The German summoned a few men and ordered them to carry out the

wardrobe, dresser and feather mattress. The doorman for her building was absolutely furious, and shouted after us, 'Oh, so you want to keep Yiddish junk, do you?!'

That's how I had Dora's belongings brought over. Of course, we had to sell some of them – we had to live.

The Jews were not the only group to be targeted by the Nazis – they also pursued a deadly campaign of persecution against the Gypsy population. Irina Sokolova witnessed the Germans surrounding a Gypsy camp in Ukraine:

> I saw savagery beyond my wildest imagination. Four people were shot on the road in front of my very eyes. A Gypsy woman and a young man were dragged outside to roars of laughter.
>
> 'Rape her!' the Germans shouted.
>
> 'That's my Mama,' the boy cried.
>
> She said something to him in their Romany language. In short, they were both shot.

We also heard miraculous tales of would-be victims escaping death by the skin of their teeth. Vladimir Sverdlov was at a children's sanatorium in the western Mogilev region when the war broke out. On that first day, almost all the employees fled, abandoning almost five hundred children to fend for themselves. The director of the sanatorium, a Jewish woman, stayed behind to care for them – many were only of kindergarten age:

> By 27 June, the Germans had arrived and at that point I realised what war was. The director was taken outside and shot, right there on the street, in front of our eyes. [. . .] The first thing that the Germans did was to sort the children. Jews – to one side; non-Jews – to the other. They fed us on frozen beetroot and cabbage and gave us 100g of bread per day. When the cold set in, many children began to die – half died from hunger. Sometimes you would say, 'Fima, get up,' and he would not – Fima was already dead. The bodies were not buried; they were

just thrown into the river through holes in the ice. The lice were terrible and so was the illness. We were in an awful state, covered in scabs! Extreme apathy set in, to the extent that by the time spring arrived we wanted to die – the sooner it all ended, the better. I remember that on 2 April the Germans brought a translator to see us. They drew up a list of all our names and told us to get ready to move to a new place – somewhere warm, bright and nurturing. We were formed into columns and the little children were sat in horse-drawn carts and transported that way. I had a friend there – he was the eldest among us at the age of twelve and a half. As we walked in our column, he turned to me and said, 'Do you know where they are taking us?'

'No!' I replied. 'Where?'

'They are taking us to be killed. If they only intended to relocate us, the guards would be unarmed. But look, we are surrounded by men carrying automatic rifles.'

I decided to escape and made a run for it. [. . .] All the children were shot.

Frida Palko recalled:

My first experience of occupation was in the city of Starodub, in the Bryansk region. I hadn't yet turned fourteen. [. . .] For the first month following their arrival, the Germans didn't lay a finger on the Jews. But then they made an announcement on the radio: all Jews were to assemble – men, women and children – with their most essential possessions. [. . .] My mother gathered together what she could and we were herded into one place. There were a lot of Jews in Starodub. We formed a column. There was a kolkhoz (Belovshchina) outside the city – we were taken there and corralled in a small area. Some stood, while others sat or lay down as best they could. At 6 a.m. a German came in and ordered that all men aged fourteen and above were to leave for work. They never returned – they were shot that same day. [. . .] The women and children were left alone. We were settled into the kolkhoz houses, which were surrounded

> by barbed wire and guarded by Russian policemen. They were the real professionals – they wouldn't let anybody out. We lived in a room with fifty people and were given nothing but frozen onions to eat. I looked like a Russian girl – blue-eyed and fair. There was another kolkhoz next door called Berezovka, where some of my school friends lived. I carefully crept through the wire and sometimes got hold of a few potatoes. They didn't have much themselves. [. . .] As time went on it became more dangerous, and I began to cross the wire less often. We lived in that ghetto for five months. But one wonderful day my friends got together and dug a hole for us. One friend, Motya Podolyako, told me that I needed to escape if I could, for the Germans were planning to shoot us all in the coming days. I begged my mother to let my sister, Lucy, come with me. But she refused. 'Are you mad?' she said. 'You'll be killed. Absolutely not.'
>
> [. . .] Our mother hadn't even let us go to Pioneer camp. But I left anyway.
>
> 'Let them shoot me in the back, let them kill me. I'm not staying here with you,' I said. I should have taken my sister with me, but I . . . She held on to my mother's skirt and wouldn't come with me. [. . .] This was in February. They were all shot on 2 March.

Frida managed to escape from the ghetto. She took a Russian name and was later deported to Germany.

'We lived between two fires'

We heard very few descriptions of Partisan and underground activities from the people we spoke to. The future *Ostarbeiter* were still very young when the Germans invaded, and the majority never played a part in resistance efforts. However, a few of them did encounter Partisan units. Regina Lavrovich (Osovets, Belarus) said:

> In December 1941 the Partisans knocked on the door of our home. They covered the window, lit a torch, and told us that

> there had been a battle outside Moscow, and that the Germans had been trounced. [. . .] There were a lot of Partisans – by 1943, practically the entire village was involved in feeding them and washing their clothes. [. . .] In March 1943 we went to live in the forest. The whole village upped and left.

However, just the slightest suspicion of links to the Partisans could have dire consequences:

> Nine people in our village were shot – they were said to have been working for the underground. An entire family was killed that same day too – the father, mother and three children. Somebody had informed upon them, claiming that they had set fire to the hay at the farm. We were made to watch, so that it would serve as a lesson to everyone. (Pavel Mikhailov, Zaporozhye region, deported in September 1943)

> People were shepherded out onto the small park square to see those who had been hanged – each with a sign reading, 'Partisan'. There was no reason whatsoever for them to have been hanged. [. . .] Take our Komsomol organiser, for example. He wasn't a Partisan, but he was hanged nonetheless. It was simply designed to show people that the master had arrived, and he could do whatever he liked with people. (Taissa Tolkachova)

> The Germans herded us all out onto the square. They had hanged a twelve-year-old boy there, with a sign reading 'Partisan'. And a German announced that they would do the same to anybody who dared to disregard the German authorities. (Galina Shalankova, Ordzhonikidze region)

Sometimes the Partisans behaved very differently from the way that they were portrayed in Soviet books and films:

> We lived between two fires; between the Partisans and the Germans. I'll give you an example: our Partisans planted mines

> in the village, just tens of metres from our huts. The logic was that when a column of Germans came through, someone would undoubtedly be blown up. So what did the Germans do? They gathered all the villagers and marched them down the road in front of them. They made them hitch up the harrows to their horses, and the column of soldiers would follow behind. [. . .] Well, you had to walk along, and the devil only knew whether you would step on a mine or not. (Leonid Osipov, Khuralevo, Gomel region)

> The Germans would turn up, and we'd run into the forest, to the Partisans. When they left, we'd come back out of the forest. In the end, the Germans burned down our village. (Victor Shuldeshov, Kryukovo, Kursk region)

The non-violent population often paid the price for the Partisans' activities. Some people talked openly about the reprisals they witnessed, while others were more cautious. Tatiana Teplova (Griva, Kalinin region) described what happened when a German, one of three stationed in her village, was killed:

> The death squads arrived the next day. They shot two fourteen- or fifteen-year-old boys. We were all lined up and told to bow our heads. We kissed each other goodbye – we thought that they were going to shoot us right there. But they didn't shoot us. They just burned down the village.

Some remembered the slaughter of former Red Army soldiers who had become trapped in the villages and farms located in occupied territory during the chaotic retreat in the early days of the war. Some of them became 'live-ins' – soldiers that local women pretended were their own spouses. Others lived in empty huts and went to work as normal. They were known as *pripisnyaki*.* At first the Germans left them alone. Nikolai Bogoslavets remembers:

* A word derived from the Russian verb *pripisat* meaning 'to attach' or 'assign'.

> These young men lived among us until 1943. And then one day the Germans gathered them together in the school and began to inspect and sort them, deciding who they would take, and who would be left behind. They took about seventy healthy young men out into the fields and shot them, claiming that they had the potential to become Partisans. For a while afterwards the Germans wouldn't allow anyone to collect the bodies; but later, they granted permission for relatives to take them home. They were all buried at their homes, not in a mass grave.

The first mass deportations of Soviet citizens to Germany began in 1942. People living in areas with active Partisan cells often fled into the forests in the hope of avoiding the Germans' net. Vadim Novgorodov, who was deported from Taganrog, remembers: 'The Germans often complained that the Partisans in Ukraine never gave them a moment's peace. Our train took us the whole way through Ukraine, and I waited expectantly, especially at night, hoping every minute that the Partisans would hold up the train and set us free.'

The survival skills that the *Ostarbeiter* had acquired during occupation would stand them in good stead in Germany. But they paid a high price for their experience, witnessing betrayal, opportunism, greed, cruelty and, worst of all, mass killings.

For many people, memories of occupation were even harder to discuss than memories of their time in Germany. One of the most traumatising aspects of life under occupation was the constant fear of deportation to an alien land. Lyudmila Vasilkovskaya, who lived through occupation in the Poltava region, spoke of this:

> Occupation was the most frightening time of all. You had no idea what lay ahead. One day you were living your life, and the next, you could be grabbed by the scruff of the neck and dragged off to the labour exchange to be assigned to heavy manual labour. [. . .] They could take anyone born between 1922 and 1925 for compulsory labour. I fell within this bracket.

PART 2

Deportation

The men and women sent to work in Germany hailed from all walks of life. Some were taken from the countryside; others from the cities. Some were very young; others were much older. Some were highly educated, while others could barely read or write. But all were united by a common fate: they were *Ostarbeiter.*

The way the deportations were carried out depended hugely on when they occurred. In the spring of 1942, every city and village in German-occupied territory was ordered to provide a defined quarterly quota of manpower, comprising equal numbers of men and women that they were to send to Nazi Germany.* Previous measures intended to entice workers to Germany had proved insufficient, and though up until early 1942 most of the workers who left for the Third Reich did so voluntarily, the number of volunteers was beginning to dry up. Meanwhile, Germany was suffering from a shortage of manual labourers. Mass deportations were deemed to provide the answer, so by spring 1942 most of those who found themselves on deportation lists had invariably received a summons from their local German employment office (*Arbeitsamt*), which had been established by the new Nazi administration. Deportations from occupied territories peaked in the spring and autumn of 1942, and they became gradually more forceful and violent in nature.

To some extent, there was also a correlation between deportation dates and the arduousness of the labour to which people were assigned. As a rule, the first work parties to be deported were sent from Ukraine to work in Germany's mines. This work was

---

* Ulrich Herbert, 'Forced Labourers in Germany: Soviet Workers and Prisoners of War 1941–1945', in Memorial's *Tough Words: The Fate of the Eastern Workers* (SPb: Memorial, St Petersburg, 2000), p.12.

especially gruelling, and these *Ostarbeiter* were treated particularly badly, especially in the early days of the war, when attitudes towards them were at their worst. Vladimir Shchebetyuk was in one of the very first work parties to be sent to Germany. He remembers his departure from the small village of Isakovtsy (in the Kamenets-Podolsk region) in March 1942:

> The Germans came, and I had nowhere to hide. I was the first to be taken to Germany. I should not have been taken – I was only fifteen. But what could I do? I was in the first party to leave – there were nine of us – and we arrived in Germany in March 1942. My mother cried, even though I told her that I would be fine there.

Many *Ostarbeiter* were able to recall the exact date of their departure, for it drew a definitive line under a former life and marked the beginning of their stay in the Third Reich. Others were less clear about when they were taken, remembering only the month, or perhaps just the time of year. Tatiana Veselovskaya (Novo-Troitskoye, Zaporozhye region) was just fourteen when she was deported in the summer of 1942: 'It was either summer, or autumn. Oh, do you know, I can't actually remember when they took me. It was as soon as the Germans took Ukraine – we were deported as soon as they reached us in Novo-Troitskoye.'

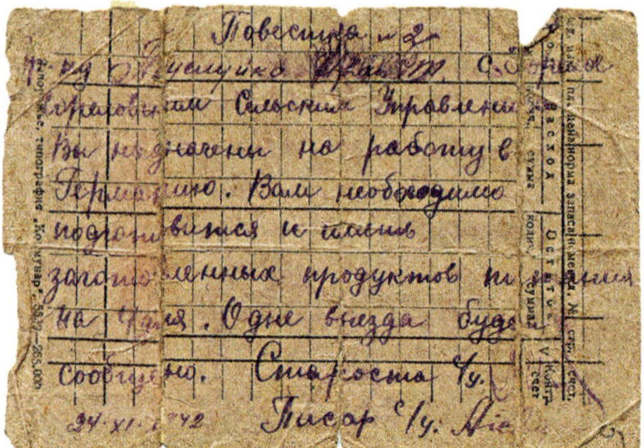
Повестка
Распоряжением Сельского Управления
Вы назначены на работу в
Германию. Вам необходимо
подготовиться и иметь
продуктов
О дне выезда будет
сообщено. Староста с/у.
24.XI.1942 Писарь с/у.

A notice of labour conscription, 24 November 1942.

> Summons No. 2: To citizen Potseluiko, Ivan T. [. . .] The Agricultural Committee has conscripted you for work in Germany. You are required to prepare for departure and to ensure that you have adequate supplies of pre-prepared food for four days. You will be informed of your departure date. From: Village elder and scribe (of the Agricultural Committee)

In some cases, the apparent difficulty of remembering a departure date proved to be a facade, rooted in deep-seated and persistent fears. Those who had been deported in the early work parties seemed worried that we would suspect them of having gone to the recruitment centres voluntarily, after deciding to leave for Germany of their own free will (before the spring of 1942, this was fairly common). Their fears were not unfounded; during the checks in the Soviet NKVD 'filtration camps' following Germany's defeat, this question of timing was one of the most crucial, and dangerous, of all. The *Ostarbeiter* carried the fear of being accused of 'leaving voluntarily' with them for the rest of their lives. In spite of all our efforts to reassure them that they could talk freely about their departure date, for it was inconsequential to us as we knew they had been forced into labour on arrival in Germany anyway, they found it much easier to say that they had been swept up in the mass deportations and couldn't remember the details.

One such conversation that omitted all 'unnecessary' details went as follows: 'We travelled around, exchanging things, and then later found ourselves being taken to Germany [. . .] There had been a round-up in a village in 1942 – everyone was taken, including us, and we ended up in Germany.' (Nadezhda Izmalkova, Kiev, May 1942)

Fear of judgement provoked secrecy and engendered contradictions. In 1941, Arkady Kozhaev was a young engineer managing a small mine in the Donbass region. He told us that he was seized from a market during a mass round-up in early February 1942. Just half an hour later, however, he mentioned that he took a German language textbook with him when he left for Germany. Even after so many years, he was still afraid to admit that the hunger and desperation in his homeland had driven him to volunteer his services as a mineworker in Germany.

Nina Odolinskaya, a student in Odessa, spoke openly and in great detail about the circumstances and reasons behind her voluntary decision to leave for Germany in April 1942, but she was one of very few to do so:

> I hesitated for a long time when the Germans announced that they were recruiting workers to go to Germany. Life had become unbearable – we were hungry, there was no question of being able to study and there was no work. [. . .] The front was creeping further and further eastward, and this caused an ever-increasing sense of wild despair and a sense that there was simply no way out. Signing up for work in Germany seemed to be the only realistic answer to our problems, especially since nobody seemed to know how long this chaos would last. So I went to the recruitment centre. A sign hung beside the door, encouraging people to sign up for six months of work and promising good wages in return. I really wanted to believe what I read. I was comforted by the knowledge that I would be given food and a roof over my head, and that I might also be able to help the loved ones I would be leaving behind in Odessa. The recruiters recorded my passport details and informed me that I would be notified of my departure date. There were lots of us volunteers – we filled an entire train of goods wagons. Don't imagine that this was some sort of 'train of counter-revolutionaries' packed with enemies of the people or evil traitors to the Motherland. No, these were people who had been driven to despair by their circumstances, people who couldn't adjust to the new situation or had lost everything – homes and loved ones – and were left feeling that they had nothing and nobody left in the world.

'There was nowhere to hide'

In all of the German documents relating to the *Ostarbeiter*, the transportation of eastern workers to Germany is described using the word *Werbung*, or recruitment, which implies a voluntary process.* Before 1942, this term was more or less accurate; those who made the journey to Germany at that time often did so of their own free will. Of course, there was plenty of promotional material designed to encourage them to go, and the Germans usually organised celebratory send-offs as an incentive for others to follow suit. One German propaganda leaflet addressed to 'all women and girls' asked:

> What kind of lives do women and girls have in Germany? Your Bolshevik executioners know full well that the ideal that they merely promise you has been realised in full by Adolf Hitler. [. . .] In Germany, women and children are given good apartments, nourishing food, good-quality clothing and medical care, and they really live a free and truly happy life. [. . .] Women and girls, your future is in your hands. Go and work! Your new life will provide you with things that have been mere empty words for the past twenty-five years: freedom, humanity, peace and true happiness!

Pavel Mikhailov was deported from Lozovoy hamlet, Zaporozhye region, in September 1943:

> At first people were hired to go and work in Germany. They put up adverts, photographs and propaganda posters, all showing how good life there would be. You would work, they said, and be paid in return. Two people from our farm signed up to go voluntarily.

* During the winter of 1941/42 the workforce in occupied territories was reorganised into a series of *Anwerbkommissionen*. A new post of General Plenipotentiary for Labour Mobilisation (GBA) was introduced in March 1942, which was filled by Fritz Sauckel. He circulated memos stating that all men and women between the ages of seventeen and thirty-five were eligible for *Werbung*. However, the Germans began to take teenagers and older people almost immediately. In April 1943, the age group was extended to include entire families with children younger than fourteen, and sometimes children as young as ten, providing they were strong and healthy and therefore considered fit for work.

Maria Vitkevich (Krasnoye Selo, Leningrad region) was deported in January 1944: 'As soon as the Germans arrived, they began registering everyone and suggesting that people left to work in Germany. They hung out notices stating that anyone wanting to leave would be given a good job, ration cards and monetary assistance.'

Vera Fedorchenko (Romanovo, Zhytomyr region), deported in July 1942, said that: 'The first recruits left to the musical accompaniment of a wind orchestra.'

Young people were driven to the recruiting centres for a number of reasons including hunger and unemployment, fear, and, in some cases, circumstances that left them with no other choice. We even heard of instances where Jews living in occupied territory with falsified documents decided to volunteer for deportation, in the hope that they would find it easier to disappear away from their villages where everybody knew them. Nadezhda Izmalkova's friend Dora was one of those who did just this (Kiev, May 1942): 'She changed her surname to Lovich, instead of Sagalovich. And she lived in Germany with these documents.'

Photographs from the German propaganda bureau entitled 'On the status of eastern workers'. Voluntary *Ostarbeiter* leave for Germany, 1942. (State Archive of the Russian Federation, F7021 Opis. 128, Delo. 286, List 25. 28)

Valentin Karvatovsky's father (Muksha-Borishkovetskaya, Kamenets-Podolsk region) was repressed before the war, leaving Valentin with a choice: either join the Polizei or volunteer to work in Germany. He recalls being encouraged by a friend in the Polizei to join him in the summer of 1942:

Propaganda poster inviting women and girls to go and work in Germany. (From the collection of M. Poizner)

> 'Come and join the *Schutzmannschaft*,'* he said. 'Your father was repressed – they'll take you.'
>
> 'No, Misha,' I replied. 'Why would I want to join the *Schutzmannschaft*? I'd be better going to Germany.'

However, as coded messages began to filter back with off-putting reports about the realities of life abroad, the flow of volunteers dried up. Victor Shuldeshov, deported in spring 1942, remembers a conversation he had with his mother before he left for Germany:

> She accompanied me to the assembly point in tears.
>
> 'Write to me once you get to Germany,' she said. 'If things are bad there, draw a flower on your letter – that could mean anything, they won't guess. They check the letters there too. If everything is OK, don't draw anything.

Reports that 'life isn't good for us there' also came back via some of the earliest volunteers, who had been sent home by the

---

* Translator's note: The Auxilary Police or *Schutzmannschaft* were the collaborationist auxiliary police of native policemen serving in areas of the Soviet Union and the Baltic states occupied by Nazi Germany during the Second World War.

Germans due to ill health or having become incapacitated for work. Rumours of the realities of work and life in the Third Reich spread like wildfire, and the number of volunteers dwindled rapidly, leaving the Germans with significantly fewer workers to deport than they had counted on. Underground activists had also begun to distribute leaflets appealing to young people not to leave for Germany – Lyudmila Stanyeva (Haichur station, Zaporozhye region), deported in July 1943, describes her work for the Resistance: 'I don't really remember now what we wrote on those leaflets. Something along the lines of 'Don't go to Germany . . . our soldiers will be back to liberate us soon.' We pasted these leaflets all over the place.

A letter dated 11 February 1943 from Senftenberg to the Kamenets-Podolsk region:

> My dear friends, you ask me to pass on your greetings to Petka Melnikov, but I'm not with him. We three all journeyed here together – Petka, Fanas and I. But I'm on my own now because Fanas has died and I've been told that Petka has gone home because he is unwell. [. . .] I tell you, it's so boring here with these foreign lads. Please write to me lots, my dear friends Fedya and Vanyusha. Well, on that note, I'd better say goodbye. I'm sending you a firm handshake and look forward to your swift reply.

From a letter dated 3 August 1943 from Nuremberg to Poltava (translated from Ukrainian):

> . . . my dearest little brothers, listen to Mama and Papa – I would listen but I have ended up here with none of my loved ones around me. Mama, life here is good – do you remember how Nastya Kazachka lived? Get Nina to sing 'The Cuckoo Flew from the Ravine to the Valley' to you.
>
> My little niece, you might be unhappy, but at least you have your Mama, whereas I . . .
>
> Remember me, my Mama, even just once an hour. And I will think of you seven times a minute.

If you can, please send me a parcel and put as many stamps on it as you can. The other girls here receive one parcel a week. But my clothes are falling apart Mummy, and I am now practically naked [. . .] Don't grieve for me; I will grieve for myself. We will live, and some day we will return. Write and tell me what years people were taken, and who went. Or were we the only ones? I am sending you a photograph taken on 22/VII-43. We often reminisce about life in Nedoharky, but we do live better here.

Pass on my warm wishes to all the family, the girls, our neighbours and friends. Write back, if only to tell me how all the family are doing. Well, goodbye for now – keep yourselves alive and well. I send you both a firm handshake, Mama and Papa. We are living in a city called Nuremberg.

As it became increasingly apparent that this was likely to be a protracted war, Germany realised that it would require extra manpower if it was to sustain its industries. The recruitment campaigns soon gave way to forced mass deportations.

NOTIFICATION OF DUTIES

By the authority of the 1st decree of the Reich Ministry for the Occupied Eastern Territories on the introduction of labour duties in occupied eastern territories as of 19.XII.1941, you are required to work beyond the borders of the occupied eastern territories and must present yourself for duty on 14 May 1943 at 12 p.m. You should bring with you any shoes and clothing that you may have. You will be compensated up to [ ] for any clothing supplies you bring with you. Your work will be carried out in standard working conditions and you will be paid at a fixed rate. Failure to report for duty will result in the employment of necessary measures of enforcement against you or your family. Furthermore, non-compliance with labour duties will be punished by arrest and either a prison sentence or deportation to a labour camp.

Regional (city) Commissar.

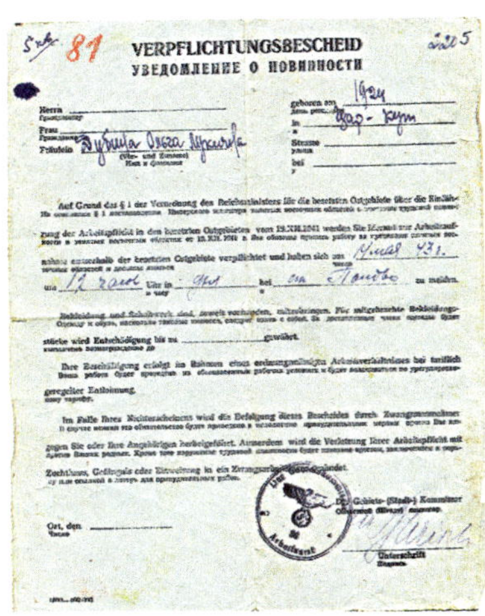
VERPFLICHTUNGSBESCHEID

Notification of labour duties, Zaporozhye region, 1943.

Prior to this, methods of coercion had included promises of good pay and assurances that nobody would have to stay in Germany for long. In the cities, all those selected for deportation received a summons to their recruitment office. In the countryside, however, lists of workers singled out for deportation were drawn up by the German-appointed village elders, and turnout at the assembly points was enforced by members of the community who had joined the Polizei. Zoya Yeliseeva (Dzhankoy, Crimea), deported in June 1942, recalled:

> Lists were drawn up. There was nowhere to hide. And, besides, the lists had been compiled by people who knew the community well – they knew exactly who lived where. We were all notified as to where and when we were to assemble, and told to bring our belongings with us. 'You're off to work!' they said. And that was that. We were warned that if we failed to show up at the assembly point, we would be taken by force.
>
> 'You won't be gone for long,' we were told. 'You'll work for three months, maybe six, and then you'll come home and it'll be someone else's turn to go.'
>
> Well. We just got on with it. I was only sixteen years old . . .

In the villages, the first names on the lists were always those of any new arrivals – anyone that the war had displaced into a new village or community. This is exactly what happened to Moscow student Raissa Pervina and her friends while on a summer field trip to Belarus in 1941. Irina Sokolova (Perevalochnoye, Chernigov region), deported in June 1942, was also one of the first to find her name on a deportation list. A military nurse, she had managed to escape from German captivity and find work as an aide in a cottage hospital. She remembers talking with her colleagues while on duty one day:

> 'Have you heard?' one of the girls said. 'They're going to deport ninety people – that's the quota they're demanding from this village. And there are rumours going round that we're going to be taken to fulfil the quota.'

> 'We need to get out of here. If we don't, we're going to wind up in Germany,' I said. [. . .] As we sat there talking, we heard a loud 'tap-tap' at the door. Two policemen entered. They escorted us all to an outbuilding. From there, we were taken by cart to the railway station in Pryluky, where we were loaded into train cars. The doors were closed and they only opened again once we were in Poland.

The accounts given by the *Ostarbeiter* indicate that certain groups were singled out for deportation first. These included former Komsomol members, elder children from large families and children from poor families, who did not have the means to buy their way out of trouble.

Anna Basarab (Nikolayevka, Sumy region), deported May 1942, remembered:

> Anyone who had a family was told to provide one person; the eldest child. They made it sound as though this was some sort of concession.

German soldiers guard vehicles packed with people to be deported to Germany. (From the Russian State Film and Photo Archive. Krasnogorsk. Fond.2, Opis.530, Sn.2)

'Mama,' I said, 'I'll go – I'm intrepid, and literate.'

'Wait! Where do you think you're going?' my mother replied.

'What other option do we have? The other girls can't even read and write.'

I really was an intrepid girl. [. . .] But the people presiding over the deportations chose which of the poor were to go, and kept their own children safely at home.

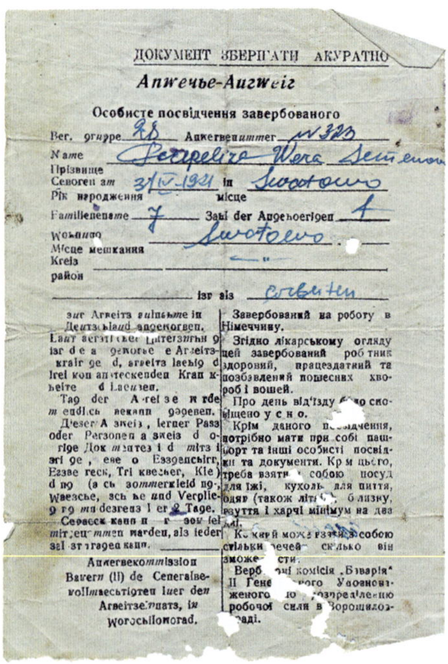

Identity document for a recruited worker, Voroshilovgrad region, 1942:

LOOK AFTER THIS DOCUMENT CAREFULLY

Recruited for work in Germany

In accordance with the medical examination, this recruited worker has been found to be healthy, fit for work and free from infectious diseases and lice. They have been informed verbally of their departure date.

Aside from verification documents, you will need to take your passport and other personal identification documents and papers with you. You will also need to take dishes and implements for eating, clothing (summer clothes too), underwear, shoes and enough food supplies for at least two days. Each person may take as many belongings as they can carry.

Recruitment Commission 'Bavaria'
General Envoy for the Distribution of Labour in Voroshilovgrad.

Others also remembered the prejudiced selection process. Nadezhda Kepet (Pukhovichy), deported in March 1944, said:

Our village elder was my friend's father. He had four daughters and a son. When the Germans gave him the order to produce

> people to take to Germany, he took them from everyone else's families, and didn't send any of his own. [. . .] The Partisans later beat him up for this.

More and more people were taken, in quick succession. Anna Shtepa (Rostov-on-Don), deported in October 1942:

> My brother Ivan and sister Lyuba were taken in the earliest groups during the summer of 1942. In the autumn, the village elder came to our house and said, 'Anna must go too. If she doesn't go, they may well shoot you.'
>
> My father deliberated over what to do. They decided to send me.

A letter sent to Germany in 1943 from the Zaporozhye region:

> A letter sent on 18 August. Greetings, my dear friends, Lida, Marfusha and Olya! It is me, your friend Mila. I hasten to tell you first of all that I didn't receive your letters, but somebody did pass on your greetings and so I decided to send you a letter. I shall tell you quickly that those born in 1926 and 1927 are being taken from our village now – the 1926 group went on 16 August – i.e. yesterday. The 1927s are leaving on 24/VIII-43. There aren't many of the 1926 group – just seven train cars. They didn't take anyone from our factory, but they took them from everywhere else. Dusya Samsonenko is going on the 24th, as is Tonka Skripka's son Vanka Konovalov. Pavlik Moroza's [child] will surely go too, but he's at the employment exchange commission at the moment. Fedka Belousa's Dusya and Zhenya were due to leave on 24 August but now they're not going. Until they hear otherwise, that is. That's all my news for now. Everything else is as it should be. On my day off on the 22nd we're thinking of going for a walk either here, or in the outskirts. That's all for now. Write to Klava. Goodbye. I'm sending you a kiss and look forward to your reply. Mila

Sometimes an entire family would be sent, including the children. Iraida Zhukova was deported from the Leningrad region in August 1942. She remembers:

> We lived in Krasnoye Selo. The Germans forced everybody to work. My mother dug peat. She often took me with her, afraid to leave me behind at home. You never know – I was ten years old after all. [. . .] One day the Germans announced that everybody was going to be taken to work in the Volosovsky district for a week, so we needed to bring some undergarments. [. . .] But my grandmother lived with us. My mother asked the Germans who she could bring with her. Children were permitted, but not the elderly. It was very lucky that my mother did take me with her, because we never came home. We were deported from there, and that was that.

Many of the *Ostarbeiter* held the Polizei entirely responsible for their deportation to Germany. Valentina Sekhina (Stalino), deported in August 1942, said:

> I remember one awful member of the Polizei – his surname was Drobot. He chose to work for the Germans and wouldn't leave us in peace. We hid from him and hid from him, but eventually he caught us. He came to our house one day when we were at home and beat my sister with his rubber whip. Then he grabbed me by the arm and dragged me off. He told my mother that I was being taken away to work, but he took me to the Lenin Community Centre. I think they held us there for about a week, at which point we were loaded into an awful, filthy train car, and taken away.

Domnikiya Skiba was deported from the village of Zasluchnoe (Kamenetsk-Podolsk region), in April 1942. She remembered:

> The first selection took place in the spring – I ended up going to Germany with this group. The Polizei drew up the lists

> – after all, they knew everybody. They wrote down the names of all the young people, of which I was one. The traitors! They knew everybody, and yet they still turned people over to the Germans. That's the type of countrymen we had.

Elizaveta Krestyantseva (Kirovograd) was deported in September 1943:

> It was our Russian policemen who went round the houses taking people away to the assembly point. I was sixteen at the time. My mother had gone out somewhere and left me at home with my brother. The Polizei appeared and asked where my mother was. I told them that she wasn't home. My brother started to scream.
>
> 'Please don't take me right now,' I said. 'My mother should be back soon.'
>
> 'We don't have time to wait,' they replied. [. . .] And they took me away.

Efforts to beg or persuade the police to remove names from lists were usually in vain. Zinaida Komissarova (Vyazhishche village, Pskov region), deported in April 1942, recalled:

> The district elder began to draw up a list of seventeen-year-olds – he put all of them, boys and girls, on this list. He arrived at our house and said, 'You and you are going to Germany.'
>
> My mother had six children, of which I was the eldest. We cried and begged them not to send us, but nothing helped.

Was it possible to avoid deportation? Many described their futile efforts to stay at home. One young girl who did manage to 'legally' avoid appearing on a list was Lyudmila Vasilkovskaya (Poltava). She told us her story:

> It was early 1942. I was on my way to the labour exchange when suddenly I bumped into a few of my classmates. They told

> me that they were on their way to enrol at the vocational land management school that was about to open. 'Come with us!' they said. So I enrolled too and thanks to this I wasn't deported. The Germans were opening these vocational schools in preparation for a shift in land use structures. You see, the kolkhoz farms were to be abandoned in favour of private farming.

Lyudmila was one of the few lucky ones – cases like hers were extremely rare.

Teenagers who found themselves on lists for deportation to Germany sometimes tried to run from their villages and farms, but more often than not they were unsuccessful in their efforts to escape. Valeria Fyodorova (Dashkovichy, Brest region), deported in March 1944, described her attempt to avoid deportation. In the months that preceded the outbreak of war she had been sent from Leningrad to spend the holidays with some relatives in Western Belarus, from where she had been unable to evacuate. She and her mother were labelled *Sovyetki** in the village where they had become trapped. One day, Valeria discovered that she was on a list of youngsters due to be deported to Germany. She decided to run away:

> As I was walking, I heard a horse and cart coming up behind me. It was some old chap heading for the market in Porozovo. With childish naivety, I accepted a lift and began chatting to him – by this time I was fairly fluent in Belarusian. Of course, he realised that I was a *Sovyetka*. [. . .] As soon as I reached the market square in Porozovo, I was approached by two policemen, and promptly arrested. They had been tipped off by the peasant who had given me a lift.

Anna Kirilenko (Rostov-on-Don), deported in September 1942, described how a 'stroke of bad luck' thwarted her attempt to escape deportation:

* *Sovyetka/Sovyetki* (pl.) – meaning 'Soviet' – was a derogatory name given by Western Belarusians to women from central areas of Russia.

> One day, I heard somebody bang on the gate of our house. I went outside to investigate, but there was nobody there. Then I saw a little boy peering out at me from behind a corner. 'You have a letter in your postbox,' he said.
>
> I thought that he was playing a prank on me – I even threatened him, called him a kulak. But when I opened the postbox, there was indeed a little note in there. It read simply: 'Leave – you have been informed on to the Gestapo.'
>
> I took the note to my father.
>
> 'What should we do?' he wondered aloud. 'Nobody jokes about such things any more.'
>
> He took me to the edge of town and pointed down a road. 'Follow this road until you get to Kuteynikovo,' he said. [. . .] We had some friends there – I could hide with them. And so I set off. I walked and walked for about four hours. Suddenly, I saw Germans ahead of me. They were armed with automatic rifles and herding a small column of women down the road. There was nowhere to hide – just open fields all around me. Then I spotted some trenches. I jumped into one! It just so happened that the women needed to stop too. '*Klosett, Klosett!*'* shouted the Germans. Well, of course, all the women jumped straight into the trenches to relieve themselves. Then they were ushered out and a German walked along, checking all the trenches to make sure that nobody had stayed behind. And there I was. He grabbed me by the scruff of the neck and dragged me into the column. [. . .] That's how I ended up in Germany.

Deported in September 1942, Lyubov Shkulyova (Kirovograd) tried to avoid deportation by feigning illness:

> The Polizei told me that I was going to Germany.
>
> 'But I'm ill, I've got a cough,' I said.
>
> 'Perhaps you've got tuberculosis,' they replied. 'You'd better get checked.'

* Lavatory.

I went to the police headquarters and our doctor was there. Bursting into tears, I told her that I didn't know what I would do if they deported me. She listened to my chest.

'There's nothing in your lungs,' she said, 'but I'll write that you have bronchitis anyway.'

But when I took the doctor's note to the German stationed at the headquarters, he told me that bronchitis was a nonsense – it was just a cough that would pass, he said. They wouldn't even let me go home before leaving. [. . .] I was shoved onto the train in my cotton *sarafan* dress.

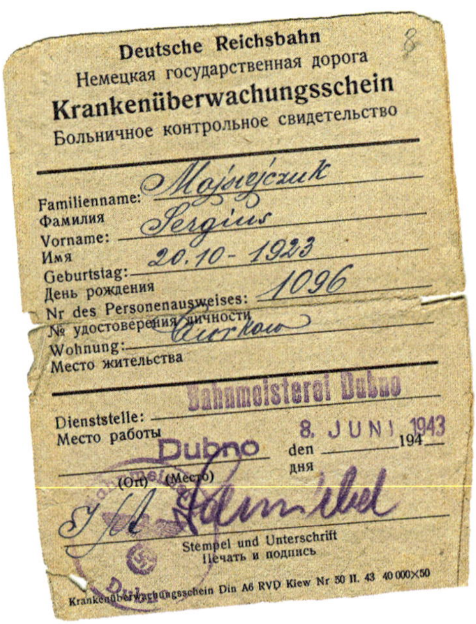

Deutsche Reichsbahn
Немецкая государственная дорога
Krankenüberwachungsschein
Больничное контрольное свидетельство

Familienname: Mojsiejczuk
Фамилия
Vorname: Sergius
Имя
Geburtstag: 20.10-1923
День рождения
Nr des Personenausweises: 1096
№ удостоверения личности
Wohnung:
Место жительства

Dienststelle: Bahnmeisterei Dubno
Место работы
Dubno
(Ort) (Место)
8. JUNI 1943
den ___194_
дня

Stempel und Unterschrift
Печать и подпись

Krankenüberwachungsschein Din A6 RVD Kiew Nr 50 II. 43 40 000×50

A medical test record issued by the Deutsche Reichsbahn (German National Railway),. Rovensky region, 1943. The following fields were included: surname; name; date of birth; identification card number; place of residence; place of work (inc. dates); stamp and signature.

Lyubov could not have known, but a diagnosis of tuberculosis could have meant a death sentence rather than a reprieve. As Antonina Serdyukova, deported from Stalingrad in September 1942, attested, the Germans were terrified of the disease: 'Before deportation we were all screened using photofluorography. I can't remember exactly how many people were filtered out during the testing – we never saw them. It was said that they were executed. The Germans were very afraid of tuberculosis.'

Sometimes, however, medical exclusions did provide a way

out. Anna Odinokova (Chernigov region, deported June 1943) remembers:

> We were taken to the so-called medical board in Glukhov. It was the sort of medical examination where they just tell you to breathe in, and breathe out. [. . .] I had a second cousin, Volodya, who had been at school with me. He was in love with me, as it happens. He told me that they weren't sending him to Germany.
>
> 'What do you mean, they aren't sending you?' I asked.
>
> 'They declared me ill,' he said.
>
> 'What's wrong with you?' I asked. 'You look perfectly all right to me.'
>
> 'There's nothing whatsoever wrong with me,' he whispered. 'The guys and I smoked like chimneys before the examination, and they diagnosed us with tuberculosis.'
>
> I burst into tears. 'Why didn't you tell me?' I cried. 'I would have done the same.'
>
> He looked at me, wide-eyed. 'It didn't even occur to me that a girl could smoke,' he said.
>
> It hadn't occurred to him! And so I was deported.

People employed various methods to avoid deportation. Zinaida Komissarova (Vyazhishche village, Pskov region) said: 'My friend was really crafty. She went to the registration point and started to convulse – she had learned how to do it. They excluded her from deportation on medical grounds. [. . .] She stayed behind, and later joined the Partisans.'

A few managed to avoid deportation with the help of acquaintances who worked for the Germans in administrative positions. Victor Zhabsky (Novocherkassk), deported October 1942, remembered: 'When I went to register at the labour exchange, I found, to my surprise, that my old German teacher from Year Five – Anna Konstantinovna – was there, acting as clerk and filling in all the documentation. She saved me from being deported in the first shipment.'

But such cases were rare.

In the cities, young men and women received a written order summoning them to their local *Arbeitsamt*. The reason for the summons was never indicated, but rumours travelled fast and everyone knew that these notes meant only one thing: deportation. Those who failed to turn up at the *Arbeitsamt* were invariably tracked down, either at home or during the regular police round-ups. Some of those caught in this manner were: Varvara Kramarenkova (Sevastopol, September 1942), Nikolai Gulyaev (Taganrog, June 1942), Antonina Serdyukova (Stalingrad, September 1942), Victor Zhabsky (Novocherkassk, October 1942) and Elizaveta Krestyantseva (Kirovograd, September 1943).

If, for the young city dwellers, there was some hope of evading deportation by hiding or losing themselves in the fabric of their city, this was not the case for those in the countryside. From the moment their names were added to the deportation lists their fate was sealed – there was simply nowhere to hide from their local administrative bodies.

Fedor Khmara (Buiskoye, Poltava region), deported January 1943, recalls:

> The Polizei delivered the order: Meet at the school or club for deportation to Germany on such and such a date. That was it – off you went. [. . .] Everyone cried, especially my father. He took me to the station [at Zolotonosha] in the horse-drawn cart. Twelve of us were taken from my village that day.

Even in the instances where it was possible to hide or find an escape route (for example, when the mass deportations began in Belarus many youngsters ran off to join the Partisans), there were serious considerations to take into account. Such steps were not taken lightly, for any loved ones who stayed behind often paid a price. Pavel Mikhailov (Lozovoy hamlet, Zaporozhye region, September 1943) explains: 'I could have escaped; I could have hidden somewhere, but there were quotas for the village. If I had run, they would have taken my mother and sister. That's why nobody ran away.'

Ukrainian workers en route to the railway station, summer 1942. (BA/BA No. 69/100/17)

Vera Dergachova (Stalin region) was deported in August 1942. She remembers:

> The deportations got underway. But we lived one house away from a lady called Marinka Fedchenkova. As soon as she saw them starting to round people up, she would begin yelling at the top of her voice, in a very unnatural way. [. . .] On hearing this sound, everyone knew to run out of their houses and make for the tall rushes in the marsh. This was her signal to us – when she started to scream, it meant that the police were coming for us, and we would run to the rushes. [. . .] Well, we ran there over and over again upon her signal. And then one day the Polizei came to our house and calmly told my parents that if I did not go, all three of them would be taken instead – my father, mother and little sister.

Nikolai Bogoslavets, deported from Taganrog in July 1943, and a friend decided on an alternative:

> There was a system in place: if you hid, they would send your parents in your place, or set fire to your home. You were free to

choose. [. . .] So my friend and I agreed that we would go to Germany, register our arrival and then do a runner.

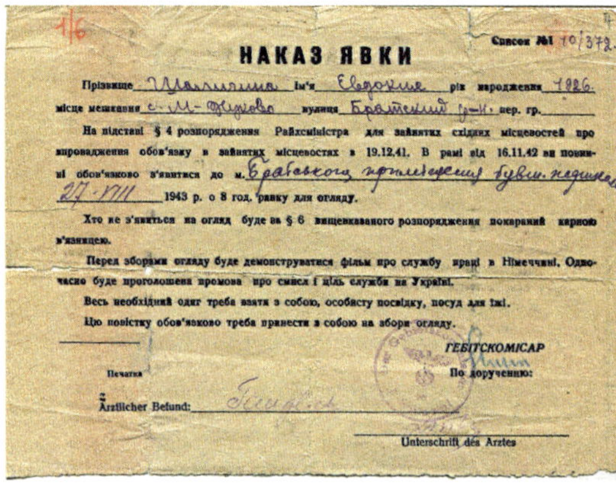

Список №1 10/372

НАКАЗ ЯВКИ

Прізвище ______ Ім'я ______ рік народження 1926

місце мешкання ______ вулиця ______ пер. гр. ______

На підставі § 4 розпорядження Райхсміністра для зайнятих східних місцевостей про впровадження обов'язку в зайнятих місцевостях в 19.12.41. В рамі від 16.11.42 ви повинні обов'язково з'явитися до м. ______ ______ 1943 р. о 8 год. ранку для огляду.

Хто не з'явиться на огляд буде за § 6 вищезказаного розпорядження покараний карною в'язницею.

Перед зборами огляду буде демонструватися фільм про службу праці в Німеччині. Одночасно буде проголошена промова про смисл і ціль служби на Україні.

Весь необхідний одяг треба взяти з собою, особисту посвідку, посуд для їжі.

Цю повістку обов'язково треба принести з собою на збори огляду.

ГЕБІТСКОМІСАР

Печатка

По дорученню:

Ärztlicher Befund: ______

Unterschrift des Arztes

Order for transportation to Germany for work, Stalin region, 1943 (translated from Ukrainian):

ORDER TO REPORT. In accordance with Article 4 of the Directive of the Reich Ministry for the Occupied Eastern Territories on the introduction of labour duties, implemented 19.12.1941, you are ordered to report for inspection at the premises of the former teaching school on 27/VIII-1943 at 8:00 a.m. Anybody who fails to report for inspection will be punished with a prison sentence in accordance with Article 6 of the aforementioned directive. Prior to the inspection, you will be shown a film detailing the system of work in Germany. At the same time, you will also be given a lecture on the ideas behind this labour service, and on its goals in Ukraine. You must bring with you all the clothing that you may require, your identity card and utensils for eating. You are required to bring this order with you at the time of your inspection.

Gebietskommissar

Vadim Novgorodov (Taganrog) gave his account:

I ran smack into a round-up near the bazaar. Luckily, a guy I knew gave me some advice – he had some sort of connection with the city police. [. . .]

'Have they taken your passport?' he asked me. 'If so, just go to the labour exchange and don't even think about hiding – I'm warning you. Your passport states your address – they'll

> go to your house. If you do a runner or don't turn up they might just decide on a whim to shoot everyone they find there – relatives or not.'
>
> That's how it was. What could I do? I had to 'show up with my belongings' at the labour exchange as instructed and . . . off I went to Germany.

Lyudmila Stanyeva (Zaporozhye region), deported July 1943, described how some people bought their freedom with betrayal. She and a group of her fellow villagers had planned to join the Partisans:

> One member of our group fell into the hands of the police. [. . .] He was taken to the police station where he was told, 'Petro, we know that someone is sticking up signs, and communication wires have been cut too. [. . .] We have been informed that there is some sort of Partisan cell operating here, but we can't catch them. If you tell us who they are, we will exempt you from deportation to Germany.'
>
> He told them about all four of us. We were arrested, of course. They took us all.

Towards the end of occupation in 1944, entire settlements and villages of people were deported from Belarus. Leonid Osipov spoke of his frustration at the inevitability of deportation in the wake of several desperate attempts to evade capture. He was deported from the village of Khuralevo in the Gomel region in April 1944:

> There was a round-up. The Germans and Polizei went round all the houses with dogs, herding everyone out onto the kolkhoz square. There we were sorted – they decided who was to go where. My father and I managed to hide, but my elder brother was taken – they hung a label around his neck and led him away. [. . .] It was just the two of us after that. And then one morning we heard the Germans coming round again with their dogs – it was another round-up.

> 'Well, what d'you think? Shall we make a run for it?' my father said.
>
> 'Where can we run to?' I replied. 'And why try, just to be shot in the vegetable patch?'

'Night falls, and the train cars rock'

Upon realising that their fate was sealed, some of the *Ostarbeiter* attempted to better their fortunes ahead of their departure for Germany. This they did by falsifying answers to certain questions in the forms that they were required to fill out (e.g. nationality, surname, age). Nikolai Kireev (Oryol region, spring 1942) remembers that, on the advice of his family, he lied about his age, hoping that if he stated he was younger, he would be assigned to easier labour duties: 'I remember the initial questions were related to who you were and where you came from. People answered as they saw fit. [. . .] I told a fib – I said I was born in '28 [instead of 1926] because my physical appearance didn't suggest otherwise.'

The extreme poverty of their situation and the scarcity of food were such that for many *Ostarbeiter* gathering even the most basic of necessities (notably food and clothes for the journey) was a struggle. Anna Odinokova, deported from Dubovichy village (Chernigov region) in July 1943, recalls:

> What could I possibly take with me? We had nothing to eat. [. . .] What clothes? Homemade ones – I spun my own yarn to knit material, then cut the patterns and sewed them into clothes. [. . .] I went to Germany in the clothes I was wearing. My mother baked some bread rusks for me to take – it was all we had, so that was all I took.

Aldona Volynskaya (Novoukrainka, Kirovograd region), deported in autumn 1942, said:

> The weather was still warm. Our matron [at the orphanage], Larisa Antonovna, used every bit of cloth she could find. She used the chintz curtains to patch together a sundress for me and

she sewed me a bra from two Pioneer ties [. . .] We left half-naked, and barefoot too.

Everyone faced a long train journey west, to the Reich. But some people first had to cover many kilometres on foot, just to reach the station from which they were scheduled to depart. Lidia Beketova (Taganrog), deported May 1942, recalled:

> We went on foot – the Germans marched us all the way from Taganrog to Sartana station in Mariupol. Cattle cars lined the track, their doors thrown open. A German stood in front of each one, armed with an automatic rifle. They loaded us into these cattle cars . . . and off we went.

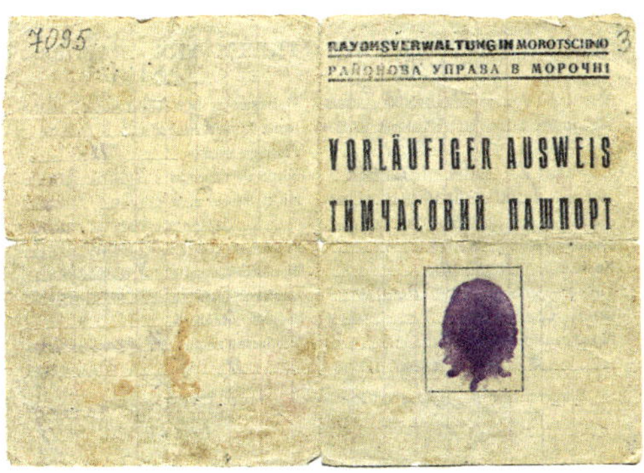

Temporary passport, Rovensky region, 1942.

Descriptions of departure followed a very similar pattern – everyone spoke of convoys, cattle cars (*telyachi*) and painful farewells to loved ones. Varvara Khabarova (Zolotonosha), deported in September 1942, described her own agonising departure:

> My mother gathered my belongings together and accompanied me to the station. A few other relatives arrived to see me off too, but the guards wouldn't let them near me. The Germans had dogs, and they surrounded us, refusing to let anybody come past. The German shepherds lunged at anyone who tried to reach us – there was no way past. We were loaded into the carriages, the guards kicking us with their boots. Everybody was shouting, 'Mama, Mama.'

> Parents were shouting too, and we shouted back, 'Mama, Mama, don't cry, Mama!'

For many, this was the first time they had left the place where they had been born. Hanna Muzalyova (Kharkov region), deported August 1943, told us: 'I had grown up under my mother's skirts. I saw a train for the first time the day that I was sent to Germany. It was my first ever journey, and it was taken under a police guard.'

Remembering the journey brought distressing emotions back to the surface. Many *Ostarbeiter* recalled having a disquieting sense that they were being treated like livestock. Larisa Shvidchenko (Rostov-on-Don), deported September 1942, said: 'They organised us into cattle cars at the station. The train inspector turned to us. "The Germans have taken cows back to Germany," he said. "You can see the straw beds for yourselves. You're going to be travelling like livestock now."'

Antonina Vladimirova (Cherkessk), deported December 1942, recalled:

> We must have travelled for about ten days. We were loaded into cattle cars – I remember that ours was red, and the floors were covered in straw. They would open the doors, throw in some food, and then close them up again. Every single person trembled with fear and hoped not to be killed. We lay there on the straw in the darkness and trundled along.

Everybody, without exception, remembers the difficulty of answering the call of nature. As a rule, the trains didn't let people out at the stops, and men and women were loaded in together. Cooped up in the cattle cars, they resorted to making holes in the floor through which to relieve themselves. Valeria Fyodorova (Dashkovichy, Brest region), deported March 1944 , said that: 'Going to the toilet was a problem. Someone used a high-heeled shoe to break one of the floorboards in the carriage, and we took it in turns to use the hole. They didn't even open the doors when we stopped at stations.'

A group of young people prior to their departure for Germany. (Russian State Film and Photo Archive, Krasnogorsk, Op.3, Delo.261, Sn.85)

Taissa Tolkachova, deported from Genichesk in May 1942, remembered:

> They loaded us into a cattle car just outside Kherson – boys and girls together. The boys relieved themselves in one corner, and the girls in the other. One girl was engaged to one of the boys in our train car though, and she was too embarrassed to go to the toilet in front of him. Her bladder burst as a result, and she died.

Sometimes they were allowed to get out of the train cars. Raissa Nefyodova (Kirovograd region), deported June 1943, said: 'The guards stood round us, holding their guns. When the train came to a halt, you got out to do your business. A German would stand over you, and you got on and did what you had to do.'

A few people remember instances when their escorts showed some sympathy. Galina Agranovskaya (Dyatkovo, Bryansk region), deported August 1942, remembers an elderly German train guard who couldn't bring enough water for the whole train car, but always shouted out '*Für kinder!*' when he handed over the water he had. This enabled the mothers to give their children something to drink.

The journeys varied in length from a few days, to two or three weeks. However, very few could remember exactly how long they travelled for – the entire episode lodged in their memories as a series of humiliations, an aching longing for home and attempts to adapt to life in the train wagons. Some remember consoling themselves by singing popular Soviet songs. Varvara Khabarova (Zolotonosha, Poltava region), deported September 1942, said: 'By evening [. . .] we had stopped crying. We decided we would feel better if we sang, to keep our spirits up. "Night falls and the train cars rock," we began. "Nobody slumbers peacefully, for our beloved city is disappearing from sight."'

Some people hoped that the Partisans would come to their rescue. Anna Odinokova (Chernigov region, June 1943) said: 'I kept thinking that perhaps my father was somewhere nearby, with the Partisans. Perhaps he would come. I lay there daydreaming – if only the Partisans would come and save us!' Anna's hopes weren't entirely unfounded. Sometimes the Partisans did attempt to free the men and women bound for Germany, as Tatiana Teplova (Griva, Kalinin region), deported February 1943, recalled:

> We waited on the tracks for a very long time [before departure]. Of course, the doors were bolted shut, but my brother managed to throw a note in through a little gap that served as a window. It read: 'When you set off, the train will stop. We will open the train cars, immediately run into the woods.' He gave the name of a place. But they didn't manage to stop the train.

Lyubov Yerokhova (Pustoshka, Pskov region), deported November 1941, remembers: 'The Partisans launched an attack on our train; they opened fire, and many people escaped from the train cars. But we were too afraid to run.'

Lavrenty Novokhatko (Seletskoye, Dnepropetrovsk region), deported in June 1942, and his friend also considered escape:

> We wanted to run away when we got to Lublin. We planned to somehow make a hole in the floor and then throw ourselves out of it while the train was moving. But in the end we were too afraid to do it because we were being guarded by SS men and they had threatened to shoot us.

Antonina Serdyukova (Stalingrad), deported September 1942, also realised that attempts to escape would be futile:

> We travelled for exactly one month. Sometimes we'd be moving, at other times we'd be stationary. Usually we would stop in an open field where there was absolutely nobody to be seen. They let us out at night to relieve ourselves. But where could we have run? There was nothing and nobody in sight, as far as the eye could see.

Zoya Yeliseeva (Dzhankoy), deported June 1942, raised the same point: '[. . .] Run? Where could a sixteen-year-old girl possibly run to? I had neither family, nor acquaintances there. One girl got left behind by the train at a stop, but she caught us up again the next day.'

Valentina Sekhina (Stalino), deported August 1942, gave in to her impulse to escape from the train, but she too soon realised that there was nowhere to hide:

> The first time they let us out in Kraków to drink some water, my mind started to race. Shouldn't I hide? So I did. The train left, my suitcase with it, and I stayed behind. I wandered about in bewilderment – I didn't know where to go, or who to speak to. Anyway, I was soon caught again and taken to the assembly point where others like me were gathered. In the end I caught up with my previous train, and found my suitcase.

For almost all the deportees, this was the first time they had set foot abroad and the already slim chance of any successful escape was further diminished by the fact that most didn't speak the local language of the countries in which they found themselves. Those

A stop en route to Germany, summer 1942. (VA/VA Nr 86/3359/17A)

who didn't have the nerve to run had good reason to be afraid, for harsh punishments were meted out to anybody caught trying to flee. Nevertheless, there remained a pervading sense among the *Ostarbeiter*, particularly those who were slightly older at the time of their deportation, that they had somehow allowed themselves to be taken. As a result, they were haunted for the rest of their lives by feelings of guilt for failing to seize opportunities to escape or for not making a stand. Yevgenia Savranskaya (Sumy region), deported June 1942, said: 'You must understand that it is very difficult to banish these thoughts from one's mind. They convinced me that I was guilty, and I live with the guilt to this day.'

PART 3

Life in Germany

'You are *Ostarbeiter* now'

The journey to the Third Reich stood out in our conversations with *Ostarbeiter* as one of the most dramatic chapters in their stories. It was clear that this had been a time of significant emotional turmoil; many had been just sixteen or seventeen years old at the time, while some were even younger. Torn from their beloved families and subjected to terrible travelling conditions, they wrestled with fears about what awaited them as captives of a frightening and pitiless enemy, and contemplated what the future held in store. With no idea where they were headed, they prepared for the worst.

'They hung some kind of placard on a chain around our necks'

The shock of the experience was so severe that some had no recollection of how long they had travelled or where they finally disembarked.

A postcard dated 5 June 1943 from Remscheid to the Sumy region (translated from Ukrainian):

> A letter from your daughter, Motya. In these first lines of my letter I would like to send a bow of greeting to you – Mama, Grandmother, my sisters and little brother Lyonya, who I miss very much. Mama, I have arrived safely and didn't lose anything on the way – everything is safe. We travelled for fifteen days, and there were two approval panels. The panel rejected one girl from Pavlovsk – we posted her letter home from Poland. Mama, Dunya is here with me. Lida and Nastya are a little further away but we still see each other every day. [. . .] It rains a lot here,

> and there are heavy hailstorms. [. . .] The same plants grow here as at home. I don't know where our lads are – we all arrived at the same place together, but then we were split up. Think of me Mama, even just once on a Tuesday, and meanwhile I will think of you forty times a day. Pass on my greetings to the aunties and uncles, the lads and the girls, and to all the neighbours from me. That's all that I wanted to write in my postcard for now. Motya.

A postcard dated 23 July 1943 from Gotenhafen to Kitaigorod, Kamenets-Podolsk region:

> Good afternoon, my precious Mummy!!! First of all, I am sending you my heartfelt greetings! Mummy, I'm in Poland. We are near the city of Gotenhafen and work right by the Baltic Sea. [. . .] Mummy, I got separated from the others I came with, and don't know where they went. Valya

Vadim Novgorodov recalls that when his train stopped over in Poland, he witnessed Jews, who had been brought from the ghetto, being forced to clean the train. He never forgot the cruelty with which they were treated: 'At Peremyshl I saw how the Jews were treated – they appeared to be Polish Jews. They were forced to wash out the wagons once the trains had been unloaded – the guards harried them with sticks. [. . .] They looked absolutely awful; they must have lived in the ghetto.'*

Many people mentioned the compulsory medical inspections and disinfection procedures that took place in Peremyshl and Poznań. The fear of epidemics was so strong among the Germans that the frightened new arrivals were subjected to the humiliation of having their hair cut and clothes boiled. A few of the women recall the fear and embarrassment of undergoing gynaecological inspections as young girls. Alexandra Mikhailova (Belaya, Moscow region), deported in summer 1942, said:

* V. Novgorodov was probably not mistaken. He was deported in May 1942, and the ghetto in Przemyśl had not been liquidated by this time.

> We were loaded onto the train and taken to Germany. We had no idea where they were taking us. But how could we have known? I cried and cried. They unloaded us in an unfamiliar city already teeming with people. And they hung some kind of placard on a chain around our necks – it displayed a number.

The trains didn't usually stop for long until they had crossed into another territory – most remember that they first broke their journey in Poland:

> We stopped in Poland. How did I know that we were in Poland? Firstly, because I could see that the signposts were written in Polish, and I could hear Polish being spoken. But I could also tell from the change in the railway – we have wide tracks and they have narrow ones. (Antonina Serdyukova)

> We travelled for two days and nights. On the third day, we arrived – as I later discovered – in Poznań, where there was a transit camp. They held us at this transit camp for two weeks. They did give us a little more bread, and some hot, watery soup. The bunks were wooden, and arranged on two levels. We were given one blanket. The mattresses were made from straw or perhaps seagrass. [. . .] We were put through a sanitary inspection and had X-rays taken. Anyone who was ill was sent home. (Yevgeny Goryainov, Kursk, deported in spring 1942)

Tatiana Teplova had grown up in the countryside and remembers the medical inspection well:

> When we were taken in for our medical inspections, we girls were put into a chair, the like of which I had never seen before. The German doctor held a big mirror in his hand, and we stood there, tense, naked and miserable. Then they lined us up and took photographs of us.

Photographs from registration documents. Left: Tempelburg 1943. Right: Altengrabow, 1942.

Aldona Volynskaya also remembers a medical inspection: 'A man led me off somewhere for the medical inspection. I was naked, and he poured water on me and smeared me with some cream. It was so humiliating – an awful procedure!'

Iraida Zhukova (Leningrad region) was deported alongside her mother at the age of ten (August 1942). She recalls:

> They took us into some sort of building. Everything was dingy and dark. Everyone was made to undress – men and women together – and once stark naked we were led off down a corridor. One German sat on one side, and another sat opposite. They held little sticks in their hands, which they used to inspect all the hairy parts. I felt so uncomfortable in front of the men. Next, we were herded into a chamber with little objects in the ceiling. I heard the adults say, 'Perhaps they are about to turn on the gas.'
>
> There was such a sense of terror! And then suddenly water came out from those little objects. Everyone breathed a sigh of relief . . . it was a shower.

It is worth noting that word of the gas chambers could not have reached the *Ostarbeiter* by 1942 – at that time, nobody knew that this was how the Germans were conducting mass exterminations at Nazi concentration camps such as Auschwitz. The ten-year-old

Iraida's memories of fear must have been formulated at a later date, when she learned of liquidation methods at the concentration camps.

The girls felt further traumatised and degraded by the mandatory haircuts – some had their plaits cut off, while others had their heads shaved completely:

> We were stripped stark naked. I had such a lovely long plait back then. A typical German with a redheaded mug came up to me and cut it off. I remember standing there, thinking that I was probably about to be killed. (Lidia Beketova, Taganrog)

> We were taken into the bathhouse where they had birch-tar soap ready. We were rubbed all over with some sort of awful-smelling cream and then they checked our heads for lice. But how could we possibly have washed on the journey? They found nits and, just like that, my head was shaved Kotovsky-style.* I came out looking like a boy – I was so upset! I had always had such lovely thick hair. When we came out, nobody recognised one another. (Anna Gulyaeva, Novoduginskaya, Smolensk region, deported spring 1942)

Nadezhda Izmalkova (Kiev), deported in May 1942, was a little older than some of the other girls when she was deported, and she could speak some German. She described how the new arrivals were organised 'according to race' before being washed and taken to a large camp at Przemyśl where 'all sorts of doctors, including general practitioners and gynaecological and tuberculosis specialists, were sitting behind a table. We had to walk up to them, naked, and they would say: "*Das ist eine neue russische sowjetische Rasse*" (This is a new member of the Russian Soviet race).'

Victor Zhabsky, who also spoke a little German, remembers his arrival in Germany:

* Translator's note: Grigory Kotovsky was a Soviet military and political figure with an iconic bald head.

> We travelled for about two weeks. One day the guys looked out of the window and said, 'All the signs are written in German. What do they say – we can't read them.' [. . .] Early one morning, the train doors were thrown open by a German shouting, '*Raus!* Get out! *Alle raus!*'
>
> We climbed down and looked around at the station. I spotted a sign that read, Kisterbach.*

Photograph from a registration document, Bogen, 1942.

Very few could remember their first few hours in Germany with any clarity; for most, they passed in a frightening and bewildering blur. The arrivals were unloaded from the trains and organised into columns to be escorted or transported into the unknown by soldiers with dogs. Antonina Sizova (Gdov, Pskov region), deported in summer 1943, said:

> We didn't know where they were taking us. We were unloaded in the drizzling rain and organised into columns in silence. They escorted us with dogs to a building where we found others just like ourselves, already waiting. Everybody was given a coloured patch to attach to the left-hand side of their chest; either red, yellow, green or blue. We were given yellow patches, which assigned us to the distribution camp.

There were insufficient numbers of these distribution camps, so many of the *Ostarbeiter* found themselves at temporary distribution

* Translator's note: It is possible that Zhabsky is referring here to Kelsterbach in Hessen, Germany.

points, which had been hastily established in any available large buildings. It was here that they spent their first days on German soil. They were registered, photographed with their allocated numbers and had their fingerprints taken.

Raissa Pervina (Baranovichy, Brest region), deported spring 1942, found herself at a camp that housed Soviet prisoners of war, most of whom had been deported to Germany before the *Ostarbeiter.* She described the terrible living conditions:

A camp at the Bogler Werk factory in Düsseldorf, 1942.

> I think we were sent to a camp on the outskirts of Verdun first of all [. . .] No, it was Soltau actually, Soltau. The prisoners-of-war camps here were large, and surrounded by barbed wire, just like in the film *Professor Mamlock.** There were barracks with stacks of greatcoats heaped outside that had belonged to our deceased prisoners-of-war. There was no lavatory; just a hole under one of the watchtowers. And you were expected to use this hole in full sight of the guard, who might just take a pot

* A reference to the 1938 Soviet film directed by A. Minkin and G. Rappaport that depicted the cruel persecution of Jews by the Nazi regime. The film was based upon a play by F. Wolf.

> shot at it for fun, to watch you get splattered with excrement. [. . .] They mainly fed us boiled potato skins. But we weren't there for long.

Anna Odinokova described a similar experience:

> They took us to Breslau.[. . .] We were herded into a camp bordered on all sides by barbed wire and watchtowers. [. . .] And then they shepherded us into a barracks with an earth floor. We stayed there for a month. I had a cast-iron bowl that held about half a litre of liquid. They'd pour in some water and you'd get three little pieces of swede which floated about in it – that was what they fed us.

Some also remembered being registered, photographed and having their fingerprints taken while in the distribution camps. Prior to having their photographs taken, a cardboard panel displaying a number would be hung around a person's neck. Varvara Kramarenkova (Sevastopol, Crimea), deported September 1942, recalls: 'The first thing that really crushed our spirits was having a panel with a number on it hung around our necks.' And Anna Odinokova said: 'They gave us a placard and everyone was photographed for the second time holding one. My number was 904. I held it up.'

Victor Zhabsky said:

> They began to write up our documents. They made a note of your name and surname, where you were from, your date of birth, registration number and faith. When they asked me about my religious orientation, I told them that I was a non-believer.
>
> 'Don't say that again,' I was told.
>
> 'And what should I say?' I replied.
>
> 'Say that you are Christian.'
>
> 'But we are Pioneers, how can we be believers?'
>
> 'Christian,' came the reply.
>
> [. . .] We were registered and assigned with numbers.

> 'This is your number,' we were each told. 'Remember your camp number. And woe betide you if you forget it.' [. . .]
>
> Well, we learned them. They were seven or eight digits long though – I can't remember mine now. I was photographed with my number.

'Nobody bought me on the first day'

The *Ostarbeiter* had clear memories of being assigned to their workplaces. After all, this was to mark the beginning of a new life. The process was usually carried out at the distribution camps, where labour exchanges had been established specifically for this purpose. They could be allocated to any number of jobs; some were sent to work in the mines, in factories, or in construction, while others were dispatched to work for farmers, or in homes as domestic helpers. The German distribution camps based their decisions on where to send the workers upon the information provided in the forms that had been filled out by the local and regional employment offices prior to the deportation of the *Ostarbeiter.*

Once the new arrivals had been categorised, employment office officials would usually set a date for representatives from a firm or enterprise to come and choose workers from a pool of suitable candidates, in return for a fee. When selecting their workers, employers would take education and professional qualifications into account, but they were generally more interested in assessing the physical condition of an individual. Much hinged on whether a person was physically suitable for a certain job, particularly since many of the *Ostarbeiter* were too young to have acquired professional qualifications and, in most cases, their education had been rudimentary at best.

Anna Kirilenko remembered:

> The selection process went as follows: they looked at us to see whether we were in good physical health and then checked whether our arms and legs functioned properly – they wanted to make sure that we would be up to the work. For the factory where I worked, they chose young, agile people of a light

A worker (in the background) with his employer, Linz, 1942.

> build. [. . .] The bigger, stronger, fitter ones were assigned to heavy manual labour.

Antonina Serdyukova said:

> There was a colossal distribution point in the forest at Frankfurt an der Oder. The factory directors would come there to select workers for their teams. They were most interested in whether or not you had finished school. The young and fit among us were taken to work at the *Lautawerk** aluminium-vanadium factory . . .

Anna Sechkina recalled:

> Fifty of us were taken into a large room with benches lining the walls. We were told to sit. Then the managers came in and set about choosing their workers. Not everybody was selected – the elderly and children younger than ten were rejected. The managers said that feeding them would be a waste of bread.

For many, the selection process was redolent of a slave market, where labour was purchased and sold. It was soul-destroying and painful to be hand-picked, like livestock at a market, and many described their dehumanising 'transition to slavery' in these terms. Time and again, we heard the word 'buy' used in reference to the selection procedure: '. . . the farmer bought us'; 'everyone had been bought, except for me'.

Georgiy Tkachov, deported in October 1942, described his experience:

* Translator's note: In Lauta, Germany.

> Everyone had been bought; I was the only one left. A man of around fifty walked up to me; he was thickset, portly. He turned out to be an estate owner with a farm. He was the German who bought me. I don't know how much he paid for me.

Lev Tokarev was deported in 1942. He told us:

> When we were taken to the labour exchange, everybody was chosen, but nobody took me. I was scrawny, and was left standing on my own. I could see an elderly man and woman standing nearby, staring long and hard at me. Eventually they walked over.
>
> 'Are you a Jew?' they asked.
>
> 'No, I'm Russian,' I replied.
>
> They talked and bartered, before eventually handing over some money to somebody. Then they took me away to work for a large-scale gardening enterprise.

The selection process was often crude and random:

> People from the countryside mainly chose peasant workers. [. . .] They would inspect your face, eyes, ears, feel your muscles . . . It was just as if we were livestock! (Yevgeny Goryainov)

> The manager of the *Glasfabrik* [glass factory] came over. He needed twenty girls. We were instructed to form a line, and he counted out twenty – as though from a herd of animals.
>
> 'I'll take these,' he announced.
>
> And then he left. Moments like that stay with you for life! (Zinaida Valikhova)

> We were unloaded. A policeman acting as a translator announced that we were going to be sorted for work duties. People began to walk up to us. [. . .] They inspected us as they would have done a horse: from the legs up. Then they handed over some money, signed a form, and led their chosen people

> away. Nobody bought me on the first day – I was sold the day after. It all happened so calmly and quietly. [. . .] You needed to experience it to understand. It's not something that can be put into words; you had to feel it. You were purchased, like an object. (Irina Sokolova)

The more erudite among the deportees compared the selection process to the slave trade; many had read *Uncle Tom's Cabin*, a popular Soviet school text in the 1930s. The experience of having one's muscles squeezed (to determine suitability for physical labour) and teeth checked (to avoid costly medical fees at a later stage) conjured visions of slave markets and powerful emotions that stayed with them for the rest of their lives.

Lavrenty Novokhatko recalled:

> We were taken to Erfurt. There was a huge, empty wooden barracks there where people were bought and sold for labour. Land owners, government officials, widows and wives of soldiers all came to choose workers to suit their needs. They would walk over, line us up and feel our arms and shoulders. Then they would look into our mouths. It was just like a slave market.

The sense of humiliation was compounded by the fact that the well-dressed and well-fed 'buyers' often looked down their noses at the Soviet arrivals. Many regarded them as chattel and 'savages', and had no qualms about dividing families. Galina Agranovskaya told us:

> The labour exchange was in Frankfurt railway station – not in the passenger section, but in the cargo area. We were unloaded from the train cars and stood around while they selected from among us. We were amazed at how well dressed the people who came to choose us were. They regarded my father with a look of revulsion – he looked haggard and gaunt, and his clothes were tattered. They felt his muscles, but there weren't any to feel. He had been a strong and handsome man once [. . .] I remember feeling unbelievably ashamed of how my parents

looked. Back home they had always been such attractive and respectable people. But here, my Mama and Papa looked ragged and pathetic. I was a tall, albeit skinny, fourteen-year-old, and a masculine, bony German woman with glasses chose me. As I was led away, my mother cried out after me, 'My darling daughter, my daughter!'

But my father's condition was such that he couldn't even react. I don't remember how we parted; I remember only my mother's cries. [. . .] They ended up on a farm and I was sent to a factory. But I was glad that I wasn't with them. Witnessing their humiliation would have been too much to bear.

Frida Palko miraculously escaped from the Starodub ghetto before it was liquidated, and was then deported to Germany under a false name in 1942. She lived in constant fear of being found out and remembers her labour exchange experience as one of the most frightening moments of all: 'Some people entered and they were told to choose whoever they wanted. They chose me, and I joined a column of others. Well, I thought we had been selected to be taken away and shot. That was it in my mind. Curtains.'

It was a blessing when fellow villagers, friends and countrymen were assigned to the same workplace. Nadezhda Izmalkova used her quick wits and knowledge of German to ensure that she and her friend were allocated to the same household: 'They wanted to separate us in Erfurt, but we kept our heads and said that we were sisters. They didn't split us up.'

Many were less fortunate.

A letter dated 13 April 1943 from Osnabrück to the village of Rudyakiv in the Kiev region:

Good day, my dear parents. My darling Mama, and little brother Petya, and daughter Olya. I am sending you my heartfelt greetings from Germany. I want to let you know that I am still alive and well, and to wish you all the very best in your lives. We arrived safely and are now living in a camp in the city of

> Osnabrück. I don't know anyone here – there's just one girl, [her surname is] Benkova, here with me – the other girls from Rudyakiv were all taken on to some other town. [. . .] My dear Mummy, don't cry. We will see each other again sometime (but please pray for me).

Anna Odinokova remembers:

> They chose from among us and made a note of who was selected. One by one, everyone around us was led away until Pasha and I were the only ones left. I was tall and spindly, and she was small and skinny – she only came up to my shoulders. We clung to each other and stood there; two orphans. Nobody else arrived. Suddenly an old lady walked up to us. [. . .] She approached and looked at us, trying to decide who to take.
>
> 'What kind of workers d'you call these?' she said. 'I need someone for the farm work – to plough, sow, feed and water the livestock, milk the cows and shift manure.'
>
> Then she pointed at me. 'You there, let's go,' she said. She told them to sign the paperwork.
>
> 'What about me?' Pasha asked. 'I won't be separated from you, I won't let you go!'
>
> 'Take us both! I beg you, please, take us both,' I implored the old woman. But no, she wouldn't give in. I don't know what happened to Pasha.

'It was a different world'

To the eastern workers arriving from the hunger and deprivation of their war-torn homes, Germany appeared clean, prosperous and orderly. They were amazed at the lack of a divide between the cities and countryside.

Georgiy Tkachov had been studying at a vocational college in his home city of Novocherkassk when he was deported at the age of fifteen in October 1942. He was assigned to work on a farm near Greifenberg:

> A German man chose me at the labour exchange and took me back to his village. There were lots of things that caught my attention along the way. The city of Greifenberg itself was an old and provincial little town. The roads were paved with cobblestones, laid neatly stone to stone. And I noticed that every twenty metres or so, there were little grilles along the sides of the pavements, where the rain drained off. The rain came down, but the roads were dry! Fruit trees lined the roads – I saw apples, pears, plums. It wasn't an asphalt road, but it was scattered with gravel and rolled smooth, so it felt as though it was asphalt. There wasn't a single pothole or bump.

A letter dated 3 June 1943 from Lauterecken to the Poltava region (translated from Ukrainian):

> Good day, my dear family!!! 3/VI-43 I am sending you my ardent greetings and wish you all the very best. I am alive and well and am living in a small town among some high mountains. Wherever you go here, you are in the mountains. There are just a few little villages below us, and a flat road that goes around the mountains, linking them all together. If you go out on the mountain, there is nothing but mountains as far as the eye can see. And yet there is not a single patch of land left untended. Everyone has a wonderful garden, not at home, but out in the fields or here at the base of the mountain. There is no vegetable patch or well where I live. There are lots of grapes here too, but my employer doesn't grow any. When I go out onto the mountain and look around me, I picture my home, and it makes me yearn for my beloved simple hut. How I long to hear the voices of my dear mother and father. I only wish I could read some words from you, but I haven't anything to read. I received one postcard, but nothing more. Or have you not written? I write to you often. Send me your news. On that note, I'll say goodbye. I'm sending everyone a handshake and to you, a kiss. Greetings to all the family. Your daughter.

A photograph of a German family, Garmisch-Partenkirchen, 1944.

Anna Odinokova, whose family formerly worked on a kolkhoz in Chernigov, described her first impressions of Germany: 'There were flowers on the balconies and all along the sides of the roads. It was beautiful – I had never seen anything like it! We had flowers, but not in such abundance. I remember thinking, Good Lord! What a place we've come to!'

Victor Zhabsky, a teenager from Novocherkassk, was stunned by the bicycle racks: 'I noticed bicycles parked outside the station. Germans would cycle up to the station, dismount, and just leave their bicycles. There were no guards, and yet nobody used a lock to secure them. We were astounded – how was it that nobody stole them?'

Yevgeny Goryainov came from a poor family with many children. He was amazed to discover how workers on the outskirts of Vienna lived: 'Every worker had his own little dacha. Every single one! It would be two, three, maybe five kilometres from the factory where he or she worked. It was clean and cultivated – many grew roses.'

The better-educated girls were taken aback by the outward appearance of the Germans. Aldona Volynskaya told us: 'Even the people at the railway station looked to me as though they had just stepped off the pages of a fashion magazine. It was a different world.'

Galina Agranovskaya was amazed to see the clothing that the Bavarians wore:

Postcard with a view of Lippersdorf, 1942.

> Some very well-dressed people stood on the platform. They looked as though they had come straight from a fairy tale; they seemed from another world. The men wore hats with feathers in them, and leather shorts. Back then, we hadn't seen any foreign films [. . .] I was in a state of shock!

Nikolai Kireev had a similar reaction:

> I guessed that we had arrived in Europe, although I knew nothing about the place and had never seen it. But I guessed from the sight of the clean and tidy children in smart little jackets and trousers. It was another world entirely – it was clear that we had arrived in Germany. We were unloaded from the train, and lined up in front of a few respectable-looking people in raincoats. They had such an air of prosperity.

When Victor Zhabsky first laid eyes on Germany, he described it as 'a little corner of heaven': 'I tell you, Germany must have been created as a paradise. Not heaven itself, but a little corner of it. Everything was clean, beautiful, and tidy.'

Among this milieu of prosperity many of the arrivals from the Soviet Union were left feeling painfully aware of their own poverty. Yevgenia Savranskaya remembers how the female registrar at her labour camp reacted upon seeing her and her fellow deportees:

> She treated us with such disdain; it was as though she was disgusted by us. Oh Lord, I suppose my clothes were in such a state that she could hardly have looked at me in any other way. Then my head was shaved. In short, I looked a fright!

A photograph sent to the Volyn region from Linz, dated 5 April 1943. On the reverse is written: *This is me with all the girls I work with, and that's our master. I am wearing a dress that I was given at the camp.*

A memento of one of the German families that an *Ostarbeiter* worked for; Albertstadt, 1943.

Photographs from registration documents: Left to right – Birkenhof, 1943; Dresden, 1943; Delitzsch, 1943.

Aside from the disdain, the arrivals had also to contend with animosity and aggression, often directed at them from German teenagers. Nikolai Bogoslavets remembers:

> The Germans would line the streets when we were being escorted back from work. Each would stand on his own doorstep and the children would fire little stones at us from their catapults. The Germans would laugh when one found a target. You would walk along, eyes peeled. You would never know when . . . Aha! . . . A little child would leap out. But on you went, wondering whether or not you'd be hit.

Of course, not all Germans viewed the arrivals from the Soviet Union as slaves, and many did show them compassion and sympathy. Maria Pudyakova remembers:

> I was deported alongside some others in May 1942. I can't remember whether they took us to Dresden or Leipzig. All I remember is that when they took us out of the station into the middle of the street, there were women lining the pavements. They cried when they saw us, and threw us clothes.

Varvara Gritsenko remembers that her German employer fed her potato pancakes as soon as she arrived:

> We sat down to eat [. . .] And I kept eating and eating – as many as she made, I ate! I was starving – we had been travelling for six days. Finally, she put down the frying pan and asked, '*Noch?*'
>
> I didn't understand that she was asking if I wanted more, so I nodded.

In the mines, the munitions factories and the large manufacturing plants, where the new arrivals were housed in work camps, the *Ostarbeiter* were treated very differently. As soon as they arrived at the distribution camps they encountered the rudeness of the guards, the police with dogs and the lack of humanity.

Before she was deported to Germany, Lyubov Shkulyova managed to complete her ninth year at school in Leningrad. She told us of her disbelief at the treatment she and her fellow deportees received: 'The train stopped in Wuppertal. There were a number of barracks there, designed for prisoners, I believe – they were surrounded by barbed wire. But we weren't prisoners of any kind – after all, we had been brought here as workers, not criminals, hadn't we?'

We asked Arkady Kozhaev whether he had expected better from life in Germany: 'Of course I expected better . . . there had been propaganda, and various promises had been made. I did not expect to be taken to a barracks surrounded by three rows of barbed wire. It was completely unexpected.'

In the distribution camps, the moment an individual was assigned to a labour category was profoundly significant, for each category dictated a very different experience and could therefore dramatically alter the course of a person's life. Work conditions, food provision, access to medicine and daily life varied hugely, depending on which of the three main labour categories a person was assigned to. They might be allocated to a work camp affiliated with a large or small manufacturing enterprise, for example, or assigned to agricultural work, helping a farmer or estate manager to work the land. The third category, domestic work within German families, was reserved for women only. In short, one fleeting decision at the distribution camp had the potential to determine their fate.

During our discussions with the *Ostarbeiter* about their deportation to Germany, many shared stories about their lives at home before the outbreak of war, and the injustices they had suffered. Not only had they and their families been subjected to starvation and repression during the collectivisation process, but many had faced further anguish during the Great Terror. As war loomed, they had been mobilised into manual labour units, digging trenches and building defences in a last-ditch attempt to halt the enemy troops. But despite all the hardship and oppression, in the Soviet Union they had lived as free citizens. It was clear that this was not to be the case in Germany. From the moment they arrived there was a distinct sense among the *Ostarbeiter* that they had fallen into captivity, and were now condemned to slave labour.

Life with an 'OST' badge

Very few *Ostarbeiter* we interviewed were able to show us the OST badges they had worn on their chests.* The small square of fabric bearing the white letters 'OST' set against a blue background (the standard size was 80 x 77mm) had to be worn on the right-hand side of the chest, on the outermost item of clothing. Not only was it a tangible symbol of the tragedy that had befallen them, but it also marked them out as second-class citizens, deprived of their civil rights. It is not coincidental that many *Ostarbeiter* referred to these pieces of cloth not as badges, but as 'patches', 'cloths', 'rags', 'swatches' and 'tags'. When they returned home to the Soviet Union, many rid themselves of their badges, not only because they reminded them of a chapter in their lives that many would rather forget, but also because there were risks associated with keeping them.

Maria Artemyeva worked for the owner of an estate on the outskirts of Mannheim. She told us: 'We found it so dispiriting having to wear those OST swatches so that people could see who we were.'

Anna Odinokova worked for a farmer in Lower Silesia and remembers:

> They gave me a patch – a little scrap of flimsy blue material with OST written in white letters upon it. I was told to sew it to my chest and to wear it at all times. On no account was I to remove it, or I would be punished.

---

* A special badge was introduced for *Ostarbeiter.* Refusal to wear it was punishable by a fine or even a prison sentence. In the summer of 1943, a new rule allowing badges to be worn on the left sleeve was introduced as a reward for good work. When the regime for the workers began to relax a little at the end of April 1944, it was decided that the OST badge would be replaced by a badge bearing the wearer's traditional national symbol. It was suggested that the Russians would wear the cross of St George and the Ukrainian symbol was to be an oval garland of sunflowers with a blue and yellow trident in its centre. The Belarusian badge was to be a red and white gear wheel. This proposal never came to fruition.

Some of those we spoke to appeared to have forgotten about their badges entirely. Taissa Tolkachova, who worked in a munitions factory in Seebach, only remembered about hers when we asked her about it directly:

> Ah yes, I forgot to mention that. As soon as we arrived, they handed us our overalls and OST cloths. We were all photographed, and they gave us a few pieces of blue cloth bearing the white letters OST. We were told to sew these onto our outer clothing and instructed never to come to work without our 'tag'.

Zoya Yeliseeva worked in a textile factory in Frankfurt am Main: 'We had to wear a badge: a little piece of white cloth with a blue background and OST written on it. We were required to sew this to our outer clothing. It was so demeaning – we weren't used to being marked out like that.'

The letters 'OST' soon became deeply embedded in *Ostarbeiter* lore, but not for their primary purpose as indicators of the workers' origins. They became symbols of ignominy, mockery and danger. Tatiana Teplova was a railway worker: 'We were given trousers, a coat, and a patch with the letters OST on it. Do you know what we said it stood for? "Beware the Soviet creature".'*

Ekaterina Kriklivets, who worked in the Fallersleben Volkswagen factory, came up with a different meaning for the letters: 'We were given these greenish-coloured jackets with blackish spots to wear, and that "OST" patch – we said it stood for "Beware the Soviet Comrade".'

Any person leaving a camp wearing one of these badges found themselves under the unwavering scrutiny of the

* Translator's note: Tatiana refers to the acronym she made using the words *Ostergaisya Sovyetskoi Tvari* (Beware the Soviet creature).

German population, who were often keen to ensure that *Ostarbeiter* adhered to the rules that had been imposed upon them. Georgiy Tkachov worked in a ship-repair factory in Stettin:

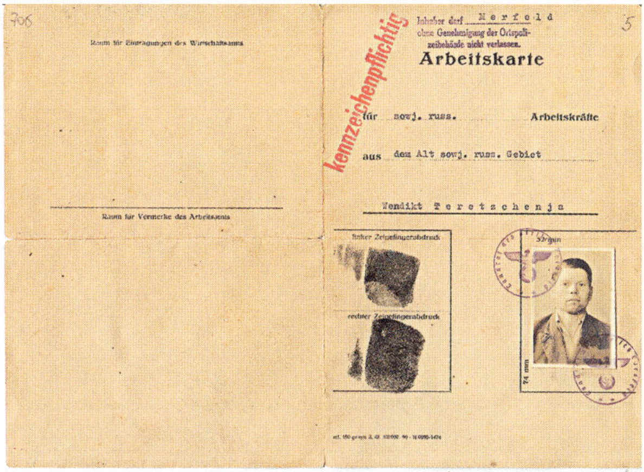

kennzeichenpflichtig

Inhaber darf Merfeld ohne Genehmigung der Ortspolizeibehörde nicht verlassen.

Arbeitskarte

für sowj. russ. Arbeitskräfte

aus dem Alt sowj. russ. Gebiet

Wendikt Teretschenja

A work card stating that 'The wearing of badges is mandatory', Merfeld 1943. The stamp states: *The bearer of this card does not have the right to leave Merfeld without the permission of the local police authorities.*

> We were free to walk around the city – we wore our pieces of cloth here on the right side of our chest. It was a blue cloth, with OST written on it. It had to be sewn onto our outer clothing, to show we were from the east: Russians. We were allowed to use the trams, but sometimes we were thrown off them. I remember one occasion when a German man chased us off the tram we were travelling on. 'Get out of here!' he said. [. . .] We didn't hang around for a second invitation to leave – we scarpered.

The badges were also a constant reminder that other nationalities enjoyed far greater privileges than the Soviet workers. Raissa Pervina worked in an aviation factory in Delmenhorst. She remembers:

> There were also Czechs working as labourers there, but they were free to come and go as they pleased. The Polish were also free, although they wore the letter 'P'. But we were marched around in convoys, and we wore a blue badge with OST written in white lettering.

Factory workers, Wuppertal, 1943. Text on the reverse says: *I am sending you my photograph from Germany as something to remember me fondly by. I ask that you keep it safe, but if you don't like it, then I would ask that you burn it.*

Despite the risk of fines or punishment, *Ostarbeiter* would remove or hide their badges when they wanted to regain a sense of freedom. Antonina Maxina said: 'If I managed to get into the cinema, I would take off my OST badge.'

Photograph for a work pass, Dresden, 1942.

Similarly, Anna Kirilenko recalled that her employer would tell her to hide or remove her badge when they went into town together, so that the police wouldn't bother them.

It wasn't until the spring of 1944, when the Germans began to relax the rules for foreign workers, that the police became less stringent in enforcing the wearing of badges.

In a State of Captivity

While some *Ostarbeiter* could describe their daily lives in Germany in great detail, others remembered very little. There were a number of factors at play here but, ultimately, much depended on personal curiosity, powers of observation and the level to which a person had been educated. The ability to speak German was also key, for even the most basic grasp of the language could prove life-changing. Years later, not all of the *Ostarbeiter* could remember the name of the place, company, factory or plant where they had worked, and some of those who worked for German families struggled to recall the names of their employers. This is understandable, especially when we consider that very few spent all of their time in one place. An *Ostarbeiter* might initially be sent to work on a farm, or at a small private enterprise of some sort. They might then be transferred to a factory, from where they could be sent to a punishment camp (*Straflager*)* or even a concentration camp following some small misdemeanour or an attempt to run away. Ultimately, in the final weeks of the war, some *Ostarbeiter* found themselves wandering across Germany on an Odyssey-esque journey. Though their stories are sometimes complicated and confusing they do enable us to attempt to paint, albeit with broad strokes, a picture of their lives in a foreign country.

'That was how we lived'

Most *Ostarbeiter* soon discovered that there was a sharp contrast between the pretty and well-kept German towns that had so

---

* *Straflager* were disciplinary camps to which prisoners (or workers) could be sent to be punished.

impressed them on their arrival and their own living conditions. Having left the distribution camps – about which few had a good word to say – life became particularly tough for those sent to work in the coal mines or large munitions factories. They were placed in camps (usually separate ones for men and women) not far from their workplaces. Occasionally, a 'family camp' would be mentioned, although these appear to have been much less common.

A camp at a metallurgical factory, Siegen, 1943.

Ostarbeiter who had the misfortune to be assigned to one of these work camps found themselves living a life of captivity, confined to barracks even after the working day was over. Many were able to give detailed descriptions of the layout of their large work camps. Antonina Serdyukova, who worked in the Lautawerk aluminium-vanadium factory, described her accommodation:

> Each barracks was divided into rooms . . . there were thirty people to a room, and wooden bunks in each. On each bunk there was a canvas sack stuffed with wood shavings, and two flannel blankets – one to use as a bed sheet, and the other to cover yourself with. The walls of the barracks were just one plank of pinewood thick and the rain would drum down on the roof, which leaked. There was an iron stove in the centre of the room.

> [. . .] In winter, we were given nine or ten bricks of brown coal each day. Each brick would burn out in just five minutes.

Taissa Tolkachova described a very similar set-up at her work camp in Seebach:

> The barracks were in the woods, encircled by a high fence with a single watchtower. A policeman with a dog stood on guard in the tower. [. . .] Within the barracks, there were ten people to a room, and each room contained bunk beds; both the upper and lower levels were wooden.

Larisa Shvidchenko lived in a similar barracks at a camp in Düsseldorf: 'The barracks was divided into rooms – each slept twenty people, on bunk beds. The washbasin and toilet were both outside. There was one small cabinet to share between four people – but what did we have to put in a cabinet anyway?'

The larger barracks were sometimes 'furnished' differently. Galina Agranovskaya was sent to work at a large leather factory in Frankfurt am Main. She remembers that rather than the usual two-storey bunk beds, she and her fellow workers slept on triple bunks. Aside from this, her barracks was much the same as the others.

Valentina Gridchina was deported from Taganrog with her mother and grandmother to a camp in Zwickau in summer 1943, where they were housed in a former theatre:

> It was a really huge theatre! Both men and women were mixed in together. There was a huge auditorium with an entrance to one side and toilets and washbasins over here [she points]. The walls were lined with beds – these bunks were allocated to families. The back half of the auditorium was for the women, and the men were given the other half, in front of the stage. There was a wide passage between the beds, which were laid out in an interesting fashion, like a chessboard! The *Lagerführer**

* Translator's note: The *Lagerführer* was the camp commandant.

Inside a barracks at a munitions factory camp, Königsberg, 1942.

'Cheery songs and games help to pass the time swiftly while waiting at a distribution camp.' A photograph from the German Bureau of Propaganda entitled: 'On the status of eastern workers in Germany 1942–1944'. (State Archive of the Russian Federation. F.7021. Op. 128. D.268.L2)

> would stand in the doorway, which was set on a diagonal so that he had a good view of the whole theatre. We were not allowed to hang curtains between the beds, and you weren't allowed to sit on anyone else's bed either. You would come home from work, climb up onto your bunk or bed and lie or sit there. You couldn't even sit in twos or threes on another bed. There were several large windows, beneath which stood a large table with long benches running alongside. You could sit there and drink coffee or have something to eat.

Hygiene conditions varied from camp to camp, and many spoke of bedbug infestations and lice. Pavel Mikhailov worked at a metallurgical plant in Saxony:

> We were crawling with lice. We shaved, and they sent us to a washhouse where they put us in a special room and released a gas [to kill the lice], but we'd be covered in lice again within a week. And lice weren't the only problem. People were weak – some didn't even get up in the night to go to the toilet – they just wet themselves right there in their beds. It was so bad that maggots hatched in their mattresses. That was how we lived.

Nikolai Zubkov described the appalling living and sanitary conditions in the punishment camp to which he was sent:

> We were given one blanket to share between two when we slept. The lice were terrible – we were eaten alive by them! [. . .] So here's what we did: those who had the strength would hold up a blanket by its corners, and burn the lice over the stove. That's what we had to do.

'You couldn't escape the bedbugs,' recalled Vera Fedorchenko, a worker at a munitions factory in Nindorf, when we asked about the barracks at her camp. Taissa Tolkachova experienced similar conditions: 'We would freeze under those blankets in the winter, but we were plagued by bedbugs. And mice! There were mice, mice, everywhere – in every bedside cabinet.'

There were, however, camps with altogether different approaches to hygiene. Nadezhda Kepet was housed in a camp affiliated to the hosiery factory in Düsseldorf:

> Twenty-four people lived in our room, but the place was spotless. This was because of our camp supervisor, who we all feared, despite the fact that she never actually hit anybody. On every day off, she would inspect us personally for lice, and God forbid if she ever discovered one! Our beds had to be made to military standards – with the white flannel blankets perfectly folded. The windows had to sparkle and we washed every day in the showers.

Lorenz factory camp, Berlin, 1943.

Some remembered that the Germans were particularly fastidious about hygiene in the camps because they feared outbreaks of diseases such as typhus. As a result, anyone flouting hygiene regulations would be punished. Pavel Mikhailov remembers:

> One day the *Lagerführer* went round the rooms doing a hygiene inspection. He spotted Grishka Klimenko, a lathe-operator, lying down in his clothes, with dirt on his face. He hoisted him up and took him to the shower to wash. He set him down on the floor in the shower room and made two guys scrub him with soap and then rub him with floor mops. He stood there, watching.

Work camp routines were defined by production cycles. Arkady Kozhaev lived in a work camp affiliated with a mine in Herten:

Camp at a munitions factory, Sömmerda, 1943.

> We were woken at 5 a.m. Everybody went outside and lined up in rows. Roll call followed . . . *eins, zwei, drei* . . . [. . .] There were often instances where someone had fallen ill or couldn't stand, in which case the roll call would stop. Then the counting would begin again. This would happen two or three times. Finally, everyone would be accounted for. We were then grouped into fours and given the command, 'Forward, march!' The working day began at eight o'clock – it took us two hours to walk there. [. . .] At two o clock there would be a changeover [. . .] You would be covered in dirt so you'd have to go and undress, wash, get dressed again and go back outside, where once again you would be counted . . . *eins, zwei, drei* . . . At 3 p.m. we were taken back to the camp, but first we had to go through the whole rigmarole of being lined up and counted again. Sometime after 4 we would finally get back to camp, and we would run as fast as we could to the canteen block, where we would be given a bowl of soup.

Varvara Kramarenkova was placed in a work camp for the BMW factory in Eisenach:

> We were woken at 4 a.m. and formed into threes. Well-trained German shepherds lined up on either side of us, and we were marched from the camp to the factory. [. . .] We returned in the evening – sometimes in the rain, sometimes in snow. We would often be soaked to the skin by the time we got back but there was nowhere to dry our clothes. We slept in our wet garments, and got up in them, still wet, the next day.

A camp 'elder' was elected with the express purpose of supervising the camp residents and overseeing barracks life. They were often chosen from among the Polish or Western Ukrainian populations, but occasionally a Russian would be nominated. Almost nobody had a good word to say about these supervisors, and there was also animosity towards those who opted to act as translators.

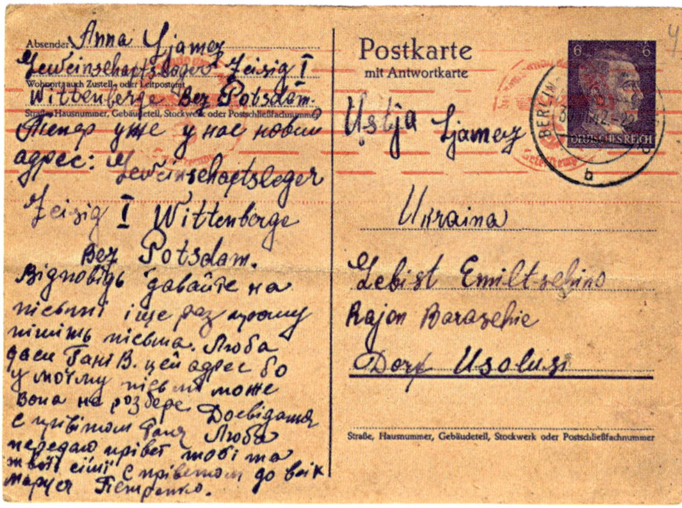

A letter from Potsdam to the Zhytomyr region, dated 15 November 1942 (translated from Ukrainian):

A letter to Mama and my sisters, and my brother-in-law and the little children. Greetings, my dear family. I am currently alive and well, and hope that the same goes for you. [. . .] The police even escort us to and from work – I really have no freedom at all. Lyuba, I don't even know whether there are people here who are free to walk about, but you ask me to write you a letter by registered post. [. . .] Lyuba, write and tell me why your cow was taken. In your letter you said: 'they took the cow'. I think perhaps I can guess what happened [. . .]

Mummy, life has become much harder for us now. We have already had our work shifts extended from eight hours to ten. We go to work at six in the morning and return at four p.m. It is dark when we leave and dark when we return. I am doing the same work as before. If Teklya is at home then get her to describe exactly what the work is like. Mummy and Lyuba, thank you so so much for the ration card.

When I realise that it will soon have been half a year since I left, bitter tears spill down my cheeks. Once I have had a good cry, my heart feels lighter for a while, and I can return once again to my frightening life. [. . .]

I'll leave it at that. Goodbye. Your daughter.

Taissa Tolkachova:

We lined up outside. Among us was a translator from Kiev – she could speak German. We knew a little German too – we had studied it for a while at school. But she was close to the camp manager. [. . .] She was essentially his assistant. We had to listen to her, because all the instructions for tasks we were to carry out

A camp affiliated with a cellulose factory, Darmstadt, 1944.

> came through her. She issued us a warning: 'Don't even think about running away,' she said, 'because the police here have dogs, so they'll catch you . . . and shoot you on the spot. If you want to live, listen to instructions and do as you are told. You are a subjugated nation – our men have already taken Moscow. They are already there, in the [Soviet] Union. You will now work here with us.'
>
> Well, what choice did we have? Where could we run? We were surrounded by forest, and in a completely unfamiliar land.

Grigory Kulbaka was sent to the Wellendorf camp on the outskirts of Kiel: 'The camp had its own Polizei – they were our people, from Western Ukraine. They oversaw absolutely everything in the camp. My, they were cruel guys. We were scared of them.'

Raissa Pervina lived in a camp affiliated with an aviation factory just outside Bremen: 'The supervisors were capricious; sometimes they would leave us in peace, while at other times they might throw a cat into someone's face as they slept. One was crueller than the other – the kindlier one was an unhappy woman, a Ukrainian German.'

Nonetheless, conditions in even the very worst of the work camps were significantly better than those in either the punishment or the concentration camps. For a start, the work camps were less heavily guarded, so it was often fairly easy to sneak out of them. And as of autumn 1942, *Ostarbeiter* were granted permission to leave camp precincts during their free time.

Going to work at a container factory work camp, Hirschberg, 1943.

Ivan Krasnov lived in a work camp in Danzig:

> A camp is just a camp, you know. You find your people there. There is gambling and card playing, and you take your turn at the table. That's just normal camp life, you see. [. . .] There are escape routes; you find holes that you can get out through at night. You might go to the port and get hold of some denatured alcohol to bring back and sell. You could make some money that way. You might find a loaf of bread to buy and resell, or swap for something to smoke. We could come and go freely – there were holes all round the camp and the guards didn't stop us from leaving – they knew we didn't have anywhere else to go.

Conditions for Soviet prisoners of war were notably worse. Though they often shared the same work camps with the *Ostarbeiter*, they were guarded much more strictly and given significantly poorer food. Mikhail Chernenko (Kharkov), deported in spring 1942, worked in a factory on the outskirts of Berlin. He recalled that the prisoners of war were kept in a separate barracks within his camp, behind a barbed wire fence: 'They lived in truly awful conditions. [. . .] They were given different food, brought in from the *Stammlager** in thermoses. It was far worse than ours.'

* *Stammlager* or *Stalag* was the name given to the prisoner-of-war camps in Germany that housed the non-commissioned ranks of military prisoners.

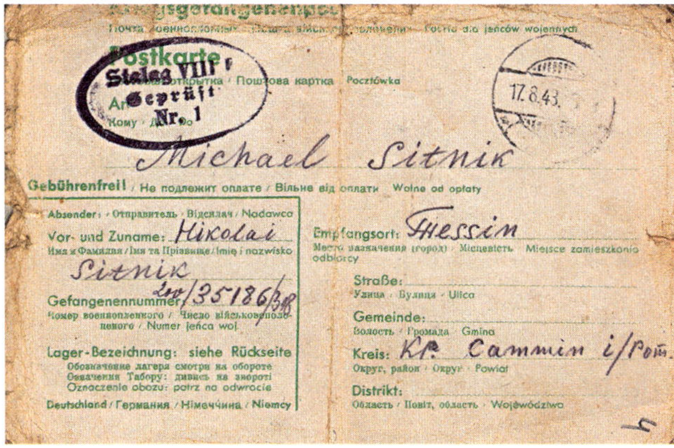

Postcard from a prisoner-of-war camp at Tessin to the Kiev region, 1944:

> Greetings, my darling daughter, Nadya. This is a letter from your Papa. I want to let you know that I am alive and well, and hope that you are too. [. . .] Nadya, I am housed in the same place as before, and working in the same place as before. Nadia, life is not too bad, but not a moment goes by when I don't think either of you, or our family at home, or Vanya. I wonder whether or not he is alive. Sending you a kiss, greetings to everyone.

Nikolai Kireev worked at a munitions factory in Spandau, Berlin: 'Sometimes we were lodged alongside the prisoners of war. The prisoners of war died there. [. . .] I would watch as first one, then a second, and then a third body was carried away. You got used to it after a while.'

Nikolai Gulyaev said: 'We lived in a long barracks of sorts. There were twenty-one of us living there. We lived in one half, and Germans lived in the other.'

Vladimir Shchebetyuk told us that: 'At night, the police would keep watch from their hut [. . .] We slept under lock and key – they would let us out in the morning to go to work. And in the evening, we would be locked up again in our quarters.'

And Lidia Beketova recalled:

> Our employer had a two-storey shed made from reinforced concrete that stood in the middle of an empty field. They made wooden beds for us on the top floor and gave us straw mattresses and pillows, as well as two nasty-looking grey blankets – I have

> no idea where they got hold of them. That's how we lived [. . .] Our employer lived nearby and I would walk the half kilometre to his farm to work.

A large proportion of *Ostarbeiter* were sent to work in the agricultural sector – on farms and private smallholdings. Those who worked for large farming enterprises were usually allocated living quarters. But more often than not, *Ostarbeiter* sent to work on farms would be housed in barns or cowsheds, sometimes sleeping alongside the animals. Franz Marmurash said: 'I slept in a shed next to the cows. It was actually pretty warm there.'

Sometimes *Ostarbeiter* were given their own rooms, but they were rarely provided with heating, even during the winter. Ivan Krasnov remembered: 'I slept there in the house, in a box room, without any heating. In the winter my employer would heat up a brick for me. I'd come home from work at night and she would put a brick in my bed.'

Anna Odinokova told us:

> They showed me to my room – it was a small, separate bedroom, with an iron stove. But they didn't light it once during the winter! And they didn't give me any fuel so that I could light it myself. They did do things differently there though – it was the only place I ever saw people cover themselves with a duvet. You would sleep on a mattress, and cover yourself with a duvet.

The absence of communal bathhouses (*banya*s) in German towns also surprised the *Ostarbeiter.* Georgiy Tkachov expressed his astonishment at not being able to visit one: 'As for the *banya* – we never went. There wasn't one! Not a single one anywhere! There was a small stream though, so I'd take a dip in there. I'd strip off and jump stark naked into the stream to bathe.'

Conditions were significantly better for those who were hired as domestic helpers by German families. Galina Agranovskaya said: 'There were two of us working as housemaids – a girl from Poland,

and myself. We lived in a semi-basement containing a laundry, a boiler room (which heated the house), two narrow beds and a small table. We hung our dresses on the wall.'

Similarly, Lidia Dadzis recalled: 'I had my own room, with a bed and a feather duvet and feather pillow. There was a wardrobe and a marble washstand. I had everything I needed.'

Wooden-soled shoes

Very few of those we spoke to managed to bring any essential items of clothing with them to Germany. Most had nothing to bring in the first place. Maria Ausheva remembers:

> I had one waffle fabric blouse – it was the only one I had – and no bra or shirt. I had absolutely nothing! Well, there wasn't much for a bra to hold up then anyway, but in any case it would have kept me warmer. I would wash this blouse and hang it

A memento from Mainz. This photograph was sent to the Cherkasy region in 1942. The text on the reverse of the photo reads: *I am sending you this photo as a fond reminder of your daughter, Mariika, who is in Germany. I sent you a photo, my dear parents, and await your swift reply.*

Remember me, Mama, on the blue steps of our home and I will think of you on a distant road. Remember me, Mama, as you sit in the evening, and I will remember you, while neither drinking, nor eating. And no matter where I go, or what I do, my dearest parents, I cannot forget you.

> out to dry on the burdock. And then I would sit there, naked, among the burdock, waiting for it to dry. I had done it this way even back before the war. Afterwards, I would crumple it up in my hands and put it back on. My Mama had made me a little skirt. That's what I wore to Germany.

Anna Odinokova was sent to work on a large farm. She remembers:

> I arrived there practically barefoot [. . .] I had neither stockings, nor trousers . . . I had absolutely nothing. Nobody had trousers there – we did without them. [. . .] I went around half-dressed, in my own get-up. Later, my employer gave me an old dress to wear – presumably one that belonged to her daughter-in-law.

The *Ostarbeiter* sent to work camps affiliated with factories were usually provided with some sort of overalls. These varied in line with the type of work: those working at the Singer factory were given a coat and trousers, the cloth factory workers wore a grey overcoat, the food-processing factory workers wore a boiler suit, and those on the factory floor would wear overalls or a protective coat. The farm workers were sometimes given cotton trousers and a coat to wear.

At the farmstead, Saxony, 1943.

Tatiana Tolkachova described the distribution of clothing in great detail:

> We were given soap, but it looked like a sponge. It didn't lather – I don't know what it was made from, presumably some sort of sand. We made do and managed to clean our underwear. They explained to us that we were to wear the dresses they gave us. Most of us had nothing to wear underneath them. We were given a robe to wear in the *banya*. It was a green dress with

A domestic worker with her employer, Frankfurt am Main, 1943.

some sort of design on it [. . .] The shoes were clogs – they were wooden, with straps [. . .] They clacked as we walked along, and everybody shared the same thought: They're packing us off, like convicts to Siberia.

A postcard depicting a view of the city of Büttelborn, 1943. On the reverse is written: *A little something for my sister to remember me by. This is my home and this is my bedroom – the first window with the white curtain.*

Galina Agranovskaya described her transformation into an *Ostarbeiter* in similar detail:

> I didn't know where I was being taken. It turned out to be some sort of medical unit: they checked us, presumably for lice, and then cut our hair very short before lathering coal-tar soap all over our heads. This

Triumph factory workers, Nuremberg, 1942.

> was followed by a primitive shower of sorts; the water came from a metal tank overhead. I had absolutely nothing to wear, so I was given a stripy dress sewn from rough cotton fabric, along with some tattered old shoes, knitted socks and a headscarf [. . .] What's more, we didn't get knickers – no underwear was provided.

Ostarbeiter working on the railways, Hamburg, 1943.

Mikhail Chernenko was deported to Germany as a teenager. For youngsters such as him, life could be very tough, particularly if they were assigned to work in munitions factories. They had no clothes other than those they wore on the workshop floor:

> We were naked under our oil-soaked overalls. We had absolutely nothing to wear but these overalls – no coat, no trousers, no

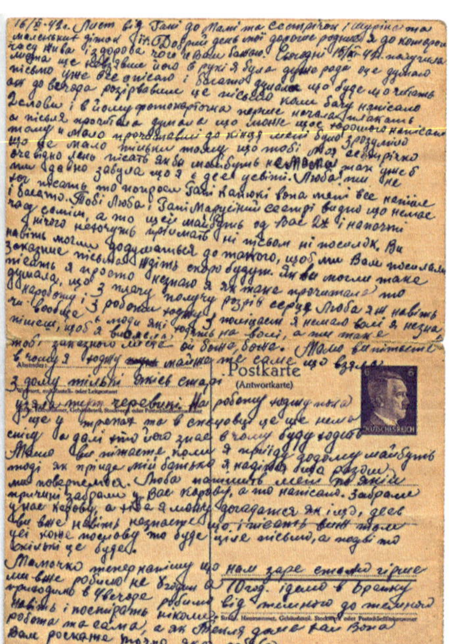

A letter sent from Potsdam to the Zhytomyr region, 1943 (translated from Ukrainian):

. . . Mama, you asked in your letter what I have to wear. I am wearing the same clothes that I took from home, although I did pick up a pair of old shoes here. I am still going to work in tattered old clothes and a boiler suit. It hasn't started snowing yet – I have no idea what I'll wear when it does. Mama, you ask when I am coming home. Perhaps it will be at the same time as my father – I hope we will return together. [. . .] The weather here is not yet very cold. The first snowflakes fell on the 14th November, but they had all melted by lunchtime. It's cold in the mornings for those without clothes, of course, but naturally those with clothes are warm enough. Mama and my dear sister, in the month of December we will not be permitted to write letters home. I beg you to write to me. Don't forget . . .

> underwear . . . nothing. [. . .] We wore some sort of hessian sacking on our feet, and stuffed them into these wooden . . . clogs [*Holzpantoffeln*], which reduced your feet to a bloody mess. That was all we had. If you were infested with little beasties, you couldn't get rid of them – you couldn't change your clothes. It was an utterly depressing state of affairs.

Almost everybody cursed the wooden clogs carved from pieces of wood that they were forced to wear to work. 'We couldn't walk in them,' remembers Zoya Yeliseeva.

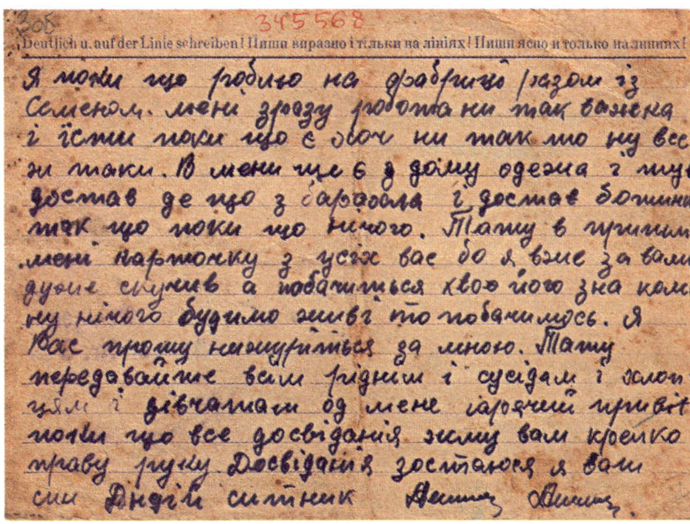

A letter from Nordhausen to the Poltava region, dated 8 June 1943 (translated from Ukrainian):

Greetings, my dear Papa, Mama and brother Antoshka. Before I write any more, I hasten to pass on my warmest and most heartfelt good wishes. I want to let you know that I am alive and well and am wishing you all the very best in your lives. I received your letter, dated 7/VI.43. For now I am still working at the factory, alongside Semyon. The work isn't particularly hard at present, and there is still food to eat, and although it's not that great at least we have some. I still have my clothes from home, and I got hold of some old clothes from the scrap pile and some boots too, so I don't need anything for now. Papa, send me a postcard from you all, because I already miss you all hugely, and who knows when I will see you next. Never mind, we'll see each other again if we survive. Please don't upset yourselves over me. Papa, pass on my best wishes to all the family, the neighbours, the lads and the girls from me. That's all for now, goodbye. I'm sending you a firm handshake. Goodbye. I remain for ever your son, Andrei.

Vera Dergachova said:

> They gave us these mules to wear, with wooden soles and canvas across the front. We walked to work in our column, plodding along like horses . . . clop, clop, clop. We were given a uniform too – a dark grey coat and trousers. That's how we went about; like prisoners. I can still hear the sound to this day.

According to Raissa Nefyodova, who worked at a food factory, these clogs were issued for three months. 'But they wore down in time, and everybody had to go about barefoot.'

Sometimes old clothes would be brought into the camp, and the *Ostarbeiter* were allowed to choose something to wear. Vadim Novgorodov remembers:

> They even brought some second-hand German suits into the camp. [. . .] I got hold of a suit jacket and a pair of trousers. They didn't match, but I took them anyway. [. . .] You could take boots too, and I took a hat for my head – a beret.

Vadim Novgorodov thought that the clothes brought into his camp were simply cast-offs from German citizens. Others, however,

Workers at the fish packing plant, Cuxhaven, 1942.

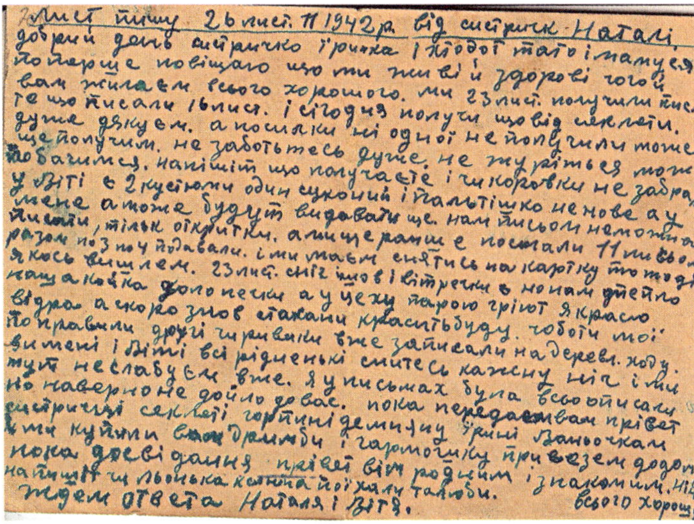

A letter from Engerau to the Nikolaev region, 1942 (translated from Ukrainian):

. . . Greetings, my dear sister Irinka, Papa and Mummy. First of all, I want to let you know that we are alive and well, and are wishing you all the very best. We received your letters on 23 November [. . .] but we haven't received a single parcel – maybe we will get one soon. Don't worry too much, and don't grieve – perhaps we will see each other again. Write and tell us what is growing and whether the cow has been taken. Vitya has two suits – one made from wool cloth – and I have a second-hand coat. But we might even be given more. [. . .] My boots are now mended, and we have put our names down for some wooden shoes. Vitya and I dream about you, our dear family, every night, though we no longer pine so terribly [. . .] We have bought you a *drumba** and a small accordion – we will bring them home for you . . .

were more suspicious about the origins of the items being handed out at the camps. Vera Dergachova:

> They brought in all the old clothes and then let us in to look through them – first one barracks, then the second, then the third. [. . .] When I began picking through the jumble, I noticed that there were dark reddish stains on some of the clothes. For some reason, it never occurred to us what they were. Perhaps our brains just weren't going there. It was only later that we realised they had been taken from those who had either been

* Ukrainian musical instrument played in traditional folk music.

> terribly injured, or murdered and incinerated in the ovens. They had been stripped naked and here were their clothes. [. . .] 'Take whatever you want,' we were told . . . I got a black pullover.

Some camps actually sold the old clothing that they brought in for the workers. Antonina Serdyukova was housed in a camp affiliated with an aluminium-vanadium factory. She remembers:

> They gave us clothes. I understand now that they were clothes that had been taken from the Jews burned in the concentration camps. The clothes were sterilised in a hot wash, laundered and handed out to us. The first time, we were given them for free, but later we had to pay for them. You could go once a month to buy something. I remember that I bought a laundered wool sweater, taken from some Jewish woman. I now know that before the Jews were incinerated, they were stripped of all their clothes, and good clothes they were too. See! [she points to a photograph] Look at the coat I was wearing – it was a good one. It had a squirrel-fur collar.

These episodes describing the distribution among eastern workers of clothes taken from the bodies of dead Jews warrant further comment. Both women relayed their memories in an exaggeratedly prosaic manner – Antonina even remarked upon the quality of her coat with the squirrel-fur collar and she repeatedly commented that the clothes had been taken from Jews. Were it not for the fact that previous conversations with Antonina provide us with some appreciation of the constant state of fear in which she lived during her time in Germany, this apparent indifference could sound a little unnatural. After all, her mother was a Jew, and Antonina herself had been informed upon once – she only escaped deportation to a concentration camp by the skin of her teeth. The absence of empathy in her description of clothes being stripped from people murdered by the Nazis was a form of defence. It was a phenomenon that we often encountered when talking to people recounting the most terrifying times that they had been forced to live through.

The following extract from an interview with Aldona Volynskaya confirms just how terrible such experiences could be for the *Ostarbeiter.* She insists that, even then, she understood what was going on, and was horrified:

> They gave me some sort of ticket, and I went into a gloomy room filled with piles of clothes. I rummaged and rummaged about. They showed me some sort of hook that I could use to dig through the dirty clothes. And then I spotted a little dress – a child's dress – covered in blood. And suddenly it dawned on me . . . I threw down the hook and ran out. I ran from the room, without shedding a tear, but a long wail escaped me: 'Oooooo.' You see, there I had been, just rummaging about, and it had come as such a shock when I suddenly realised that those were the clothes of people who had been murdered, shot. Do you understand? It was truly nightmarish.

The young women were painfully aware of how shabby they looked in comparison with their well-dressed German contemporaries, and they tried to find ways to adapt and restyle even their uniforms with needle and thread. Antonina Maxina:

> When we arrived, we were issued with cotton uniforms. Well, they were blue suits with wide trousers designed for men. We sewed them up ourselves – I sewed some darts into mine. And how did we make use of these pantaloons we made? Well, you could steal a few potatoes and stuff them down inside – you could hide far more in these trousers than you could in the original ones. On the whole, I loved to sew – to tailor things to fit me, rather than wearing clothes that looked like a sack. And before long all the girls were doing it. [. . .] What did we do next? We were given two blankets each – new ones, made from flannelette. Some were plain, and others patterned. We took them and cut patterns for warm dressing gowns. Why didn't those bastards just give us some warm dressing gowns in the first place? It was so cold!

The girls adapted to their new environments and often evoked the sympathy and compassion of the German girls they worked alongside. Anna Gulyaeva says: 'Our boss was such a kindly old chap. He looked a little bit like our Lenin. And his wife was lovely too. They brought us their clothing cast-offs and we made a few alterations to them. By then we had learned to knit ourselves scarves and berets.'

Ostarbeiter outside the camp barracks, Schwarz (Saale), 1943. The text on the reverse reads: *A keepsake from Senya for my dear brother Vanya to remember me fondly by while I am away working in Germany. If we are never to meet again, if fate is to be cruel to us, then let my name and handwriting serve as a memento.*

A postcard from Remscheid to Mariupol, dated 1 June 1943:

> Greetings, my dearest Mummy and little brother Igoryochek.* Sweet Mama, I am alive and well, and life here is the same as before. I miss you though. But never mind, this will pass, and we will return to our good and happy lives once again – if only the war would hurry up and end. Mama, did you receive my postcard? I send you two postcards every month. Mummy, write to me more often. Mama, don't feel sorry about selling the odds and ends – sell them all. Take care of yourself so that

* Translator's note: A diminutive form of the name Igor.

> when I come back you are just the same as before – plump and healthy. Mummy, how is Igoryochek's health? Does he do what you tell him? They gave me a dress – it was too big but I altered it so now it fits. Mummy, I made myself a skirt from a canvas bag – I sewed it all myself – so when I come home I think I'll design clothes and hats for women. Life here is the same as before. Katya gets more letters from home than any of us. Don't be sad, don't cry – we will see each other again soon. Keep an eye on Igoryochek and make sure that he doesn't turn into an unruly little boy. Keep yourself alive and well. Goodbye for now and pass on my best wishes to Klava, Lyusenka, Granny, Uncle Vasya, Lorochka and all the others. Yours for ever, your daughter.

The understandable attempts to make themselves look and feel more human did not always end well. Raissa Pervina was sent to the punishment block for failing to affix her OST sign to her clothing, having travelled to another camp to have a coat altered:

> I needed to have a coat altered and was given an overcoat to wear in the meantime. There was a tailor in the other camp. You had to take the train to reach this camp – so off I went.

> [. . .] I could easily have passed for a German woman, but a document-check was carried out on the train, and I didn't have any documents.
>
> 'Why aren't you wearing your badge?' the police shouted, and seized me on the spot. They took me back to the camp – straight to the isolation unit.

The girls used their meagre wages to purchase cheap soap, hairpins, bead necklaces, and even perfume and lipstick. To earn extra money, they took on any work they could find, and this enabled them to make dresses for themselves out of old clothes. The young *Ostarbeiter* were also eager to send home photographs that showed them looking both well dressed and well-to-do.

A memento photograph, Loburg, 1942.

The text on the reverse reads: *To my dear sister Zoya from your dear sister Nyusya – something to remember me by while I am here in Germany. I love beer, I love* kvass, *but most of all I love you, Zoya. Photographed in Loburg.*

Memorial's archives contain numerous examples of these photographs: essentially 'ceremonial portraits', taken specifically to be sent home to families and loved ones. But despite their best efforts to improve their appearance with what little they had the *Ostarbeiter* couldn't escape the reality of their situation. Far from home and deprived of their rights, most were now half-starved manual labourers clothed in little more than rags.

Shchi-slop

If some of the *Ostarbeiter* had harboured hopes that a comfortable and prosperous life awaited them in Germany, and that, at the very least, they would not go hungry there, most found such hopes vanished immediately. Maria Volobueva wrote in a letter:

> I thought of nothing but food. The trough back home where my mother would mix up the swill for the pigs swam before my eyes. I remember thinking that if I stayed alive and made it home, I would first eat my fill at this trough and then go to find my family.

Almost all those in the work camps recalled a constant feeling of gnawing hunger. During a conversation Lyubov Shkulyova explained:

> You have to understand what it is to be hungry. Hunger is not simply a desire to eat. Hunger is when there is constantly nothing to eat. Nothing! Your vertebrae cling to your stomach, you feel nauseous, your head spins and all you can think about is how to get hold of some food. For just one small piece of bread, I would have given absolutely everything. I met my work quota, I met it! You had to; if you didn't, you wouldn't get your ration card. I worked my fingers to the bone – I met all my quotas. [. . .] I worked because my life depended on it.

Life was particularly hard for those who lived in camps affiliated with mines and factories. Taissa Tolkachova describes her first breakfast in the camp:

> 'Form a line!' somebody barked. We duly got in line and filed into the kitchen where we were given three little pieces of bread. They were teeny-tiny pieces, spread with a tiny bit of what looked like butter, but turned out to be a scrap of margarine. When we were leaving, we were told to take our

Camp canteen, Bavaria, 1942.

mugs and dishes with us. I think they were our own ones. We got a cup of coffee, and three pieces of bread.

'Go and have your breakfast,' we were told. 'And then form a line and go to work.'

Lunch at the camp, Barth, 1942.

The camp inmates would take their own bowl and spoon to receive a portion of 'soup' at the canteen. More commonly referred to by the *Ostarbeiter* as 'swill', it was usually made from partially rotten and frosted vegetables – predominantly cabbages or turnips. Maria Ausheva remembers the swill she was fed while living in a work camp in Göttingen: 'There were potato peelings in there and mainly turnips. Sometimes they would add some pasta or noodles, but they were always spoiled. [. . .] You could smell the stench from three kilometres away when it was time to go to the canteen to eat this food.'

Sometimes the food was so grisly that despite their hunger they could not bring themselves to eat it. Yevgenia Savranskaya described one such meal at her work camp:

> The beetroot had started to go sour, and nobody could bring themselves to eat it. But one girl among us called out, 'Girls, anyone who can't eat theirs, give it to me – I'll eat it up.' We gave her our portions and, in return, she washed the floor of our room in the barracks.

Victor Shuldeshov worked on a smelting factory floor in Leipzig. In scenes reminiscent of the Soviet film *Battleship Potemkin*, he remembers finding worms in his bowl of slop. Upon seeing his squeamish reaction, his camp comrades simply burst out laughing, 'Close your eyes and eat it,' they said, 'otherwise soon enough those worms will be eating you.'

Nikolai Kireev described the bread the *Ostarbeiter* were given at his work camp in Berlin:

> We were woken at 5 a.m. and had a cup of coffee, or *kava*, as the Poles called it. You carried your dish with you everywhere – it was your main weapon – just in case somebody somewhere poured you something to eat. You'd get a loaf of bread, generally made from . . . Actually I don't know what was in there. But you'd take it, despite the fact that it looked as though it had been made from compressed sawdust. Just sawdust. We ate it anyway – it was actually quite tasty. [. . .] You'd share one loaf between five.

Rations for the eastern workers were so meagre that people often fell ill. Malnutrition combined with back-breaking labour soon rendered many incapacitated for work. Galina Agranovskaya:

'Towards the end of my time at the factory I began to suffer from furunculosis.* I was taken to the medical unit, where they smeared some cream on me and shaved my hair, which was all matted with pus. [. . .] It was a classic case of malnutrition.'

Pavel Mikhailov said: 'We were nothing but bones – the skin was hanging off us. How did we stay on our feet? It was our youth that saved us.'

On Sundays and celebration days, the food was sometimes a little better. Antonina Maxina recalled that: 'On Sundays we lived like kings. We'd get a piece of meat in our jacket potato. We only got this on Sundays – on normal working days we'd get *shchi*-slop, made either from kohlrabi or turnip.'

Nikolai Kireev remembers that on Hitler's birthday they were each given:

> . . . a portion of margarine the size of a matchbox. There was an abundance of frogs around – whole armies of them! We were often given frogs on celebration days. [. . .] Their hind legs were chopped off where they met the body and they were marinated in some sort of sauce. It was excellent food – I always tried to get second and third helpings, because I really loved it. Then they'd also give us red sugar cane – sometimes you'd have a cane this thick [gestures] in your hand. I don't know what that cane was, but it was sweet, with lots of those long stringy bits throughout. [. . .] The feeling of hunger was relentless.

Unlike workers in the occupied countries of Western Europe, who received food rations in line with those of German workers and assistance from the International Red Cross, the *Ostarbeiter* relied heavily upon food parcels sent from home. Such parcels were rare, however, and after 1944 they stopped arriving altogether.

---

* Translator's note: A deep bacterial infection of the hair follicle that can lead to the formation of abscesses. Possible contributory factors include malnutrition, anaemia and poor hygiene.

A letter from Kassel to the Kamenets-Podolsk region, dated 13 December 1942 (translated from Ukrainian):

> Good day, my dear family! I am sending you my greetings and wish you all the best in your lives. I received your letter, for which I was very grateful. [. . .] You write that you would like me to tell you everything – about my health, where I'm living, how life is and all the rest. I am living in Kassel and working as a freight handler in a factory. I'm being housed in a barracks in a room with some other lads from our village and the next one over, and from the regions around us. The food isn't too bad – at 6 a.m. we are given a cup of coffee and 300g of bread, then we leave for work at 7 a.m. We have a 15 minute break at 9 a.m. and at 12.30 we break for lunch – a bowl of soup. At 2 p.m. we get back to work. I work until 5.45 p.m., but some of the others go until 7 p.m. We are given another bowl of soup in the evening. You write that you might be able to come and see me in the spring. Write and tell me how life is at home. You say that Papa has started working as a caretaker at the school, but that you stay home. Write and tell me whether the cow has been sold, and how much bread the kolkhoz made. You ask whether to send me a parcel. I asked in a previous letter whether you could send me some tobacco [. . .] Send me as many dried plums and dried biscuits as you can. And send as much butter and as many other provisions as you can too. You know how to send them. Perhaps the rest of the family could send something too, and don't let my friends forget about me. Write and tell me who has been taken prisoner, about whom you have heard news, or who might be alive and where. Goodbye for now, I'm sending you a firm handshake. Pass on my greetings to Papa, Mama and all the family. Your son, Grisha.

Those carrying out heavy manual labour sometimes received a little more food. Tatiana Veselovskaya: 'They gave us a little loaf of bread this size [gestures]. And because I was a *Schwerarbeiter*,* I got an extra half – so I got a loaf and a half in total. [. . .] Life was good for us as a result.'

Mikhail Chernenko told us:

> Yes, there was a constant sense of hunger, but we weren't going to starve to death. Not at all. Those doing hard manual labour (*schwer*) were given extra food, and those who did the hardest labour (*schwerst*) got further rations. I can't remember exactly, but I think once or twice a week the *schwer* labourers got an extra good-sized chunk of bread. And the *schwerst* labourers would get an extra loaf of bread along with a bit of margarine or sausage.

A letter from Neumarkt to the Volyn region, dated 1 August 1944 (translated from Ukrainian):

> . . . Thank you so much, my kind-hearted brother and dearest aunt, for your parcel, which has already arrived. The parcel contained salted fat, a couple of pieces of bread spread with lard and, to my surprise and joy, at the bottom I also found your photograph, Auntie! You look so old; you have changed so much. I look at the photo a lot, and remember my dear mother. If only you knew Auntie, just how sad I am about my mother. She was so good to me . . .

Procuring extra food became the primary goal of the *Ostarbeiter.* If an opportunity arose to steal something to supplement their diet, they would invariably seize it. Sergei Bogdanov remembers:

> We gave ourselves a helping hand by supplementing our meagre rations. Our camp was on the outskirts of the city and it was a kilometre and a half to the mine adit. The road there was lined with potato fields and if the policeman escorting us

* A person performing heavy manual labour.

> was a decent sort of man, he would turn a blind eye as someone dashed out of the column, dug up a few handfuls of potatoes and stuffed them into his pockets.

Nadezhda Izmalkova remembers that she once managed to take double the permitted portion of two potatoes per person at the camp canteen:

> I arrived at the canteen to find Sheffin, a shrill-voiced German woman, in charge. 'Come and get your portion . . . *zähl aber laut! Ich muss hören!*'* she was shouting.
>
> I started to count . . . '*eins, zwei . . .!*' But instead of picking up one potato at a time, I took double.

Handing out bread at the steel factory, Düsseldorf, 1943.

Canteen at the gunpowder factory, Magdeburg, 1943.

Many people resorted to stealing whenever the opportunity arose. This they did despite the risk of bring caught and beaten by the guards or, worse, sent to prison or a concentration camp. Taissa Tolkachova:

> The police kept watch day and night [. . .] Our girls found out that the Germans hid beetroots in holes. A few of the braver girls dug up the holes and took a few beetroots. Perhaps they

* 'Count out loud so that I can hear!'

> didn't fill them in again afterwards . . . Anyway, the Germans found out that a few of us had been digging up their holes and stealing the beetroot. They called everyone together: 'We'll shoot the lot of you!' they threatened.

Driven to their very limits, people were prepared to risk everything just to steal a raw potato that they could cook later in the barracks. The prospect of punishment, at times extremely brutal, was no deterrent. Victor Shuldeshov:

> There was a canteen for the workers. I remember that I stole the potato and beetroot peelings sometimes. I had a little jar that I boiled them in. I was desperately hungry – I'd have eaten almost anything. And then one day I was caught. They took me from work, straight to the police department. I was given a month and a half in prison. The food in prison was actually better than at the camp!

Extra food supplies were easier to come by in the smaller camps, where the regimes were sometimes slightly more relaxed. Lavrenty Novokhatko worked on the railway and remembers: 'We got our extra food supplies from the vegetable gardens and orchards by the roadside. We would slip out of the toilet window at night and go and gather up some apples and vegetables.'

Such missions were risky, however, as Pavel Mikhailov explains: 'The fields were private land, and they were guarded. One of our guys got hurt – he was shot in the leg by one of the landowners.'

It goes without saying that none of those we spoke to would have considered resorting to thievery under normal circumstances. But the *Ostarbeiter* looked upon stealing during their time in Germany very differently. They almost always described the food they stole as though it did not belong to anyone in particular; potatoes were taken 'from the fields' for instance, and apples 'from a garden'. And even when they did steal directly from people, it was the enemy they were stealing from. The *Ostarbeiter* remembered only too well how the German soldiers had helped themselves to anything they wanted during the occupation. They had stolen from the occupiers then too, and they continued to employ similar methods to obtain food in Germany. They spoke of this as though it was an accepted fact of life; as if it went without saying that we would understand. Peter Marunchak recalled:

> We hung about in Vienna and on the outskirts of the city. We'd pick people's pockets. What could we pinch? Money and ration coupons. It wasn't just me. There were a few of us doing it. One day there'd be five of us, the next day seven, then the next day two would be caught, and we'd be five again.

Lavrenty Novokhatko remembers what the railway workers would do:

> A few of the guys working on the railway were 'brake shoers' [. . .] Those working the night shift would get some proper food supplies. If it was a Pullman train, let's say, carrying apples, they would position the brake shoe closer to the carriage, so that the train would slam into it, tipping out the apples.

A lucky few managed to earn a little extra money by conducting some business on the side. Vadim Novgorodov said:

> Before the war, one of my school friends had taught me how to repair watches and alarms. So I started mending watches in the camp – I mended some for the Germans too. [. . .] I repaired a wall clock for a farmer and he brought me some potatoes a couple of times. He also gave me some creamy, full-fat milk.

Antonina Maxina told us:

> We had the opportunity to go and do some paid housework [. . .] I only went in the afternoons, after work. I'd go there and the old lady, who worked as a foreman, would immediately offer

> me breakfast. '*Frühstück, Frühstück*,' she would say, and I would sit down to eat.
>
> 'Today we're going to do the washing,' she'd say afterwards.
>
> And when I set off home, she'd give me something else to take with me – either an apple or some other sort of fruit.

Georgiy Tkachov sold toys made by the Soviet prisoners of war to the Germans:

> There was a lack of children's toys. The shops were full, but there were no children's toys to be found anywhere on the shelves. The Germans really prized them. [. . .] Back home before the war, we had these little stick toys. You'd turn two little wheels and either a butterfly or a cockerel would flap its wings, or a little carousel would turn. The prisoners of war would throw them over the wire. They made them, and we would sell them and split the profits. They'd get a little extra food, and we could survive on the proceeds.

A letter from Chemnitz to Baranovichy, Brest region, dated 23 October 1942:

> Greetings, my dear parents! First of all, I'd like to reassure you that I am alive and well, and hope that you are too. Life here is good. I am living with our lads. [. . .] We are living in Chemnitz – I work in the factory. Please, dear parents, please could you send me some tobacco and dried biscuits as soon as you can. We can no longer receive parcels any larger than 200g, but you can send even ten of that size – you just need to address them to different surnames. Please send me news of what you are doing, my dear parents. Is everyone alive and well and still at home? Goodbye for now, dear parents, don't miss me too much and please send letters and parcels as soon as possible. Send my best to all the family and friends. Greetings, my dearest father! I wish you good health. I cannot forget you. Farewell, then. Write and tell me how your work is.

The *Ostarbeiter* rarely managed to procure much extra food. To do so, they had to be able to hide it, sneak it into the barracks, and then cook it. Antonina Maxina remembered:

> We weren't allowed to cook in the barracks, but in the winter we could put potatoes in the stove – there were a few potbellied stoves in the barracks. There were boilers to heat the water during the summer, so we would get hold of some potatoes, wash them, put them in our little handbags with long cord straps, and drop them into the water. The water would boil, and our potatoes would cook.

Anna Gulyaeva worked in a potato warehouse near Schwerin. She also described in detail how they cooked the potatoes that they managed to secrete away:

> When we unloaded the freight cars, we'd each pop three potatoes in our pockets to take home. We had a round stove in the barracks, and we asked the guys to make us a grater. So what we would do was grate the potatoes into a bucket, wash them, squeeze out the water and then strain it off. Then 'plop', we'd pour the gratings out onto the stove. And . . . Hey presto! A little while later they'd be ready! We'd split them between all twenty-four girls.

Not everybody shared the spoils. Many stories directly contradict the widespread myth that Soviet citizens always provided unconditional assistance to their comrades. Georgiy Tkachov was housed in a work camp for the Todt Organisation on the outskirts of Berlin. We asked him whether the men at the camp got on well together:

> We got along well, but to tell the truth it was the law of the jungle in there. There was no stealing. But as for sharing . . . nobody shared. If you wanted to live, you got hold of something, and you traded it. But if I went out and found something to

> eat, I'd bring it back for myself. Everybody had his own little compartment and locker, but you didn't lock anything up. Nobody would go into your locker – not so much as a crumb would be taken.

Friendship played an important role, both for those in the camps and the domestic and farm workers. We were told stories of friends helping and supporting each other in any way they could, often at great personal risk.

Camp kitchen at a munitions factory, Berlin, 1943.

Nadezhda Izmalkova remembers that a friend helped her out when she was transferred from the German village where she had been working to a new workplace at an aerodrome. There she was fed very badly: 'Some people had these ration coupons that you could use to buy blood sausage in shops. [My friend] stole some sausage coupons from her employer and sent them to me in a letter.'

The factory workers welcomed any days when they were reassigned to temporary agricultural work, for farm work provided an opportunity to get hold of some extra food. Leonid Osipov worked in an aviation factory:

> Sometimes during the summer a farmer would come to the camp and select a few people to work for him – planting

> tomatoes, irrigating the cabbages and such like. They fed you well there – good, hearty bowls of food. [. . .] But you could only go on your day off. You'd leave in the morning, and in the evening you'd return to the camp.

Relationships between workers and employers in the countryside were very different from those between factory workers and their managers. This disparity manifested itself in food rations too – generally, the diets of those working in the countryside were far better, although this depended entirely on the employer. Vladimir Vishnevsky worked in a hamlet called Kronstorf, not far from Enns in Austria. He recalls working for two very different employers, one of whom gave him nothing but a small piece of bread to eat each day. 'The other one gave me as much bread as I wanted – I was fed practically five times a day,' he remembers.

Nadezhda Izmalkova also compared life with different farming families for whom she worked around the city of Weimar:

> We all ate at the same table. [. . .] Our employer was an excellent cook. She had conserved meat, chicken . . . she even made *Biersuppe* and all sorts of other soups. My first employer, Frau Shenke, also made lots of different soups, and when I met other German women and they asked what Frau Shenke had cooked, I said, 'Pea soup, bean soup, cabbage soup, carum soup.' Gossip spread through the hamlet because I had told everyone what meals she had cooked.

Food on the farms depended on relationships with employers and individual family traditions. Workers and the families that employed them often laboured side by side in the fields, and shared lunch together. Some farming families sat down with the *Ostarbeiter* at the same table to eat, as had been the tradition for many years. This they did despite Nazi orders that explicitly forbade it. Victor Smirnov: 'We ate together at the same table, but I never had enough food. My employers didn't eat much themselves – they were very miserly.'

Vera Dergachova said:

> We ate whatever they were eating. There was no difference. But, Lord no! We never sat together. Even if there was nobody around, Lord no, you couldn't sit next to them. They sat down to eat together, and we sat about ten paces away. They said we didn't have the right to sit with them.

Though the domestic helpers tended not to go so hungry, for many of these women food became a status symbol. The food itself was less important – what mattered was whether they ate with the family, or separately.

Some of the women were ambivalent about whether they ate meals with their German employers, but for others eating separately was yet another humiliating reminder of their subordination. Frida Palko worked for the owner of a warehouse and usually ate her meals separately. We asked her whether there were ever any exceptions. 'Actually,' she said, 'now and again I sat at the end of the table on special occasions. [. . .] But I never said a single word to the master of the house.'

Irina Sokolova didn't go hungry either – she worked for a doctor: 'I ate whatever they ate [. . .] But I ate in the kitchen. There was a fridge in there and if I wanted a little piece of something, I could help myself. I could take beer to drink, and nobody ever said anything about it.'

Galina Agranovskaya worked as a domestic helper for a German family in Frankfurt am Main. She remembers:

> We ate separately from the family. Generally, we were fed on heaps of those *Gemüse*.* It was turnips mainly; for some reason I remember those kohlrabi turnips particularly well. We were also given some sort of bread. Well, as you know, bread isn't really a German speciality. We had grains too. In any case, I wasn't going to faint from hunger.

* Vegetables

Aside from the fact that the food was often scant and of poor quality, it was also completely unfamiliar. Few had ever encountered *Gemüse* such as those that Galina mentioned prior to their arrival in Germany. Anna Odinokova, who worked in Zagan, Lower Silesia, remembered: 'I couldn't eat the spinach – it made me retch when I put it in my mouth. It was all soft and slippery – not even pigs would eat it!'

They remembered how their hunger would be exacerbated by the abundance of food in the German shops and homes. Georgiy Tkachov:

> They wanted for nothing. The shops were so full they were practically bursting at the seams. Black bread, white bread, all sorts of bread rolls, pastries, gingerbread, biscuits, sweets . . . even chocolate ones, and jam and honey. [. . .] They had every type of grain – barley, oats, rice and buckwheat – and many types of pasta. In short, they had absolutely everything, right down to fruit jellies. But everything was distributed by weight. Take barley, for example. You'd get five grammes per person. It was the same story with the various sausages – either ten, fifteen or twenty grammes. You could fill your basket with produce. The Germans had more than enough food. They said there was a famine. It wasn't true. They didn't know the meaning of the word.

Preparing vegetables in a farming household, Germany, 1944.

In the face of the inhumanity and cruelty to which they were subjected, the *Ostarbeiter* appear to have maintained great composure, and remarkably their stories were often devoid of blame and condemnation. It was plain to see, however, that the injustice and humiliation had cut deeply. Galina Agranovskaya remembers that the Polish girl she worked alongside for a family in Germany once said: 'Our boss thinks that you and I are living in seventh heaven here.'

Taissa Tolkachova recalls the hurt she felt when the starving *Ostarbeiter* were mocked: 'We girls were so very hungry. The Germans lined up to watch us eat. If one of us ran up to the cooking pot and cried out "Give me more, more!" they laughed.'

A postcard from the Kiev region to Neheim-Hüsten, 12 August 1943 (translated from Ukrainian):

> Postcard dated 12/VIII-43. Sunday. Greetings, my sweet, darling daughter Zosya. First of all I wish to tell you that we are still alive and well. I sent you a parcel on [Apple Feast of the] Saviour Day. I dried a packet of rusks, 8 packets of groats, 2 packets of onion and a cube of butter. I think Semyon also sent two half-kilo jars of oil. Don't worry – everything here is fine. On [Apple Feast of the] Saviour Day I received five postcards from you, which you wrote on 29/V, 09/VII, 10/VII, 27/VII and 18/VII. In them we learned that you received our parcels containing a shift and a blouse. But you haven't yet received the parcel containing the piece of linen – you only received the little postcard from Yanov. Zoska,* I have described everything at home as it is. If you receive my letters, then you must know what's going on. Don't believe what you hear from others. [. . .] I'll leave it there. Goodbye.

All those we spoke to felt an enormous sense of gratitude towards the people who had treated them with kindness in Germany. They could recall every sympathetic gesture and every little piece of bread

* Translator's note: A diminutive form of the name Zosya.

Domestic workers having lunch, Liebau, 1943. The reverse reads: *Photo from my time in Germany. Photo taken at lunchtime in the courtyard. A memento for Mummy and my sisters, from Katya. In the photo: We all work in this house. Vita – cook, 32 years old; Katarina – housemaid, 19 years old; Dora – waitress, 20 years old; Anya – seamstress, 50 years old. Anya and I share a room. She is like a mother to me here.*

that was slipped to them on the quiet. It was usually the young teenage girls who elicited the most sympathy. Tatiana Veselovskaya: 'When I arrived [at work], and opened up my desk, I would always find a sandwich and some other little morsel inside. I never knew who put them there, because the Germans were afraid of each other.'

Forced Labour

Some *Ostarbeiter* had only cloudy memories of where they had worked and what they had done in Germany, which is perhaps unsurprising considering that few remained with one family or at the same factory for the full duration of their two or three years abroad. The German employment offices shuffled the eastern workers about like a deck of cards, shunting them from one place to another as and when required. They were sometimes obliged to evacuate during episodes of heavy bombing, and towards the end of the war, as the Red Army advanced, many found themselves on the move every few months.

'I work down a mine'

As time went on, the *Ostarbeiter* grew to understand the nature of the production they were involved in. Vera Dergachova recalled:

> We were sent to Wittenberg, to a place they called 'a factory'. To my mind, factories were places where food products, or knitted goods, were made. But this was a manufacturing plant where they made parts for aeroplanes. [. . .] Soldiers with pilots' epaulettes would cross the factory floor, which made me think: Why would pilots be walking about unless this was an aircraft factory?
>
> I worked on the milling machines and lathes.

A postcard from Osnabrück to the Kiev region, dated 13 April 1943 (translated from Ukrainian):

> We are working at the factory now – it's 3km from the camp on

foot. I wouldn't say the work is hard, but it really takes its toll on my feet – they hurt, and I have to stand on them all day. We work 12-hour shifts. We take over at 6 p.m. and work until 6 a.m., and then in the morning the day shift takes over, and they work until 6 p.m. We are fed three times a day. In the morning we get coffee and 150g bread, at lunch we have soup and 150g bread, and in the evening just soup. My dear, beloved Mama, Petya, Olya, Godmother, Auntie Kulina and Uncle Petro and sister Paraska, I send you my wholehearted greetings, from the very bottom of my heart, to the ends of the damp earth. Mama, don't cry for me – I'm fine here. They gave us mattresses and two blankets each as well as a mug, spoon, fork and towel. Well, that's all for now. Send my best wishes to the family and all the neighbours . . .

Camp at a metallurgical factory, Salzwedel, 1943.

Galina Agranovskaya changed workplace many times: 'In Frankfurt am Main I worked at the munitions factory. It was a closed camp; we lived behind barbed wire. My job was to bore holes: assault rifles have hand guards, you see, and I drilled holes in them with these special twist drills. I switched the drill bits in and out myself.'

DWM Ausweis

Zuname: Pljasan

Vorname: Vera

Geburtsdatum: 2.8. 23

Ausländerlager Schönholz

Deutsche Waffen- u. Munitionsfabriken Akt.-Ges.

Berlin-Reinickendorf-Ost 1

1213 Lager-Nr.

32067 Kontroll-Nr.

14. 10. 42 Eintrittsdatum

Pass for a munitions factory, Berlin, 1942.

Below left: Workers at a processing plant, Wiesen, 1942. Below right: Workers at a metalworking factory, Siegen, 1943.

Regardless of where the *Ostarbeiter* were sent to work, and what kind of labour they were assigned to, they rarely worked less than ten- or twelve-hour days. Life was hardest in the mines and munitions factories. Antonina Serdyukova worked in the Lautawerk aluminium-vanadium factory. She remembers:

> We were woken at 4 a.m. but given nothing to eat. No matter the weather, we had to stand outside in columns three people wide, and wait for the police and dogs to come and escort

> us to the factory workshop. We had to be at our positions and ready to work by six o'clock. Eventually, our German escort would arrive, and we would be recounted at the gate. They would count, lose count, and then start again. And we would stand, and stand, and stand by the gate. Finally they would finish counting us and then we had to run, run . . . [. . .] We'd run to the factory and would barely have had time to undress before they began shouting, 'Samples! Let's have a sample!'* We'd work like dogs until 2 p.m., scurrying to and fro. At 2 p.m. the whole rigmarole of earlier in the day was repeated – we lined up in threes, were led out of the factory, and recounted again at the gate. Somebody would invariably be missing, having been left behind or run off somewhere. My goodness, it was torture.

Larisa Shvidchenko was sent to a work camp in Düsseldorf:

> We worked for twelve hours at a time. When you worked the night shift you'd come back and fall into bed. 'Get up, its time to eat,' someone would shout.
>
> But you wouldn't be able to open your eyes.

A postcard from Tuttlingen to the Kamenets-Podolsk region, dated 27 October 1942 (translated from Ukrainian):

> Greetings, my dear cousin. In these first few lines of my short postcard I want to tell you that I am alive and well and to wish you all the very best in your young life. I also wish for you to live happily there in the little village in which you were born. Be sure to work hard to stay there, in your home village, so you can continue to live there until the day you die.
>
> I will tell you about my work. At present, my work is very bad – I am building a barracks. It is autumn and it rains a lot.

* Translator's note: Antonina was required to test the percentage of vanadium content of samples in the laboratory.

> We are deep into autumn here and we contend with rain and frost, without any winter clothes. I work for ten hours a day, the food isn't much to write home about, and none of us have any idea how long we will be working here. I'll leave this short letter there. Pass on my greetings to my cousins Mikhail and Ivan, and to your dear mother and Yakov too. Don't forget me, and please send a reply. I'll write more another time, but for now don't be upset that I'm writing so little. There are lots of girls working here too, as well as old men and many others – none of them live too well either. Goodbye, from your cousin Ivan.

Valeria Fyodorova was housed in a work camp in the small village of Tharau:

> I worked on the pressing machine, making bricks. It was absolutely exhausting and the work made my hands swell [. . .]. We worked on a conveyor belt, so if I was desperate for the toilet I'd have to yell at the top of my voice to call over the manager. He would then turn off the master switch so that I could run to the toilet. But you can't imagine how much he would then curse and swear at me for stopping the press and reducing output.

Galina Agranovskaya described the exhaustion brought on by the inane and robotic work:

Railway work, Dresden, 1942.

> Night time . . . the monotonous hum . . . the milling cutter whirred as you worked. You had to remember to lubricate it with emulsion from time to time, to reduce the friction – you had to be careful to do this. All degrees or qualifications were obsolete – it was a case of endless, unthinking, robotic movement.

The slightest misdemeanour or act of disobedience, or a failure to fulfil quotas, could result in being forced to work a double shift. Managers could also mete out beatings or other punishments for any flawed items produced, despite the fact that many of the workers were teenagers, sitting behind a workbench for the first time in their lives. Yevgeny Goryainov worked in Vienna:

Factory pass, Ruhr district, 1942.

> Apparently the factory where I worked used to manufacture motorcycles, but during the war it began to produce military haulage trucks and tractors. I drove the forklift, but they reassigned me to the machines one day, and I broke one. They were old machines – you couldn't use a torque force greater than 900. I was in a rush, and overdid it – I took the torque up to 1400 and it packed in. I was beaten, and for three days was given nothing but water and a crust of bread to eat. And then

> it was back to the factory. After that, I had to get all my work signed off to make sure that I didn't do any more damage.

Exhaustion, inadequate training and poor working conditions resulted in many of the workers suffering injuries. Maria Ausheva worked in the Winkel factory in Göttingen:

> At first, I was assigned to washing the items in acetone-benzene and Stauffer grease. My hands were swollen from the acetone . . . they didn't give us anything protective to wear – we used our bare hands. Not only was I breathing it in all the time, but it soaked into my skin. In the end it caught up with me, and I came down with acetone poisoning. The camp doctor took pity on me and gave me the treatment I needed.

Nikolai Kireev remembered his work in the Spandau area of Berlin: 'It was a munitions factory. I remember loading the weapons – automatic rifles, pistols, grenades . . . they went to the Russian front. It was heavy work but needless to say we were expected to get on with it – no allowances were made. People were constantly being injured.'

Mikhail Chernenko worked in a munitions factory in Fürstenberg:

> It was the wood-chipping machine that did for me. The medical wing bandaged up my eye, and I was sent back to work. I walked down the central aisle and, since I could only see out of one eye, I bumped into the iron bar between two carts, hurting my leg. The wound became infected but I kept going, kept working. A hole appeared – you could see right down to the bone. It was awful! Imagine, a sixteen-year-old boy walking around with a hole in his leg!

Siemens factory pass, Nuremberg, 1943.

It would be wrong, however, to say that every *Ostarbeiter* found their work in Germany to be tortuous and devoid of any meaningful value. Those who found themselves in well-established plants and factories were often quick to tell us that they had been able to learn and develop useful new skills. However, good fortune tended to favour those who had arrived in Germany with professional qualifications and a basic grasp of the German language. Like many of the young *Ostarbeiter* men, Yevgeny Goryainov took an interest in the latest mechanical instruments:

> I was young and interested in everything. I watched it all – I was curious, you know. I was practically a savage. [. . .] An elderly German man taught me how to drive the forklift buggy. He was about fifty years old, and spoke half in Russian, half in Polish. He was a foreman. First he showed me how to operate the forklift buggy. It was a manual, but a good little machine – it was pretty speedy. To tell the truth, the first time I drove it I got up to the third speed setting, so they limited the speed settings after that. 'That Russian is racing about,' they said. 'He almost killed the foreman!' I moved items around the workshop. At first I drove about with him, then he handed the forklift over to me and I drove it and moved things myself.

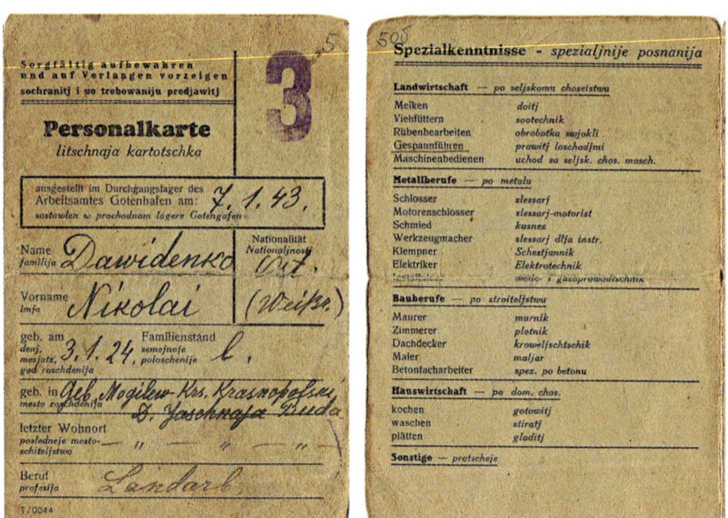

Sorgfältig aufbewahren und auf Verlangen vorzeigen
sochranitj i po trebowaniju predjawitj

3

Personalkarte
litschnaja kartotschka

ausgestellt im Durchgangslager des Arbeitsamtes Gotenhafen am: 7. 1. 43.
sostawlen w prochodnom lagere Gotengafen

Name *familija* Dawidenko — Nationalität *Nationaljnosti* Ost.

Vorname *imja* Nikolai

geb. am *denj, mesjatz, god roschdenija* 3. 1. 24. — Familienstand *semejnoje poloschenije* l.

geb. in *mesto roschdenija*

letzter Wohnort *posledneje mesto-schiteljstwo*

Beruf *profesija*

T/0044

Spezialkenntnisse – *spezialjnije posnanija*

Landwirtschaft — *po seljskomu choseistwu*

Melken	*doitj*
Viehfüttern	*sootechnik*
Rübenbearbeiten	*obrobotka swjokli*
Gespannführen	*prawitj loschadjmi*
Maschinenbedienen	*uchod sa seljsk. chos. masch.*

Metallberufe — *po metalu*

Schlosser	*slessarj*
Motorenschlosser	*slessarj-motorist*
Schmied	*kusnez*
Werkzeugmacher	*slessarj dlja instr.*
Klempner	*Schestjannik*
Elektriker	*Elektrotechnik*

Bauberufe — *po stroiteljstwu*

Maurer	*murnik*
Zimmerer	*plotnik*
Dachdecker	*kroweljschtschik*
Maler	*maljar*
Betonfacharbeiter	*spez. po betonu*

Hauswirtschaft — *po dom. chos.*

kochen	*gotowitj*
waschen	*stiratj*
plätten	*gladitj*

Sonstige — *protscheje*

Record card with a German–Russian workplace vocabulary list. Gotenhafen, 1943.

Handlers at the paint and varnish factory, Krefeld, 1942.

Many were impressed by German discipline and orderliness. Georgiy Tkachov worked in a ship repair factory in Stettin: 'In terms of discipline, Germany was the ideal paradigm. If you left something out, nobody would ever come along and take it or use it.'

Some *Ostarbeiter* voiced pride in the new skills that they acquired in Germany. Vadim Novgorodov worked at several mines in

A postcard from Metz to Proskurov (translated from Ukrainian):

Good day to you all, my dear family and relatives. And greetings to my wife Yefimiya Ivanovna and my dear children Gapya, Dunka and Vanka. [. . .] I wish you all success in your lives. I am alive and well for now. My health is a little better, but I go to the doctor quite a bit, though nothing really helps me. I work down a mine for 9 hours a day. The work is hard but it's good that it's warm down there and I work with the same guys – Yakov and Makey. The food isn't much – cabbage, potato and turnip, and 600g of bread. Nothing else. There is no winter here. Our camp is 20 kilometres from Metz. [. . .] It's a former depot. We aren't allowed to send letters. I handed one in to the post office, and a few days later it was returned to me. I don't know what the situation is in Ukraine, whether letters are getting there or not . . .? [. . .] Write and tell me your news – what's going on at home and in the village? They pay us very little. I received your postcard – thank you so very much. Goodbye for now. I look forward to your reply.

Bochum. He remembers that he gradually earned the trust of his German co-workers:

> The mine worked in conjunction with an on-site coke-processing plant. We worked in the plant. [. . .] Before long they began to trust us to do more than just carry bricks and remove rubbish. We began to learn from the engineers and the blacksmith. Within a few months I had learned how to make fertilizer – I made ammonium sulphate and monitored the production process because the specialist who worked there had no chemical education. I, at least, had learned some chemistry in school. They trusted me to monitor the machinery – I would update the specialist, and he would take measures accordingly.

An *Ostarbeiter* work team clearing the Traisen river, 1944.

Antonina Serdyukova described how she became an experienced laboratory technician in Germany:

> I was assigned to the workshop floor, where they were smelting vanadium – it was the foundry. Vanadium is a strategic metal; it was smelted into nut-like granules that were then packed into iron tins, which were then stamped. It was all done very precisely by weight. Anyway, when a job sweeping this

smoky, fire-spitting workshop floor was foisted off on me, I lost my appetite for brandishing a broom! So I tried striking up conversation with some of the Germans – asking what apparatus did what. The general foreman came over – he was in charge.

'*Können Sie Deutsch sprechen?*'* he asked.

'I learned it well at school,' I replied.

He transferred me to the laboratory to test the vanadium content percentages of samples. They taught me how to do it, of course. First of all I learned all the German names for the chemicals. The system was as follows: I arrived at 6 a.m. and immediately took a sample to test. From then on, I did the same thing every hour. '*Stichproben*'† [random sampling] they called it. I would weigh out one gramme, sprinkle it into a test flask, pour in the required acid and heat it on the stove. It would simmer there for half an hour, then I would let it cool for a minute or two and titrate it. I'd do the calculations and jot down my findings in a notebook.

Arkady Kozhaev was a junior engineer with a good command of German when the war broke out. After working for some time in a mine, where conditions were extremely tough, he was transferred to a factory manufacturing V-2 rockets. He described an incident when he identified a product defect:

I remember one particular episode.

'Arkady,' someone said, 'you've made a mistake somewhere.'

'*Nein, nein,*' I replied, '*Das ist unmöglich.*'‡

I searched for the problem and took an instrument to test it. There was pressure here [gestures] . . . and there . . . but here, no! Aha! I thought. That's why! The company manufacturer was called, and he apologised. Everyone praised me.

* Can you speak German?
† Random sampling
‡ 'That's impossible.'

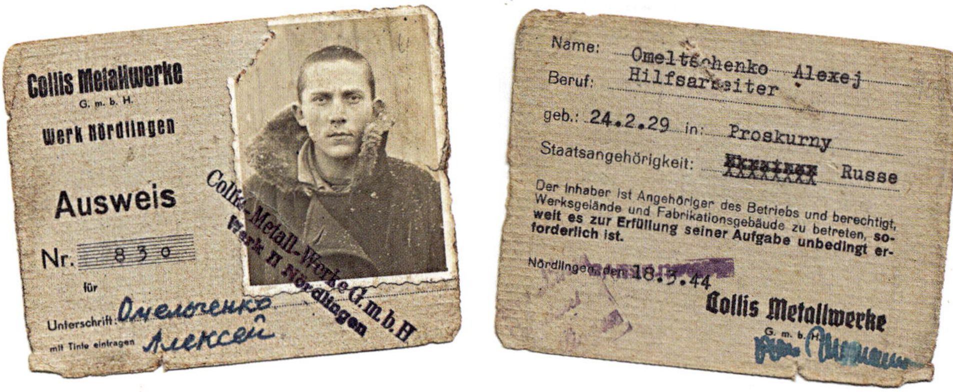

Factory pass, Nördlingen, 1944.

Many expressed their admiration and respect for the German engineers and foremen who taught them. Vadim Novgorodov:

> In 1943 we were assigned to construction. The bombing had intensified and the infrastructure at the coke-processing plant was regularly destroyed. They'd bomb it, and then four or five of us – all Russians – would fix it. There was another guy, Leo Liss, a quiet, calm German man. He couldn't stand this 'Fascist system', as he called it. It was from him that I learned to work with scrupulous attention to detail. He never hurried, but did everything with meticulous care and attention. The managers held him in high regard because he was an exceptionally good specialist.

From a letter sent from Nuremberg to Poltava, dated 3 August 1943 (translated from Ukrainian):

> I wrote this letter on 3/VIII-1943. Greetings, Papa, Mama, brother, sisters and my niece Nina. First of all, I want to let you know that I am still alive and am sending you my very best regards. I am working in a factory, alternating between 12-hour day and night shifts weekly. I get 300g of bread twice a day. We live in a camp, with sixteen people to a room. I have sent you two letters, but I haven't received a single one from you. If only I could hear just one word . . .

A stamp on a postcard: *Ostarbeiter* camp, Steyerberg, Weser.

A postcard from Senftenberg to the Kamenets-Podolsk region, dated 11 February 1943 (translated from Ukrainian):

> Good day or good evening, my dear comrades. I am sending you my warm and ardent greetings. My dear friends Fedya and Vanyusha, my first task in writing this letter is to let you know that I received your letter and to send you my heartfelt thanks for not forgetting me. I will also tell you about the weather in Germany. By our standards, the weather here is good. It's warm – it got down to minus sixteen once, but now it's warm. The only thing that's bad is that it rains a lot. But here, come rain or shine, we still have to work. I can tell you, the work isn't very hard though. We work for 8 hours, and they give us 300g of bread and soup twice a day. Dear friends, you also write that 1933 is coming closer, but 1933 is already almost with us here.*

Antonina Serdyukova told us that she owed a debt of gratitude to her German manager:

> He took me to the manager of the workshop floor – a highly intelligent engineer called Oscar Menikh. He sat me down and began to ask me questions about this and that. After the war, I wanted to thank him – he really did a lot for me.
>
> I remember bumping into him in the corridor sometime

* Translator's note: Possibly a reference to the Holodomor famine of 1932–3.

before New Year. 'What would you like as a New Year's present?' he jokingly asked me.

'A dictionary and a piece of bread,' I replied.

He did give me a little dictionary – I still have it. You could say that he continued to help me out for the rest of my life.

Workers at Heinrich Niemann's logging company, Hanover, 1943.

Arkady Kozhaev became a prominent electrical engineer in the USSR during the 1960s. He believes that his post-war career was heavily influenced by the experience and knowledge that he gained in Germany.

Laundry workers with their foreman, Magdeburg, 1943.

Railway workers, 1943.

> They taught me a lot . . . things that I could only have learned in Germany. They didn't teach such things here. There, I learned to do things well the first time round. 'If you do something twice,' they said 'you'll do it badly both times. You were to do things once, and only once! I got a lot of practical experience in Germany. If I told somebody at the factory to do something in a particular way, I would always follow up and check that it had been done the way I asked. For this reason, despite being politically neutral, I was given responsibilities when I returned and people looked up to me. Germany was a training ground for me, but I brought it all back – all the knowledge I had acquired. I brought it back to the Soviet Union with me. I gave back.

'Do your work badly and you'll be sent to a concentration camp'

Work on the farms could be punishing, especially for the youngsters who had grown up in the city and were not accustomed to the physicality of farming life. Varvara Khabarova remembers:

> First, we were taught how to milk the cows. We went to a lesson in the village and the milkman showed us how it was done – how to milk the very last drops. My employer had five cows. My legs would shake as I milked them, and my hands would go completely numb. I tell you, it took a lot of strength!

> After milking, I had to muck out the cowshed, the pig shed, and feed the livestock.

Yevgenia Savranskaya was sent from a factory to work for a farmer. She found the farm work far worse, and recalls the cruelty of her employer:

> She was so unkind to me. I had cut my finger open and couldn't sleep at night. It was frightening, of course. I told her that I couldn't milk the cows because I had hurt my finger and it was causing me a lot of pain.
>
> 'No, you're going to milk the cows,' she told me.
>
> In short, she could make me do whatever she wanted.

Anna Odinokova had a similar experience working on a farm in Germany:

> They'd wake me with a knock on the door at 3 a.m. I'd get up and go and fetch the heavy wooden wheelbarrow. Then out I'd go with the scythe to cut clover for the three cows and the bull. I needed to feed them each morning and had to take it all in

Workers at a bakery in Cloppenburg, 1943.

one go. Then I fed the other animals and prepared the bread. On top of all this, I had to pile up the manure so that it composted, and put down straw on the floor. After that, I milked the cows under the watchful eye of the mistress. I would wish for her to leave so that I could gulp down some milk, but no, she never did. Once I had finished the milking, I had to prepare the swill for the pigs. Then there was the vegetable garden to weed. And so it went on . . . endlessly. In the winter I had to chop branches in the woods, saw and chop the firewood and then stack it away in the log store. I was so overstretched that my stomach was displaced. [. . .] But all that the mistress said was, 'Do your work badly and you'll be sent to a concentration camp.'

Nina Woronezka. Ukraine.
Stadtgut Lippehne. bei Werner Ketelhut. Kreis Soldin.
Postkarte
An, Кому: Anatol Woronezki. Perejaslaw. Staro-Kiewska №18. Perejaslaw. Kiew.
Дорогі батьки! (29/VI-43 р.) Нарешті одержала я від вас открютку 26/VI-43 року. Це велика для мене радість. Пишіть почастіше, тому що нам дозволено писати лише дві открийки на 1-ий місяць. Я дуже по-

A postcard from Soelden, Austria, to the Kiev region, dated 29 June 1943 (translated from Ukrainian).

My dear parents! At last, I have received your postcard, dated 26/VI-43. It brought me such great joy – please write more often, because we are only able to send two postcards per month. I've lost a lot of weight – I'm now the same size as I was during the exams in Year 10. I'm not quite sure why though – it might be down to the work, or perhaps the heartache of missing home. Work isn't too hard at the moment – we weed the beetroot and potatoes, plant turnips and rake the hay – but for me, even this work is very hard. Work is horrid during the autumn months – it's cold and rains a lot. It's a terribly rotten, cold climate here. Winter is even worse – all winter, we will thresh the wheat for the bread in the frost. You can find out about our food and dormitory from Shura's mama – she wrote all about it. Write and tell me absolutely everything – I want to know about the goat, the ginger cat, the garden and the vegetable patch. Sending you both a kiss.

Your Nina

Sometimes the workload was so onerous that the *Ostarbeiter* were driven to complain about their employers. Ivan Krasnov worked on the outskirts of Danzig:

> We were sent out to cut ten-kilo chunks of turf. We put them in the wheelbarrow, but I couldn't lift it, let alone push it. I told my employer that the work was beyond my strength.
>
> 'You came here to work, didn't you? So get on and work,' came his reply.
>
> 'I can't,' I replied. 'I'll leave.'
>
> 'And go where?' he said.
>
> 'To the police department,' I replied.
>
> I went to the police and told them that I couldn't work for him. 'It's such heavy labour,' I told them, 'and I'm too weak.'

It sometimes paid to complain, as Yevdokiya Verkholantseva discovered:

> I went to the employment bureau as soon as it opened one morning. A woman sat inside. 'What's the matter with you?' she asked.
>
> I explained that I was crawling with head lice, but my employers wouldn't let me scratch my head, and that the work was beyond my strength.
>
> 'I'm hungry and drained, and they give me all the men's work to do even though I'm small,' I said.
>
> 'All right,' she said, 'we'll call and find you a job somewhere else in another village.'
>
> But my employer had already sent Anton running to find me at the employment bureau or, as they called it, the *Arbeitsamt*. He looked at my tear-stained face. I'm not

Agricultural work on the outskirts of Freiburg im Breisgau, 1944.

sure exactly what the woman told him – it was all in German – probably something along the lines that they were going to find me a position in a different village. But Anton told her that our mistress wanted me to come back.

'You're good and kind,' he said. 'She's going to let you do whatever you want – you can scratch your head, wash your hair, have a day off . . .'

So I went back with him. [. . .] From then on she began to treat me better. She stopped yelling at me and when other Germans walked past, she would praise me aloud, saying, '*Gut, gut.*'

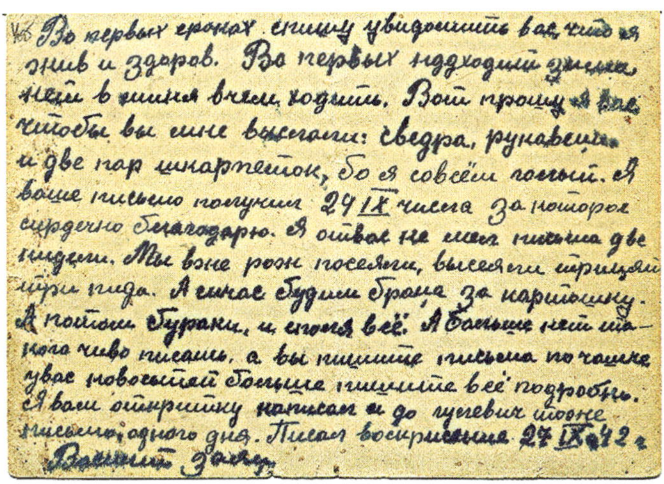
Во первых сронах спишу увидомить вас что я
жив и здоров. Во первых надходит зима
[illegible] в [illegible] всем ходить. Вот прошу я вас
чтобы вы мне выслали: светра, рукавиц
и две пар шкарпеток, бо я совсём голый. Я
ваше письмо получил 24 IX числа за которое
сердечно благодарю. Я от вас не имел письма две
недели. Мы вже рож посеяли, высеяли тридцать
три пуда. А сичас будим брать за картошку.
А потом бураки, и [illegible] всё. А больше нет та-
кого чиво писать, а вы пишите письма почаще
у вас новостей больше пишите всё подробно.
Я вам открытку написал и до [illegible] тоже
письмо одного дня. Писал воскресенье 27 IX 42 г.
Василий [illegible]

A letter from Angerwiese, Kaliningrad region, to the Kamenets-Podolsk region, dated 27 September 1942:

In these first lines I hasten to tell you that I am alive and well. Firstly though, winter is approaching, and I have nothing to wear, so I ask that you please send me the following, as I am completely naked: a sweater, mittens and two pairs of socks. I received your letter dated 24/IX, for which I send my heartfelt thanks. I haven't had a letter from you for two weeks now. We have sown the corn already – 33 poods of it – and now it's time for us to dig up the potatoes. Then it'll be time to bring in the beetroot and other field crops. I don't have much else to say, but please do write more often – you have more news, so write it all down in detail. [. . .] Written on Sunday 27/IX-42. Vasily.

Working on a farm. Offenberg, 1942.

The organisation on the farms impressed some of the *Ostarbeiter*, and several remembered labouring alongside their employers. Georgiy Tkachov worked on a farm in Greifenberg:

> I remember their surname was Shmelinkh. The family had a daughter, Lina, and two boys: Fritz, and Hans. Hans, the eldest son, was in the army. They all worked and all milked the cows. And I was made to help out. Lina would milk first, and then the mistress would finish off milking the cows. There were twenty head of cattle and two fields. One of the fields was an experimental one, where they grew wheat and potatoes. The potatoes weren't very big, but they were evenly rounded and there weren't any tiddlers. When you dug up a plant, you'd get a bucketful of potatoes – up to a hundred at once! There were also turnips and sugar beet – we gave the turnips to the cows and pigs, and all the sugar beet went to the factory. They had a sort of reaping machine that cut the crops, bound the sheaves and spat them out. Our job was to collect the sheaves and tie them together.

Working in the countryside gave rise to a number of comic episodes too, as Nadezhda Izmalkova, who worked on a farm on the outskirts of Weimar, recalls:

Potato harvest on the outskirts of Offenberg, 1943.

A female worker on the farm with the family she worked for, Düsseldorf, 1944.

Gathering potatoes alongside the employers on the outskirts of Rochlitz, 1944.

Working on a farm on the outskirts of Leibnitz, Austria, 1943.

> We needed to plant the cabbages, so I was summoned to help. I had a reputation in the village for being lazy. There were eight of us working there in the fields – an Italian, a German girl called Vera, and the rest of us. I had always loved to sing and remember singing 'Nobody in our district knows Chilita, she's so clever and beautiful'. The Italian began to sing along in Italian too. It turned out that the song 'Chilita' was famous the world over. And so we sang it together! The Germans toiled away at their work, while we sang. [. . .] Some time later, Vera came to tell me that the master had gone to inspect the cabbages in the field and discovered that they hadn't all taken root. He couldn't for the life of him understand why, and cursed aloud: '*Schweinehunde also!*'* But Vera had realised exactly what had happened.
>
> 'Nothing has grown in the places where you and Gino were working,' she told me. 'You just sang songs and never actually did any work.'
>
> Of course, the master was at a loss as to what had happened. We roared with laughter about it.

The domestic work tended to be less physically demanding, revolving principally around cleaning, housekeeping and childcare. German families usually chose the younger women for these roles; they had a preference for blonde, fairly well educated girls who could pick up the language quickly. These girls were hired to look after the children of city-based doctors, lawyers, bankers and civil servants, and their employers sometimes grew attached to them, feeding them well and treating them with kindness and sympathy. In some cases these young *Ostarbeiter* women almost became part of the family. Their young charges often grew to love them, which usually helped to win the parents round too.

Tatiana Zhelamskaya remembered:

> The house had 14 rooms. [. . .] The master of the house was the general director of ReiseBank. I had to sweep the floors

* 'Those bloody bastards!'

> and clean them with a wet cloth, then polish the metal handles with a wire pad until they shone. The children were lovely – they were always kind and polite to me. I always held the eldest, Anna-Laura, in high esteem – she had just finished school. The younger ones – Klaus and Gita – were just wonderful. I remember sitting at home on my own one day, singing a song. Klaus overheard, and afterwards he would often ask me in German, 'Tat-yana (that's how he pronounced my name), sing!' [. . .] My life there wasn't bad, and I didn't wear my OST badge with them.

Tamara Selivanova worked as a housemaid for the director of the Torpedo-Werk enterprise in Frankfurt am Main:

> I worked from half five in the morning until twelve thirty at night – I was exhausted. I remember that I even fell asleep once while sitting in the kitchen. The master of the house saw and I heard him give his wife a thick ear. After that she started sending me to my room to rest for an hour after lunch.

With an employer's children, Innsbruck, 1944.

A housemaid with the children of her employer, Eltville, 1943.

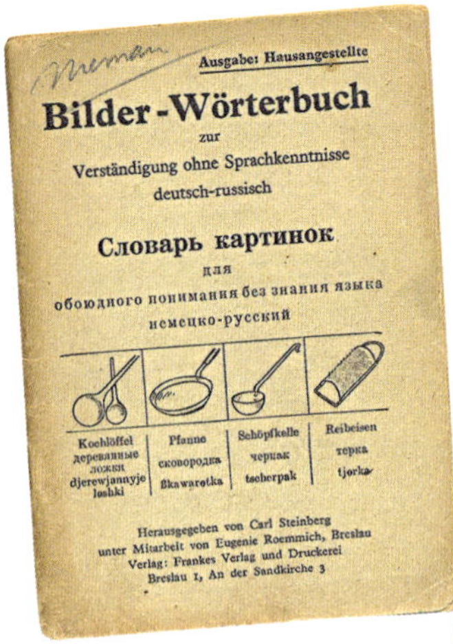

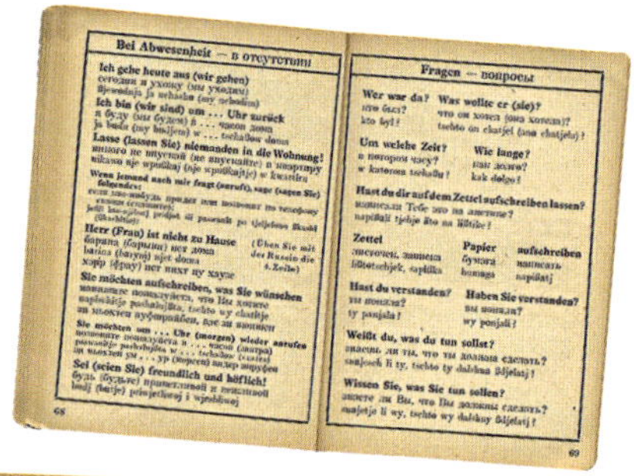

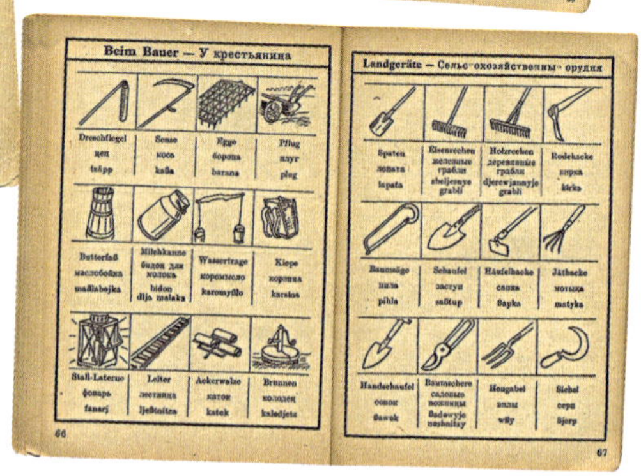

A German–Russian dictionary, with pictures, published by Frankes Verlag, designed for domestic workers, Breslau, 1943.

Despite the fact that domestic work was considered less demanding than factory or farm work, there was no escaping the fact that it was forced labour. The young *Ostarbeiter* girls living with German families were acutely aware of their second-class citizenship, which they found both humiliating and degrading. Their situation was made more difficult by the fact that the quarrels and insults levelled at them were often of a more personal and explicit nature. We share two such stories below.

Irina Sokolova never forgot one particular conflict that arose while she was working for the family of a doctor in Freising. The conflict with her mistress came about when Irina left the house one day, forgetting to leave the keys behind. As a result, her employers were obliged to wait for her to return and let them in. Upon her return the mistress flew into a rage, screaming blue murder:

> 'You . . . you . . . you . . . Russian dog!' she spluttered at Irina.
>
> 'People are products of the lives they live. Give us a dog's life, and what do you expect?' came Irina's reply.
>
> 'Go to your room!' she screamed. 'I don't want to see you.'

> 'And I haven't wanted to see you for the last two years,' Irina responded, throwing the keys at her and storming off to her room.
>
> The mistress's voice rang out from the bedroom, 'Don't forget that Dachau is just eleven kilometres from here . . .'

Galina Agranovskaya was sent to work as a domestic helper for a businessman in Frankfurt am Main. She remembers her joy at discovering a large library in his house, with a portrait of Leo Tolstoy hanging on the wall and many of the Russian classics in the bookshelves.

> 'Good Lord!' I thought. 'At last I can tell them that my Papa is a writer, and my Mama is a teacher.'
>
> But one day that wonderful woman who read Tolstoy and had given birth to these lovely children slapped me across the face for the most trivial matter. She claimed that I was peeling the potatoes too thickly.
>
> 'It's wartime now, and we must economise,' she said. 'Germany is having to spend vast sums of money to beat your monster.'
>
> [. . .] It was then that I realised that I meant nothing to her: I was nothing but a Russian *Schwein*.

'You could use it to buy needles and thread'

In accordance with a directive issued by Hermann Göring on 7 November 1941, all businesses were officially required to pay their eastern workers a wage. For the large plants and agricultural enterprises, this wage was to be paid weekly. This same directive also stipulated, however, that the pay was to be minimal – no more than pocket money. Farm workers and domestic helpers living with German families had very little security, and wages would often be paid intermittently, or sometimes not at all if an individual was considered to be working for their keep. The wage system vacillated constantly and payments depended not only upon the category of labour and whether or not

Harvest time on the outskirts of Ortelsburg, 1943.

A souvenir photograph from Kleve, 1943. On the reverse is written: *This is our employer – we work for him. The housemaid is sitting to his right – she works for him, and cooks lunch.*

quotas were met, but also on the politics relating to the use of foreign workers at any particular time. The *Ostarbeiter* explained that there were regular deductions for food and living costs, in addition to occasional further deductions for clothes, shoes and sometimes even transport to work. As a result, they were rarely left with more than three to five Reichsmarks in their pockets each week. Worse still, those working in the camps were often paid in camp tokens, with which they could only purchase items in their camp stores.

Frida Palko worked in a chemical factory in Ludwigsdorf. She said: 'They didn't pay me so much as a penny.'

Lidia Beketova worked in a factory producing optical instruments in Wedel: 'They paid us each week. We got one [Reichs]mark and a few pfennigs.'*

Fedor Khmara worked on a farm in Zwickau: 'Our employer paid us ten Reichsmarks per month.'

Olga Smirnova worked in the Siemens factory in Stuttgart. She said: 'They paid us in tokens, instead of money.'

Some described how they spent their money and what they were able to buy with their meagre wages. Georgiy Tkachov said: 'Money? Yes, we were paid. [. . .] But there was nowhere for us to spend it. It sat in our pockets like dead capital.'

---

* Translator's note: The pfennig was a monetary unit equal to one hundredth of a mark.

Eastern workers on a farm, 1942.

A memento, Dramburg, 1942. The text on the reverse reads: *The house belonging to my employers.*

Zinaida Valikhova remembered: 'There was a kiosk at the factory where I bought soap.'

And Vera Dergachova told us: 'They paid us once a week – just a small sum of money. You could use it to buy needles and thread at the shop. I remember buying sanitary towels and washing powder there too.'

Fedor Khmara recalled: 'I couldn't buy a single thing. I never even saw a shop in our village.'

Antonina Serdyukova told us:

> We bought things in the canteen shop. Later they began to pay us in Reichsmarks. It cost three sets of wages to buy a clean woollen jumper. [. . .] Those who worked in the 'hot' workshop were paid much more. They could go to the canteen shop once a month and buy whatever they needed. There was a small room in one of the camp barracks where a German man ran a shop, but only at certain times and on certain days.

'. . . to hurt those bastards'

Virtually none of the *Ostarbeiter* described taking part in any sort of underground activity. This is perfectly understandable – not only

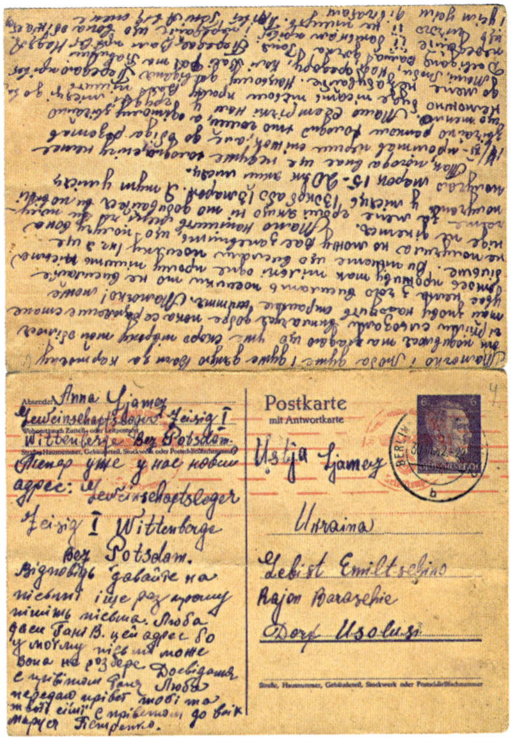

A postcard from Potsdam to the Zhytomyr region, dated 30 November 1942 (translated from Ukrainian):

> . . . Mummy, perhaps you don't have anything to put in a parcel, in which case don't worry about sending one. I'll make do. I do ask one thing though – please write more letters. You wrote that you sent a 1kg parcel. I haven't received it yet but I can assure you that I will get it – it won't get lost. Mama, write and tell me whether you received compensation for me. If not, then you must insist that you do. You should receive 130 *karbovanets** or 13 Reichsmarks per month. I get 15–20 Reichsmarks per month, depending on the month.

were most very young when they were sent to Germany, with no experience of underground movements, but those labouring at plants and factories were locked up in closed camps under the constant supervision of strict guards. And at the other end of the spectrum, the domestic and farm workers were usually utterly

* Translator's note: The Ukrainian *karbovanets* was the country's official currency for three separate periods of the nineteenth century.

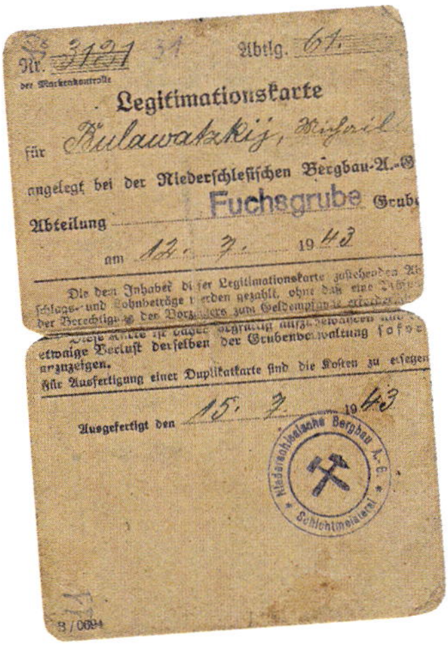

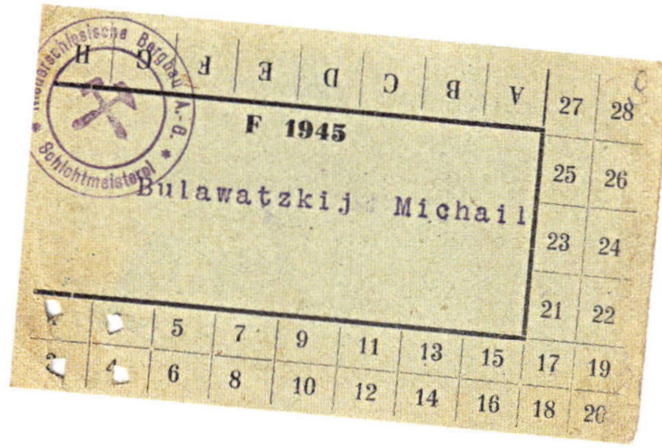

A wage card and an identity document belonging to a mineworker. Lower Silesia, 1945. The text on the reverse of the wage card reads: *Wages will only be paid upon presentation of this card alongside supporting identity documents. [. . .] Money must be counted immediately upon receipt; all later grievance claims will be disregarded.*

A photograph from the German Propaganda Bureau entitled: 'On the Status of Eastern Workers in Germany, 1942–1944.' (The State Archive of the Russian Federation, Fond. 7021, Opis'.116, Delo.389, List.74)

isolated, and therefore rendered incapable of playing a part in any collective subversive activities. However, rumours circulated in the camps that such organisations were operating. Mikhail Chernenko:

> A grown-up called Sergei immediately took me under his wing. He was acknowledged to be in a position of authority in the camp. People listened to him; he was the de facto boss. [. . .] He had links with the Brothers' Union of Prisoners of War [an anti-Fascist underground organisation established by Soviet prisoners of war. It operated between 1943 and 1944 and several *Ostarbeiter* joined its ranks]. He was directly involved, a real-life Stierlitz.*

* A reference to Stierlitz (Maxim Isayev), a Soviet spy who operated in the Third Reich and later became the hero of the popular Russian television series *Seventeen Moments of Spring* (1973).

Taissa Tolkachova:

> We had a Russian nurse at our camp. One day the police came and took her away. After that, people started talking – they said that she had links to the Partisans. It transpired that there was some sort of Partisan movement operating among the Russian workers at our camp – a group of people that tried to sabotage and damage things. [. . .] The nurse had been a member of this group.

Raissa Pervina also remembers an attempt to form an underground organisation, which ended in tragedy, due to betrayal:

> There was an incident where a man from another camp managed to persuade some of our guys to form an organisation of some sort. He suggested that I join too, but I didn't like him – I didn't believe the things he said. [. . .] I don't know who ratted on them, but a few people were taken away one night – mostly men. [. . .] We never found out what became of them.

Protests generally took a more mundane shape. The *Ostarbeiter*, for example, would often do all they could to help the Soviet prisoners of war, who endured significantly worse conditions in their camps. Tatiana Veselovskaya recalls: 'I remember throwing raw beetroots to our prisoners of war – they lived in such awful conditions. You had to throw them in such a way as to ensure that nobody saw you.'

Besides helping their imprisoned countrymen, some *Ostarbeiter* also made attempts, albeit only vocally, to contest their treatment as slaves by taking a stand against the insults and humiliation they were subjected to. Maria Ausheva remembers:

> There was one tall SS guy who all the Germans were afraid of. [. . .] While the battle for Stalingrad was raging, he came up to me and said, 'Maria, we're going to take your Russia. You'll be our slaves and then we'll really show you!'

He shook his big fist in my face. I thought to myself for moment, clenching my own skinny little fist, and then replied, 'And if we defeat you, then my hard little fist and I will show you.'

With that, he left, and the Germans scolded me, frightened.

'Maria,' they cautioned, 'he's SS. Even we are afraid of him. He won't think twice about killing you . . . Bang! And that will be that.'

A letter from Bremen to Weinbergen, 1944 (translated from Ukrainian):

. . . My friend, I received your letter, for which I send my heartfelt thanks – thank you for not forgetting me during these sad, unfortunate times. [. . .] I once told her [employer] that I wanted to go to the doctor, but she wouldn't let me go. She said I could go with the others once the harvest was over. But I argued with her, and told her that I was going to the doctor anyway, at ten o'clock that morning. It reached the point that we began fighting, and she told me that she would go to the police that same day.

'Go, then!' I told her.

Off I went to gather firewood, and she went to call the police. I had been sitting down for half an hour or so when she came running up.

'What have you been doing?' she asked. 'You've been out here for a whole hour and you've only got one basket of wood to show for it.'

But I had begun to work purposefully slowly, so that a task that should have taken just fifteen minutes, or at most two hours, took me four or five hours. She never spoke of our fight, but she did begin to swear at me. In turn, I took to working in such a way that she decided to send me away. My friend, I've now been at the employment office twice, and I told them everything; how she was always arguing with me . . .

Workers with their managers in a munitions factory, 1944. The text on the reverse reads: *My camp friends. The photo was taken on 14.03.44, in Germany; a land of slavery and oppression of different peoples. Duisburg*

The *Ostarbeiter* often felt compelled to defend their homeland and Soviet life when it was insulted, and in doing so, sometimes painted a picture rosier than reality. Tatiana Veselovskaya described a conversation she had with her German manager in the factory where she worked:

> 'Why d'you want to go back to Russia?' he asked me one day. 'In Russia everyone goes about in *lapti*.'*
>
> 'They do nothing of the sort,' I replied.
>
> I stood up for Russia – I was offended by his comment, even though we lived in a wooden house in Moscow where we had to stoke the stove ourselves, wash in an unlit corridor and use an outside toilet. Yes, our living conditions were poor. Whereas in Germany, the toilets even had toilet paper. [. . .]
>
> The manager pressed me further: 'Did you even have toilets like we do here, or did you go outside?'
>
> Of course we didn't have a toilet in the house. But I didn't tell him that.
>
> 'It was just the same as it is here,' I lied. 'We have the same baths, and bedding too, it's all just the same as here.'

Those who joined the Russian Liberation Army† were treated with

---

* Translator's note: Traditional Russian peasant shoes, made from bast that was woven to fit the foot.

† The Russian Liberation Army (RLA) was the name given to a collaborationist force, primarily composed of Soviet soldiers, that fought under German command during

demonstrable contempt. Anastasia Arkhipenko recalls a little ditty that the *Ostarbeiter* girls used to sing to the tune of the popular German wartime song 'Lili Marleen'. It mocked the 'Vlasovites', as those who joined the Russian Liberation Army became known.* 'We'd see an officer in German uniform bearing the emblem of the RLA (Russian Liberation Army) and by the next day we'd all be singing:

> Where once there was a privy, a big barracks now was laid,
> and there stood a Russian commander, in German uniform arrayed.
> What did you sell out the Motherland for? What was it that they gave?
> Perhaps some smelly cheese, or a spoonful of marmalade?
> Ah, Russian commander, so cheaply you betrayed!'

Anastasia's ditty was far from unique. The *Ostarbeiter* frequently used songs and poems to voice their feelings about life in Germany. An extract from a song taken from a collection in Memorial's archives goes:

> I'll tell you now, dear, about life as a prisoner;
> and all about life in the camps.
> About how the Germans hounded us with dogs,
> and the police strangled us in quiet doorways.

More often than not, protests sprang up as spontaneous reactions to persistent vexing, injustices and cruelty. But sometimes they were successful, as described by Mikhail Chernenko:

---

the Second World War. **Translator's note**: Many of the 'volunteer' soldiers are said to have been prisoners-of-war, who joined up to avoid starvation in prisoner-of-war camps. When, in 1945, it became clear that Germany faced inevitable defeat, the RLA joined the Czech uprising in Prague, fighting against the Germans. At the end of the war, any RLA soldiers unable to avoid forced repatriation faced sentences in the Gulag on their return to the Soviet Union. Several of the generals, including Andrey Vlasov, were hanged at Butyrka prison, Moscow.

* Translator's note: In reference to the Russian Red Army general Andrev Vlasov, who defected to Nazi Germany following capture during the siege of Leningrad and became the leader of the collaborationist RLA force:

> In the months leading up to spring of 1943, we had seen a dramatic decline in the quality of our bread, which very quickly deteriorated into something resembling clay. Dissatisfaction developed into something between a revolt and a hunger strike.
>
> 'Let's see if the *Lagerführer* will eat this,' someone said, throwing it at him. 'Here! Give it a try!'
>
> 'This is nothing short of clay. It's not fit to be eaten,' the *Lagerführer* agreed. Not long afterwards, perhaps just three or four days later, we had edible, albeit poor, bread to eat again.

Nadezhda Kepet relayed a remarkable tale of solidarity. At the mining plant where she worked, one of the factory floor foremen hit an elderly woman – an Italian worker. She fell and lost consciousness:

> We all got out from behind our machines, and stood up. We stood there, not just the Russians, but the other nationalities too. The chief workshop manager saw us from his glass cabinet. As a result of this spontaneous 'strike' of ours, the factory floor foreman was fired.

The workers would also engage in sabotage or petty vandalism from time to time, as Tatiana Zhelamskaya recalls: 'We were given cabbage or beetroot seeds to sow, but to hurt those bastards we would just dig a hole and bury the seeds in it.'

In some cases, when listening to stories of sabotage efforts, it was difficult to discern exactly which actions were conscious attempts by the *Ostarbeiter* to help their country fight the enemy, and which were instinctive attempts to alleviate, however briefly, their individual work burdens. Valeria Fyodorova, who worked in a brick factory in Tharau, Kaliningrad region, told us:

> When we could endure no more, we would throw stones into the clay mixture for the bricks. These stones broke the blades of the machines, and we were able to stop and rest while they were being repaired. But we couldn't do this often – if you were caught, the manager would beat you with whatever

A congratulations card, Hamburg, 1944 (translated from Ukrainian):

Happy 1st May, Yusya!!!
Congratulations, my dear friend, on the Great International 1st of May Holiday! Yusya, do you remember how we celebrated this day the proper way back home three years ago? We looked back on all our achievements with such enthusiastic optimism on that great day! We were so happy back then. And now? Now whole rivers are flowing with the blood of our fathers, brothers and sisters at the front. We too, the young workers of our country, agonise over the situation at the front. We cry bitter tears within the damp confines of these factories. Yulia, this is the view of the factory where, for two years now, we have been breaking our backs for these kulaks. But all this is merely temporary . . . any moment now the sun will come out and light up the road to a better future.

> he could lay his hands on, and threaten to turn you over to the police. That meant only one thing – arrest, followed by a concentration camp sentence.

Valeria also recalled that the camp inmates would deliberately inflict wounds upon themselves:

> You'd do it with something sharp – a knife, pin or a needle – you had to gouge out a little wound and then rub in some fresh buttercup. The buttercup juice and leaves ate away at the wound. It was painful, but when you were so tired that you were barely conscious, you could tolerate it. The wound would deteriorate overnight and in the morning you'd go to work and show it to the manager. The Germans had an absolute horror of infections of any sort.

Galina Shalankova recounted a frightening personal experience of her own:

I deliberately chopped off two of my fingers. If the Germans had found out that I had done this because I didn't want to work on the workshop floor I would have been taken straight to the Gestapo. [. . .] I placed two fingers down, and pressed . . . I didn't pass out, but I pretended that I had. I was taken away immediately – straight to the hospital. I was there for two weeks and then I was transferred to the laboratory to work as a cleaner.

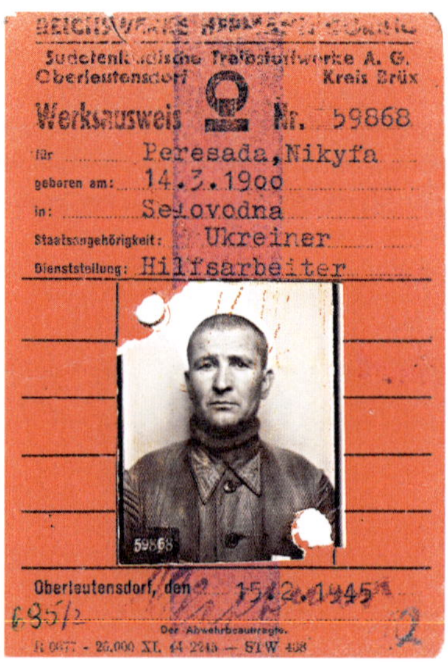

Sudetenländische Treibstoffwerke A. G.
Oberleutensdorf Kreis Brüx
Werksausweis Nr. 59868
für Peresada, Nikyfa
geboren am: 14.3.1900
in: Selovodna
Staatsangehörigkeit: Ukreiner
Dienststellung: Hilfsarbeiter
Oberleutensdorf, den 15.2.1945

A work pass for the railway, Hildesheim, 1943.

Владельцу сего разрешается выход из помещения единственно ради работы.
Arbeitskarte
für sowjetrussische Arbeitskräfte
aus dem altrussischen Gebiet
Inhaber ist nur zum Zwecke der Arbeitsverrichtung zum Verlassen der Unterkunft berechtigt.

A work card, munitions factory, Schönholz, Berlin, 1942. The print on the reverse reads: *The bearer of this card has permission to leave his area for work purposes only.*

The objectives of those who chose to harm themselves varied, and some preferred not to discuss the reasons behind their decision. Some hoped that they would be reallocated from heavy manual labour to something less demanding; others longed to be sent to the hospital for a brief rest. Perhaps some also believed that they might be sent home. Among all the stories that we heard, however, there were a few that left us in no doubt that their protagonists had acted out of a reluctance to work for the Germans.

Aldona Volynskaya recalled:

> We were sitting in the barracks when Lyonya – I can't remember his surname – came in. He held out his hand, which was bleeding, to show us the deep wound he had given himself between his thumb and first finger with an axe.
>
> 'To hell with them,' he said. 'I don't want to work for these people.'

Sometimes it was difficult to make sense of how injuries in the workplace had occurred. Taissa Tolkachova said: 'We made these little wheels. A few people were missing a finger, or half of one. They had been working on machines and had lost concentration for a minute, causing a finger to slip into the machine – just like a meat-mincer.'

Accidental injuries such as these, and similar incidents that occurred as a result of the inadequate training given to *Ostarbeiter* prior to starting work in the factories, often transmuted in people's minds over time into acts of protest. This was especially common during the post-liberation interrogations at the 'filtration camps', when many people sought to varnish their actions with patriotic 'intent'. Very often, these minor fabrications would become so deeply assimilated into an individual's personal myth that they too would come to believe them. It wasn't until the 1990s, when attitudes towards former *Ostarbeiter* began to change, that a few of the former 'eastern workers' admitted that while working in Germany, survival, and not sabotage, had been foremost on their minds.

Lidia Beketova worked in a factory manufacturing optical instruments in Wedel: 'We generally worked against our own people, polishing lenses that were clearly intended for some military purpose. But we didn't think about this – for some reason it wasn't something we ever considered.'

Of course, many *Ostarbeiter* were troubled by the knowledge that, directly or indirectly, their work was aiding the enemy. Many felt powerless and suffered from an acute sense of guilt towards family

Postcards depicting views of Dremmen, 1943. The text on the reverse reads: *A keepsake for my dear and beloved sister, Zinochka. From Valya. Dear Zinochka, this sequence of photos shows the village where I am living. The top one is a general view. The left one shows the main street and the right-hand one shows the former monastery, which is now the Russian camp. This is where I live. It looks very pretty from the outside, but life on the inside isn't great.*

members fighting at the front. Anna Odinokova describes her pain: 'I cried. Oh God! I thought, my father is on the front line right now. I'm fighting against my own father [. . .] And I'm helping the Germans . . .'

Having been sent to prison following an unsuccessful attempt to run away from her workplace, Anna Basarab assured her cellmates that it was better to be stuck in prison than to be making weapons for the Germans in a munitions factory. She recalls:

> The girls were all crying.
>
> 'What are you crying for?' I asked them. 'Lord knows, what will be will be. Surely it's no better to be there, building shells to be used against your brothers.'
>
> We weren't blind you see.

Sometimes the protests took an unexpected turn and had far-reaching consequences. Anna Kirilenko, who worked in a fabric factory in Düring, remembers that she and her fellow workers decided to celebrate the 1st of May holiday:

Workers at a munitions depot, Halberstadt, 1944. The text on the reverse reads: *This was taken in winter, now it is summer. But we aren't being given a work rotation [. . .] We thought there was truth to be found, and we searched for it. It's very hard for us to bear, especially as we have now found out . . .*

> I got a little red blouse from someone and hung it from a pole in place of a flag. Our colony sang as we marched along: 'Morning paints with a gentle light the walls of the ancient Kremlin. The whole of the Soviet land wakes up with the dawn.'* There were twenty of us. The foreman reported us – he recorded everything himself. [. . .] We were arrested shortly afterwards.

Following her arrest, Anna was transferred to Ravensbrück concentration camp.

'Where could you possibly go, if you looked like a "Russki"?'

The most common form of protest against the back-breaking labour and degrading treatment was escape. Many attempted to run away from their camps or employers, but it wasn't until the final months of the war, when Germany was on its knees and there were refugees everywhere, that chances of success increased. Up until this point, almost all of the escapees were captured although, remarkably, some did manage to make it as far as the western borders of Poland. Several of those we interviewed described escape efforts, namely: Galina Agranovskaya, Fedor Apyonkin, Anastasia Arkhipenko, Vera Bobrovskaya, Nikolai Bogoslavets, Vasily Demchuk, Grigory

* From the Soviet song 'Moscow in May'.

Dmitrash, Valentin Karvatovsky, Nikolai Kireev, Ivan Krasnov, Grigory Kulbaka, Igor Malitsky, Maria Mudrak, Neonila Rozhkova, Ivan Zapirin and Nikolai Zubkov.

The runaways were all very young when they made their escapes and, with the spontaneity of adolescence, they often set off with little preparation, and without pausing to consider the possible consequences of their actions. It wasn't difficult to wriggle out under the barbed wire or through the gates of the camp, and those living on the farms or with families often had no physical barriers standing in their way. But they usually failed to appreciate the challenges they would face having made their escape. First and foremost, where could they run to? After all, they were in an unfamiliar country, and most didn't speak the local language. Several runaways recalled that hunger ultimately drove them to seek assistance from local people.

Nikolai Kireev worked in a factory in Berlin. He told us:

> Life had become intolerable. Two experienced adults had run away the day before. [. . .] That planted the idea of escape in my mind. The work was beyond the limits of my endurance. I hid my OST badge – pinned it so that it couldn't be seen. I decided to quickly share my plans with Petka, who had the bunk next to me. We needed to run away, I told him, while we still could. So we ran away together.

Kireev and his friend spent their first night of freedom in an air-raid shelter at the other end of the town. However, hunger eventually drove them to steal, and they were caught one day while wandering about on the outskirts of Berlin. As a result, they were sent to a concentration camp.

Nikolai Bogoslavets managed to remain on the run for three whole weeks following his escape from a camp in Frankfurt an der Oder:

> All three of us ran away on Trinity Sunday. Before we made our escape, we took enough bread, tinned meat and salt from

Logging workers, Dietzhausen, 1944.

> our employer to get us started. And then we set off across Germany on foot. Now, I would think more carefully about what to take. [. . .] It was easy to run while we still had supplies of bread and meat. We'd sleep during the day, often in a copse or hidden among the corn, and then run through the night. The fields weren't big so you couldn't split the corn too much. And if you were hiding there, you had to lie very quietly so that any passers-by, or their dogs, didn't notice you were there. You covered yourself with wheat sheaves and had to lie there in line with the corn – if you lay crossways, you could be seen from the road.

Their supplies ran out, at which point they were caught:

> Our supplies ran out after three weeks, and Mitya began to cry because he was hungry. Another two days and we too would have been crying from hunger. Mitya couldn't bear it any longer – he went to ask some cowherds for a little food. That evening they invited us into their house, fed us, and put us up in their barn to sleep. In the morning we woke to find ourselves in handcuffs.

An extract from a letter written by Maria Fursevich to Memorial:

> I ended up with an employer who treated me very badly. I decided to run away from him. His wife had gone to a funeral that day – her sister had died – and I managed to escape that evening – I threw my things out of the window. I had persuaded one of the other girls to bring me some bread and accompany me to the woods. I walked through the night for two days, sleeping during the daytime. On the third morning I walked out onto a road and was caught by a policeman.

Stories circulated of people who had managed to escape and join up with the Partisans operating in the countries bordering Germany. Ivan Kosarevsky described his unsuccessful attempt to escape from a camp in Wuppertal:

> We decided one night that we needed to get out of there. Rumours had reached us of a Partisan cell operating in the mountains of France. [. . .] Six of us left one night. The barbed wire wasn't electric, so we just climbed over it and headed out of the city.

Agricultural workers, Eschwege, 1942. The text on the reverse reads: *The Russians and Ukrainians who helped me run away. I'm in the black dress.*

A factory camp, Lichtenberg, Berlin, 1943.

Deep down, many of them knew they wouldn't make it out of Germany. They ran away, not in the hope of reaching home, but in an effort to escape the gruelling factory work or the cruelty of their employers. Many hoped to find another workplace; somewhere where their lives might be slightly easier. This was Alexandra Mikhailova's goal, when she ran away from the munitions factory where she worked: 'What were our reasons for running away? We thought we might find a private employer to work for. We weren't afraid of work. We just wanted to eat; we wanted to escape the hunger.'

Alexandra and her friend roamed about Germany, looking for Russians who were working on farms:

> We arrived at some town, and asked whether there were any Russians there. I saw a girl approaching and asked her in German, 'Where are the Russians?' [. . .]
>
> We worked there for a couple of months. One morning I woke up and went down to the kitchen to find a policeman standing there. It was me he was after.
>
> 'You don't have any documents,' he said. 'You need to come with me to Lüneburg.' Off we went, and when we arrived, I saw them . . . Gestapo.

Alexandra was taken to Auschwitz concentration camp on 29 June 1944, before being moved to Mauthausen two months later, where she remained until the camp was liberated on 5 May 1945.

Vera Dergachova and her friend ran away from a camp at a munitions factory in Wittenberg:

> We ran off together. Lord, half of the camp was looking out for us, trying to help. They kept an eye on the guard – told us where he was going, where he was standing. There was some sort of shed on the other side of the camp. People helped to drag out a chair, then a table. We stood on the table, then climbed onto the chair, and up onto the barn roof. Then Maria and I jumped off the other side. [. . .] We went to the station, boarded a train, and off we went.

Vera's story is one of the rare accounts of a successful escape.

After many trials and tribulations, both she and Maria found work in the same German village, where they were able to remain until the end of the war.*

A postcard from Hof, Germany, to Nordhausen, Germany, dated 13 May 1943 (translated from Ukrainian):

> Greetings, Shura Vasilyevna! I'm sending you a handshake and a kiss on the lips today, when you receive my short letter. Shurochka, I wish you happiness and the best of health – may you return home in good health to begin your happy life once again. And may you forget this terrible sorrow, which now abides within everybody. Your heart and mind will carry the memory of the jacket potato and spinach to the grave – that food which sapped your vitality and wore you down, leaving whatever life blood remained to be drained by the padlocks, fences and cumbersome OST badges.

Aldona Volynskaya ran away from her employer with her girlfriends for company:

> I still can't remember why we ran away. The others just came up to me and said, 'We're leaving.'
>
> 'But what about me?' I replied.
>
> 'Well, pack your things then,' they said.
>
> And that was that.

A postcard from Kassel to the Vinnytsia region, dated 18 April 1943 (translated from Ukrainian):

* Translator's note: Vera was employed by a kindly woman called Frau Mainz. Vera credits Frau Mainz with saving her life, for when the Gestapo arrived at the village one day demanding to see the girls' documents (which neither possessed) Frau Mainz insisted on accompanying them both to the Gestapo's headquarters. This she did, despite warnings from the military police that she would not make the journey home should she choose to go with them. Following a humiliating interrogation described in a later chapter, both girls were issued with documents and returned to the village with Frau Mainz.

> To my Ukrainian homeland. Good day, my parents; my Papa, Mama, Styopa, Ganya, Petya, Tanya. I am sending my cordial greetings from great Germany. As I wrote in a previous letter, there are six of us here together, in the same place as before. My life and health are just as before. I can tell you though that there are only three of us left from the group that came to the mine. Ivan T. died on 30/III. [. . .] Please write and tell me whether you are working on the collective farm or planting at home (this is of great interest to me). How many lambs did Styopa's sheep have? [. . .] I wrote a postcard to tell you (so that you didn't write to me) that I was considering sharing the road with three girls, but plans fell apart. It's good that we didn't go in the end – it's not the right time.* Write and tell me about life with you – are things better or worse now? [. . .] Happy Easter! Write and tell me what dues you are paying. And perhaps someone else has returned home . . .?

For an escape to be successful, an *Ostarbeiter* had to dress carefully, so as not to attract attention. Considering their circumstances, this was far from easy. Aldona Volynskaya recalls that she had nothing to wear but an old dress belonging to her employer:

> It was absolutely riddled with moth holes – it took me about two weeks to darn them all. It had these whalebone hoops in the skirt – it must have been from the eighteenth century! I wore it with knee-high lace-up boots. In short, I had nothing normal to wear. My friend had to give me a skirt. [. . .] Elka took a little Spanish suitcase from her employer – she was very proud of that little lacquered case. I was also guilty of some thievery – I took some little 'Farewell, youth'-style boots† to wear.

* Translator's note: Possibly an allusion to the failed escape attempt of Aldona Volynskaya and her two friends.

† Translator's note: The name given in Russia to a certain (unflattering) style of short winter boot, made from felt.

Despite their apparent naivety, Aldona and her friend succeeded in making it as far as Poland:

> First, we bought tickets to Berlin. We sat there on the platform and ripped up our documents – our identity cards . . . everything. Then we went and bought tickets to Poland [. . .] The train crossed the Polish border and stopped at a small station. We saw a group of policemen approaching the train, so we ran to the carriage at the rear, and jumped out. We ran down the tracks until we reached a fork. We didn't know which to take, so we asked someone which track led to Russia.
>
> 'The military police headquarters is over there,' came the reply. 'Go and ask there.'

The unsuccessful runaways all remembered the moment they were either turned in, or caught by the police. Encounters with German teenagers were particularly dangerous – their training in the Hitler Youth organisation had imbued many with an alert watchfulness from which it was difficult to hide.

Ivan Kosarevsky fell foul of the Hitler Youth:

> All of a sudden, three boys tore past on their bikes. It must have been they who noticed us and tipped off the Gestapo. An hour or so passed, maybe more, and then suddenly motorcycles appeared, first from one side, then the other. 'Ah! Russians! Come here, quickly, you swine.' Then, crack! They started shooting from their rifles. Well, there was nothing we could do. That was that; we had been caught. [. . .] We went over to them, they seized us . . . and took us to the Gestapo.

Nikolai Kireev: 'Where was there to run, when every boy around you was German? They paid them a reward for catching Russians. And catch us they did. So where could you possibly go, if you looked like a "Russki"?'

Nikolai Bogoslavets described his own failed attempt at escape: 'It was only later that we found out that every Pole who caught a

Camp at the Salamander factory, Kornwestheim, 1942. The text on the reverse reads: *Girls of misfortune, I won't forget you. Dusya*

fugitive received a reward. They just handed us over to the German police headquarters and we were sent to a punishment camp.'

The captured runaways were often beaten ruthlessly; some were beaten to death. The punishments meted out to escaped prisoners of war were particularly brutal. Mikhail Chernenko recalls: 'In the first few days following our arrival at the camp, two people escaped from the prisoner-of-war barracks. They were caught, and shot. Their corpses were brought back to the camp, to make a point.'

Vera Fedorchenko: 'Two lads ran away from our camp. [. . .] They were caught three days later and beaten to death – blood flew in all directions.'

According to Vadim Novgorodov, the punishments meted out to runaways depended very much upon on the individual camp authorities:

> I remember returning from the night shift when suddenly the camp director walked up to me. 'Fetch your things and come with me,' he said. [. . .]
>
> He needed me to translate for him. We drove to another camp where we found a young lad from our own camp. He had escaped, and then been caught. The camp commandant hit him, put him in the car, and didn't lay another finger on him. He scolded him all the way back to camp. This director never sent a single runaway to a concentration camp – there were

cases where people had escaped, been caught and brought back, and then stayed on to work in the camp.

Work camp at Wilhemshafen shipyard, 1943.

A postcard from Osnabrück to the Zhytomyr region, 1943 (translated from Ukrainian):

> An enduring memento for my beloved family while I am away in Germany working at a furniture factory, from your daughter and sister, Nadia. I send a greeting to my loved ones in my dear Ukrainian motherland from the far reaches of this foreign country.
>
> Together we lived and walked the German roads,
> Awaiting our fate and when we would be free.
> Expect my return soon, and please remember me.

Typical punishments for captured runaways included a spell in a solitary confinement cell, reallocation to heavy manual labour, or a month-long transfer to prison or a punishment camp. Others paid a higher price and were transferred directly to a concentration camp. This was the fate that befell two friends who ran away together: Vera Bobrovskaya and Neonila Rozhkova. They were caught on their third day on the run. They described the moment of their arrest: 'Like many runaways, we lied and said that our train had left us behind. They threw us to the floor and beat us with whatever they could lay their hands on – sticks, whips . . . Then they took us to Mauthausen.'

'The *Appell* went on for ever'

Almost all of the *Ostarbeiter* spoke of the punishments they suffered. These varied in severity from a slap in the face from an employer, to being sent to a concentration camp.

In the factories it was usually the workshop managers who meted out the punishments, which could be administered for a variety of 'transgressions', from a careless blunder or a mistake at work, to behaviour that was considered impertinent. In the work camps, it was the guards and *Lagerführer* who decided on the reprimands for failure to adhere to camp rules and routines, or other such minor offences. But captured runaways, or workers suspected of sabotage or theft, were handed straight to the Gestapo. Following an interrogation during which they were beaten, they would be sent to prison, and from there to a punishment or concentration camp.

Vladimir Shchebetyuk was fifteen years old when he was deported to Germany and sent to work on a farm. He ran away, and managed to make it as far as Slovakia, where he joined the Partisans. However, a short time later he was caught, along with some of the Partisans, and taken to the Gestapo: 'They kept us there for a week, and beat us. After the interrogation we were sent to the central prison in Vienna. It was a frightening place. Some people were shot on the spot, and the others were sent to a concentration camp.'

Lavrenty Novokhatko was accused of sabotage and arrested while working at a railway station in Neudietendorf:

> There was a preliminary detention cell at the police station, but it felt like a prison cell – the walls were absolutely covered with different swear words and curses. I can still remember the following quatrain written on the wall in Russian: 'Don't lose heart, Russian folk/ You suffer now, but don't lose hope/

Above: Mine workers, Schöneberg, 1944.

Left: Mine workers, Holzwickede, 1942.

Someday your loved ones will justice restore / routing the Germans and settling the score.'

I was held in that prison for 46 days – we were each kept in solitary confinement.

Nikolai Kireev was badly beaten by the Gestapo on a number of occasions and sent to two punishment camps (at Grossbeeren and Buchenwald), having been caught stealing and attempting to escape several times. He was later transferred to Mauthausen concentration camp:

The first camp was Grossbeeren – it was a punishment camp on the outskirts of Berlin. There was a specific punishment camp system: two months' imprisonment, and then *Entlassen**, they alleged. They claimed that if you served your sentence with good grace, you'd be freed. But it was all just a game, nothing but lies and deceit. Some people really, truly believed – and

* Release.

I too believed – that we would be freed. But it transpired that they had a system in place – at the end of your two months, they'd take you straight back to the Gestapo, and you'd repeat the whole torturous process. The Gestapo would keep you for a while, and then you'd be sent to a different camp.

A memento sent from one friend to another – both Ukrainian *Ostarbeiter* women working in Germany. From Bremen to Weinbergen, 1944. The accompanying text (translated from Ukrainian) reads:

Greetings, my dear and esteemed friend, Dasha. Before I begin my short little letter, I shall let you know that I am alive and well, and hope that you are too, in your young and blossoming life. [. . .] Life is just as before, and I'm still in the same place. I don't have a boyfriend so I'm still alone for now. Dasha, I have five cows to look after – I really wish they'd go to hell, because my fingers really hurt. And we have a cow that lives in the house and only gets let out in the mornings. Don't be angry, Dasha, and don't go there with those guys. I wanted to take the train to Filsen, Dasha, but I ended up being grounded instead for seven weeks as punishment for returning home late one night. [. . .] Life was terribly depressing when I first got here, but now after this, it is even worse. I'll leave my short letter there. I'll await your reply like the nightingale waits for summer. Don't forget to write.

According to the *Ostarbeiter* we spoke to, life in the punishment camps differed very little from that in the concentration camps. Nikolai Zubkov told us:

> I spent two months in Lanzendorf punishment camp. Life there was such that when we were taken out to work there would always be some people on the brink of death – already of no use to anyone. They would die right there in the truck – just roll over, dead. It was the same story on the way back – two or three people would be dead. [. . .] The bodies were taken away – there was no crematorium there. Anyone who was still alive two months later was transferred to a concentration camp.

Nikolai Kireev described the beatings at the punishment camp he was sent to:

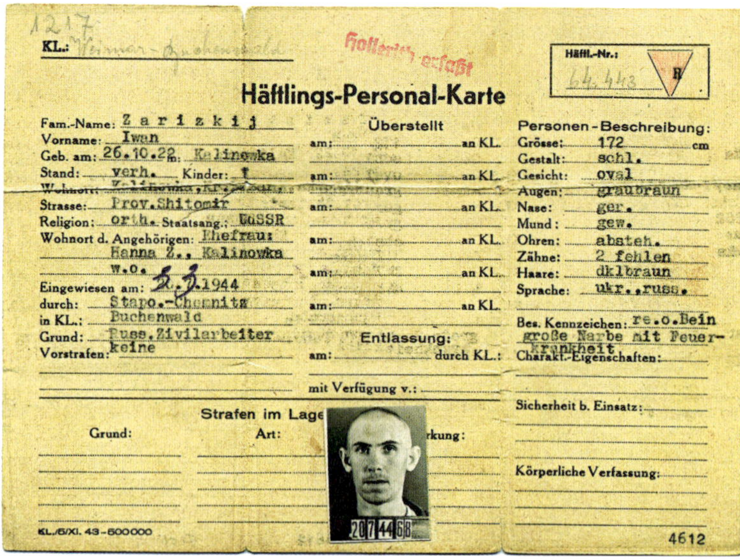

KL.: Weimar-Buchenwald

Hollerith erfaßt

Häftl.-Nr.: 64.443

R

Häftlings-Personal-Karte

Fam.-Name: Zarizkij
Vorname: Iwan
Geb. am: 26.10.22 in: Kalinowka
Stand: verh. Kinder: 1
Strasse: Prov.Shitomir
Religion: orth. Staatsang.: UdSSR
Wohnort d. Angehörigen: Ehefrau: Hanna Z., Kalinowka W.O.
Eingewiesen am: 3.3.1944
durch: Stapo.-Chemnitz
in KL.: Buchenwald
Grund: Russ.Zivilarbeiter
Vorstrafen: keine

Überstellt
am: an KL.

Entlassung:
am: durch KL.:
mit Verfügung v.:

Personen-Beschreibung:
Grösse: 172 cm
Gestalt: schl.
Gesicht: oval
Augen: graubraun
Nase: ger.
Mund: gew.
Ohren: absteh.
Zähne: 2 fehlen
Haare: dklbraun
Sprache: ukr.,russ.

Bes. Kennzeichen: re.o.Bein große Narbe mit Feuer-krankheit
Charakt.-Eigenschaften:
Sicherheit b. Einsatz:
Körperliche Verfassung:

Strafen im Lager
Grund: Art: Bemerkung:

20744

KL./5/XI. 43-500000

4612

An identity card from Buchenwald concentration camp, 1944.

> Twelve, or *zwölf*, was considered an appropriate number – twelve strikes with a flex cable, on the same area of skin. You had to lie down on a bench. Well, these twelve strikes were delivered with such force that you couldn't even get to your feet afterwards. You had to slide yourself off the bench, somehow put your trousers back on and shuffle away. They had heavy cables, with lead cores, so each strike felt as though it was a hammer-blow.

Generally, however, life in the concentration camps such as Auschwitz, Ravensbrück and Mauthausen was infinitely worse.

Olga Smirnova was sent to Ravensbrück when she was caught trying to run away. She remembers:

> We were woken at 5 a.m. for *Zählappell**, where we were counted. [. . .] People died every single day – they hanged themselves in the toilets or electrocuted themselves because the *Appelle* were so grim - they went on for ever. Some of the prisoners were Jehovah's Witnesses, who had been sent to the

* Roll call.

Auschwitz registration photograph, 1944.

> camp purely because they did not support the war.* As soon as the signal was sounded – like a war trumpet – they all had to cover their faces with their arms and sit down on the ground. They sat right where they were, and we had to drag them into rows and count them. Come rain or snow, they had to sit, covering their faces with their hands.

Domnikiya Skiba was sent to Ravensbrück for singing a Soviet song with her friends in the barracks of her work camp. First, the girls were beaten, and then they were taken to the concentration camp: 'I felt that I had landed in hell on earth. There were hordes of people walking about like corpses; they were emaciated, nothing but bones.'

Dina Stefanenko was a prisoner at Auschwitz. She remembers: 'The dead were removed from the barracks each day and piled up outside. The barracks supervisor counted up the dead and the living. Nobody attempted to do a runner or hide.'

Vladimir Shchebetyuk was transferred from prison in Vienna to Mauthausen concentration camp. He describes his first impressions:

> No sooner had we begun climbing down from the train cars than we were assailed by whips, truncheons and dogs – they

* Translator's note: Jehovah's Witnesses endured intense persecution by the Nazis, in part due to their commitment to peace, and hence their opposition to war.

> met us with automatic rifles, whips and dogs. We knew then that we had arrived somewhere even worse. [. . .] 'Remove your clothes!' they shouted. We were taken to the bathhouse where they seized our clothes. We were given a stripy uniform instead, and wooden clogs. Anybody with any hair had it shaved off with a machine that left neat little paths across their head. Then we were escorted to Block 17 and I remember going up to one of the prisoners of war and saying, 'Hey, Mister! When will we get out of here?'
>
> And he just looked at me, that prisoner of war. He was older than me. Then he replied, 'We'll all find our freedom through that chimney over there.'
>
> He pointed to the crematorium next to Block 16, where all those who died were incinerated. To this day I cannot stand the smell of burning skin.

Some of our interviewees spoke of the difficulty of putting up with other *Ostarbeiter*, who had been given responsibilities by the Germans in the work camps, either as 'elders' or 'brigade leaders'. But in the concentration camps, the cruelty and disloyalty suffered at the hands of 'one's own people' were far worse. Valentina Sekhina recalls:

> There was one encounter with an *Aufseherin** that I remember – it happened the first time I went to get water or have a wash. She was a prisoner herself, believe it or not – the *Aufseherin* were chosen from among the prisoners. They truly went out of their way to give us a hard time. This particular time, she really whacked me on the head. I didn't fall, but I saw stars. I couldn't fathom why she had done it. What had I done? I gathered later that I had splashed a few drops of water on the floor. It was hardly a crime.

* A female overseer or supervisor appointed by the Germans from among the prisoners.

Life in the work camps seemed almost normal when compared with the concentration camp regime. Alexandra Mikhailova recalls:

> When I was sent to the concentration camp, I completely switched off. I didn't think about anything. In the work camps, my thoughts had sometimes wandered to my father, mother and brother. But in the concentration camp I thought of nothing and no one. I didn't think about myself either . . . I felt as though I had flown away somewhere; as though I had left Earth entirely. [. . .] Perhaps this is what saved me. I had often cried at the work camp, and spent a lot of time worrying. But at the concentration camp, I neither cried nor laughed. All thoughts had flown from my head; it was as though I was no longer living on this Earth.

'The *Revier** was next to the crematorium'

Remembering their lives in Germany, many *Ostarbeiter* recounted tales of illness, injury and death. For those detained in concentration camps, sickness was akin to a death sentence. Vasily Domoratsky described his experience in Mauthausen concentration camp:

> Each day we went to work. And then I became ill with phlegmon [inflammation of the soft tissues]. My foot swelled up completely and I could no longer walk on it. I fell down. I was immediately transferred to a different group, in the *Revier*. The *Revier* was next to the crematorium. It consisted of a couple of barracks, and we lay two to a crib on bunk beds, sleeping head to toe. I shared with a Polish guy. I lay down for a while and felt him go cold. He was dragged away.

Anyone who had suffered the misfortune of falling ill in a concentration camp expressed their surprise and amazement at having

* *Revier*: an abbreviation of *Krankenrevier*, the German word for sickbay. For many, the word was synonymous with death.

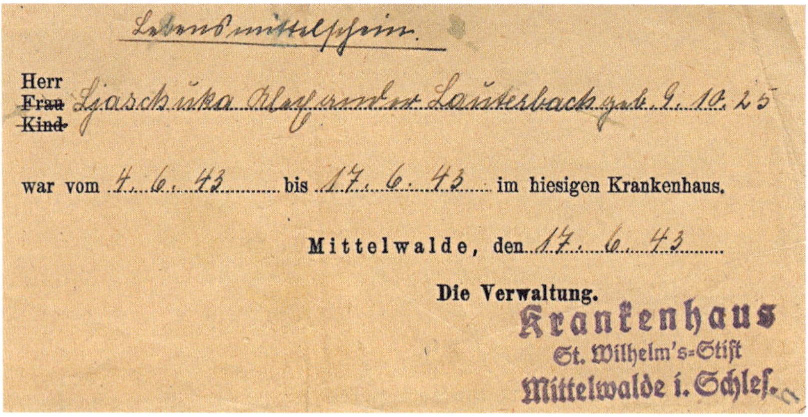

Lebensmittelschein.

Herr ~~Frau~~ ~~Kind~~ [illegible] geb. 9. 10. 25

war vom 4. 6. 43 bis 17. 6. 43 im hiesigen Krankenhaus.

Mittelwalde, den 17. 6. 43

Die Verwaltung.

Krankenhaus St. Wilhelm's-Stift Mittelwalde i. Schles.

A hospital note confirming that the bearer underwent treatment for the amputation of a left hand, Mittelwalde, 1943.

survived. Looking back on his time in Mauthausen concentration camp, Mikhail Daragan said:

> I remember the cold of winter. [. . .] I once fell ill with a temperature of 40 degrees. But there was a mandate that anyone who developed an incurable illness was to be shot on the spot. I was lucky to be examined by a Russian prisoner-of-war doctor. He said that my illness wasn't life threatening, but he whispered in my ear that I had pleurisy. I was sent to the *Revier*, where I lay for two or three weeks. But the food was a bit better there, so my condition improved, despite having virtually no medicine.

Sometimes a helping hand meant the difference between life and death. Anna Basarab described her experience in Auschwitz:

> I ended up in the hospital wing with inflammation of the lungs. [. . .] But the barracks supervisor was a good Polish woman. Some other Polish people brought her some pills to give to me. [. . .] I was so ill that I couldn't stand, but thankfully my body was still healthy. The Polish woman would sneak me the pills when nobody was looking. I would take them, silently, and my health began to improve. I lay in the hospital for a month, barely lifting myself from the bed. When I was ready, she came

> and took me back to her barracks – she was a good woman. Her name was Stasya.

Even the tough conditions endured by *Ostarbeiter* labouring in the mines and factories were preferable to those in the concentration camps. Cases of people falling ill and dying were far less common in the work camps. Particularly in the early years, most *Ostarbeiter* deported to Germany were strong, healthy young men and women, and medical assistance was usually provided to those who fell ill in the work camps or on the farms. The most frequent health issues to arise were workplace injuries or illnesses such as typhoid, dysentery, tuberculosis and scabies. Some also recalled suffering from boils, pleurisy and inflammation of the lungs. Victor Shuldeshov:

A memento from Wedel, 1944. The text on the reverse reads (translated from Ukrainian): *This is how I looked in late September 1943 in the far-off country of Austria. I was working in a factory in the city of Wedel. In mid-December 1943 my left arm was permanently damaged there. I am now missing one hand.*

> There was an outbreak of typhoid in the camp – it was spread by lice. The camp was quarantined and the management figures all ran away. We weren't allowed out though – they went to great lengths to coop us up and nobody was allowed to come within a hundred metres.

Mikhail (Misha) Chernenko said:

> I contracted typhoid in the winter of 1942. I was taken to the camp hospital ward for infectious diseases, where I lay unconscious for eight days. Somehow, I recovered. [...] A few months later I returned to the camp, where it was widely

> believed that I had died. I can still remember walking past an open window by Barracks One. One of the 'Easterners' was cleaning the glass. His jaw dropped, and then he let out an awful scream and fell to the ground. I had no idea why he was screaming, but it later transpired that he thought he had seen the ghost of Misha!

Vadim Novgorodov told us: 'Lots of people contracted lymph node tuberculosis. Some even died from it, especially the Ukrainians from the Vinnytsia and Zhytomyr regions. It was either brought on by the damp climate or lack of food.'

A postcard from Hermsdorf to Bremen, dated 2 March 1944 (translated from Ukrainian):

> Good day, my dearest and most esteemed sister, Marusya Ivanovna! I am sending you my candid, sad, sisterly greetings from the very bottom of my heart. Marusya, I am still alive and well, and hope that you are too. I also hope dearly that I will soon return to my homeland of Ukraine for a happy reunion with my elderly parents, brothers and sisters, and all my friends. You know all about my life. I do the washing; the work is hard. I've been left on my own because my first friend at work, Galya, is lying ill in the infirmary for the third week in a row, and she isn't getting better. They suspect she may have tuberculosis – a dangerous illness. Tina is also in the infirmary – her wisdom teeth are coming through. Katya left yesterday. Other than that, everyone is alive and well for now. I received your postcard, Marusya, and I send you my heartfelt thanks for not forgetting me in this alien country. Goodbye for now, a thousand kisses on your ruby red lips. Galya.

Anna Basarab remembered:

> One day I developed a rash out of the blue. I sat and cried – my skin was red all over. Christya told me not to cry. 'I'll bring you

> a cream to clear it up,' she said. It was a sulphur ointment and, sure enough, after three applications the blotches disappeared. But that rash was frightening all the same.

Aldona Volynskaya and Anna Miftakhutdinova, who lived with the families they worked for, remember going to the dentist. The costs of the visits were covered by an insurance fund, to which the employer was required to contribute. It was for this reason that future employers looked into the mouths of those that they were considering hiring at the labour exchanges – they wanted to make sure that their teeth were strong and healthy. The same insurance fund also covered appendix removals. Anna Miftakhutdinova recalls having hers taken out: 'I was taken to the hospital with appendicitis. The doctor removed it under anaesthetic.'

A postcard from Metz to Kamenets-Podolsk, 30 July 1943 (translated from Ukrainian):

> Good morning or good evening to you, my dear family! This is to you, Yefimiya, as well as the children: Ganya, Dunka and Vanka. I am sending you a warm greeting and wish you all the very best of success in your lives. May God bless you with health and happiness. I am alive and well for now. I'm in a camp in the same place as before and, as of 8 June, I had about two months off work following my operation. But now I have been sent back to work – I started again on 28 July. I work at a mine – on the surface, but the work is hard there too. My health is a little better for now, but who knows whether it will remain so. They gave me some sort of belt to tie around my waist after the operation. I haven't received any letters from you, except the one dated 25 May. But I sent you four postcards. [. . .] There is just one problem – I haven't got any thread with which to mend my clothes. You can't get any here. Write to me with all your news and let me know about the harvest. Goodbye then, good health to you all. S.A.

Some suffered from afflictions brought on by the psychological stress of life in Germany. Following her miraculous escape from death in her hometown of Starodub, Frida Palko lived in the Third Reich under counterfeit documents that disguised the fact that she was a Jew. Living in constant fear of discovery took its toll, however, and she developed a nervous disorder:

> What brought it on? You know, I was afraid of everything. If I spotted a person resembling someone from my hometown of Starodub I would think they were going to kill me. One day, I had a fit. It was as though I had epilepsy – I quivered for three days straight. A German man called the doctor, who gave me a pill of some kind. It was my nerves that caused the fit. Oh well, I remember thinking, the sooner I die the better; at least I will be spared this torment.

Frida managed to recover from her illness, but others were less fortunate. Victor Zhabsky recounted the tragic story of a teenage boy from Novocherkassk, for whom life in Germany proved too much to endure. Zhabsky, who was just fourteen years old himself when he was deported, recalls that Nikolai Yefimov began to cry, at first silently, almost immediately after their group departed their home city:

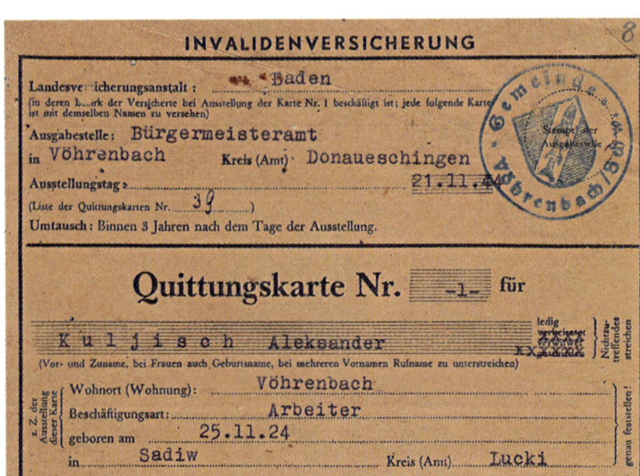
INVALIDENVERSICHERUNG

Landesve[...]icherungsanstalt: Baden
(in deren B[...]rk der Versicherte bei Ausstellung der Karte Nr. 1 beschäftigt ist; jede folgende Karte ist mit demselben Namen zu versehen)
Ausgabestelle: Bürgermeisteramt
in Vöhrenbach Kreis (Amt): Donaueschingen
Ausstellungstag: 21.11.44
(Liste der Quittungskarten Nr. 39)
Umtausch: Binnen 3 Jahren nach dem Tage der Ausstellung.

Gemeinde Vöhrenbach
Stempel der Ausgabestelle

Quittungskarte Nr. -1- für

Kuljisch Aleksander — ledig
(Vor- und Zuname, bei Frauen auch Geburtsname, bei mehreren Vornamen Rufname zu unterstreichen) — Nichtzutreffendes streichen

z. Z. der Ausstellung dieser Karte:
Wohnort (Wohnung): Vöhrenbach
Beschäftigungsart: Arbeiter
geboren am 25.11.24
in Sadiw Kreis (Amt) Lucki
genau feststellen!

Disability insurance document, Vöhrenbach, 1944.

> He was a grown up boy of fourteen for goodness' sake! It was a disgrace the way he snivelled and cried. He had never been away from home, you see. Not even to a Pioneers' camp – he had never been far from his parents' side. [. . .] He cried as we walked along the road to Rostov, cried on the train, cried and snivelled at the camp. 'What's all this crying for, Nikolai?' I'd ask him. It was clear that he was losing his mind. He was taken to the infirmary. [. . .] I went to see him one evening after work. None of the other guys went to see him, but I did. He lay in there for three days, and then on the fourth day I was told that he had been taken away.
>
> 'What do you mean, taken away?' I asked. 'Where has he been taken?'
>
> 'He died,' came the reply.
>
> He was our first fatality.

The *Ostarbeiter* had fond memories of the German doctors and nurses who helped them. Victor Shuldeshov remembers the camp doctor who gave him a tetanus vaccination:

> The camp commandant had a German shepherd. It was always biting us and also got me once. I've still got the scar. [. . .] There was an Austrian guy at our camp – I'm not sure whether he was a doctor or just a hospital attendant, but he was very kind to the Russians. I went to see him and showed him the bite mark.
>
> 'I'm going to give you an injection,' he said. 'It's one that you can't get in Russia. It will last your whole life – dogs can bite you all they like and you'll be fine.'
>
> After that, when I was bitten by a dog, I didn't have to go to the doctor. It was a special sort of injection that lasted your whole life.

A postcard from Hof to Nordhausen, dated 13 April 1944 (translated from Ukrainian):

> Shurochka my dear sister. Our little Ukrainian birdie. I'll describe my life for you [. . .] I'm alive, my sister, but I won't be able to live like this much longer. I'm reaching my limit. I haven't written to anyone and haven't said a word to anyone back home – I don't want them to know of my sorrows until I die. Then the girls will write and tell them everything. Oh, Shurochka, how I have suffered. There isn't a hospital left in this city that I haven't been to, but nothing helps. [. . .] At first, I tried to find cures myself – I went to the steam room. But then the doctor gave me an injection and some tablets. Now, however, the doctor refuses to give me another injection. He says that I must write to my director and request time off work. I haven't worked for a week now and today the general supervisor said that I would be sent home. But I don't know when or where they will send me. Shurochka, God only knows whether the transport will take me back to Ukraine. Perhaps I will be taken to another camp where I'll starve to death more quickly. [. . .] So there you have it, Shurochka – I've briefly described my life and sorrow. Please send me some food coupons – if you have them. [. . .] Goodbye, my dear sister. Write and send me a letter as soon as you can, because I may perhaps soon leave this unhappy life behind me for ever. Sonya.

Irina Sokolova worked for a German doctor who helped one of her friends when he was ill by providing him with medicine:

> When Misha fell ill, the lads told me that he was going to die. I begged the doctor on my knees to go and take a look at him.
>
> 'I can't go and see him,' he told me. 'If I went, it would likely cause some unpleasantness for him. You go, and come and tell me what his symptoms are.'
>
> He appeared to be suffering from a twisted bowel. I came back and described Misha's symptoms to the doctor, who gave me some medicine. I didn't have permission to pass through the factory, so I handed the medicine to the lads and told them what to do. They gave him the medicine to treat the

> obstruction, and he survived. I was very grateful to the doctor for agreeing to help.

Sometimes the Germans they worked with also helped. Larisa Shvidchenko remembers: 'The German women would give us medicine if we needed it – if we had a temperature or injured a hand, for example. Unlike us, they had a pharmacy in their living quarters. We worked in the lathe workshop, and hot chips were always flying about.'

Fatalities in the work camps and private workplaces were fairly rare. Mikhail Chernenko recalled: 'There weren't many fatalities. I can remember all those who died in the first work camp, although unfortunately I can't remember them all by name. Let me see, there were . . . one, two, three, four. I can't remember if there was a fifth.'

Raissa Pervina also remembered: 'A few people caught colds, but there weren't many fatalities. The first year was especially difficult – lots of people fell ill that year.'

Galina Shalankova recalls an explosion at the factory where she worked: 'The shockwave propelled us out onto the street. Nobody was hurt, except for one girl: Anya Kalabukhova. She died, and we buried her there in the cemetery.'

As the end of the war drew closer and the bombing intensified, the number of fatalities among the *Ostarbeiter* began to rise. Those who worked in munitions factories were particularly at risk, as these manufacturing plants were targeted on a regular basis. Georgiy Tkachov said:

> Quite a few bombs fell on our factory. [. . .] Everyone who was inside at the time perished. They laid the burnt bodies out between the fields and the camp, and then the scorched corpses were taken away. I never went to the cemetery, but some of the other guys went. [. . .] They said that it was a very orderly cemetery. It was here that they were buried – in Stettin. Everybody was buried separately, rather than in shared graves. I'm not sure whether they just wrote numbers on the gravestones, or whether they stencilled people's surnames onto them.

A camp affiliated with the Telefunken factory, Berlin, 1944.

Antonina Serdyukova told us:

> Then the bombing started in Germany. It was the English bombing us. They wanted to bomb the factory where I worked, but bombs landed on our camp instead – they couldn't be entirely accurate. There was an enormous blast at our camp one day. More than two hundred people were killed outright. We buried them in a mass grave just beyond the camp fence. We dug a vast ditch and laid them out in rows ourselves. This was already 1944.

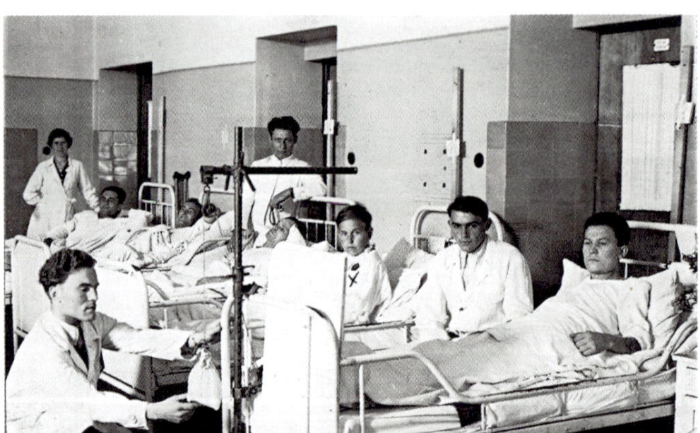

Men recovering in hospital following a bombing raid, Frankfurt an der Oder, 1945.

Many of the elderly *Ostarbeiter*, those who survived into old age, blamed the war, and their forced labour in Germany, for health problems that plagued them later in life. Tatiana Teplova said:

> I haven't yet mentioned this, but for me working on the railway was hardest of all. I had to clean the steam trains and stoke coal into the furnaces [. . .] I really busted a gut; it made me very ill.

Similarly, Nadezhda Bulava recalled: 'My poor head put up with so much. And my feet too! My feet, my head . . . I can't tell you how they hurt. It's the war that's to blame for it all.'

After Work

'Here in Germany, our youthful years are passing by'
In spite of the lack of information on the reality of the lives of *Ostarbeiter* in Germany, one oversimplified stereotype persisted. People spoke of back-breaking labour, beatings and OST badges worn upon chests, but very little was known about what the workers did in their spare time. Had they, in fact, enjoyed any free time at all? For many years the *Ostarbeiter* sought to avoid all discussions on this topic, afraid that they might convey an impression that life in Germany hadn't been entirely bad.

A postcard sent to a friend in a work camp, Stuttgart, 28 November 1943 (translated from Ukrainian):

> An enduring and memorable keepsake for my dear friend Zhenya Romanyuk . . . during the difficult minutes of this German life in the city of Stuttgart. 28/11-43. Nadya + Zhenya are friends. With fondest wishes, Nadya.

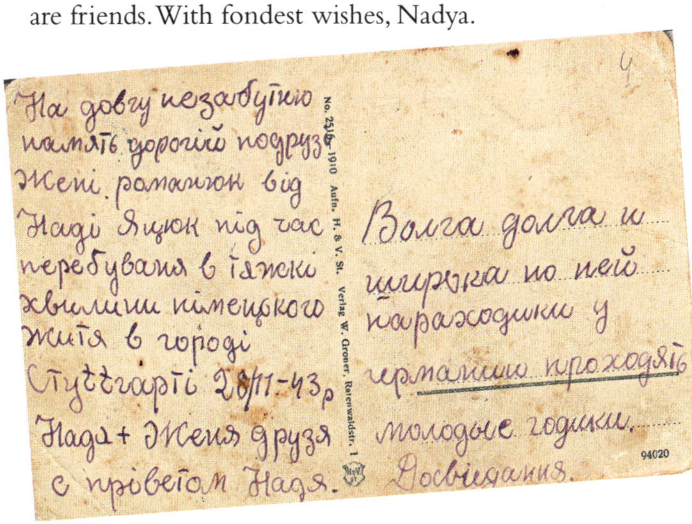
На довгу незабутню
память дорогій подрузі
Жені романюк від
Наді Яцюк під час
перебування в тяжкі
хвилини німецького
життя в городі
Стуттгарті 28/11-43 р
Надя + Женя друзя
с привітом Надя.

Волга долга и
широка по ней
пароходики у
германии проходять
молодые годики.
Досвиданния.

A tin factory work camp, Hamburg, 1944.

A metalworking factory work camp, Berlin, 1943.

Steam boats puff slowly
Down the Volga, long and wide
But here in Germany
Our youthful years are passing by.

Officially, *Ostarbeiter* were required to work six days a week, with a day off every Sunday. But in both the work camps and private enterprises much depended upon the individual in charge, be that the camp authorities or the employer. A ten- or twelve-hour shift in a munitions factory or a mine left workers with precious little free time. All they really wanted to do when they finished work was sleep; sometimes they lacked even the energy for a conversation. In an extract from his memoir, Lev Mishchenko (a prisoner of war) says:

> Strangely enough, I spoke more to some of my comrades while at the factory than I did back at the barracks. We generally didn't speak much at the barracks to be honest. The working day was long and once 'home' you still had domestic tasks to do – mending clothes, washing . . . There would be some short, general discussions at bedtime, as we lay down on our bunks and turned out the lights in our quarters. We'd tell stories about events in our lives, recount native fairy tales or spin fantastical yarns. Arguments broke out over different ways of life and customs, particularly those concerning village life.

> We would discuss what had happened at the factory that day, or things that had occurred within our teams. We also talked about people who had begun working harder (too diligently) or were perceived to be behaving in an un-comradely fashion. Scathing views were often voiced on this subject, and some people adopted a different voice to speak so that you couldn't always tell who was saying what.

As noted by Lev Mishchenko, any free time in the camps tended to be taken up by mundane practical tasks such as the repair of clothing and shoes, doing laundry and such like. A black market operated in every camp, in which all sorts of things could be traded, despite the official ban on such activities. Alexander Bulavin remembers: 'A bazaar was set up between the barracks. You could exchange a portion of bread for some tobacco, or vice versa. But if the Germans caught you, you'd be in for it.'

A laundromat work camp, Klagenfurt, 1943.

A postcard from Osnabrück to the Kamenets-Podolsk region, dated 10 May 1943 (translated from Ukrainian):

> Postcard sent on 10/V-43. Greetings, Romik, Olya, Vitya and Volodya. I am alive and well, but I wish you all the very best life that the world can offer. [. . .] I enjoyed three happy days of Easter celebrations and a further two days off in May. The weather here is warm and I am doing the same work, but I am already being paid more than I was. I now get 9 [Reichs]marks instead of the 4 that I received previously, so things are already better. I can't buy anything except for postcards and stamps, but you can get a loaf of bread from the guys for 10 marks, so I will

> buy one. My dearests, I have already had my photograph taken three times, but I haven't yet received the prints. I will send them to you as a memento as soon as I get them. [. . .] Well, I'll leave it there since there's not much else to say. Sending my best wishes. Your loving Anna.

Sometimes they would exchange items with the Germans. Lyubov Shkulyova remembers:

> We were provided with washing powder and laundry overalls. [. . .] We'd go and knock on the Germans' doors and ask one of them, '*Wollen Sie haben Waschpulver?*'*
>
> 'Oh yes, yes,' would come the reply.
>
> Sometimes they gave us bread vouchers in exchange. Once, we were given some pieces of liver sausage and black pudding. We'd save up our washing powder and then go and exchange it. That was our main source of joy.

All sorts of odds and ends could be bought at the bazaar within the camp precincts. The salaries of many *Ostarbeiter* were paid in special vouchers called 'bonds', which they saved up to make a purchase at the bazaar. Nadezhda Bulava recalls: 'They gave us these bits of paper called 'bonds'. On Sundays, a little window would open up in the barracks. They sold lipstick there – I would wear all sorts of different ones.'

Elizaveta Krestyantseva told us: 'We wanted to look pretty, even if it was just for each other. We mixed soap and soot to use as make-up on our eyes, eyelashes and brows. We sat and sang songs together.'

Larisa Shvidchenko explains:

> We didn't work on Sundays – we just sat in the barracks and rested. 'Feel free to go out into the courtyard,' we were told.
>
> . . . And do what exactly?

---

* Would you like some washing powder?

'Not even the sun shines in quite the same way here'

It was often during their spare time that they felt most despondent. They missed their families, and pined for home. Antonina Maxina said: 'It was an unfamiliar country, with an unfamiliar language, and unfamiliar customs. Some of the girls were just thirteen or fourteen years old – they were only children! It was very hard for them.'

The teenagers were not alone in finding life hard. Irina Sokolova remembers:

> At night you would dream that you had returned home. You would see your Mama, and all your friends and family. But it was as though they looked right through you. It was painful; hard to bear. And when I woke, my whole pillow would be soaked with tears. I really missed home.

Besides the aching homesickness, many also experienced a gnawing sense of hopelessness. This was often especially pronounced

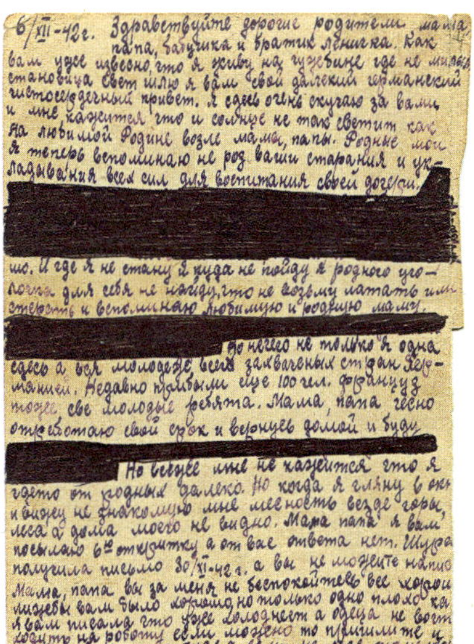

6/XII-42г. Здравствуйте дорогие родители мама,
папа, бабушка и братик Лёнечка. Как
вам уже известно, что я живу на чужбине где не [illegible]
становится свет шлю я вам свой далекий германский
чистосердечный привет. Я здесь очень скучаю за вами
и мне кажется что и солнце не так светит как
на любимой Родине возле мамы, папы. Родные мои
я теперь вспоминаю не раз ваши старания и ук-
ладывания всех сил для воспитания своей дочери.
[erased]
[illegible]мо. И где я не стану и куда не пойду я родного уго-
лочка для себя не найду, что не возьму латать или
стирать и вспоминаю любимую и родную маму.
[erased]
до нечего не только я одна
здесь а вся молодежь всех захваченых стран Гер-
манией. Недавно прибыли еще 100 чел. французы
тоже все молодые ребята. Мама, папа честно
отработаю свой срок и вернусь домой и буду
[erased]
Но все же мне не кажется что я
где-то от родных далеко. Но когда я гляну в окн[illegible]
и вижу не знакомую мне местность везде горы,
леса а дома моего не видно. Мама папа я вам
посылаю 6ю открытку а от вас ответа нет. Шура
получила письмо 30/XI-42г. а вы не можете напис[illegible]
Мама, папа вы за меня не беспокойтесь все хорош[illegible]
лишь бы вам было хорошо, но только одно плохо ка[illegible]
я вам писала что уже холоднеет а одежда не [illegible]
ходить на работу если можно то пришлите и
с [illegible] что нибудь а если не льзя то не [illegible]

A letter from Witten to Mariupol showing lines erased by censorship (6 December 1942):

As you already know, I am living in a foreign country; where my world has lost all light and meaning. I am sending you my heartfelt best wishes from Germany. I miss you terribly, and it seems to me that not even the sun shines in quite the same way here as it does in my beloved homeland, beside my Mama and Papa. My dear parents, I often think now of the efforts and great lengths to which you went to raise your daughter. [*the following lines were erased by censorship*]

And no matter where I find myself, no matter where I go, I cannot find a corner to call home. Whether I am doing the washing or the mending, I remember my dear and beloved Mama. [*the following lines were erased by censorship*]

In any case, I do not feel far from my loved ones. But when I look out of the window and see the unfamiliar landscape – mountains in all directions, forests . . . but not my home . . . [. . .] Mama, Papa, don't worry about me. Everything here is fine – I only hope that all is well with you too. There is only one problem – as I wrote before, it is beginning to get cold here, but I don't have any warm clothes to go to work in . . .

in the early months following their arrival in Germany. Vadim Novgorodov: 'We couldn't believe entirely that we would be returning home. We wanted to – we missed our friends and family. But in time, our powerlessness became such that it was hard to imagine how we would ever return home.'

Lyubov Yerokhova worked on a farm with several other *Ostarbeiter.* She remembers that even singing brought tears to their eyes:

> We would finish our work in the fields and come home tired and hungry. I remember my friend Tonya saying, 'Come on girls, let's go into the cornfield and sing our hearts out!'
>
> Tonya sang, while we cried.

A postcard from Waldheim to the Chernigov region, 1943 (translated from Ukrainian):

> Something for my Papa, Mama, Olya, Styopa, Shura and Tolechka to remember me by.
>
> The cottonwoods and willows whisper
> Ruffled by the breeze
> Remember, my dear family,
> Who is writing, please.
> It is your daughter; yes, she who misses you so,
> In a foreign land
> Where the warm sun doesn't glow
> She is without her beloved mother
> But no one shows compassion.
> The photograph on this postcard shows the city where I live.

They reworded popular Soviet songs such as 'The Sea Stretches Out Widely', 'The Gull Flies Bravely By' and 'Blue Handkerchief'. Many *Ostarbeiter*, particularly the women, recalled how the songs served as medicine for the soul, helping to alleviate their sorrow.

Zinaida Valikhova said:

> I remember a film* that came out before the war, which included some songs. I wrote lyrics to set against the melodies, and we sang them:
>
> Mama, I have flown off to a far-away place
> And, perhaps, will never return,
> And perhaps, will never see
> My green garden, Mama's gaze,
> And home so familiar to me.

A postcard to Storkow from the Kamenets-Podolsk region, dated 22 July 1943 (translated from the Ukrainian):

> A letter from Ganya to her darling daughter. Good morning or good evening, our darling daughter. I write to tell you that we are alive and well, and hope very much that you are alive and well too. Sweetheart, our little birdie, our ladybird . . . we could never forget you. We miss you terribly – it feels like for ever since we saw you last. We hear you, we see you and we dream about you; we miss you so. Darling daughter; our little ladybird, don't cry, and don't be sad. Perhaps God will bring you home again. [. . .] Your Papa is already home – he has completed his six months of forced labour. Goodbye. I'll await your reply like the nightingale waits for summer.

They sang to the tunes of old songs from the 'cruel Romance' genre. Anastasia Arkhipenko remembers singing one particular song, which was probably written by a group of her fellow *Ostarbeiter*:

---

* The film *The Fighters* (1939, director: E. Pentslin) featured the song 'Comrades Fly Away to a Far-Off Land' composed by N. Bogoslovsky, words by E. Dolmatovsky.

The clogs we wore they crushed our feet
They pressed to our chests a swatch marked OST
The keys and prisons of the police
Rendered hope of freedom lost.
Why, Mother, did you give me birth?
Why did you bring me onto this Earth?
For you bestowed this wretched fate upon me,
To surrender our culture to another country
A country that holds our culture in contempt
And won't let us leave, nor even attempt
And fills its prisons from among these people of mine
And calls us by the name of Russian *Schweine*.

Such songs were rewritten and learned by heart. As such, many remembered them for the rest of their lives.

A letter from Leipzig to the Sumy region, dated 2 March 1943 (translated from Ukrainian):

> . . . It rains a lot. Sometimes it's dreary, but sometimes the sun comes out. But you said that there is no sun here. While I am sitting at work, the sun shines so brightly through the window that it makes me want to cry. It is a shame that I think only of Ukraine as a good and happy place – it's happy because you are all there together, my dearests, while I am here, alone. Here, as at home with you, the girls and young men go out and enjoy themselves, but here they do not have so much fun. We also have a guitar, just to cheer us up a bit. Sometimes we come home from work, have dinner, and then play the guitar and sing. We cheer each other up and don't lose heart, because if we did we

A factory worker, Genthin, 1942. The text on the reverse reads: . . . *You will have forgotten me within a year, and all the more so after two. May seeing this photograph keep me within your thoughts. Keep it, if you haven't already forgotten me. And if you have forgotten me, then tear it up.*

> would send ourselves to an early grave. God willing, we will return home and live together again. We don't have any news to tell you. Write and tell me your news. What is everyone up to back home? How is life? Who is still at home? Who has gone where, who has arrived, which men and women have married and who has been born into the world . . .?

Yevdokiya Verkholantseva remembers an *Ostarbeiter* friend of hers, a girl from an educated family, with whom she wrote a poem in Germany:

> It was Maya who taught me how to write poetry [. . .]. She wrote poems herself, you see. One day I decided to write one too – I read it out to her.
>
> 'You write well, Dusya,' she said, '. . . so neatly and skilfully.'
>
> In those days, I spent a lot of time thinking and writing – what else was there to do?

Vadim Novgorodov had a friend who composed a few verses about Taganrog. When we spoke to him, he tried to explain just how much these lines had meant to him:

> One of the lads from Taganrog, Oleg Frolov, [. . .] was blessed with a musical ear and a talent for poetry. He wrote a song about Taganrog – it became a sort of anthem for us and brought us together. He only wrote two couplets though; they were about how we missed Taganrog, what Taganrog was like, how our mothers missed us, and how we would either return, or not; neither she, nor we, could know. We sang those lines when we returned to Taganrog. Well, those of us that were left alive, that is.

Some of those we interviewed recalled writing songs and poems in exercise books or notepads that they took with them from home or acquired in Germany. However, for a number of reasons, very few of these records have survived. Hardly anyone held on to their

The work camp at the Krupp factory, Berlin, 25 April 1943. The text on the reverse reads: *Barracks No. 3, Room No. 9.*

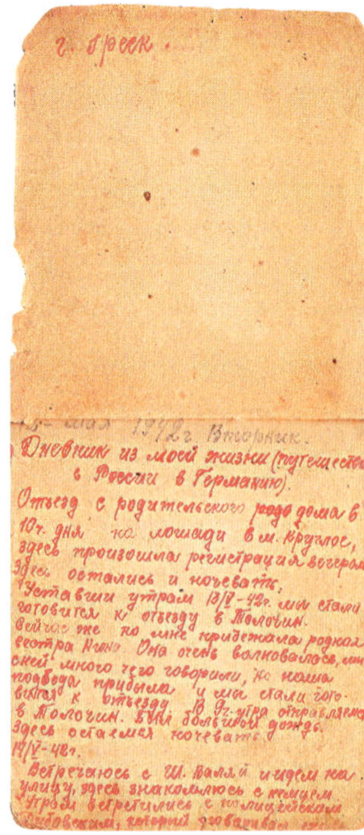

г. Брест

Дневник из моей жизни (путешествие с России в Германию).

Отъезд с родительского дома в 10ч. дня на лошади в м. Круглое, здесь произошла регистрация вечером здесь остались и ночевать.

Уставши утром 13/V-42г. мы стали готовится к отъезду в Толочин. Сейчас же ко мне приезжала родная сестра [illegible]. Она очень волновалось, мы с ней много чего говорили, но наша подвода прибыла и мы стали готовится к отъезду. В 9ч. утра отправляемся в Толочин. Был больший дождь. Здесь остаемся ночевать.

14/V-42г.

Встречаюсь с Ш. Валей и идем на улицу, здесь знакомлюсь с [illegible]

Zhenya Kisselkova's diary, 1942–3, entitled 'A Diary of My Life: The Journey from Russia to Germany'.

teenage diaries, despite the fact that before the war writing a diary had been popular among teenagers. Memorial's archives contain only one such example. It belonged to Zhenya Kisselkova, who wrote it between 1942 and 1943. Within its pages, she penned short and fairly generic notes about what had happened to her each day.

'Mama, you ask whether I cry'

Ostarbeiter told us of the letters and parcels that they received from home, and often remembered distinctly the words that their loved ones had written to them. In the years that followed the war, however, such correspondence was often used by the secret police as evidence of collaboration. As a result, a significant portion was destroyed. Maria Ausheva recalled:

> Mama burned everything.
>
> 'It's enough that you were taken in the first place,' she said.
>
> She destroyed all of my letters and notes [. . .]. All of them. I cried so much. I resented her doing it. They had been good

> letters – it seemed such a shame. But she burned them all – every single one.

A postcard from Angermünde to the Kamenets-Podolsk region, 1943 (translated from Ukrainian):

> Friday 19th February. Good day to you, my darling Mama and Vasya. I am writing to let you know that I am alive and well, and hope that you are too – I hope that you are living as best you can back home. Mummy, I have already received lots of letters from you! I got the letter that you wrote in red ink and when I read it I was so proud of how well you wrote. Write to me often, because I miss my home and family terribly.

Nevertheless, a considerable number of letters sent to and from Germany did survive, and several are now stored in Memorial's archives. As of July 1942, the *Ostarbeiter* were permitted to send two letters home per month, but this allowance changed in November 1942, and they were told they could only write postcards. Every letter or postcard had to pass through censorship in Germany, where any lines inferring that life in the Third Reich was not all that it might have been were erased. As a result, very few letters contain any specific details, and many of their authors resorted to allusions that they hoped the recipient would interpret correctly. A letter from Germany to Ukraine, for example, noted that the sender was eating 'just as heartily as in 1933'; a thinly veiled reference to the terrible man-made famine that became known as the Holodomor. The postcard below contains a similar insinuation.

A postcard from Remscheid to the Sumy region, 5 June 1943 (translated from Ukrainian):

> . . . Mama, we work in a factory. We work twelve-hour shifts, and they provide us with a bed, a mattress and rubber aprons. Mama, life here is good – they feed us very well – just like 1933. We are very happy here and sing every day. It rains a lot,

and there are heavy hailstorms too. Write and tell me whether everyone is alive, and whether Pasha is still at home. Tell me how the vegetable garden is looking . . .

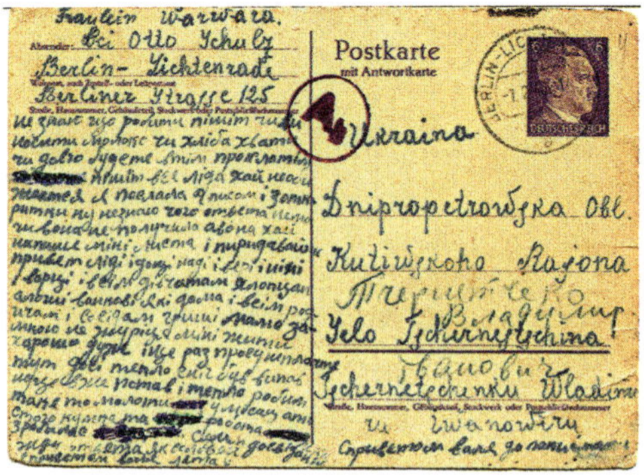

A censored postcard sent from Berlin to the Dnepropetrovsk region on 1 February 1943 (translated from Ukrainian). Several words were struck out by censorship.

Many also noted that letters did not appear to be arriving at their designated addresses.

> Letter sent on 01/II-43. A letter from your daughter Valya, to her dear Papa, Mama and Kolya. In the first lines of my short letter, I wish to let you know that I am alive and well, and hope that the same is true for you. From the bottom of my heart, I am sending you a low bow of greeting – all the way from the dawn sky, down to the damp earth – and countless kisses to you my Papa, Mama and brother Kolya. I am extremely grateful to have received your letter dated 21/I – I feel much happier now that I know you are alive. You say that you are upset not to have received a letter from me though. My dearest Mama, I have sent countless letters, but I don't know why you aren't receiving them. I'm not sure what can have happened – they must have got lost on the way. Mama, I have received nine letters from you. If that's how many you sent, then I have received all of them. The letters from you are getting through, but I don't know why mine are not. They aren't even letters, but postcards, because they send any letters we write back to us. I wrote one a while back, and sent it, but it was returned to me two weeks later. We were told to write postcards instead, and I have already sent four or five to you. I don't know whether they will arrive

> or not. Mama, I implore you to send me a photograph of you, Papa and Kolya. I asked you to send one ages ago – please do, because I miss you terribly and just want to glance at a photo to see you as you are now. Mama, you ask whether I cry. Mama, I don't think that anything can help me, and as I wrote here before I will serve my year and then come home. As for whether I cry, in truth, I do Mama, whenever I think about you, and how you are . . . I don't know what to do about it. If I had wings, I would fly away home to you. Mama, I dream about Kolya every night too. I often dream that he too has been taken to Germany – the dreams are so vivid that I don't know what to do with myself when I wake up. [. . .] Mama, don't be sad for me. Life here is good, so again, please don't cry. [. . .] I'll leave it at that, goodbye. I await your reply like the nightingale waits for summer. With fondest wishes, Valya.

Lidia Beketova told us: 'I wrote letters home, but my sister later told me that when they arrived almost all had been heavily censored. And I never received a single letter from her.'

Letters from home, Feldkirch, 1943.

Hanna Muzalyova said:

> I always tried to write that everything was OK, so that nobody at home worried about me. But what could possibly have been OK? I missed home at first – I cried for a year and couldn't adjust to my new life. I got used to it in time . . . Because, well

> . . . I didn't want to die. [. . .] We had to place our hope in something.

Taissa Tolkachova remembers that she only ever received one letter, but a few small food parcels arrived from her family from time to time:

> I don't know why, but we never received any letters. It wasn't that we didn't write – we wanted to write and so we did send letters. [. . .] But my Mama later told me that they hadn't received a single one from us. Our parents went to the military police headquarters to find out whether they could send parcels to us. 'Yes, you can send parcels,' they were told. 'You can send two hundred grammes of millet and a few pillowcases.'

A postcard from Yanov to Neheim-Hüsten, 23 June 1943:

> Greetings to our darling children, Zoska and Nastya. We are writing to let you know that your parents and family are alive and well, thanks be to God, and we all hope that the Good Lord bestows the same rude health upon you. For so long, we have waited, aching with sorrow, to hear from you. We had no news from you for such a long time, but, praise the Lord, we have now received your letter and, having heard from you, we feel a little better. We are sending you a Whitsun parcel – it will be the fourth that we have sent. I have given Zoska 21 rusks, and Simon gave 28. Your Auntie Anna made these 21 pieces – you must write and thank her. Zoska, you write that you haven't received any letters from us. I have written lots, but I don't know why we are receiving yours, while ours are not reaching you. We are desperate to know whether our parcels and letters have arrived. We send them, without knowing whether or not you are receiving them. Try to send us word somehow, even if only via somebody else. [. . .] We are sending you a deep bow. Both your parents and all the family send you their very best wishes too.

Lyubov Shkulyova told us:

> The Germans permitted our families to send us parcels [. . .] just little packets weighing no more than 200g. They could send a piece of salted fat from home, but if the packet weighed more than 200g it wouldn't be accepted. Mothers and grandmothers would bake biscuits and put them into little packets, or weigh out 200g of seeds to send. A few of the girls received parcels – some got as many as fifteen, others only five or so.

Mikhail Klintsov was almost arrested after sending a letter to his brother, in which he had complained about the Germans:

> I don't think my letter ever arrived – I must have written too much. [. . .] Some SS men came to talk to me one day.
>
> 'Well, what do you say, shall we take you with us?' they asked.
>
> They didn't take me in the end – I was just a youngster after all; only a lad.

A postcard from the Vinnytsia region to Hagen, Germany, 26 February 1943:

> Good day, my dear sister Marusenka. We are sending you our ardent greetings and wishing you all the very best. Marusenka, today (26/II) we received your second letter, which you wrote on 6/I. It has taken fifty-six days to reach us, Marusenka, and we are so grateful to have received it. We have had to wait such a long time for it, and were starting to grow weary of waiting. Marusenka, while we were overjoyed to receive your letter, we found no words within it that could bring us any joy. You have been dealt a great deal of sadness in your young life, Marusenka. I think about you all the time and cannot quite comprehend how this misfortune befell you. If we had the means to do so we would help you more than ever. But the trouble is, it's wartime now, and we have to accept the limitations of the times. It's just a shame that we have been forced apart and now have to

> endure the sadness of life without you, while you go hungry. We really want to hear more news from you, and I would like to write much more, but unfortunately we are not allowed to write letters. I will leave my postcard there. Wishing you the best of health and happiness. We are sending you a kiss.

Until 1944, most *Ostarbeiter* were able to maintain correspondence with loved ones they had left behind in occupied territory. However, some were less fortunate, and in 1943, as the Red Army began to regain control of certain areas, some found that their lines of communication with home had been cut. Of course, the *Ostarbeiter* could continue to communicate freely with friends and family living within Germany until the very end of the war. Galina Agranovskaya exchanged letters with her parents, who worked on a farm in a different part of the country; Nadezhda Izmalkova wrote to a friend; and Nikolai Kireev found his sister, having discovered that she too had been deported to Germany.

Writing letters home, Feldkirch, 1943.

Needless to say, however, these letters could never contain anything of a critical or seditious nature. Galina Agranovskaya was given some guidance by the Polish girl she worked alongside: 'When I started receiving post from my parents, Regina explained to me that when I replied I needed to write like this: "Everything is great here. I am very grateful to my employers . . ."'

Vera Dergachova recalls that a translator at the camp offered some advice to a friend of hers:

> I had a co-worker, Maria, whose aunt was working in Berlin. They would write to each other, and one day her aunt wrote

in a letter: 'These Germans! I'd drown them in their chamber pots if I could.'

Those were the sorts of letters she wrote! [. . .] The translator told Maria to write to her aunt. 'I have to read all your letters,' he explained. 'And am obliged to inform the camp authorities about anything inappropriate. And she's writing about chamber pots! Write and tell her not to say such things again.'

'She and I would sit and try to remember our algebraic equations'

Many *Ostarbeiter*, particularly those who had received an education prior to their deportation, longed to lay their hands on a Russian book. Although some of the work camps were equipped with libraries, conditions in these camps were such that few enjoyed opportunities to read. Those employed privately were even less likely to encounter a source of Russian reading material – it was virtually non-existent.

A postcard from Leipzig to the Sumy region, dated 2 March 1943 (translated from Ukrainian):

> Greetings, my dear Uncle Kolya, and my darling Mama and brother Kolya. In these first lines of my short letter I wish to let you know that I am alive and well, and hope that the same is true for you. I send a low German bow to you all. I am living in the city of Leipzig, where I work in a factory. My work is good – it is clean, and not too hard. They feed us well: bread, butter and coffee in the mornings, and soup for lunch and dinner. It's all pretty good. On our day off, we go to the cinema in town, and to church – the choice is ours. But although life is good here, we long for home and cannot wait for that day, that minute, when we return home. If only you knew how boring it is in this foreign and far-off land, with neither friends nor loved ones for company. [. . .] How is my Mama's health? I hope that she does not worry about me, and that instead she looks after her own health, and that of my Papa – I am well aware that

none of you are in the best of health. I implore you to look after yourselves and wait for me, for if you grieve for me, you will die before I can return home to you. I will return, and you won't be there. Send my best wishes to all the family from me.

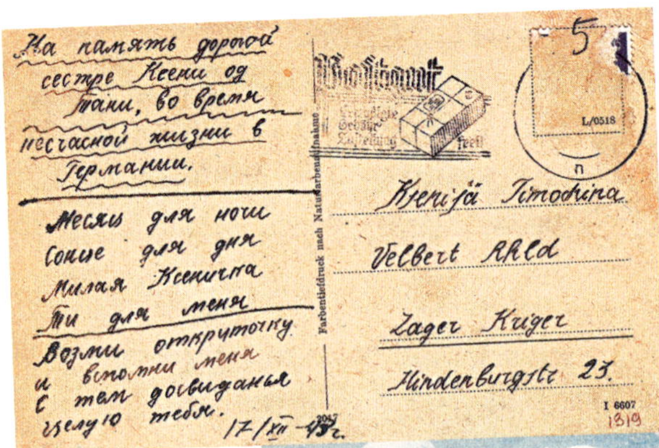

A postcard sent from an *Ostarbeiter* in Berlin to her friend working in Velbert, 1943.

Below: The museum, theatre and St Peter's Cathedral in the central square of Chemnitz, 1943.

Galina Agranovskaya told us of her joy at discovering some of the Russian literary classics, albeit in German translation, in the library of the family home where she worked as a domestic helper in Germany. Nadezhda Izmalkova described a similar discovery:

> Later, when I moved and went to work for a new employer, I was given a room filled with books! It was a whole library! I found books by Dostoevsky, Tolstoy, and Dumas – all printed in German. My hands began to tremble when I saw *The Count of Monte Cristo.*

Vera Dergachova and her friend Anna tried to remember the lessons they had learned in school: 'Anna had also completed Year

Ten. [. . .] We didn't have a single book to use. So she and I would sit and try to remember our algebraic equations and geometry . . . sine, cosine and such like. We analysed and pondered over it all.'

Mikhail Chernenko remembers reciting, at the request of his friends, a satirical novel by Ilf and Petrov called *The Little Golden Calf*, which he knew almost by heart.

Nadezhda Izmalkova had completed Year Ten at school in Kiev before the war, but she remembers feeling terribly worried that her education had been interrupted. As a result, she acquired an English dictionary in an effort to expand her vocabulary: 'I worried that I would suffer as a result of not being able to study once war broke out. I was afraid that I would never be able to make anything of myself; that I would never be more than a housemaid.'

However, the dictionary aroused the suspicion of the Gestapo, who subjected her to repeated interrogations:

> 'Where did you get this English dictionary and textbook?' they asked. 'And what's it for – are you waiting for the Americans?'
>
> 'How could I possibly be expecting the Americans to arrive, when you are the all-conquering force?' I replied. 'No, I am learning English – I studied it in school and am falling behind.'
>
> They continued with their questioning: 'And how did you obtain such books from our shops?'
>
> 'I received them by post – I paid a few Reichsmarks for this dictionary and textbook,' I replied.
>
> 'Where did you learn to speak German?' they asked.
>
> 'I went to secondary school – a gymnasium.'
>
> 'Look over there,' they pointed. 'That's Buchenwald* . . . we'll send you there.'
>
> Every day that week they drove up on their motorcycles and interrogated me.

Some camps circulated propaganda newspapers in Russian and Ukrainian; we heard of two publications in particular – *The Voice*

* Buchenwald concentration camp, Weimar.

and the weekly *New Word* newspaper. Some *Ostarbeiter* recalled that by reading these papers, they were occasionally able to glean some information about the situation at the front. Nikolai Gulyaev said:

Ostarbeiter after work. A photograph from the German Propaganda Bureau entitled: 'On the status of eastern workers in Germany. 1942–1944.' (State Archive of the Russian Federation. Fond.7021, Opis'.128, Delo.268, List.27)

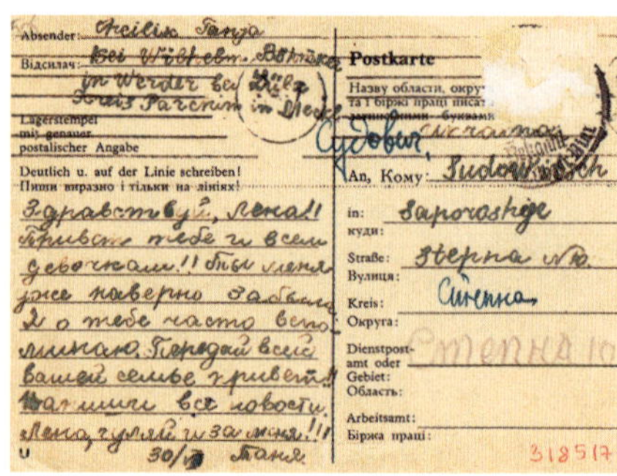

'Easter Greetings' postcard sent from Lyubets to the Zaporozhye region, 1944. On the reverse is written: *Greetings, Lena! Hello to you and all the girls!! You have probably already forgotten me. I often think about you. Pass on my greetings to all your family. Write and tell me all your news. Lena, go out and have fun for me!!! Tanya.*

An Easter postcard from the Brent region, western Prussia. Sent to the Chernigov region, 1943.

> There was a newspaper called *The Russian Word*, which contained articles about how good the lives of the Russian workers in Germany were. In short, it was a propaganda paper. It would also tout the victories of the triumphant German army, announcing that they had taken this city and that. It revealed that a battle was underway for Stalingrad, and later informed us about [the battle of] Kursk. One February day we received a newspaper with a printed black border and mournful tone. But it didn't say anything about Stalingrad. We learned about that from the Germans.

'There were prayers in every language'

Having been raised in the militantly atheist Soviet school system, the majority of the young *Ostarbeiter* were non-believers at the time of their deportation to Germany. However, the hard labour, hunger and aching homesickness began to take its toll, and as the bombing intensified, and with it fear for their lives, many of the young workers began to seek comfort in faith. Some remembered reciting prayers that they had overheard at home. Lidia Beketova recalled:

> We had been taught not to believe . . . I was a Pioneer, and a member of the Komsomol. [. . .] There was a Ukrainian girl called Motya in our camp – I will never forget her, she was such a sweet person. She taught me 'The Lord's Prayer' and told me to recite it whenever life was hard. I believe this was the only thing that really helped me in life.

Nadezhda Bulava told us:

> I had never prayed before I went to Germany. I didn't know a single prayer, despite the fact that my mother was religious and went to church. We were all Pioneers, and members of the Komsomol – how could we possibly have been believers? But life was so hard there [in Germany]. So I would pray: 'Help me, Oh Lord . . . Help me, Oh Lord . . . Help me, Oh Lord . . .'

Similarly, Maria Ausheva said: 'The Lord kept me safe because my mother prayed all the time. I'm sure I would never have survived otherwise. Never.'

A postcard sent from the Poltava region to Eilenburg, 10 April 1943:

> Greetings, my dear daughter, I am sending you my parental blessing and good wishes, and hope that you will be so fortunate as to pull through these times and return home. My darling daughter, pray to God, for God will help you in your grief, and I too will pray ceaselessly that the Lord has the grace to look upon you. My darling, I would gladly assist you by sending you a parcel, but they won't accept them. May God help you with the strength of his own hand and may He give you strength. If they accept parcels, then you can expect to receive one. Goodbye. God willing, we will see each other again.

The *Ostarbeiter* were permitted to go to church, and many of those we spoke to recalled attending services. We asked Vera Bobrovskaya whether she had prayed at the camp. 'Everybody prayed at the camp,' she replied. 'There were prayers in every language.'

Varvara Khabarova worked on a farm not far from a church: 'My employers allowed me to go there to pray. We would go, and if there were some other Russians attending the same church, we were able to meet on Sundays.'

Yadviga Shpakova wrote in a letter:

> We worked on the railway at Bad-Rappenau. On Sunday afternoons we met in the meadow outside the camp precincts. Former officers of the White Army – emigrants – would come there to join us, and together we would sing 'Evening Bells'. We cried, and prayed for our swift release and an end to the war.

Yevdokiya Verkholantseva remembers praying alongside her employer – each prayed for victory for her own side:

Right at the outset, my employer told me what to do: 'Let's pray to God that the Russians perish,' she said. But I was Russian! And so she would pray for the Germans, and I would pray for Russia. [. . .] What mattered was that she prayed for her Germans, and I prayed for my own people at the very same table. What else was I going to do? Pray that our Russia fell?

An unsent postcard from Salzwedel, 1944.
The text on the reverse reads:
A memento for Papa, Mama and my brothers and sister, from this far and foreign, dreary corner of Germany. My dear family, set your hearts on that sacred mountain, where we will find our eternal home and Father: our benevolent, dear Saviour. And we will live there together for eternity. I pray for this, and believe that our Lord will bring it to pass, and that we will see each other again soon.

Textile factory work camp, Wuppertal, 1944.

Weaving factory work camp, Dornbirn, Austria, 1944.

'We got hold of . . . a mandolin'

Memories that the *Ostarbeiter* held of their time in Germany varied hugely; some were bright and gay, while others were quite the opposite. Many recalled gatherings with their peers, where they sang songs, danced and made friends. Some even formed romantic attachments. Fedor Khmara worked on a farm, and remembers that his employers would allow him to gather with friends on Sundays to play the accordion.

Aldona Volynskaya worked at the aerodrome in Cologne and remembers running off with her friends to attend dances in the neighbouring camp:

Mining work camp, Kamen, 1943.

> We had to find a way out through the wire in order to get there. They had some sort of *Ostarbeiter* orchestra in their camp, composed of some lads and girls from Kharkov. We danced the foxtrot, and the tango – just as we had done before the war. We sang 'I've got a secret, this secret is you.'*

Ostarbeiter formed their own musical ensembles, playing in their

* The romantic song 'Secret', music by V. Sidorov, words by A. D'Aktil.

own camps and any neighbouring ones. Anna Kirilenko worked in a textile factory in Düsseldorf. She remembers:

> A group of Polish men and women would often come to our camp with their musical instruments. We would all gather, and a large orchestra would be assembled, composed of Russian, Polish, Dutch and Ukrainian workers. The Germans would come along too. The band would play the Tango and the Foxtrot – they were very fashionable at the time.

Zoya Yeliseeva, who worked at a weaving factory, described an inter-camp amateur theatre group that the *Ostarbeiter* formed:

> A few of our girls made friends with some of our men working in the other factory. [. . .] Together, they decided to stage an opera – *Natalka Poltavka*.* They made wonderful stage decorations and sewed Ukrainian costumes – we went to watch the performance. The Germans sat in the front rows, and we sat behind.

Workers at a sewing factory, Winterdorf, 1943.

* Translator's note: An opera written by the Ukrainian composer M. Lysenko in 1889 based on the play of the same name by I. Kotlyarevsky.

Vadim Novgorodov took part in concerts alongside some of his friends from his hometown of Taganrog:

> We got hold of some musical instruments including a guitar and a mandolin. [. . .] We organised a trip to perform a concert and sing our songs in another camp in the same city. We sang 'Katyusha',* of course, as well as some songs by Kozin, such as 'Masha' and 'Autumn . . . chilly morning, sky as if shrouded in fog'. We also recited a few poems.

Vadim also described an episode from one concert reminiscent of a scene in a later Soviet film:

> I remember performing in a concert staged at our camp. [. . .] We sang songs, and I read Lermontov's 'Death of the Poet'. When I came to the line 'but you, arrogant offspring' I turned towards the portrait of Hitler hanging on the wall, addressing it in just the same way as in the film *The Young Guard*.† Once I had finished the poem, I felt a cold sweat creeping down my spine. What if the Germans had noticed? But no, I got away with it.

'We'd be let out in groups of six'

Every *Ostarbeiter* dreamed of slipping out through the wire and escaping from the supervision of their employers, supervisors, or the families for whom they worked. But not everybody had the opportunity to do so. Those in the work camps usually had the least freedom of all – particularly the new arrivals, who were forbidden from leaving camp premises for the first few months following their arrival in Germany. Later, they were allowed out, but only in formation, and under guard. In time, as a reward, they might be allowed to leave the camp in groups, but time away from camp was

---

* Translator's note: 'Katyusha' was a popular Soviet wartime song composed in 1938 by Matvey Blanter with lyrics by Mikhail Isakovsky.

† *The Young Guard,* based on a novel by Alexander Fadeyev, was a 1948 Soviet film directed by Sergei Gerasimov.

always strictly regulated. Lyubov Shkulyova worked on a crane at the Krupp factory in Oberhausen:

> We were allowed to leave the camp to go into town, providing we didn't break any of the rules. We'd be let out in groups of six. You left as a six, and had to return as a six. Nobody was allowed to go off on their own, not even in twos. If you couldn't find five others to go with you, you had to stay in the camp.

Anna Kirilenko said: 'We had been working in the weaving factory in Düsseldorf for about two months before they started letting us go into town on Sundays – from two in the afternoon until six in the evening.'

Of course, much depended on the camp's regime, or the restrictions of a particular enterprise, or an individual guard. Elizaveta Krestyantseva worked in a rubber factory in Berlin. She remembers:

> Sometimes the gatekeepers would let you pop out when you told them you really needed to go somewhere.
>
> 'OK then, off you go,' they would say, 'but make sure you're back on time.'

Zinaida Valikhova worked in a factory in Gladbeck. She remembers:

> Our guard was physically handicapped. I think he was called Heins. He wasn't old, but he had a problem with his leg, which meant he had not been sent to war. Anyway, our girls would go up to him and say, 'Heins, listen. Could you just go round the corner and stay there for ten minutes or so?' Off he would go, and they would slip out over the wire – it wasn't very high – and take off!

Pavel Mikhailov was housed in a work camp near the village of Weinstadt:

Workers from a munitions factory on an excursion into town. Magdeburg, 1944. The text on the reverse side reads: *The German woman takes us to work every day, but on the weekends she takes us on excursions into town.*

Workers from an aviation factory on a walk into town, Rangsdorf, 1943.

> We could come and go freely from the camp despite the fact that it was fully enclosed with barbed wire – this didn't serve any purpose. There was also a security gate, but God knows what it was there for. A Polish guard was always sat there on duty, but he never paid anybody the slightest bit of attention.

Georgiy Tkachov remembers that *Ostarbeiter* were checked at the exit of his work camp (associated with the ship-repair factory at Stettin) to ensure that they looked 'decent' and were wearing their OST badges:

> When we lived in the camp, we were free to go into town. But we had to be more or less 'decently dressed' in their eyes. [. . .] We couldn't look like ragamuffins. We wore blue patches of cloth bearing the letters OST. They had to be sewn onto our outer clothes to show that we were from the east: Russians.

Ostarbeiter who worked on farms or as domestic workers for German families were at the mercy of their employers; it was they who decided what they could and couldn't do in their free time.

Tamara Selivanova worked as a housemaid for the director of the Torpedo-Werk enterprise in Frankfurt am Main: 'After lunch on Sundays I was given some time off until seven o'clock in the evening. But my employers were very strict about what I did; under no circumstances was I permitted to meet up with anyone.'

Working on a farm on the outskirts of Leipzig, 1944.

By contrast, Zinaida Komissarova, who worked on a farm, was free to go where she liked. She worked alongside her employers, and could go off on her own after work:

> In the mornings we looked after the livestock, then we'd have breakfast and drink coffee before getting into the cart and going out to the fields together. We would finish work in the evenings, and then I could go and see my friends, or invite one of them over. I could take the key to the house – my employers couldn't have cared less. I could have stayed out all night if I wanted to, but there were patrols* – you could be caught.

Vera Fedorchenko was punished for becoming separated from her friends in town one day and returning to the camp without them. 'I had to clean the toilets after work for a whole month,' she remembers.

The *Ostarbeiter* were limited in terms of where and how they could spend their free time. Very few were able to speak German, especially during the early years, and almost nobody knew anything about the area where they had been sent, or the town or city they

* There was a long list of punishments for transgressions committed by *Ostarbeiter* during their free time. Anyone caught in breach of the rules could face a concentration camp sentence, or even the death penalty. It was forbidden, for example, for *Ostarbeiter* to go anywhere without their ID Card (*Ausweis*) or to return to their camp after a specified time.

were permitted to go to. In theory, they could go to the shops, but they had little if any money to spend and their ration coupons only enabled them to buy the bare necessities.

A postcard from Rangsdorf to Novgorod-Volynsky, dated 31 August 1943 (translated from Ukrainian):

> Postcard written 31/VIII-43. Good day or good evening, my dear parents. First of all, I want to let you know that I am still alive and well. I was discharged from the hospital today and don't feel too bad at the moment. I have received seven parcels from you, which were sent on the 31/VII, but I haven't received any letters for a long time – I don't know why this might be. Either you haven't written, or they haven't arrived. They are feeding us just the same as before – I don't even want to write about it. We used to be free to leave the camp at will, but now they won't allow us out, although they say that we will be allowed to go out again soon. [. . .] I've still got clothes for now, but my boots are starting to fall apart. I might be able

Workers at a smelting factory, Eisenberg, 1944. The text on the reverse reads: . . . *As dawn breaks over the sky, illuminating the face of a dear friend, in a place where budding years pass by. Where happiness evaporates on the wind, like clouds in autumn. And every day, youth withers in a far-off foreign land.*

Workers at a shoe factory, Speyer, 1943.

> to buy a pair somewhere though. If you are able to send me a parcel, then please do. The parcels that you have sent me previously have helped me enormously. I don't have any more news. Write and tell me all your news – how life is with you and whether you are all still at home. Send my greetings to all the family, friends and acquaintances. I will send a photo. With fondest wishes, your son, Kolya.

Many of the eastern workers were astounded at the trust that German shopkeepers placed in their customers. Irina Sokolova remembers:

> You would go into a little shop and somewhere, right in the back of the shop, a bell would ring. There would be ration cards lying out, money, groceries . . . everything . . . But nobody in sight! And you'd just pick up whatever you needed from the shelves. I could never understand it.

Aside from going to the shops, the girls sometimes went to the hairdresser. Tatiana Veselovskaya remembers: 'I would go to the hairdresser – after all, we were paid a little bit. I would take off my OST badge on arrival, get my hair done and pay. Everyone there knew that I was Russian.'

They also went to the photography studio so that they could send attractive photos of themselves home.

Towards the end of the war, as Allied bombing raids intensified, precipitating a wave of refugees, the Germans struggled to control the movement of millions of foreign workers across the Third Reich. Little hotspots of semi-clandestine black-market activities began to crop up around Germany – in Berlin, one such place was the central square: Alexanderplatz. Mikhail Chernenko remembers:

> Alexanderplatz was right in the centre of the city [. . .] There was a beer bar right outside the metro station. It was a real den of iniquity – you could find all sorts there and buy or sell anything you liked. [. . .] And I have no doubt that there

were all sorts of criminal dealings going on . . . and Gestapo lingering about too.

A postcard from Berlin to the Kamenets-Podolsk region, dated 30 September 1943 (translated from Ukrainian):

> [. . .] Good day or good evening, my dear parents – Mama, Papa – and Granny, and my brother, Volodya. I am sending you a son's bow of greeting and wish to let you know that I am alive and getting better by the day. Soon I will return to work alongside my comrades. [. . .] My darling Mama, and all the family, I received the parcels you sent (23 items), for which I am very grateful. I would ask you though to please swap the groats* for something else, as I have no way of cooking them. Please send more tobacco, because this is most expensive to buy, and we can use it to buy anything else that we need. [. . .] I remain alive and well and am sending you and all the family my greetings, Mama. I send a bow to all the relations and my comrades. I'll leave it there. Goodbye! I look forward to your reply. Your Petya.

Even tens of years later, many *Ostarbeiter* harboured vivid memories of the beautiful landscapes, buildings and statues that they had

A picture postcard from Bürstadt, 1943.

Ostarbeiter on an outing in Berlin, 1944.

* Translator's note: Hulled grain kernels, e.g., oats, wheat, rye and barley.

seen in Germany. Zoya Yeliseeva gave an interesting account of one of her Sunday excursions into town (she worked in a textile factory in Kassel):

> They began to let us out. We had money, but we couldn't buy anything because you could only purchase with ration coupons. We weren't allowed to go to the cinema – they wouldn't let us in. But sometimes, we would remove our OST badges and try to get into the small, shabbier cinemas. We would try to filter in among the tide of the general public. [. . .] We began to familiarise ourselves with the city – Kassel was beautiful and boasted a great many medieval buildings. [. . .] There was a wonderful park outside the city, where we would have our photographs taken. A staircase fountain, similar to the one at Peterhof, climbed the hillside, and at the top stood a statue of Hercules. He was leaning on a club, and beneath him the staircase fountain cascaded down the hill. There was also a medieval castle – Löwenburg – in this park. We began to get to know the city and bought postcards – beautiful, colourful ones. I had lots of these postcards, and it wasn't just me who bought them, we all did! Of course, we didn't have much money, but the postcards only cost a few pennies.

Yevgenia Savranskaya also remembers buying a postcard:

> I knew a girl called Edith. One day she said to me, 'Genya, I can show you round Berlin if you like?' [. . .] She took me round the city, and I just remember that I bought a postcard of the painting *Judith and the Head of Holofernes.* I actually don't know why I bought it – I didn't like the painting.

A picture postcard from Oberhausen, 1944.

More often than not, the *Ostarbeiter* bought postcards as mementos of places where they had lived and worked. They hoped to take them home to show their families and, when we spoke to a number of them tens of years later, it transpired that many had held on to them.

'More importantly, I have my health, strength and good comrades'

The support of friends and fellow countrymen had a profound impact upon an *Ostarbeiter*'s fate and experience in Germany. It was always important to be near one's own people; whether this was someone from the same village or city, or merely a new acquaintance made on the journey to Germany, and many spoke of friendships that made it easier to cope with the break from home. Vadim Novgorodov, who was sent to work in a mine, remembers:

> A few of us from Taganrog were assigned to the same place. It was plain for all to see that we Taganrog lads were a close-knit bunch. Men from other cities would often want to attach themselves to us and the camp authorities treated us with respect, because we were a large group.

Antonina Maxina also spoke of her band of friends (from Rostov), as did Nadezhda Izmalkova (from Kiev). Likewise Aldona Volynskaya never separated from her childhood friends, with whom she was sent to Germany. They all benefited hugely from the mutual support and assistance that they gave to each other.

A postcard depicting a view of Möllersdorf, 1942. The text on the reverse reads: *My dear, beloved Papa and Mama, and my dear brother Vanya! I am sending you a picture of the village in which I live. I ask that you keep it until my return.*

Yevdokiya Verkholantseva recalls her fear at finding herself alone in Germany:

> My belongings were loaded into the cart beside me, and I sat there, alone. Alone! [. . .] Off I went, along the riverbank, crying as I went. I considered jumping into the river and drowning myself . . . but then I chased this thought from my head – I remember thinking that if I drowned, my mother would suffer terribly. I could hear her words in my head: 'Duska, save yourself, save yourself if only for me. Try – do whatever you can – to stay alive.' I imagined myself lying, bloated in the river. But no, that didn't fit with the act.

A postcard from the Zaporozhye region to Mecklenburg, 1942 (translated from Ukrainian):

> Good day or good evening, to our daughter Ulya Matveevna. First of all, I wish to tell you that we are all still alive and are sending you our deepest regards – from myself, your Mama, and brothers Petya and Fedya, sisters Zina and Nadya, and Grisha, Polya, Varya, Pavlo and their children, and Paraskeva Agafonovna too. We all send you our regards, Ulya Matveevna, and wish you all the very best in your life. We hope that you will work to the best of your abilities while you are required to do so, and then return safely to us again, back to your home in the Motherland. We can now tell you, Ulya my daughter, that we received your letter, for which we were very grateful. We discovered that you arrived safely and that life is not too bad. Do your best, my daughter, to ensure that nothing bad befalls you – work to the best of your abilities so that you are respected for your work and obedience, rather than scolded. Perhaps we may even see you again, although I must tell you, my daughter, that I am in poor health. But perhaps God will grant that we see each other again. Petya is still at home for now – he is working at the kolkhoz. We received your letter dated 14 February. Winter is cold here with us currently – there is a great deal of snow. God is helping us to live for now, but I must tell you, my daughter, that I am often ill, and you are often in my thoughts and dreams. Would that I live until you

> return home to tell me about your travels. How is life there? You write, Ulya, that you girls are all together. Do you mean with one employer, or just in the same city or camp? The other girls' mothers come and ask me questions, and I don't know how to answer them. I simply say that you wrote that you are all together, and that is all. With that, I bid you farewell, our daughter and sister. We are all alive for now and wish you all the very best in your life. Petya sends his sister a kiss on the right cheek and says goodbye to his sister Ulya. Everyone is safe and well here at present, and now your Papa says goodbye to his daughter too. All the best to you, daughter dear. Your Papa, M. Redka.

A postcard from Berlin to the Kamenets-Podolsk region, dated 14 January 1943 (translated from Ukrainian):

> Postcard sent on 14/I-43 [. . .] Good day to you Mama, Papa, Grandma and my little brother Volodya. I send you a low and heartfelt bow of greeting. I thank you from the bottom of my heart for your New Year greetings. In these first lines of my letter I hasten to let you know that I am alive and in good health, and wishing you all the very best that this world can offer. I also wanted to tell you that I received your three parcels, for which I send my thanks. You asked in your letter, Mama, Papa and you, my little brother Volodya, how I am dressed – what clothes I am wearing. I have clothes, but, more importantly, I have my health, strength and good comrades – just two: Volodka and Vaska. [. . .] Could you send more parcels, because some of the other guys have already received more than thirty parcels containing salted fat and tobacco. Write and tell me whether anyone else has left for Germany. Please send me the addresses of those in Berlin, and tell me how things are at home – how is the bread, the cow, and what duties are you paying? Has anyone joined the army? Tell me all that is new in the village because I have no news. I'll leave it at that. Goodbye. Send my heartfelt greetings to all the family. [. . .] Write and tell me all the news

> from the village and our hut. I eagerly await your reply!!!! Your son, Petro.

For those who were sent to the concentration camps, the support of others became a prerequisite for survival. Lavrenty Novokhatko was sent to Mauthausen. We asked him how he survived. He replied:

> It was all thanks to friendship. One day I began to lose my sight – at one point I could barely see a thing. When we had to file out past the guard post, my friends led me by the hand. [. . .] That's what I call true friendship. Anyone on their own usually died straight away.

Ravensbrück prisoner Olga Golovina never forgot the help she received from an *Ostarbeiter* girl called Sasha who worked near to the camp:

> She worked on a farm . . . unloading wagons of produce of some sort. This girl, Sasha, from Kursk, did a huge amount to help anyone who fell ill. She brought dried onion and dried carrots to us – anything she could, really. She not only had to bring these things to us, but she also had to hide them on herself.

In reality, of course, not all relationships in the camps and workplaces were a perfect picture of friendship and mutual support. Unsurprisingly, conflicts and grievances arose frequently, as described by several of those we spoke to.

Yevdokiya Verkholantseva remembers that a girl called Tosya, an *Ostarbeiter* from Leningrad, claimed a parcel that had been sent to Yevdokiya from home:

A work camp at a ceramics factory, Hermsdorf, 1944.

Mine workers, Herbede, 1944.

A work camp at a chemical plant, Bitterfeld, 1943.

> 'Tosya,' I said. 'A parcel from home should have arrived for me containing a dress that I sewed myself.'
>
> I had sewn little gold buttons all around the edges, they were decent-sized ones that glistened like gold. I had also sewn them down the sleeves and around the sash. And now Tosya was sitting there, wearing my dress – and my boots too!
>
> 'Tosya,' I said. 'That's my dress, how did you come by it?'
>
> 'What are you talking about, Dosya?' she replied. [. . .]
>
> She refused to give me back my parcel. I went to my employer in tears and explained the situation, but Tosya still wouldn't give it back. That bitch from Leningrad refused to hand over my parcel.

There were also examples of disloyalty and denunciation. Nikolai Kireev remembers:

> There were snitches in every camp. You'd be lying on the top of the triple bunk, and beneath you, on the lower bunk, there might be a snitch. He would be the type of person who, even if he knew that he would die tomorrow, would inform on everyone and anyone in the meantime. This he would do in exchange for a reward of some kind, even one as paltry as an extra bowl of soup.

Nadezhda Bulava said: 'There was a group of five of us at the camp who slept together on adjacent bunks. We never discussed anything in the presence of others – if somebody overheard, the next day you might be given a good whipping . . . or disappear completely.'

Ostarbeiter lived in perpetual fear of being informed upon by someone in their inner circle. This fear was particularly acute for Antonina Serdyukova, whose life depended upon her Jewish identity remaining a secret: 'Someone informed upon me – they told the Germans that my mother was a Jew. They denounced me! I don't know who did it.'

Antonina was lucky – her life was saved by a translator. She recalls:

> I was called to a meeting with the *Lagerführer*. A translator translated from German for me: 'We have been told that your mother is a Jewess, and that you are a Jewess.'
>
> 'No,' I lied.
>
> The translator was an old emigrant [former White Army officer], and, as it happened, I could speak German quite well. I therefore understood when he turned to the *Lagerführer* and said, 'It's all nonsense. At the time her parents married, Russians weren't permitted to marry Jews. Of course, she's not a Jew.'
>
> The *Lagerführer* looked at me. 'Get out of here,' he said.

The difficult living conditions and the humiliation of their position sometimes provoked aggression, often directed towards the more vulnerable individuals. This also exacerbated ethical conflicts and increased animosity and resentment towards those who enjoyed more privileged positions in the Nazi hierarchy.* Stereotypes were born and strengthened: Polish people were said to be 'cruel' and 'greedy', while 'Westerners' (Western Ukrainians and Western Belarusians) were labelled 'ill-educated' and 'dirty'.

---

* Heinrich Himmler issued an order on 20 February 1942 regulating the use of forced labourers, in which he suggested dividing the workforce into several categories. The top rung was reserved for Western labourers, and beneath them in the hierarchy were the Poles. *Ostarbeiter* were beneath the Poles in this ranking system, but above Jewish and Roma people.

Registration document photographs: left to right: Apolda, 1943; Leipzig, 1943; Dessau, 1942.

For the Soviet *Ostarbeiter*, frustrations were exacerbated by the fact that virtually all other forced labourers – not only those from European countries, but also workers from the regions of Poland that had been part of the USSR prior to the war – enjoyed advantages over them. In the work camps and the concentration camps it was people from these countries who tended to be appointed as leaders and foremen, or given the less physically demanding jobs. The explanation for this divide lay in the wave of repression that had swept across the new Soviet territories between 1939 and 1942. It had left the 'Westerners' with a hatred towards the Soviet authorities and, by default, animosity towards the Russian population as a whole. Needless to say, this raised them above the Russians in the Nazi hierarchy.

Victor Shuldeshov said:

Registration document photographs: left to right: Platkower Loose, 1942; Lackenbach, Austria, 1943; Winterlingen, 1942.

> There were Poles in the camp, and later some Estonians. There were Latvians too. But they were all treated in a very different manner. We were marched to work under guard, in formation, wearing clogs. Our shoes had wooden soles . . . can you imagine! [. . .] But the other nationalities went to work on their own, and their food was completely different. They got butter, and all sorts of other things. And the French received help from the Red Cross . . . our people got nothing at all.

Many recalled conflicts with the 'Westerners'. Antonina Maxina remembers:

> There were also a few people from Ukraine. The Donetsk region was our part of Ukraine, but these people were from the western side of the country, which had joined the Soviet Union in 1939. We didn't understand each other at all. They were sort of dishevelled, and we never spoke to them. They weren't our Ukrainians, they were Western Ukrainians.
>
> 'Hey!' they would shout when they saw us, 'the Rostov beggars are coming!'
>
> We would respond in kind: 'We'll show you who the beggars are!'
>
> [. . .] 'Shut up, ragamuffin, or else you'll get it!' I would say.
>
> But they never let up. They got their comeuppance when we gave them a good beating though – they soon learned not to touch us.
>
> 'Rostov beggar, eh?' I would say. 'Well, you're a boorish slob.'

Hanna Muzalyova recalled: 'The Western Belarusians really didn't like us. "The *Sovyetki* are here!" they would shout. The Kharkov girls – city girls with sharp tongues, knew just how to respond.'

Anna Kirilenko: 'We befriended the girls from Dnepropetrovsk but we didn't have any contact with the Western Ukrainians. They really didn't like us – especially those of us from Rostov – they thought that we were all Reds.'

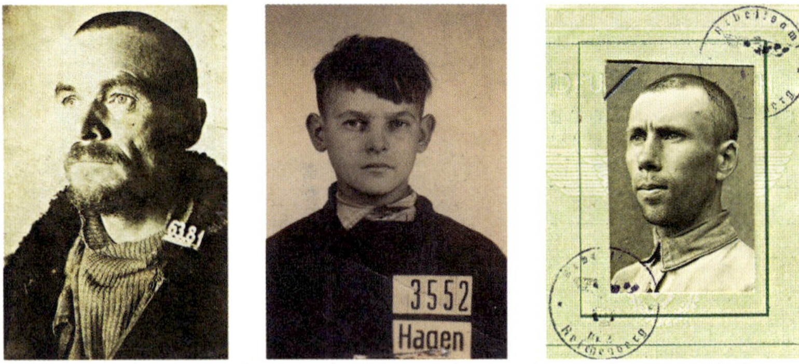

Registration document photographs: left to right: Dresden, 1943; Hagen, 1943; Gablonz,1944.

Olga Smirnova also mentioned the enmity between Russians and Western Ukrainians:

> The owner of our factory was very pleased about the fact that he had girls from Western Ukraine working for him. [. . .] They had all come to Germany of their own volition! They needed the money – the Western Ukrainians were poor. The Germans gave them duvet covers and bed sheets, but they chose not to use them – they said they'd take them home instead.

Workers at a munitions factory, Hamburg, 1944.

Relationships with Polish workers could be equally strained. Varvara Kramarenkova recalls: 'Our supervisor was an old Polish guy. One day I didn't get up when he entered the room. He cuffed me across the face so hard that everything went black.'

Nikolai Zubkov said:

> I was in the punishment camp at Lanzendorf for two months. It was like Lamsdorf* in all but name. The *Vorarbeiter*† were

* Translator's note: A notorious German prisoner-of-war camp in Poland: Stalag 344.
† Foremen.

Ostarbeiter celebrate Christmas, Könnern, 1942.

> Polish men . . . they worked for the Germans. I found them to be worse than both the Czechs and the Yugoslavians.

We also heard many positive accounts of life among people of other nationalities, and many *Ostarbeiter* took an active interest in cultures that they were encountering for the first time. Georgiy Tkachov remembered:

> There were four or five rooms in the barracks, each housing between twenty and twenty-five people. We filled two of the rooms, and there were a few Polish men, so they filled another. [. . .] There were also Dutch, French and Belgian men.

Georgiy learned to speak Polish, thanks to his friendship with the Polish men he worked with on the farm: 'We were friendly with the Poles – we never argued with them. Not once! [. . .] And what's more, I learned to speak excellent Polish.'

A hand-drawn birthday card sent from an aviation factory work camp. Dessau, 1942.

The French were remembered particularly fondly. Victor Shuldeshov recalls:

> They loved and respected us Russians as brothers. I worked with a Frenchman at one time. [. . .] I asked him to teach me French, and offered to teach him Russian in return. He agreed! We started with 'Have you got a smoke?', 'Where do you work', *ça va* – OK, *gros* and *petit* – big and small. He asked me to teach him words for the body, starting from the head – hair, eyebrows and such like. We had got as far as the word for 'waist' when we were separated. That's just how it was. But by then I could already count to ten in French, and had started to speak a little.

A postcard from Witten to Mariupol, 6 December 1942:

> Greetings, my dear parents, Mama, Papa, Grandmother and brother Lenechka. [. . .] I am not the only one alone here – there are lots of other young people from the countries that the Germans have captured. Another 100 people recently arrived from France – all of them young too. Mama, Papa, I will carry out my work sentence here honourably, and then return home. [. . .] As I mentioned in a previous letter, it is already getting cold here, but I don't have anything warm to wear to work. Please send me some food as well if you can, but if you can't then don't worry. Please write and tell me whether all is well with you, and whether there has been another round of recruitment. Is Papa working, or not? Goodbye for now, give my best to everyone.

'In a black jacket and a blue beret'

Many of the men we interviewed insisted that the women were dealt an easier hand in Germany. They claimed that the women were spared much of the heavy manual labour and did not arouse the same sentiments of fear and contempt in the local population. Some men also noted that after a couple of years in Germany, a number of the women began to dress and style their hair in the German fashion. Mikhail Chernenko said:

> Our girls lived in barracks where conditions were considerably better. [. . .] In general, they had it much better than we did. In the early days, none of the girls indulged in camp romances. These only began when the village girls arrived. Each of these girls – without exception – had a 'protector'. The French and Polish girls were always the classiest.

Left: Workers at a munitions factory, Kassel, 1942. Right: A woman working as a dishwasher in a restaurant, Stadthagen, 1943.

In truth, the lives of *Ostarbeiter* women in Germany were no easier than those of the men. They too had to endure manual labour, punishments and beatings. Moreover, for the women, the mockery and derision stung just as sharply as the beatings and therefore, unlike the men, they often spoke of the pain and humiliation of their loss of dignity and abasement. Frida Palko said:

> Sometimes you forget the bad things. They are forgotten now. But, at the time, I had to put up with all sorts – you just had to take it. Lord knows there were all sorts of slurs and humiliating incidents. Children talked down to me too. But I held my tongue through it all.

Taissa Tolkachova told us:

> Some village girls arrived – they wore those long, sweeping skirts and loose blouses and spoke only Ukrainian. They were organised into groups, as were we, and then we were marched along in formation. The first time the Germans saw them, they roared with laughter at the sight. Then they ran up to them and lifted their skirts. I was furious. 'My God,' I remember thinking. 'You Germans are supposed to be cultured people.' I would have hit someone who did that to me. […] But the girls just moved the men's hands away so meekly. […] And the Germans roared with laughter again. Someone had told them that the girls didn't have any underwear – that's why they lifted their skirts.

Left: Workers at the Sauer & Son factory work camp, Suhl, 1942.

Below: Workers at the Singer plant work camp, Wittenburg, 1944.

Ostarbeiter women were seen as easy game. They were regularly subjected to sexual harassment by the camp officials, the security guards, foremen and their private employers. Tatiana Veselovskaya remembered:

> The foreman asked me to go to work on a Sunday once. I arrived to find that nobody else was there – it was just the two

> of us. Of course, I was a little uneasy, but I didn't understand what was going on. Then he told me to go downstairs. I was just fifteen at the time, and I was only saved thanks to the intervention of a German co-worker, Otto, who looked kindly upon me. I saw him standing under the staircase. 'Don't be afraid,' he said, 'I won't let anything happen to you.'

Fellow workers could also constitute a threat. Yevdokiya Verkholantseva narrowly avoided being raped by a Serbian worker:

> It was a weekend, and everyone had gone to church. He and I had taken a horse out together – he was going to scythe the grass, and I was to throw the clover into the cart. [...] Suddenly, he grabbed me and threw me down onto the grass. I managed to wriggle free, took to my heels and ran like mad through the clover.

Some prisoners were forced to work in brothels in concentration camps. Nadezhda Bulava (Mauthausen) told us how she managed to escape this fate:

> We were woken at four o'clock and immediately ordered to line up outside. The Germans were selecting girls from this line-up. I remember an older Polish girl in our block said to me, 'Missy, take this slop pail and go inside. They are about to choose the girls they want for the brothel. [. . .] You can come out again afterwards. You're tall – they'd feed you up and do what they liked with you.'
>
> We didn't know at the time, but it transpired that they used the girls as they wished, and afterwards, so that they didn't talk, they sent them to the crematorium, and replaced them with more girls from our block.

These are the stories of women for whom things ended comparatively well – we can only surmise that those who were not so fortunate found it extremely difficult to share their experiences.

A railway workers' camp, Brandenburg, 1944.

A work camp at a sawmill, Berlin, 1943.

Indeed, most of the women we spoke to made no mention of any sexual contact, including violence.

Mikhail Chernenko told us a little more about what went on in private between men and women in the work camps:

> We had a few old men of about fifty at our camp and they had some women looking after them – they would cook for them and do their mending. But the rest of us would have a woman or girl – sorry, a girlfriend – come by. Some would have a woman visit only periodically; others would have somebody around more or less all the time.

Naturally, these romantic liaisons within the camps, not to mention the sexual violence, resulted in the birth of children

A work camp at a rope factory, Singen, 1944. The text on the reverse reads: *Children from the camp nursery. The woman in the apron holding the two children is the nursery nanny. All the other girls are pictured after their night shift.*

within the camps. Some women also used pregnancy as a pretext for avoiding manual labour, or in an attempt to get sent home. Memorial's publication *Tough Words: The Fate of the Eastern Workers* contains the following information regarding pregnant *Ostarbeiter* women in Germany: 'At first, any pregnant women from either Poland or the Soviet Union were sent home, but it soon became evident that women were purposefully becoming pregnant so as to be able to leave Germany.'*

Accordingly, as of spring 1943, pregnant workers were forbidden from returning home. Children born to *Ostarbeiter* women were removed from their mothers and sent to special-purpose orphanages where many of them died.

While pregnancy did come with an advantage in that it exempted one from work duties, this led to problems of its own. As Antonina Serdyukova explains, pregnant women often found themselves the subject of jealousy and bitter resentment:

> There were some beautiful twenty-five-year-old Western Ukrainian girls in our camp. [. . .] They already had children – mainly fathered by members of the police, who gave them extra food. They had these children, and then they didn't have to go to work; instead, they just looked after their babies. There was a special barracks for mothers and children.

The constant strain of life in the work camps upset the balance of ordinary human emotion, to the extent that something as small as a piece of butter could become a source of resentment and a catalyst for conflict. Lyubov Yerokhova remembers: 'Our Maruska fooled about with a Polish man and gave birth to a son and daughter. She didn't work, but she received butter for the little ones. We were so angry that she got butter, while we didn't.'

None of the men or women who spoke to us returned from Germany with a child, but they often spoke of dates and romantic

* Ulrich Herbert, 'Forced Labourers in the Third Reich: Soviet Workers and Prisoners of War 1941–1945', in Memorial's *Tough Words: The Fate of the Eastern Workers* (SPb: Memorial, St Petersburg, 2000), p.20.

Children of workers at an aluminium factory, Braunau am Inn, Austria, 1944.

attachments that were formed. We asked Galina Shalankova whether she had a boyfriend in Germany:

> I did. He was called Misha. [. . .] We became friends, and grew to really love each other. I remember walking along the banks of the River Elba with him once. He turned to me and said, 'Tell me, do you love me, or not?'
>
> I was silent for a while. [. . .] Then he took me by the shoulders. 'Tell me if you love me,' he repeated.
>
> 'I love you, I love you, I love you,' I replied.
>
> My God, what a wonderful man he was. So handsome . . .

Marriages between *Ostarbeiter* were permitted, and the German

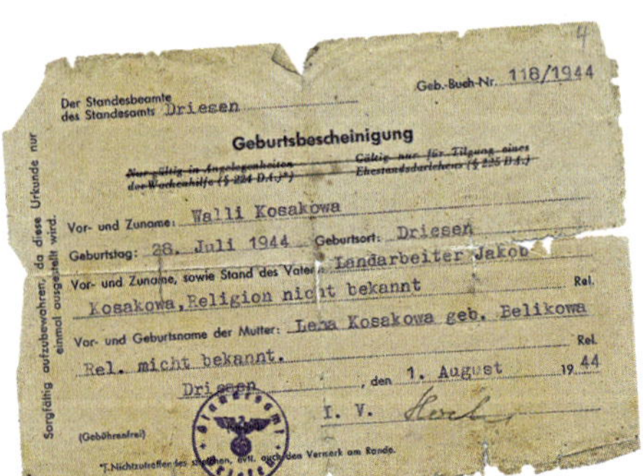

Geb.-Buch-Nr. 118/1944

Der Standesbeamte des Standesamts Driesen

Geburtsbescheinigung

~~Nur gültig in Angelegenheiten der Wochenhilfe (§ 224 D.A.)~~ ~~Gültig nur für Tilgung eines Ehestandsdarlehens (§ 225 D.A.)~~

Vor- und Zuname: Walli Kosakowa

Geburtstag: 28. Juli 1944 Geburtsort: Driesen

Vor- und Zuname, sowie Stand des Vaters: Landarbeiter Jakob Kosakowa, Religion nicht bekannt Rel.

Vor- und Geburtsname der Mutter: Lena Kosakowa geb. Belikowa Rel. Rel. nicht bekannt.

Driesen, den 1. August 1944

I. V.

(Gebührenfrei)

Sorgfältig aufzubewahren, da diese Urkunde nur einmal ausgestellt wird.

A birth certificate, Driesen, 1944.

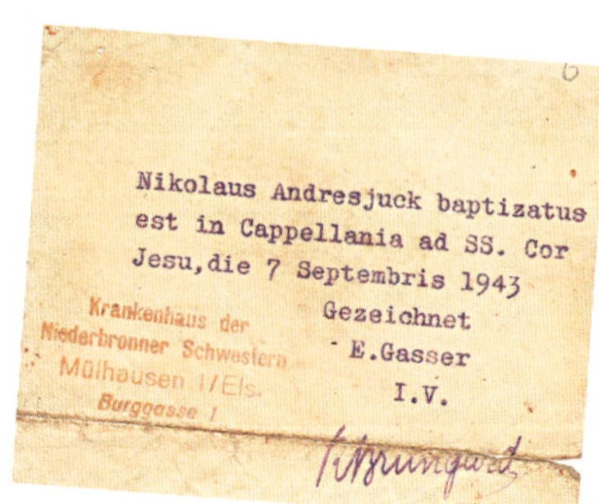

Nikolaus Andresjuck baptizatus est in Cappellania ad SS. Cor Jesu, die 7 Septembris 1943

Gezeichnet E.Gasser I.V.

Krankenhaus der Niederbronner Schwestern Mülhausen i/Els. Burggasse 1

A baptism certificate, Mühlhausen, 1943.

authorities provided written proof of any such union, in addition to birth certificates for any children born in the Third Reich.

More often than not, however, these relationships were torn apart by the war, as Anna Odinokova describes:

> One guy, a Western Ukrainian, was head over heels for me. He wrote me an entire exercise book of poems! But I lost the book . . . He gave the poems to me, and I felt uncomfortable refusing them, so I took them. And do you know what is interesting? When we were liberated and were heading home, a truck drove past us. And he was in the truck! They were being taken to the front. He and some of the other guys recognised us. We waved at them, shouting 'Goodbye!' . . . And off they went. They probably all died.

Below is an extract from a song taken from a handwritten book of songs that was brought back from Germany and safeguarded. It describes the love of an *Ostarbeiter* woman and is set to the tune of the popular Soviet song 'Blue Handkerchief':

> You met me with a
> Sweet and gentle smile
> In a black jacket and a blue beret
> An OST badge on your breast
> I remember how you smiled
> And jokingly said
> The OST patch will be ripped off
> Memories will fade
> And you will forget me.

Antonina Serdyukova worked in a chemical laboratory in a factory and met a young Frenchman in the factory hospital:

> His name was Claude Strett [. . .] He was quite some man, and of course I was mesmerised by him straight away. For his part, well, he was completely blown away by the fact that I was

> Russian. From the moment we met, we began to send little notes to each other. [. . .] Claude came up to the camp fence and cut a hole in the wire for us to talk through. At night . . . can you imagine? He would usually throw stones across the fence onto our barracks – the barracks had been built along the fence line – one stone . . . two . . . and then I would run out to the fence. [. . .] But then they started bombing us every hour of every day and night. The Germans were frightened, and they stopped repairing the fence, so I was able to slip out of the camp. We would run off into the woods together – you know what it is to be eighteen.

An *Ostarbeiter* husband and wife, Osnabrück, 1943.

Returning home after the war, the *Ostarbeiter* girls never spoke of their relationships in Germany. They had learned the necessity of silence in the immediate aftermath of the war, when they were routinely insulted by the Red Army soldiers, who called them 'German whores'. Worse still, they had been forced to endure prolonged questioning at filtration camps, where investigators did all they could to dredge up examples of 'unpatriotic behaviour'.

Suspicion that they had 'consorted with Germans' followed these women home and lingered for many years to come. As a consequence, many were denied the personal lives that they might otherwise have enjoyed.

'The Germans were all different'

The stories we heard provide a clear indication that relationships between Germans and *Ostarbeiter* were usually more complicated and contradictory than conveyed by the stereotypical characterisations of the 'oppressed and oppressor' and the 'employer and worker'. It is also significant that tens of years later, the *Ostarbeiter* spoke openly about how they felt towards the Germans. Many readily admitted that their relationships were not defined purely by a sense of fear and hatred; sometimes they also felt sympathy and gratitude towards certain individuals. However, these relationships were heavily dependent upon the category of work to which the *Ostarbeiter* had been assigned, for experiences varied enormously in the work camps, the farms, and within German family life.

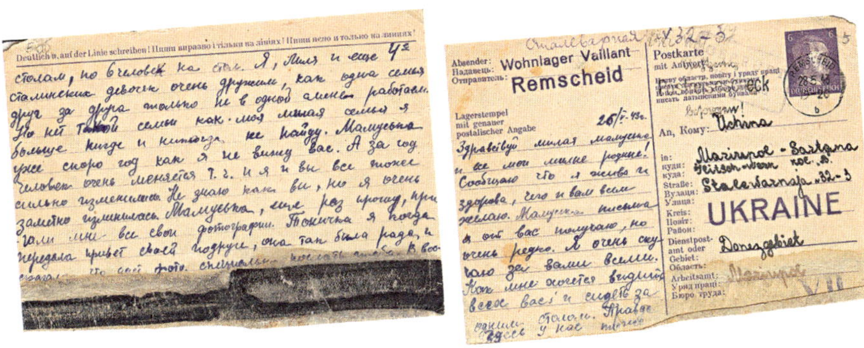

A postcard from Remscheid to Mariupol, dated 26 May 1943:

> Greetings, my dear Mummy and my darling family! I am alive and well, and hope that the same goes for you. Mummy, I do get your letters, but only very rarely. I miss you all so very much. How I wish I could see you all and sit down around the table with you. There are actually six of us here who sit down at the same table too – Lilya and I, as well as four girls from Stalino. Though we don't all work the same shift, we are so close that we are like a family. But never and nowhere will I find another sweet family quite like my own. Mummy, it will soon be a whole year since I saw you last. A person changes a lot in a year, myself included, and you will all be much changed too. Mummy, I ask you again to please send me your photograph. [*The following lines were erased by censorship*]

Nadezhda Bulava acknowledged: 'It must be said that not all the Germans were bastards – some were civil towards us. And there were good people who helped in some way. But there were also Fascists, of the first degree.'

Most of those we interviewed described their first impressions of their arrival in Germany. They recalled being met with a mixture of suspicion and contempt, and many remember being mocked, threatened and insulted. Moreover, they almost always remarked upon the loss of individuality that they sensed almost immediately, especially in the presence of German security guards in punishment camps, prisons and concentration camps. These men and women feature in their accounts as faceless figures who humiliated, beat and interrogated them. Josif Abkovich was imprisoned in the Grodno ghetto before being transported to Auschwitz concentration camp in June 1942. He remembered: 'They then started to lay into me. They beat me, for no reason other than that I was there. They all got involved: the SS, the *Kapo*,* and the assistants.'

Krupp factory, Berlin, 1942.

Metalworking factory, Peine, 1943.

Vadim Gumenny recalled: 'I worked on the railway. Those SS men would walk up and down, watching us. From time to time, they would come over and beat us savagely.'

Lavrenty Novokhatko also remembered his treatment: 'You'd be beaten by the Gestapo, and then taken straight from the Gestapo to prison. But the Gestapo, they really gave you a proper beating; they'd beat you and interrogate you at the same time.'

* Translator's note: The *Kapo* were the concentration camp prisoners assigned by the Nazi guards to oversee and supervise certain activities in the camp.

Very often, the *Ostarbeiter* had only ill-defined memories of the Germans, having grouped them into sets of caricatures: the foremen, the supervisors or the teenagers, for example. The key features of their stories were almost always the cruelty of the Germans and a painful awareness of their own helplessness. Arkady Kozhaev said:

> Working in the mines was very hard indeed, not least because we were under the constant supervision of the German miners. They were young men too – about 30 to 35 years old. They treated us terribly badly [. . .] We were put to work, despite having no idea how to use any of the equipment – so, of course, we made mistakes! They beat the guy who slept on the bunk next to me so badly that he died in the barracks the next day. It was awful, and everyone was outraged, but we couldn't do anything.

The cruelty of some Germans set them apart from the rest. Zinaida Valikhova remembers:

> I was standing, talking to a young man through the wire one day, because we weren't allowed to cross over to see each other. Suddenly I received a thumping whack across the face. I saw stars [. . .] The *Lagerführer* was a real executioner-type. It was awful, the way that he would hit the girls.

A furniture factory work camp, Dörverden, 1943.

Pavel Mikhailov told us of an incident he remembered:

> It was cold at night in the factory workshop. On one occasion I found a warm spot to curl up in and fell asleep. Suddenly I was woken by an almighty whack on my back. I leapt to my feet and saw the foreman with the workshop manager. The manager was an absolute brute.

'What's all this? Sleeping?' the foreman said. 'Off you go and pick up the chippings from under the machines.'

I began to clear the chippings away, but the foreman must have felt that he needed to prove himself to the manager . . . he hit me square in the face, and I fell to the floor. The manager started to thrash me on the back with a rubber hose. Whack, whack . . . I didn't cry out, although others often did. I held it in, but I wet myself.

Tatiana Zhelamskaya said:

> Our employer had a whip [. . .] He would call us out onto the veranda or into the barn and whip us. If you cried, he would stop. If not, he would thrash you for a long time. For some reason, I simply couldn't cry. He stood opposite me and brought his whip whistling down across my shoulders. The next day I was in so much pain that I couldn't turn over in my bed. I cried, but only later.

Lidia Beketova recalls:

> Once, I went to the factory without wearing my OST badge. On the way home, the police were there, watching us as we passed. [. . .]
>
> 'Why aren't you wearing your badge?' one of them asked me. And he began slapping me across the cheeks with his leather gloves. Of course, I burst into tears – I was still just a young girl.

Taissa Tolkachova remembered her journey to work:

> Whenever we walked to and from work, we would see these youngsters laughing at us, and children too. They would throw stones and call us 'pigs'. [. . .] We couldn't say anything in response – anyone who did retaliate would be punished. And so we waited resignedly for it to end; we waited to be freed.

A postcard depicting the Nestlé factory in Kempten, 1943. The text on the reverse reads: . . . *I am sending a postcard of the factory where I work . . .*

Workers with their foreman at a railway car factory, Frankfurt, 1944.

Irina Sokolova, who worked as a housemaid for the family of a German doctor, recalls that unknown passers-by would also hurl cruel insults at the *Ostarbeiter*: 'You would hear people talking as you walked by . . . "These louse-ridden Russians", "Russian pigs", "dogs" . . . It wasn't very nice. But you just had to keep walking – it wasn't as though you could respond.'

The scars left by the humiliation were often etched deeper than those caused by the beatings. Vera Dergachova was interrogated by the Gestapo following her escape from a work camp. She and her friend had run away, and later been caught without documents at the home of Frau Mainz. She remembers the interrogator well, because he chose to focus his attentions upon her friend, who Vera described as 'a true beauty':

> He didn't touch me, but he punched her in the face. [. . .] And then he went and washed his hands in the sink, after touching her face. Can you believe it? He also called her '*Russischer Mist*'*. He washed his hands – after touching such a beautiful face, he washed his hands! And yet it had been he who had touched her. His hands were so squeaky clean, were they?

The *Ostarbeiter* often found it particularly difficult to forget episodes in which they were insulted and humiliated by Germans they lived and worked alongside. Perhaps the pain of enduring

* 'Russian dung'.

these affronts was especially acute because they were a permanent feature of daily life. For the most part, the ordinary, well-educated people of Germany were not inherently cruel; they simply felt justified in treating the *Ostarbeiter* with a certain degree of ignominy. The German historian Ulrich Herbert explains: 'For the vast majority of the population, the *Ostarbeiter* were nothing more than a fixture of wartime life. As such, they were viewed in much the same way as ration cards, or bomb shelters. Discrimination between Russian and Polish workers was viewed in much the same way.'*

A postcard from Bochum to the Kamenets-Podolsk region, dated 18 September 1943:

> Good day or good evening, my dear parents, sisters, and all the family. I am sending you my heartfelt and loving greetings and wishing you all the very best that life can bring, at home in our beloved Ukraine. Mama, Papa and my dear sisters, don't forget that you had a son, Grisha, who has now been separated from you. I cry for you here, but please, my dear family, do not cry for me because it will not help in any way. I ask only that you do not forget me . . .

The Germans were conveniently able to attribute the position of *Ostarbeiter* to the hardships that correspond with war, and they therefore deemed it entirely natural that the workers should wear badges, labour for a pittance, and live at the mercy of their individual employers. Time and again *Ostarbeiter* heard the phrase: 'Life is tough now for everyone – there's a war going on.'

The sense of humiliation experienced by *Ostarbeiter*, heightened by being dispossessed of their rights, was exacerbated by the fact that very few were able to speak German. Yevdokiya Verkholantseva recounted a story from her time working for a farmer in Germany. The incident in question might seem unremarkable and trivial, but

* Ulrich Herbert, 'Forced Labourers in the Third Reich: Soviet Workers and Prisoners of War 1941–1945', in Memorial's *Tough Words: The Fate of the Eastern Workers* (SPb: Memorial, St Petersburg, 2000), p.22.

A brewery manager posing with workers, Munich, 1944.

it is etched in her memory as one of the greatest injustices that she ever experienced. She explained that somebody had thrown a black cloth into the vat in which the white sheets were washed:

> The damp whites were hanging out where I had put them, but somebody had thrown a dark cloth in with them. I washed all the whites at home – as if my mother would have allowed me to do that! Of course, at home we washed the whites and the darks separately. [. . .] The mistress ran over, screaming blue murder. [. . .] If she had spoken Russian, I would have explained that I would never have mixed them. Who did she think we were? Russians pigs who didn't separate our whites from our darks? I tried to explain that I hadn't done anything wrong, but she didn't understand me. I couldn't respond because I didn't speak German, so I just burst into tears.

As a result of these humiliating episodes, *Ostarbeiter* were often eager to share stories of times when they had managed to object to something, or been able to demonstrate their knowledge, gain the upper hand, or prove their worth. Anna Kirilenko, who worked in a textile factory, remembers:

> I often got into debates with my foreman. I would tell him that we were normal people; that we had libraries and went

> to Pioneer camps. I told him all this, but all he would say was, 'That cannot be true. You don't have anything of the sort.'
>
> I showed him evidence to the contrary, but he didn't like it. He was such a stubborn man.

Maria Vitkevich had completed Year Nine at her school in Leningrad before being deported to work as a domestic helper for a family in Berlin with several children:

> When we arrived, our employers told us that we had lived in a Communist country, where forty people slept together under a single quilt. When we began to quote lines by heart from Goethe and Schiller, and sing arias from operas, they couldn't believe their ears. 'Surely you don't have schools there?' they marvelled. 'Surely you aren't taught such things?'

Mikhail Chernenko had a similar experience when he discovered that not a single one of his German contemporaries working at the factory knew how to solve algebra. He tried to teach them the basics.

Vera Dergachova enjoyed reminiscing about the time when her mistress asked her to sew her some underwear 'of the type that they didn't wear':

> I sewed my mistress a bra. She was a round woman and her breasts were quite a size – they sagged down to her stomach. Well, it wasn't a very attractive sight!
>
> 'Yours look so lovely,' she said to me one day. I showed her my bra.
>
> 'Would you sew me one?' she asked.
>
> I told her that I would, and sewed her a bra that lifted her breasts off her stomach. She was transformed into such a shapely, beautiful woman.

There were many similar stories. We were told of how *Ostarbeiter* would prepare salted cabbage using Russian recipes, teach their employers' children how to ice-skate, or correct a German foreman

A farmer with his wife, Altendorf, 1942.

when he made a mistake with his calculations. Despite the near impossibility of the undertaking, in light of the constant workplace discrimination, they felt it was important to prove that there were many tasks at which they were as proficient as, if not more so, than the Germans.

Again, however, a basic knowledge of German made a fundamental difference in this respect. Nikolai Lilyeev, a prisoner of war, explains:

> I came to the conclusion that if you could speak to a German person in German, then that man would recognise you as a person, and treat you as such. [. . .] But if you couldn't speak German, you were deemed to be no better than one of the animals that worked on the farm.

A postcard sent from Berlin to the Kiev region, 10 March 1942:

> Greetings, my dear sister Zina! Surely you haven't become too grand to write? It really hurts that I have sent you letters describing every detail of my damned life, but I haven't heard a peep from you. Either you haven't had time, or perhaps you have forgotten that you cried bitterly when I left. I still count the days, and each one feels like a year. If it wasn't for the girl from my village here with me, I would have gone mad. Every evening, when I finish work, I run to her, and I feel as though I am home when I sit with her. On Sunday there were lots of other girls here, as well as Ukrainian, Polish and French lads. We danced together, and the music kept playing until 10 p.m. But I was only allowed out from 2 p.m. until 5 p.m. and then again in the evening, from 9 until 10 p.m. That's the sort of wonderful mistress I have – if only her death would be as beautiful as the many tears that I am spilling while working for her here. Take care, my darling sister. I'm sending you a kiss.

Irina Sokolova explains that learning German enabled her to stand up for herself to her employers: 'I became bold and sharp. They [her employers] weren't to blame – I just learned how to speak.'

Yevdokiya Verkholantseva recalls that she tried with all her might to learn some German words. She would listen to them, and write down what she heard using the Russian alphabet: 'I'd write everything down. Like this: *kumelika* [*Kuh melken*] – to milk cows; *shvei fedra* [*Schweine füttern*] – to feed the pigs; *Vasser* [*Wasser*] – water. I would translate them all straight away. I picked it up quickly – I seized upon every word I heard, and learned it.'

But not everybody wanted to learn German, and not merely because of the linguistic challenge it presented. Those who could understand were often disgusted by what they heard issuing from the mouths of their enemy, which often amounted to little more than orders, shouts and curses. Taissa Tolkachova said: 'I didn't want to, but I came to hate the Germans – all I heard, time and again, was "*Schweinerei*"'*

Many *Ostarbeiter* remember the cruelty of the local teenagers who, as members of the Hitler Youth, were taught in school that the *Ostarbeiter* were '*Untermensch*', an inferior race. For these children, the eastern workers were prime targets.

Attitudes among the adult population were more varied. Some had been Social Democrats or Communists before the Nazis came to power, and these men and women tended to treat the *Ostarbeiter* with greater sympathy. There were also Germans who pitied the children and teenagers who had been sent to their country to work. And despite the fact that the local population were strictly forbidden from having any personal contact with *Ostarbeiter* (e.g. giving them food or clothing supplies), some showed great compassion towards them.

A postcard from Angerwiese, Kaliningrad region, to the Kamenets-Podolsk region, dated 30 November 1943:

---

* Filth.

> In these first lines of my letter I hasten to inform you that I am alive and well and sending you the very best wishes for your life at home. I can also tell you that I received your letter, for which I send my heartfelt thanks. I had not received any letters from you for a whole month, and was beginning to worry that something was wrong at your end. I haven't sent you a parcel yet, but when my employer goes into town, he may take it to the post office for me, because I don't go into town very often. You write that mother can no longer work, so you might hire someone when you can. If you are short of money, I can send you some. Don't worry about me for now – just look after yourselves. All things permitting, this year I will come home on *Urlaub*.* Goodbye for now. I remain alive and well.

Workers at a canned-food factory, Ludwigshafen, 1944.

Acts of compassion and sympathy took various guises, but more often than not, kindness was manifested in the form of a meal, or the provision of food supplies. A considerable number of *Ostarbeiter* described how German men and women, both complete strangers and familiar faces – often fellow workers, foremen and sometimes even guards and members of the police – would occasionally 'slip them something' in secret. In bringing the *Ostarbeiter* a sandwich or a piece of bread from home, these kindly Germans were flouting the rules at great personal risk.

* Leave.

Nevertheless, these instances of kindness were undoubtedly made memorable by the fact that they were generally one-off events, and very much out of the ordinary. Vera Dergachova says: 'I remember that the foreman invited me to his house. I can still remember it now – you don't forget those moments! He lived at 18 Bergstrasse (Mountain Street). I arrived, and they fed me preserved pumpkin from containers that looked like milk bottles.'

A worker with farming family, Prignitz, 1943.

Vera Fedorchenko worked in a munitions factory in Nindorf. She remembers:

> One day at work my needle broke and I went looking for the foreman. There were some elderly German women seated at a table, sorting through some things. They were having some sandwiches for their tea – Lord, what meagre little sandwiches they were! I walked over to them, and one woman got up and slipped a piece of bread into my pocket. They didn't have much themselves – they too were hungry. Heaven forbid that someone should have seen her give it to me.

Victor Shuldeshov, who worked at the Marion factory in Leipzig, recalled:

> I worked alongside a German called Amon in the foundry. If he had something to smoke, he would give me a cigarette. If not,

> he would give me a cigarette butt. He would slip me a sandwich sometimes, and when we worked the night shift he would let me take a half-hour nap. There was a tiny room there where you could catch forty winks and he would wake me up when it was time to get back to work. He was a good man.

Lyubov Shkulyova worked in a munitions factory in Osterfeld. She remembers:

> Our guard, Matthias, escorted us to work from the camp each day. He was a very old man. [. . .] I always walked right at the back of the column, and one day he said to me, 'You all look so hungry when you walk; you meander like shadows.'
>
> 'They feed us badly,' I told him.
>
> 'I'm going to tell the camp authorities that one of my windows has been knocked out and needs clearing up,' he said.
>
> And so we went off to the camp director and Matthias asked, pointing at me, for permission to take a prisoner home to clean up the broken glass. They agreed, and he took me back to his house where we all sat down around the table, said a prayer, and ate bean soup.
>
> 'Eat up, eat up,' Matthias encouraged.
>
> Afterwards, he took me back to the camp. As I said, he was an elderly man – he was about sixty-five or seventy.

According to Zoya Yeliseeva, who worked in a textile factory in Kassel:

> The Germans were all different, very different. Some treated us with hostility and suspicion – you couldn't wear an OST badge on the trams, for example, or you would be thrown off straight away by the conductor. Others were quite the reverse – sometimes as we walked to work in formation, someone on the pavement would slip something into your pocket. [. . .] I must say, however, that such behaviour was rare unfortunately.

Tatiana Teplova was a railway worker:

> I worked alongside a tall, strong woman called Marta with a deep voice. What a wonderful woman she was! It was such a joy to work a night shift with her – she would sit me down at the table with her, pour me a cup of coffee and give me a bread roll.

Maria Ausheva also relayed an astonishing story about an unexpected display of human compassion:

> I worked at the Winkel munitions factory and will never forget one particular incident until the day I die. We were marched to work in the mornings in formation – there was always one guard with an automatic rifle at the front, and another, also with an automatic rifle, bringing up the rear. Our route took us past a house where the most beautiful roses grew – I had never seen such beautiful flowers! From the moment I first saw them, I always made sure to walk in the first row so that I could stop by the fence of this house and look at the roses for a while, before joining the rear of the column again and walking on. [. . .] I did this every day, both on the way there, and on the way back. And then one day, just when I had stopped and begun to look at the roses, a German man appeared in front of me. He wore a beaming smile on his face, and he immediately cut three roses that were only just, just starting to open. They were the most beautiful roses. And then he gave them to me! My God! I had tears in my eyes. I felt as though I had been given half of the world!

Irina Sokolova described becoming overcome with emotion as her employer wished her a Happy New Year during her final winter in Germany:

> They invited all four of us – myself, and the Polish, Ukrainian and Serbian girls to eat with them. It was New Year 1944–1945. My employer reduced me to tears when he said, 'I wish for

Irina to celebrate the next New Year surrounded by her family and friends.'

Of course, I broke down in near-hysterical tears.

A postcard from Stassfurt to the Kiev region, dated 19 April 1943 (translated from Ukrainian):

> A note [. . .] from your daughter and sister Tonya to her dear and so distant Papa, Mummy, little brother Pavlusha, and sisters Marusya and Galya. Greetings, my dear family! Before I begin writing this short letter, I hasten to send you my sincere and heartfelt greetings from a far and unfamiliar place. I wish you all the very best and pray that God grants you all that you ask of him. Allow me to wish you a happy [Christian] Bright Week; may you celebrate these days in the best possible way and may God send you happiness, good fortune, and long lives, until I return to my beloved home to live and talk among you once again. My dear family, I will also be celebrating the special day of 25 April for three days, although I do not know exactly what we will do. I am currently sitting in the courtyard outside the barracks, writing this letter to you. But my thoughts are somewhere else entirely – they are nestled close to you, in my beloved home. And all because now – around this time in particular – I can find no peace in my life, since it reminds me of 20 May, the day when I left both you, my dear family, and the region I call home, and travelled to a distant, foreign and unknown land, unaware of what lay ahead of me. I cannot forget the moment I walked over to little Pavlusha with you, my sister, and Mama asked, as she stood there crying, 'When will you make the journey back to us?'
>
> And I replied, 'Don't cry, Mama. I will be back soon.'
>
> But Papa wasn't at home. And then you and I, sister, walked up the big hill, and I gazed all around me, my eyes sweeping across the familiar surroundings of home. I saw him then, standing among the flowers, as though surrounded by milk. [. . .] Goodbye, my darling family, I am sending you infinite

> kisses. I could write until the cows come home, but I've run out of paper. Pass on my greetings to all my friends for me.

Fedor Khmara told us that his employers broke all the rules by allowing him to listen to the radio: 'My employers had a wireless and they allowed me to listen to Russian broadcasts on it. They asked only, God forbid, that I didn't tell anybody about it – "Or else, we will hang," they said.'

A domestic worker with a child in the suburbs of Munich, 1944.

An *Ostarbeiter* nanny (employed by a businessman) with her young charges, Pirmasens, 1942.

Perhaps unsurprisingly it was usually the *Ostarbeiter* who worked for families as nannies or housemaids who enjoyed the warmest and closest relationships with Germans. The strict orders that employers were not, under any circumstances, to fraternise with foreign domestic workers were often broken in the realities of daily life. Varvara Khabarova recalls that her employer once said to her, 'Varvara, you must never tell anybody that you eat with us at the same table. We do so because the children love you.'

According to Varvara, the children would refuse to go to sleep unless she was with them. We heard many such stories of children becoming attached to their *Ostarbeiter* nannies, and these feelings were often reciprocated. The *Ostarbeiter* girls, torn away from their own homes and families, frequently cherished the bonds they formed with their young charges.

Galina Agranovskaya worked as a domestic helper for a German family with several children. She remembers:

> I loved to cuddle their children. [. . .] I always felt particularly sorry for little Helga, who was constantly covered in little sores. She had terrible eczema and the poor little thing would scratch at her skin all night. I would wash her mucky pyjamas. She was an adorable little thing, and so kind. She knew that I always had a soft spot for her.

Yevdokiya Verkholantseva pitied the youngest son of the family that she worked for. He had been forced to work as an apprentice with the blacksmith who, it transpired, beat him constantly. She remembers that he came to her in tears:

> Anton came to me. He was crying, and I cried too – both for him, and for myself. And as he cried, I realised that the blacksmith really was beating him badly. He would hit him with whatever he could lay his hands on at the time.
>
> 'I won't go back there, I won't go back,' Anton cried to me.

There were also accounts of deeper relationships that formed between *Ostarbeiter* and members of the local population.

A letter from Bad Freienwalde wishing a former domestic worker (an *Ostarbeiter)* a happy birthday, dated 22 November 1944:

> Dear Tamara,
> I wish you a heartfelt happy birthday. I hope that you are happy in your new place and that work there is good. Just one year ago we were all in Berlin together and today it is one year exactly since we lost our apartment during an air raid. I haven't heard anything from you in a very long time.
>
> My new girl works daily, but only for five hours so I have enough work to keep me busy. You worked so diligently. If you ever marry, you will be so adept at managing the domestic

work. [. . .] Buy yourself some flowers for your birthday with the money enclosed within this letter. I wish you all the very best and send you my heartfelt greetings. Yours, E. Nadolny. My husband sends his heartfelt congratulations on your birthday too.

Domestic workers with the German family they worked for, Bremen, 1944.

The foreman at the factory where fourteen-year-old Tatiana Veselovskaya worked took a shine to her and when the factory was bombed during an air raid, he and his wife sheltered her at their home. Tatiana remembers that he said to her:

> My wife would like to invite you to our house. Just make sure that you remove that OST badge and put on some other clothes. I went to their house and they came out to meet me. They took me inside and put me straight into the bath. He washed and cut my hair – he was a former hairdresser – and then they styled it with curls. And then she began sewing me some clothes, altering some of her own to fit me. They let me stay the night. I remember it as though it were yesterday and will never forget their kindness. [. . .] From then on, I went to them every Sunday. She knitted things for me, she sewed me clothes.

Tatiana remembers that they tried to persuade her to stay with them at the end of the war, and she admits that she sometimes regrets not having listened to them. Instead, she chose to return home.

Despite the rules in place to discourage romantic relationships between *Ostarbeiter* and Germans, such attachments did form. For understandable reasons, however, the *Ostarbeiter* we spoke to were reluctant to enter into discussion about such topics. As a result, only one person provided an account of a relationship of this sort. Lidia Yerastova (née Balyuta), deported in summer 1943, worked on the railway in Artern, escorting freight train cargoes. Unlike most of the female *Ostarbeiter*, who lived in work camps, she lived in a dormitory residence and, if she covered her OST badge, she could walk freely into town. She shared the following story with us:

> One day, I arrived at the cinema to find that there were no tickets left. A couple of young German guys offered me a ticket. That's how I met Rolf Uetze, who I remained friends with until the very end of the war. One day he said to me, 'Lidia, my Mama has asked for you to come over to our house, so she can meet you. She knows all about you – I told her where you are from . . .'

Lidia Balyuta and Rolf Uetze, Artern, 1945.

A residential camp for *Ostarbeiter*, Saalfeld, 1944.

> . . . And so, I went. She saw me and threw her hands up in the air. 'Oh!' she said, 'what a beautiful girl.' She welcomed me in, and offered me cakes. We sat and talked. Meanwhile, Rolf was trying to tune in to Radio Moscow on the wireless.
>
> 'Is this Moscow?' he asked me when he thought he had found it.
>
> 'Yes, it is,' I replied.

We listened for a while, and then he turned it off. 'That's enough,' he said. 'I'm afraid.'

Each time that I went to his house, he would find Radio Moscow so that I could listen to it for a little while. We remained friends until the end of the war. I was happy with him. [. . .] His parents loved me, and invited me to live with them. [. . .] No, we were not husband and wife. I slept in his little brother's bedroom. We weren't yet of legal age – I was seventeen, and he was a year younger than me. We planned to wait until Rolf turned eighteen, so that we could marry. But the war ended before that, and I had to leave . . .

Many years later, I discovered that the Uetze family had looked for me for a long time. They wrote to every authority, but each one replied that my whereabouts were unknown. One day they received a different response: 'Lidia Balyuta returned to her motherland and married. There is no need to trouble her.'

In actual fact, at that time I was doing [forced] logging work in the Komi Republic. There in the labour camp, I had a recurring dream that I had returned home to Artern. I knew that if only I could reach the door and ring the bell, Rolf would open it, and we would never again be separated. But I never managed to ring it – I always woke up first.

Through the Prism of War

In the early months or years following their deportation to Germany, the *Ostarbeiter* tended to have only a very blurred picture of events unfolding at the front. The rumours that filtered back to them did little to inspire hope that the war would soon be over, let alone belief in the possibility of the Red Army's victory.

'We aren't to blame for all this – Hitler is'

Taissa Tolkachova was deported to Germany in May 1942. She describes the reaction of her factory foreman to the news that Sevastopol had fallen to the Germans:

> He was such a loathsome German. He was for ever calling us '*Schwein, schwein*' – pigs, pigs. One day he suddenly ran over to us shouting, 'Sevastopol has fallen! Sevastopol has fallen! Now I will be your lord, and you will work for me.' We watched him, with tears in our eyes.

Workers at an aviation factory, Wels, Austria, 1943.

Gennady Gribovsky remembered: 'The police gathered us together and announced, "That's it – Russia and the Soviet Union are no more. You will be here until the day you die."'

During the initial stages of their new lives in Germany, many *Ostarbeiter* harboured little hope of ever returning home. Mikhail Chernenko told us that in the summer of 1942 he did not believe that the Red Army could possibly defeat the Germans:

> After being dragged away to Germany, I fell into a state of depression. Unfortunately, I must admit that at the time I never even asked myself what the future might hold. I was convinced that Russia would be defeated. You should have seen the way our army scarpered in Ukraine.

Iraida Zhukova remembers: 'I had lost all hope of ever seeing my home or my Papa again. I thought we would die there.'

Even as the end of the war drew slowly into sight, for some it still seemed inconceivable that Germany could be defeated. Georgiy Tkachov told us that even as late as March 1945 people in the work camps were still signing up to join the Russian Liberation Army:*

> They lined us up. The officer was Russian; he was a member of Vlasov's Russian Liberation Army. [. . .] This officer came up to us, with a pretty young woman beside him dressed in the same military uniform. Both uniforms were German. He began his speech with the words, 'We are representatives from the Russian Liberation Army. We stand against the Communists.' In other words, he was in favour of a return to the old order. The essence of his speech was this: anyone who would like to join the ranks of our army, take three steps forward. Ten or fifteen people stepped forward to join them. They were immediately organised into formation and marched away.

* Translator's note: In 1944, Vlasov's army was renamed the Armed Forces of the Committee for the Liberation of the Peoples of Russia. Its goal was to overthrow Joseph Stalin's regime.

Maria Ausheva told us of her conviction, rooted in mysticism, that the Red Army would be victorious:

> In any case, I knew that we would win. I just knew. Would you like to know how I knew? From a conversation with a lieutenant who stayed in our house. One day he asked my mother whether she had stocked up on cross pendants.
>
> 'No, my son,' she replied.
>
> 'Oh! But you will need some cross pendants to wear – it's going to be a long war,' he said. 'But don't fear, Mother, victory will be ours.'
>
> I remembered his words, and throughout my time in Germany I remained convinced that we would win; that he had spoken the truth.

As time went by, the *Ostarbeiter* began to suspect that the situation at the front might be somewhat different from what they had been led to believe. Having picked up a little of the local language, they caught snatches of conversation or cast about for snippets of information in propaganda newspapers or German cinema newsreels. Some even managed to tune in to Radio Moscow (e.g. Irina Sokolova, Taissa Tolkachova and Fedor Khmara).

An *Ostarbeiter* on her employer's bicycle, Dramburg, 1944.

Largely, however, it was the perceptible shift in German attitudes towards the *Ostarbeiter* that led them to question what direction the war was taking. These attitudes were influenced by both the successes and the defeats of the Wehrmacht, as well as the content of letters that filtered back from the front lines.

Workers at a clothing factory, Berlin, 1943.

The *Ostarbeiter* first noticed a palpable shift in the German mood following the battle of Stalingrad. Some described how it was that they got wind of the news that the Germans had been encircled:

> I could read the situation at the front from the facial expressions of my mistress and her sister. If they looked gloomy, I knew that somewhere the Germans had been dealt a blow. That was for sure! Especially at the time of Stalingrad [the battle]. I remember it perfectly – endless gloomy days. I was particularly aware of it, because it affected me personally. (Galina Agranovskaya)

> We watched as all the Germans and the foreman gathered together in a huddle. They were in a terrible mood. I remember thinking that something must have happened. But no news had reached us – we didn't know where any of the soldiers were; either German or Soviet. We just went to and from work, like slaves. A German man who had previously declared that he was a Communist later told us that the Russians had taken Stalingrad. (Taissa Tolkachova)

> Stalingrad signalled a turning of the tide in terms of people's consciousness. [. . .] Some prisoners from Stalingrad were brought to our camp – they had been raked up in the early days of the battle, when their city had been all but entirely seized. When they appeared, bringing with them stories from the battle and the ensuing chaos, the mood altered perceptibly. (Mikhail Chernenko)

The situation at the front affected the attitudes of the Germans towards the *Ostarbeiter* in different ways. Tatiana Teplova recalled working alongside a German woman called Frieda: 'Her brother was killed at Stalingrad – she hated us.'

But for many of the German population, the realities of war, including the relentless bombing raids, the sharp decline in food supplies, and the deaths of loved ones provoked a very different reaction. Raissa Pervina said: 'I cannot complain about my mistress. She always treated me well – perhaps, because her son was fighting in Russia. She once said to me, "Perhaps my son will find himself in the same situation as you."'

Zinaida Komissarova recalled:

> The son of the family for whom I worked was killed. I watched them cry in the evenings. They ordered a portrait of him. They never thought for a moment that they would be defeated – they had such faith in that Hitler of theirs. It wasn't until the American bombing raids intensified that they began to understand.

Pavel Mikhailov described the mood of the German workers at the metallurgical plant where he worked at the end of the war:

> We had received no news at all from the front, but the truth can never be kept hidden for long. People had begun to hold frank conversations and we told the Germans that Hitler was *kaputt*. Of course, there were fanatics among them who argued against us.
>
> 'No, no,' they insisted, 'Hitler will show you yet.'

When describing this shift in behaviour and attitudes, many we spoke to noted that the Germans, having woken up to the situation now facing them, began to shift all blame onto Hitler. 'We're just ordinary people,' they would say. 'We have done nothing wrong ourselves.'

Anna Odinokova, who worked for a farming family in Lower Silesia, remembers:

> Rumours began to reach us that our soldiers were moving closer. My employers began to treat me better. There was no

> improvement in terms of food, but they were less rude to me. [. . .] Goebbels and his sort were always blathering away on the radio . . . blah blah blah. The Master would switch it off, cursing. 'Ah! *Schweinerei!*,'* he would say, followed by a few choice swearwords. He was trying to show me that he had no love for these men on the radio. 'We didn't even want Hitler,' he alleged. 'It was those idiot youngsters who supported him.'

Accounts by *Ostarbeiter* reveal that it was usually the elderly members of the German population who treated them with the most kindness and compassion. Rather than viewing the *Ostarbeiter* as the enemy, they tended to look upon them as hapless youngsters and victims of misfortune.

Maria Ausheva recalled an incident:

A work camp at a gunpowder factory, Frankfurt am Main, 1944.

> A woman came up to me, crying. 'Take this bread,' she said to me. 'My son is in Russia with your people. We aren't to blame for all this – Hitler is. Your mothers are crying too. Take this, in memory of my son.' We took the bread, and shared it between everyone in the barracks.

Victor Shuldeshov recalls some of the conversations that he had with German workers in the foundry of the Marion factory in spring 1945. The gist of the discussions was that both Hitler and Stalin ought to be held responsible for the war; the people themselves were entirely innocent. He recalled: 'The conversation went something along these lines: Why did Hitler and Stalin have to go head to head? We just want to have a job to go to, and food on the table!'

When the Allies commenced their mass bombing raids on German

---

* Filth.

cities, people began to sense that the end of the war was imminent. This only served to heighten the fear that some already felt towards the *Ostarbeiter*, who up until then – in the eyes of their employers – had been little more than sorry, penniless servants. Almost overnight, they began to see their workers in a very different light – these people were now on the side of their future vanquishers, and as such could perhaps guarantee their safety in times ahead:

> A woman called Frau Kurde was the head of our laboratory. I remember that she asked me one day, 'Galya, what will the Communists do when they get here? Will they hang us all?'
>
> Once the war was over, the Germans began trying desperately to befriend the Russians – they actually became kindly. (Galina Shalankova)

> By about March 1945 we had begun to notice that the Germans were treating us slightly differently. A few of them had started coming up to us and saying things like, 'Well, this means you'll soon be going home, doesn't it? The war will soon be over.' (Taissa Tolkachova)

> Our master began to curry favour with us so much that I knew the war was ending. I remember remarking upon this change in his behaviour to the Polish girls with whom I worked. 'He is being so kind!' I said.
>
> 'Kind eh?' they replied. 'His son is in the SS – he's frightened, and praying to God that the Americans get here first – not the Russians.' (Galina Agranovskaya)

'Everything was destroyed; everything was ablaze'

Before the war finally ended with the surrender of German forces across Europe in May 1945, both the *Ostarbeiter* and the Germans had to survive the relentless and indiscriminate Allied bombing raids. Despite the fact that these air raids undoubtedly reinforced the belief that the war was soon to end, those we spoke to considered this latter period of their life in Germany to have been the most

Sorting through the rubble after an air raid, Berlin, 1944.

terrifying of all. Little wonder, when so many of them worked in munitions factories, which were prime targets for the bombers.

> It was utter hell. Everything was destroyed; everything was ablaze. (Anna Yermilova)

> Aeroplanes began to circle overhead, scattering their bombs. 'We're toast,' we thought. 'It's our turn now – we're going to die.' (Valentina Sekhina)

> Trying to survive the bombing was the most terrifying experience of all. (Zinaida Valikhova)

A letter from Schwerte (unsent), dated 22 March 1945:

> An enduring and fond memento for my dear brother Pavlusha, from his sister Tonya in a far-off region of Germany. [. . .] Pavlusha, I wrote this song for you at four-thirty p.m. on Thursday, while our city was being bombed heavily and fired upon by the Americans. Our barracks shook and the window was blown out, but our factory and station went up in flames.

Vadim Novgorodov remembered:

> A bomb exploded on the other side of the hill. People started shouting and Tosya and I raced to the bomb shelter. We began to count how many of 'our lot' were in the shelter. Lidochka wasn't there, neither was Lyonya Batrachenko. Nikolai wasn't there either – I can't remember his surname . . . [. . .]. A fragment of shrapnel had pierced Lidochka through the heart, while Lyonya was killed outright by a blow to his temple. Nikolai was wounded in the back – he didn't die immediately. [. . .] There was also a man from Western Ukraine – his intestines were blown out, leaving only his spine. [. . .] When the bombing became truly unbearable in 1944, our faith that we would survive began to diminish.

While, for the *Ostarbeiter* at least, the bombing brought with it hopes of imminent freedom, this anticipation was overshadowed by the fear that they might not live to see the end of the war.

Aldona Volynskaya spoke candidly about the 'strange feeling' of solidarity with the Germans that was evoked by the fear of dying in an air raid:

> My God! I ran down into a basement somewhere and found some German men and women already there. The house began to shake and everyone in the basement crouched down. It was a strange feeling, you know. Here we all were, sharing the same fears, because the Americans were bombing us – they were bombing all of us!

Victor Shuldeshov also recalls feeling sympathetic towards the Germans and the victims of the bombing:

> I'll tell you about the bombing by the American and English air forces. The English would fly at night, and the Americans flew by day. The Americans would fly over at 12 p.m., and then the English would fly at 12 a.m. On the hour. The number

Sorting through the rubble after an air raid, Augsburg, 1945.

> of planes was just terrifying! [. . .] And when they suddenly started to drop their bombs . . . there was no warning siren – nothing at all. I don't know whether it was half the city they bombed, or more . . . The whole city was burning – the flames were so bright that they lit up the night. One of the Fascists was escorting us to work that night. He wore a Nazi armband on his arm. His entire family had been killed. He took us to work and stood under a low canopy where he took a drink, and told us that his home had been hit by a bomb, and his family had been killed – they were all lying buried under the rubble. He drank about 100g, began to cough and took off his armband. Raising it to his nose, he blew into it. Of course, if one of his own had seen him do this and reported him, I don't know what would have happened! But we understood how he felt.

From Victor's story it is clear that as the bombing intensified, and the number of victims on their own side rose, the Germans began to lose their faith in victory. As symbolised by the security guard tearing off his Nazi armband, there was an increasing sense of despair among the German population. They were aware that catastrophe was looming.

PART 4

Between Germany and the USSR

The Victors

'Our guards did a runner'

The accounts by *Ostarbeiter* of the final weeks, days and hours before their liberation were characterised by a conflation of different emotions. Excited anticipation at the prospect of freedom mingled with a fear that they might not live to see it; that they might die right in the very last moments of the war. There were also frightening rumours circulating – many *Ostarbeiter* recalled hearing that the Germans intended to kill them before the advancing Allied troops arrived. Victor Zhabsky, who was interned in a work camp in Leipzig, remembers: 'I didn't think that I would get out of the camp alive. I believed that sooner or later the Germans would slaughter us all. They would slaughter us for fear that we would take revenge upon them.'

From a letter written by Maria Volobueva:

> When the war ended, we were in a work camp somewhere near Berlin [. . .] One day our German guard said to us, 'The Russians are close. You are all to be taken out into the woods and shot. You should scatter once you're in the woods. If they don't arrive today, the Russians will be here tomorrow.'
>
> We were led out of camp and, once we got to the woods, we scattered. The Germans had no time to shoot – they were fleeing themselves.

Fedor Apyonkin was imprisoned at Mauthausen concentration camp. He recalls: 'Rumours were circulating that the SS were planning a massacre; one last act of revenge. We heard that nobody

A photographic keepsake, Gelsenkirchen, 20 May 1944. The text on the reverse reads: *A fond and enduring memento for my fellow countryman and friend, from the time I lived in Germany, in the city of Gelsenkirchen.*

Lyosha, it may be that our time here is up
And some of us will now return home.
My sweet friend, I ask you
To tell my wife about me
Where I lived and wandered in this foreign land.

was going to be allowed to leave the camp – we were all to die at the hands of this regime.'

The mass killing of several million eastern workers would never have happened. But for those in the concentration camps, the risk of such an atrocity was real. More than one hundred and thirty thousand people were killed between January and April 1945 in Sachsenhausen, Bergen-Belsen, Mauthausen, Dachau and Buchenwald concentration camps. Many more were murdered in other camps.* The SS began to hurriedly march the inmates of the concentration camps in the eastern territory of the Third Reich deeper into Germany. These became known as the death marches, and several of those we interviewed remembered them well.

Nikolai Bogaslavets was imprisoned in Gross-Rosen concentration camp. He told us:

> We were herded down little tracks. Every five or six metres there was a German guard with a dog. If anyone fell so much as half a metre out of line, they would be shot without warning. That's

* A. C. Yakushevsky, 'The Internal Crisis of Germany 1944–1945', *New and Cutting-Edge History*, 1995, No.2, pp.62–3.

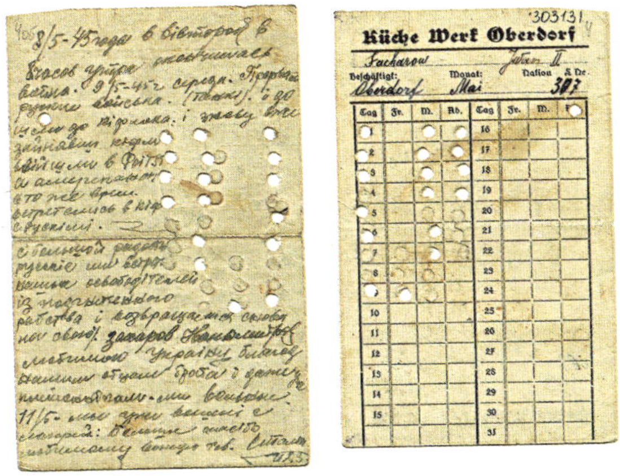

A letter written on the reverse of a pass for a mine canteen, Voitsberg, 1945.

At 8 a.m. on Tuesday 8/5-45, the war ended. On Wednesday 9/5-45 the Russian soldiers (tanks) broke through as far as Köflach and, once they had taken Köflach, they moved on to Voitsberg. Meanwhile, the Americans met the Russians living in Köflach. We Russians went out joyfully to meet our liberators. Free from the yoke of slavery we will soon be returning to our beloved Ukraine again [. . .] We are free. By 11/5 we had left the camp. Thank you, Comrade Stalin, our beloved leader.

> what happened to a Belarusian chap I was friendly with. He was walking in front of me, and needed to relieve himself. He moved ever so slightly out of line and . . . one minute Volodka was there, the next he wasn't . . . Anyone who couldn't keep pace with the group was simply shot.

Anastasia Agafonova was imprisoned in Ravensbrück concentration camp. She remembers:

> We were marched to a camp around twenty or twenty-five kilometres from Hanover. [. . .] There were no wooden bunks; we sat on the floor, huddled up against each other, and slept right there on the floor too. The dead were taken away each morning [. . .]. By 15 April we could hear the sound of gunfire – the front was drawing closer. [. . .] Then we heard the rumble of tanks, and saw that an English tank had been driven right into the camp – there were soldiers sitting on top and the driver was waving. We didn't even have the strength to rejoice.

Witnesses described seeing the concentration camp guards fleeing on the eve of the arrival of the Allied troops. Oksana Kossakovskaya recalls:

> In January 1945 [. . .] we women were moved from Auschwitz to Ravensbrück. We were locked up in a barracks there for a month – they wouldn't let us out. The barracks was packed with people, all sitting pressed up against each other like sardines. They would open the doors to bring in the slop – some got some, others didn't. [. . .] And then one day we realised that the guards were gone. We got up and left.

The men and women on the death marches also began to notice that their guards were fleeing. The prisoners tried to make the most of any opportunities to escape that this created. Sometimes, *Ostarbeiter* were able to hide fugitives from concentration camps and prisoners of war. Valentina Gridchina was in a work camp in Zwickau:

> The *Lagerführer* disappeared. Everyone disappeared. We were alone in the camp. Not long beforehand, some runaways had arrived, asking us to hide them. They had been marched out of their concentration camp and along a path through the woods. Anyone too weak to keep up was shot . . . A few of them had somehow managed to hide, and had then made a run for it. They appeared at our camp and a few of our campmates hid them under the floor. They took up the floorboards, and the runaways lay there, under the floor.

During the final weeks of the war, when many of their factories had been bombed out and production had ground to a halt, those of the *Ostarbeiter* still interned in their work camps were generally put to work clearing rubble or digging anti-tank ditches. Time and again, this work was interrupted by the wail of air-raid sirens, and this made it more and more difficult for the guards to keep tabs on the *Ostarbeiter* . . . Many of them escaped and in some instances the Germans simply set workers free.

Leonid Osipov was held in a work camp on the outskirts of Dessau:

> The Americans began to bomb us, and they hit the factory where we worked. The German in charge of us said, 'Leave, and don't come back to work. Go! Go wherever you want.'
>
> But where could we go? About thirty or forty of us went into the woods. We spent the night there. But there was nothing to eat so in the end almost everyone returned to the partially bombed-out barracks again.

Galina Yakovleva, who had been sent to Ravensbrück concentration camp, remembered:

> We were transferred to Rostock before our soldiers arrived. [. . .] One morning we were given a small loaf of bread each and herded hurriedly down to the port. There was panic among the Germans. [. . .] The woman who guarded us in our barracks abandoned us and the port commander had no idea what to do with us. Just then, a German officer arrived. He walked over to the commandant and told him that we were to be released. But we didn't know where to go – so we went back to the camp in Rostock. The Germans were retreating, but there was still no sign of our soldiers. On the way, we found two abandoned railcars; one full of bits and pieces, the other with some food supplies. There was enough food to last us for a short while.

A letter from Mikhail Zerkal says:

> When the Americans reached Essen, the Germans evacuated our camp. We walked for about two days, during which time most of our guards did a runner. We were taken to some sort of mine shaft, surrounded by forest and mountains. We weren't wanted there, so our little group returned to Essen.

Zinaida Komissarova described how the Germans tried to round up and take away the *Ostarbeiter* working on the farms. The elderly couple for whom she worked saved her from one of these so-called 'evacuations':

> As the Americans approached, the Germans gathered all the *Ostarbeiter* together, intending to take us away. I don't know where they planned to take us. But my employers, my elderly couple, hid me from them. For three days, we hid in the straw in the barn (there were two other Russian girls with me). The Germans searched for us – they came to my employers and asked about us, and even went down into their basement.
>
> 'We don't know where they are,' my old couple told them.

Irina Sokolova recalled hiding in a bomb shelter with her employers in the hours preceding the arrival of the Americans:

> We were liberated on 29 April. There was a ruckus of some sort in the night. An air-raid shelter had been built outside and my employers said we should move in there, just to be on the safe side. It was extremely crowded, but we somehow managed to squeeze in.

Many of the farmers handed over the reins to their workers and fled when the Red Army arrived. Yevgenia Savranskaya remembers: 'Our employers began preparing to leave too. They owned a large farm, with cows, calves and pigs, and my mistress said to me, "Genya, you look after the farm please – we are going away for a little while but will be back soon."'

For the workers abandoned in the camps, the first priority on discovering that their guards had fled was to find food. Galina Shalankova described her experience:

> The Germans abandoned the camp on 24 April, leaving around two hundred of us alone in the camp. They just upped and left without giving us a single thing to eat. That morning,

nobody woke us up. We raided the storehouse – you should have seen it! It was a frightening sight – two people suffering from dystrophy* were holding up a sack of flour, while a third hacked the sack open with a knife. Everybody threw themselves at the flour, stuffing it straight into their mouths. My friend and I stood, staring at the scene.

'Why are we standing here watching, there will be nothing left for us!' I said. 'Look at that old guy with bread sticking out of his pocket – he's trying to get his hands on some more. Let's go and take it off him.'

We went over and took the bread off him. Already, there were little campfires burning all over the place – people were cooking up gruel. We ate our fill and then started singing songs.

Valentina Gridchina was only fourteen at the time. She remembers:

Suddenly they all disappeared from the camp – the *Lagerführer*, the guards and all the camp personnel. The camp was left empty. For several days, while the fighting continued between Chemnitz and Zwickau, we were left to fend for ourselves.

A picture postcard with the inscription 'Greetings from Hinterweiler', 1945. The text on the reverse reads: *We were liberated in this village.*

* Translator's note: Dystrophy is the degeneration of tissue (often muscle tissue) usually due to disease or malnutrition.

> Lyusya and I ran to the railway line and watched some German women dragging boxes from railway cars.
>
> Lyusya turned to me. 'Let's take a box each too,' she said.
>
> To cut a long story short, Lucy loaded me up with a box and told me not to bend over. But I bent over, and my box fell. [. . .] One of the German women came running over and hoisted the box onto my shoulder, shouting, 'Quick! Get out of here!'*
>
> Lyusya and I arrived back with our boxes and opened them to discover hard-boiled sweets and confectionery. We divided them up between everyone right there and then.

Lavrenty Novokhatko described the reaction of the prisoners of Gusen-II concentration camp (a sub-camp of Mauthausen) upon realising that they were free:

> On 5 May we saw that there was nobody left on the watch-towers. People began to cry out, 'Freedom! Freedom! We're free!'
>
> The crowd was so great that we couldn't get out of the gates. So we threw various rags over the barbed wire, and climbed out over it. [. . .] And off we went in our striped outfits. We walked and walked, thin and weak, until suddenly we saw a little house. We went in. It must have been a clockmaker's house because the table was covered in watches and clocks. The family were eating their dinner; I remember there was a platter of some sort – I think it contained vermicelli. There were five of us, and all five stuffed a handful into our mouths. Do you understand? There was a complete absence of shame and decency.

Grigory Kulbaka was imprisoned in the Neuengamme concentration camp. He describes his first few hours 'free from supervision' following the camp's liberation:

> We walked about the town of Neustadt asking where we might find something to eat. All of a sudden, we bumped into some

* '*Schnell weg!*'

> of our lads, who pointed us in the direction of a cafeteria. [. . .] We went inside and discovered that it was indeed some sort of cafeteria or teahouse – God knows which. All the waitresses were wearing white – I had never imagined for a moment that I would ever be served by a German in whites. A plate of milky rice pudding appeared in front of me. I ate one spoonful, and then another, but I couldn't manage any more. For some reason I felt very unwell – perhaps because I hadn't eaten for so long.

Nikolai Bogoslavets was a prisoner of Gross-Rosen concentration camp. He remembers his first minutes of freedom: 'The 11th April was like my birthday all over again! I was free! I didn't know what to do with myself, what to do next. But I knew one thing – I was free.'

'Girls, you're free!'

In the north and west of Germany, where most of the *Ostarbeiter* we interviewed had been living in April 1945, chaos reigned. Some cities had come under the control of the Allied forces but often as little as ten kilometres away bombs were still falling, the SS were continuing to herd concentration camp survivors along on the infamous 'death marches', and German patrols were out capturing and shooting deserters on the spot. Teenagers were sent to defend the German cities.

Anna Gulyaeva described her reaction:

> The Germans had abandoned the city [Schwerin] by 30 April. By then, there wasn't even an army to defend it [. . .] The Hitler Youth were all that was left. These poor children, the Hitler Youth, were only about fifteen years old. One had a rifle with a bayonet twice his size – I don't know how he carried it! He had been ordered to do so. Our Komsomol members were not forced to do things in the same way that the Hitler Youth were. They were utterly committed and would go anywhere – into fire, into water.
>
> By 1 May the first American tank was rolling past our barracks.

Grigory Kulbaka miraculously escaped from a ship* that sank while transporting prisoners from the Neuengamme concentration camp. He remembers his first minutes of freedom:

> The street was filled with women wearing striped uniforms and number badges. We saw that they were prisoners. And they saw us, with our shaved heads, and realised that we too were prisoners. They hugged and kissed us. We didn't understand a thing. And then, suddenly, a tank rolled past us on the street – not a German tank, but an English one! And there were soldiers in berets. Another tank came by, followed by a third. It was then that it dawned on us that this was it – we had been liberated.

Almost all of the *Ostarbeiter* emphasised just how much they had looked forward to the arrival of their Soviet soldiers. But, as Lyudmila Stanyeva recalls, when they saw the Red Army officers for the first time, some didn't even recognise their uniforms:

> The gates opened and our soldiers came flying in.

Ostarbeiter encounter Red Army soldiers in Germany, Brandenburg, 1945. (The State Archive of the Russian Federation, Fond.9526, Opis'.4, Delo.47, Photo 68)

Soviet citizens following liberation, Copenhagen, 1945. (The State Archive of the Russian Federation, Fond.9526, Opis'.4, Delo.7, Photo 7)

* Translator's note: It is possible that Kulbaka may have been involved in the tragedy in the Bay of Lübeck, where two large ships – the SS *Cap Arcona* and SS *Thielbek* – carrying an estimated 7,000 concentration camp survivors were bombed and sunk by the British Royal Air Force. An estimated 6,600 people are believed to have died.

'Girls, you're free!' they said. But we had never seen these new uniforms with their epaulettes.

'Good Lord, who are these soldiers?' we asked each other.

'This is our new uniform!' they replied.

The first few hours of freedom were etched brightly in the memories of the *Ostarbeiter.* Nikolai Gulyaev:

> I remember a temporary wooden rostrum was knocked up. The Major, himself a Hero of the Soviet Union, gave a speech. Lots of people had gathered to watch – some sitting, some standing. He delivered his speech, and then began to cry. You don't believe me? Perhaps he paid less attention to the men, but the women were a truly awful sight. They were emaciated, their heads shaven. Can you imagine? And they were dressed in those uniforms too.

Soviet women released from captivity, River Oder, 1945. (Photographer: M. Redkin from the PhotoSoyuz agency)

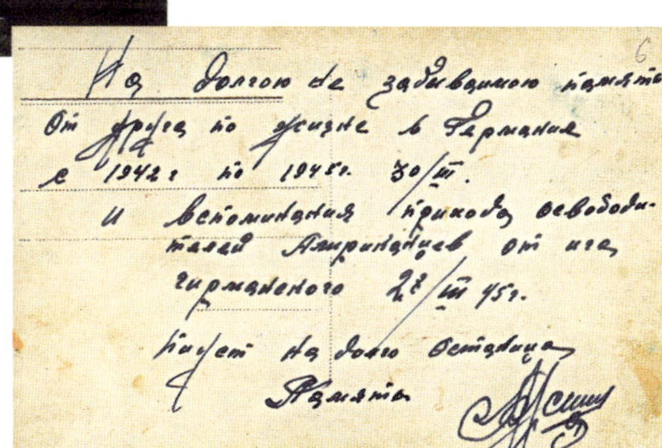

A postcard keepsake, Gelsenkirchen, 1945. The text on the reverse reads: *An enduring and unforgettable memento from a friend of life in Germany from 1942 to 1945 and a reminder of the arrival of the American troops liberating us from the German yoke on 28.03.1945. Long live the memory.*

Sergei Driga, a prisoner at Mauthausen, remembers hearing Russian voices from his camp:

> And then a tank burst into the camp – the crew were Russian. The tank commander climbed out, stood on top of his tank, put on his helmet and addressed us.
>
> 'Comrades!' he shouted.
>
> I must say, in that moment, we all felt our bodies begin to tremble and tears begin to flow. You can't be surprised! To hear such a dear, familiar word . . . And to see the rest of your life stretch out before you. What kind of life? Well, a life for a start!

To the *Ostarbeiter*, the gum-chewing Allied soldiers stepping down from their tanks in German towns and cities looked exotic. Many were tall and dark-skinned, and for many *Ostarbeiter* this was the first time – outside of the cinema that is – that they had ever laid eyes on a person with skin of a different colour to their own. Victor Zhabsky remembered:

> The Americans showed up one morning – our joy knew no bounds. They handed out food rations – a pack wrapped in wax paper. You opened it up, and there was food inside – butter, cheese, savoury biscuits. There were even cigarettes and matches. This was also the first time that I had seen chewing gum – I liked it, incidentally. We watched the way the Americans always seemed to be chomping away on something – they just chewed and chewed. 'Weren't they going to swallow it, whatever it is?' we wondered. It turned out that this was chewing gum!

Olga Kormakova recalled:

> The 7th of April was my birthday. I cried and cried – I had turned eighteen, but was stuck behind a wire fence. A bomb had fallen at the camp and been defused – we hauled it over to use as a seat and everyone delighted over the fact that it was an American one. Can you believe it? We were rejoicing over a

> bomb! Suddenly we heard someone saying, 'Hey! Girls! Don't you don't know yet? Come and meet the Americans!'

Taissa Tolkachova said:

> Our village had already been taken and everybody had left. There were no police, nobody! Just us. Oh, how we hugged and kissed each other – we were free! The Americans had taken over the cafeteria. They were listening to such cheery music – it was the first time we had heard American music.

They would remember the moment of their liberation for the rest of their lives – it was filled with a sense of promise at the prospect of peace and freedom, and accompanied by expectations of a bright and happy future. Yevdokiya Verkholantseva recalled:

> One of our officers was playing the accordion. He played so well; so lightly, and one of the lieutenants was dancing to the music. He was a good-looking young man, that lieutenant, and he danced away for a while. Before the war, I too had enjoyed dancing. I made up my mind to join him – it was my own choice, nobody pushed me. The lieutenant, still dancing, asked, 'Would anyone like to join me? Please don't let me down.'
>
> I stepped forward. Well, I didn't think I would let him down – I thought I would make a pretty good dance partner! My soul was glad – the war was over!

Liberation was particularly overwhelming for the concentration camp prisoners. Valentina Sekhina remembers: 'When the Americans arrived at Mauthausen [. . .] we knew that we were free. We should have laughed and celebrated, but instead we just sobbed.'

Galina Sivoded remembered:

> We heard men jumping out of the barracks, shouting, 'Hurrah!'
>
> You know the bellowing sound that cattle make? A bellowing herd of cattle? That's how the cries of the men sounded.

Many of the concentration camp survivors remain convinced that they were saved just in time. Varvara Gritsenko explained that she and her fellow inmates wanted to go outside and greet their liberators, but couldn't:

> By then, I couldn't leave the barracks. We had been given nothing to eat for the last few days, and I had begun to bloat. Shortly afterwards – about a day or two later – the Americans arrived in trucks. They began to take photographs of us. I wanted to embrace them – some of the girls threw themselves upon the soldiers – but I didn't have the strength.

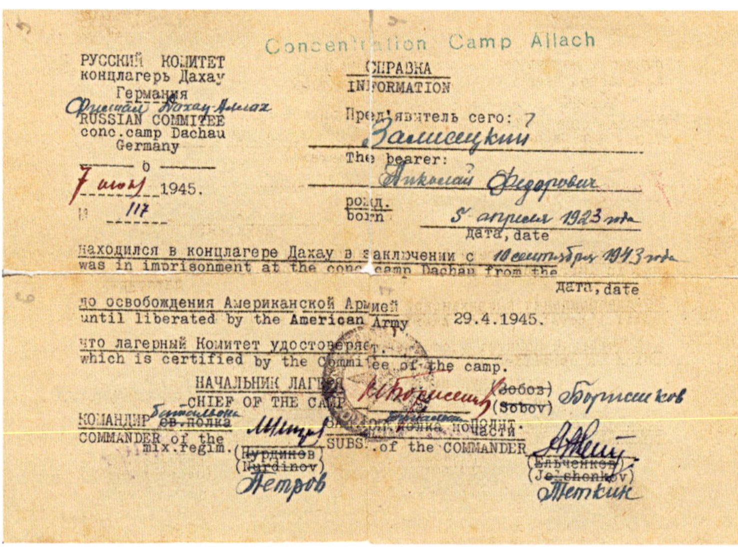

Concentration Camp Allach

РУССКИЙ КОМИТЕТ
концлагерь Дахау
Германия
RUSSIAN COMMITEE
conc.camp Dachau
Germany

СПРАВКА
INFORMATION

Предъявитель сего: Замосецкий
The bearer: Николай Федорович
рожд.
born 5 апреля 1923 года
дата, date

7 июня 1945.
№ 117

находился в концлагере Дахау в заключении с 10 сентября 1943 года
was in imprisonment at the conc. camp Dachau from the
дата, date

до освобождения Американской Армией
until liberated by the American Army 29.4.1945.

что лагерный Комитет удостоверяет.
which is certified by the Commitee of the camp.

НАЧАЛЬНИК ЛАГЕРЯ
CHIEF OF THE CAMP (Зобов) (Sobov) Борисенков

КОМАНДИР батальона
COMMANDER of the mix.regim. (Нурдинов) (Nurdinov) Петров

SUBS. of the COMMANDER (Ельченков) (Jelchenkov) Петкин

Notice of internment at Dachau, dated 7 June 1945.

Ekaterina Kriklivets remembers the pity that she inspired in an American officer:

> I remember it well. I was holding on to the barbed wire, and the American – a tall redhead – was holding on to the wire on the opposite side. I was crying and though he spoke very poor Russian, I understood when he said, 'I have a daughter like you.'
>
> I cried, and so did he.

The concentration camp survivors all remember that the Americans immediately began to hand out food. But often neither those who fell upon the supplies, nor those who handed them out, appreciated the care with which this needed to be done. Nadezhda Bulava (Mauthausen) told us: 'Then the Americans arrived and began to feed us. Oh, but so many died from the food – they simply weren't accustomed to it. There was fresh pork with pasta or potato. And men sat around these vats of food . . . dead.'

Nikolai Zubkov (Mauthausen) said: 'People were starving, emaciated. The Americans warned us not to eat too much at once, or else, they said, we could kill ourselves.'

'It was revenge'

There was a thirst for revenge in the hours that followed liberation, and it manifested in immediate reprisals against members of the camp administration, supervisors and barrack monitors.

Nadezhda Bulava said: 'Our prisoners of war beat up lots of the SS men – even the commandant. Everybody took it in turns to beat him or give him a jab with their foot.'

Valentina Sekhina remembered:

> Then someone said: 'Let's go and drag out all those *Aufseherinnen** who tortured us and get our own back on them.'
>
> They really roughed up those they got their hands on – they poked forks into them and beat them.

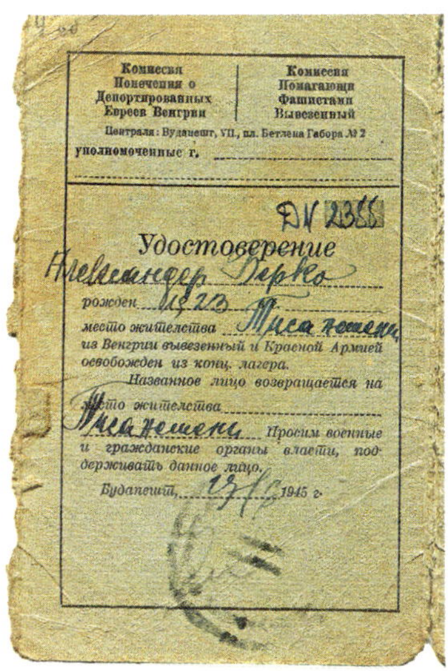

Комиссия Попечения о Депортированных Евреев Венгрии | Комиссия Помагающи Фашистами Вывезенный

Централя: Будапешт, VII., пл. Бетлена Габора № 2

уполномоченные г.

Удостоверение

рожден

место жительства

из Венгрии вывезенный и Красной Армией освобожден из конц. лагеря.

Названное лицо возвращается на место жительства

Просим военные и гражданские органы власти, поддерживать данное лицо.

Будапешт, 1945 г.

Document affirming an individual's liberation from a concentration camp, Budapest, 1945.

* Femine plural form of *Aufseher*: a camp overseer or supervisor.

Vladimir Shchebetyuk recalled:

> It was then that I witnessed the most dreadful tragedy of all: prisoners killing other prisoners. The butchering began: they caught the remaining *Kapo*, the *Blockältester* and the *Stube* monitors.* They beat them black and blue, and dragged them off to the crematorium. It was revenge for those that they had killed. It was awful.

It wasn't only the concentration camp prisoners who took revenge against the cruellest guards and supervisors – *Ostarbeiter* in the work camps often did the same. According to Zoya Yeliseeva: 'The young lads at our factory were so embittered that when the Americans arrived, they beat one of the foremen to death.'

No matter how justified they may have considered these acts of vengeance, almost all those who witnessed the violence acknowledged that it was dreadful. They sought to emphasise that there had also been demonstrations of magnanimity and compassion towards the defeated population. Anna Basarab provided one such account:

> Horns honked and sirens sounded. Flags were pulled down. By 3 May the camp supervisors and overseers were coming up to us and saying, 'Girls, you are free now, but our hearts are heavy – we don't know what will happen to us.'
>
> They would burst into tears, but we would console them.
>
> 'Don't cry,' we said. 'Our people aren't like yours. Yours shot, killed and burned. But our people aren't like that.'

'I found a piece of material and a green suit hanging up . . .'

Even tens of years later the hundreds of thousands of *Ostarbeiter*, prisoners of war and concentration camp survivors who witnessed

* *Blockältester:* barracks monitor; *Stube* monitor: supervisors of a particular room or section of a barracks.

the aftermath of liberation were reluctant to cast their minds back to the looting and theft that accompanied the chaos and lawlessness. They were often disinclined to discuss such events at all.

'Should I tell you everything?' Yevgenia Savranskaya wondered aloud when we asked her about her experience of this time.

Likewise, Victor Shuldeshov deliberated over how best to respond. 'I don't know whether to talk about this,' he said. 'Perhaps there's no need.'

The *Ostarbeiter* who were prepared to speak of such things were quick to condemn the looting and rape. Moreover, their accounts make it clear that the starving and bedraggled people hunting for food and clothes were not governed by moral strictures. They also hastened to stress that many of the homes and shops that were raided had been abandoned and appeared at the time to be unoccupied. Nadezhda Bulava told us: 'People had abandoned everything in their homes. They had just abandoned them and run – they were afraid. They had been told that the Russians were coming, and that they would kill everyone. And so they had all fled.'

Anna Gulyaeva remembered those days: 'The younger, stronger people dashed into town. They began to loot the shops, taking clothes and anything else they could get their hands on, including medicine and groceries. They brought it all back here to the camp.'

Grigory Kulbaka thought back: 'We went about in a group of five, looting the farms. After all, they had cows, sheep and geese.

Ostarbeiter following liberation, Berlin, 24 April 1945. (Photographer: A. Ustinov, PhotoSoyuz Agency)

We would take a cow by the horn, raise a pistol and . . . crack! And we'd start by feeding ourselves with that.'

For most of those we interviewed, reflection on the extent to which such behaviour was permissible only occurred much later. Mikhail Chernenko said:

> I did pity the Germans too, to some extent. But how could I not take from them, when at the time I was freed I was walking around half-naked, and practically barefoot. I didn't do it because I wanted to line my pockets. During my time in the camp I'd had quite a few recurring thoughts. One was that I'd like to get hold of a pair of good boots and one of those turtleneck pullovers. So, to tell the truth, on the first night, I pinched a turtleneck for myself.

As is often the case, it was usually easier for people to talk about unseemly events that others had been involved in, rather than describing events that implicated themselves. Vadim Novgorodov told us:

> When we were liberated, the guys went on the rampage – both in the shops, and among the farming communities. They slit the throats of cows and did whatever they liked. [. . .] They might ransack an apartment or rob a farmer, or break into a house and rape any women they found – German, Russian, whoever happened to be inside.

It is worth mentioning that when Vadim Novgorodov discussed the rape and looting, he tried to provide an explanation. 'There were some real lowlifes among the eastern workers in Germany,' he told us. 'Some were bona fide criminals, who had gone there in search of an easy life. Perhaps that's why the ugliness that followed liberation was so awful.'

Of course, it goes without saying that the career criminals were not the sole perpetrators of these acts of violence and vandalism. On the whole, they were outbursts of stifled hatred and aggression, or born from a desire for vengeance in return for the suffering and humiliation that many workers had endured. It was common for such sentiments to give rise to meaningless acts of vandalism, as Pavel Mikhailov described:

> While we were at the Magdeburg transit point, we wandered about the city – we were free to walk about by that point. There was a half-empty house near the camp and for some reason we decided to have a rummage about in some of the rooms. The rooms had already been partially ransacked. [. . .] There was a grand piano in one and we were idiotic enough to stamp on it with our feet.

Heading homeward, Lower Silesia, 1 March 1945. (Photographer: A. Ustinov from the PhotoSoyuz agency)

In an effort to bring a halt to the unbridled and indiscriminate looting, the Allied administration imposed its own obligatory contribution system upon both companies and private employers. Lidia Dadzis recalls: 'Our employers supplied us with everything we needed to ensure that we didn't return home in a sorry state. We were given a coat, a suit, a dress, a blouse and shoes.'

Zinaida Komissarova says: 'The Americans began to gather us together in one place. We were even able to occupy houses that Germans had left. I remember that we lived for a few days in a house that had beds and linen.'

And according to Lavrenty Novokhatko: 'The American soldiers ordered the German proprietor of one house to accommodate and attend on us.'

Former concentration camp prisoners and Soviet officials were given lodgings in German houses. Anna Kirilenko:

> Our Soviet command headquarters wasn't far from the camp. They came to an agreement with the Germans living nearby, requesting that they took people in.
>
> 'There aren't many of them,' they said.
>
> The Germans didn't demur – an elderly couple took me in. I was given a bedroom on the very top floor – it had a lovely bed, and bed linen too! Of course, I had a bath and washed all the clothes I had. The elderly woman gave me other clothes to wear.

According to the *Ostarbeiter*, in the early days following liberation the atrocities that took place in the Soviet zone were worse than those in the territories liberated by the Allies. Pavel Mikhailov said: 'If our soldiers took a town, they wrecked shops and broke into homes – they stole valuables, and killed too.'

We heard a number of stories similar to that of Iraida Zhukova:

> 'Why are you going home empty-handed?' some soldiers chided us. 'There was a war in Russia don't you know – there's nothing left there. You should take something with you from here.'*
>
> 'And where should we take things from?' we asked.
>
> 'Come in here,' they said, leading us into a house of some sort. [. . .] Whoever had lived there had fled. We looked into the rooms – there were a few things left – some bed sheets, a quilt, some bits of fabric. We took them.

* The Department for Repatriation issued a decree concerning the *Ostarbeiter* (No. 21) stating that as of 1 April 1945 any citizens seeking repatriation could legally take any property home to the Soviet Union with them, including livestock and work tools.

A notice from the military commandant in Arnswalde, 2 June 1945:

> Transport notice. Issued to citizen Anna Fedotevna Talalaeva, together with her two children. Liberated from German occupation by the Red Army on 4 March 1945. Registered at the Command Headquarters in Arnswalde on 2 July 1945 to be returned to her home country.
>
> Request to provide transport assistance.
>
> Arnswalde Assistant Military Commandant, Captain Shendrik.

Anna Gulyaeva and her friend were talked into helping themselves to some clothes by a prisoner-of-war they knew:

> He came up to us and said, 'You're preparing to go home, are you? Come on then – surely you're not planning to go in the clothes you're wearing? You need to wear something else.'
>
> 'And where will we get these other clothes?' we asked.
>
> 'Right here!' he said. 'Go down the street and look in the houses.'
>
> He took us to a house and we looked inside – there was nothing to be found. He led us to another. [. . .] He opened one wardrobe, followed by another.
>
> 'Take everything you want,' he said.
>
> Holy Moly! We didn't know what to take! Valya found a suitcase and, quick as a flash, she stuffed everything into it. I looked to see what might suit me. I found a piece of material and a green suit hanging up. Then I found a couple of dresses – I tied them up into my bundle too.

Waiting for transportation home, 22–25 February 1945. (Photographer: A. Ustinov, PhotoSoyuz Agency)

Anna Basarab remembered:

> The Germans were all heading off somewhere. I grabbed a suitcase from one of them.
>
> 'Oi!' he shouted.
>
> But I needed something to wear, didn't I? Anything! After all, we were still wearing those striped uniforms.

Not everybody managed to make it home with their loot. Many *Ostarbeiter* recalled having it snatched by their fellow countrymen. Anna Gulyaeva:

> We were granted permission to return to Russian territory, so we crossed back over. We saw hordes of our prisoners of war at the border. These guys had already amassed a good haul – they had everything . . . suits, even gramophones and records! The Red Army soldiers later rummaged through it all and relieved them of everything. They tipped it all out onto the ground and helped themselves.

Anna Gulyaeva's story is striking in that even many years later you can hear her judgement of both those who stole and those who helped themselves to the stolen goods (this despite Anna having earlier described stealing from the Germans herself). She was not the only one to recount a story of looting with a note of judgement in her tone.

Following liberation Nadezhda Bulava was hired by the Soviet secret service. She recalls an officer being publicly tried by a military tribunal after revealing items he had stolen:

> We were standing in the training ground with the officers. A military tribunal was passing its judgement. The officer had served for the duration of the war. And yet he was shot – for looting. Just imagine, you survive the entire war, you're an officer, not a mere foot soldier. You've led your men forward. And for that . . . they hold up a bra, they go through the jumble

> of other things, lifting things up, holding them out for all to see. The tribunal sentenced him to be shot.

Some *Ostarbeiter* shared examples of instances where Germans who had helped them were treated with fairness and decency. They highlighted examples of people who they remembered fondly. Vadim Novgorodov said:

> Willy, I don't remember his surname, treated the boys like sons. One young lad, who hadn't yet turned eighteen, caught a chill and became very ill. Willy brought him medicine and made him cups of tea. The boy pulled through, and the other lads were very grateful to Willy [. . .] When we were liberated, he came to the camp on his bicycle to check up on us. The lads hugged him and gave him presents and food to show their gratitude. Food was the most significant present you could give. He cycled off, overcome with emotion at the kindness they had shown him.

Far more frequently, however, we heard stories of a very different nature. These were often very difficult for the *Ostarbeiter* to recount.

'You wouldn't believe it . . .'

The *Ostarbeiter* spoke uneasily and with condemnation about the looting, theft and vandalism. But it was even harder for them to relive and discuss the scenes of violence that they had witnessed as Soviet soldiers brutalised the German civilian population.

In the end, we heard a number of these accounts, though many tried hard to skirt around them. This was hardly surprising; for many years, such episodes were never officially discussed, as they simply didn't fit into the retrospective war narrative. Only rarely does the topic surface in Soviet films, and books tend to focus on the perspective of the Red Army soldiers brimming with revenge and rage as they entered Germany. There can be no doubt as to the intensity of these sentiments, particularly since Soviet propaganda published during the war years had incited hatred towards the

German population as a whole, never distinguishing between 'Germans' and 'Fascists'.*

Galina Agranovskaya recalls a typical episode. Following liberation, the family she worked for were obliged to take in two Soviet officers. She recalls that they invited her to dinner one evening:

> It transpired that both officers, Pavel and Igor, had been philologists before the war. Oh, how uncomfortable I felt when the mistress of the house and her daughter attended on us – they served our food and pandered to us, and the officers never objected. We were the victors, and they were now the vanquished and humiliated ones.
>
> 'Do you have to behave this way?' I asked the officers.
>
> 'No!' came Igor's response. 'We ought to just shoot these people.'

Of course, the blame did not lie solely with the propaganda. The outpouring of violence and aggression was primarily a product of the protracted and bloody war. The immense losses and pitiless military commanders who placed no value on the lives of their soldiers certainly played a part in spawning the violence, not to mention the wake of destruction left in regions formerly occupied by German forces. On top of this, the punishing conditions of daily life were taking their toll on the Red Army soldiers. Almost all those who witnessed or partook in the violence divulged that

* In Soviet propaganda during the war years, the words 'German' and 'Fascist' were synonymous. The slogan 'Kill the German' featured heavily in propagandist materials of this period. It often appeared on posters and leaflets alongside lines from a poem by K. Simonov: 'If Your Home is Precious to You' (published 18 July 1942) and an essay by I. Erenburg entitled 'Kill' (published 24 July 1942). The slogan ceased to be used following the publication in *Pravda* of an article written at Stalin's behest by H. Alexandrov entitled 'Comrade Erenburg Oversimplifies' (11 April 1945). This shifting of responsibility onto writers and journalists was another propaganda move by Stalin. When it became evident that the violence and looting were beginning to taint the image of the Soviet army and word got back that the German population was fleeing en masse from the Red Army towards the Allies, politicians saw the need to act. Any crimes committed by members of the Red Army were punished harshly. However, this could not halt the violence and theft entirely.

such acts were often committed under the influence of alcohol.

Discussion around this topic had been forbidden for so long, that even many years later, those we spoke to questioned whether they should really talk of such things. Galina Shalankova said: 'You know, I really don't know whether you should record this. After all, these are Soviet soldiers I'm talking about.'

Varvara Khabarova also had concerns – she believed that people would doubt the veracity of her account: 'I won't say anything about the Russians. You wouldn't believe it anyway.'

Nevertheless, we did hear a significant number of stories . . .

Valentina Sekhina spoke of the violence directed at German women: 'The German women hid – they were afraid of the Russian soldiers because they made sport of them, and raped them. They slashed the feather beds so that the down flew in all directions. They didn't behave well.'

Fedor Khmara told us that the elderly farmer he worked for, as well as his wife and daughter, were shot by Russian soldiers when the *Ostarbeiter* who worked for them told the soldiers that they were 'mean people': 'They lined them up and told them that they were going to be treated the same way that they had treated us.' Even after so many years, Fedor spoke of this episode as though it were simply a matter of course.

Eagerly awaiting liberation, Lidia Yerastova never imagined the danger that her own soldiers would present:

> As our soldiers began to arrive, the Germans began questioning me.
>
> 'Please, tell us what will happen,' they asked. 'What will they do?'
>
> 'You have nothing to worry about,' I told them. 'Nothing will happen. Everything will be OK.'
>
> And would you believe what they did? They raped my Rolf's* auntie. [. . .] By the time I arrived, the soldiers had left.

---

* Translator's note: Rolf Uetze, Lidia's German boyfriend, whose family she was living with at the time.

> She was sitting there, crying. Her husband didn't know what to do. 'I was stood in the corner,' he said, 'while they raped her.'

German women were not the only ones to fall victim to the violence – *Ostarbeiter* and female prisoners only recently freed from concentration camps were targeted too. Instead of being treated as fellow Soviet citizens released from servitude, these women were often held in contempt and viewed as prostitutes who had elected to consort with the Germans.

As soon as she was liberated, Raissa Pervina was assigned to work in a Soviet hospital, but this did not spare her from harassment:

> Of course, it was the men who gave us the most trouble. They even had a saying that went like this:
>
> For the German men – you're willing,
> But us – you rebuff.
> Well, if you're going to be so unyielding
> You won't be heading home.

Maria Vitkevich recalled that when she complained to a Soviet colonel that a captain in the secret police was pressuring her to go to bed with him, his response was, 'So you put out to the Germans, sweetie, but you don't want to go with us?' Then he threatened, 'A couple of weeks in solitary and you'll be coming to us yourself.'

Accusations that the *Ostarbeiter* girls had not only been working for the enemy, but had also 'gone to bed with them' became a pretext for sexual violence.

Galina Shalankova shared her story on this subject, although not without first questioning whether it ought to be committed to paper:

> A car pulled up. Two soldiers grabbed me under the arms and bundled me into the car.
>
> 'You're coming with us,' they said. 'We'll go for a stroll and then bring you back.' We drove out of town, to where their unit was stationed. They took me into a large hall, where about twenty girls were sitting at tables. Every 'suitor' had already

chosen himself a 'bride-to-be', along with a drink and an appetiser. I began to wonder how I might escape. The drinking session ended, and each man took his 'bride-to-be' and left. I was picked by a man called George. He led me to a room and began trying to make his case, telling me what kind of women we were – that we had chosen to consort with Germans etc. [. . .]

'Now I'm going to shoot you,' he said, 'and nobody will know where you are.'

'Oh come on, stop waving that gun around,' I replied. 'Who's to blame for the fact that we ended up in Germany, eh? You are – you abandoned us.'

We bickered back and forth like that for a while until he called a halt.

'All right, all right. That's enough. Take your clothes off.'

What choice did I have? He was right, if he shot me then, nobody would be any the wiser. So I undressed, down to my shift. Suddenly, I told him that I needed to go to the toilet.

'Here,' he said, handing me his overcoat. 'Put this on. I'll take you.'

Just then, someone called his name and I bolted out onto the street and through the gate. A soldier standing at the gate shouted after me, 'Stop! I'll shoot.'

'Please don't shoot, Sir!' I shouted at him. 'Save me!'

It worked. He led me to the chief of staff and I told him everything. The chief of staff turned to the soldier and ordered him to fetch the culprit.

'And bring her clothes too!' he shouted after him.

George was brought in and the chief of staff began to berate him. Oh, you should have seen how he begged for forgiveness – I actually started to feel sorry for him!

'I'll marry her, if she agrees!' he said. 'There's no need to punish me.'

I don't need a husband like that, I thought to myself.

Most of the women told us stories that ended favourably. In reality, this was not always the case, but such was the ignominy and pain of these events that, even tens of years later, many women were still reluctant to talk about what they had endured.

Contempt for the *Ostarbeiter* women among military circles was so deeply rooted that measures taken to deter perpetrators of sexual violence rarely prompted a change of attitude. Many soldiers looked upon punishments imposed for sexual violence as nothing more than a necessary formality – the main thing was not to get caught.

The second part of Galina Shalankova's story is a case in point:

> The chief of staff handed me over to two soldiers and told them to escort me back into the town, to the hospital where I worked. And as we walked, these two soldiers turned to me, 'Won't you go with us, darlin'?' they asked.
>
> 'What d'you mean, "go with you"?' I replied, confused.
>
> 'Well . . . lie with us here – on the grass,' came the reply.
>
> I burst into howls of tears.
>
> 'All right, all right. Stop your blubbering. Let's go,' they said.
>
> We arrived at the hospital and one of my co-workers telephoned the chief of staff.
>
> 'We have punished him,' was all they were told.

This story serves to show that while one man was indeed taken in hand, the remaining twenty or so 'suitors' that evening went unpunished, having been left to spend the evening with their 'brides-to-be'. And the young soldiers who had been ordered to escort Galina home after her miraculous escape had felt confident enough to proposition her too.

Female Red Army personnel could be equally unsympathetic; they invariably treated the *Ostarbeiter* women with animosity and, on occasion, hostility. With their German clothes (often mere rags) and new hairstyles they were viewed as the very embodiment of venality and betrayal. Yevdokiya Verkholantseva was hurt by a comment made by a nurse to a Soviet lieutenant as he introduced himself to her: '"What are you doing, shaking the hand of a German prostitute?" the nurse said as he extended a hand to me. This was a woman speaking, and a nurse no less! My heart sank immediately.'

In a letter to Memorial, Tatiana Savenko also recalled the sting of injustice: 'Almost the first thing our lieutenant said when he met us was that we were traitors; that we had sold out to the Germans. It was so hurtful to hear.'

Repatriates

The mass repatriation of Soviet citizens to their homeland began soon after Germany's surrender. In fact, the USSR had commenced preparations as soon as the Red Army began pushing the Germans back across Eastern Europe.* In line with pacts made at the Yalta Conference, it was agreed that all Soviet citizens who had been displaced abroad during the course of the war were to be returned to their country. From the outset it was clear that this was to be compulsory, rather than voluntary, repatriation. Each and every Soviet citizen, without exception, and irrespective of personal wishes, was to return to the Soviet Union. It made no difference where they were living – in Germany or elsewhere – or whether it was the Soviets or the western Allies that had liberated them – every single citizen was to be forcibly repatriated.

'All I needed was to get home'

In the summer of 1945, the Soviet Union began sending home any *Ostarbeiter* who had been liberated by Soviet troops and were now living in Soviet-occupied areas. Elsewhere, the Allies were under obligation to hand over any Soviet citizens to the occupying Soviet forces. But this took time, and those who wished to stay in the West did their utmost to cross over into Allied territory. Antonina

* In October 1944, a government department was established – the Department for Authorised Delegates of the Council of People's Commissars of the USSR (as of 1946, the Council of Ministers) – for the matter of repatriation, and its members began to conduct investigations into 'displaced individuals'. This department oversaw the containment of these people in various transit camps and was responsible for working with the NKVD to establish the 'integrity' of each person through a process known as 'filtration'. Once successfully 'filtered', the department would arrange for a person to be returned home.

Serdyukova was one of those who made such a journey. Alongside Claude, the French prisoner of war she had fallen in love with, she tried to reach the American zone:

> Claude and I ran away. [. . .] Dresden was burning in front of our eyes. We walked through its charred remains and made it to Magdeburg, which was under American control. There were already trains leaving from Magdeburg – cattle cars loaded with French and Belgians – everybody was fleeing. Claude and I left on one of those trains.

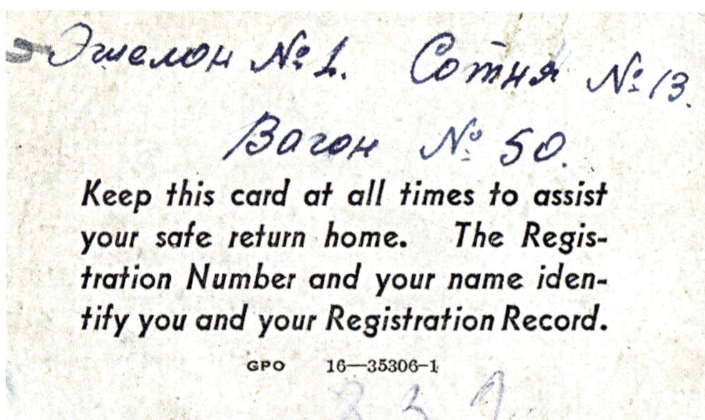
Эшелон №1. Сотня №13.
Вагон №50.
Keep this card at all times to assist your safe return home. The Registration Number and your name identify you and your Registration Record.
GPO 16—35306-1

A registration card from an Allied-occupied zone, 1945.

Some *Ostarbeiter* told us that employers or Germans they had befriended over the years tried to persuade them to stay.

Irina Sokolova worked as a domestic helper on a small country estate. She remembers that as soon as the Americans arrived, the owner not only asked her to stay, but also promised her an attractive future:

> 'Irina,' he said to me, 'perhaps you would like to stay? We will help you to master the language and assist in preparing you for university.'
>
> Though his words really tugged at my heartstrings, I replied, 'You know, going home matters to me most of all. I won't stay.'

An extract from the memoir of Zinaida Komissarova:

> I lived with my elderly couple – they were sixty-four by then. When the Americans began arriving, they said to me, 'Why are you going back to Russia – there's going to be a second war there. America is going to attack you now. Why don't you stay here with us?'

Zoya Yeliseeva was also asked to stay, although in her case it was the director of the textile factory where she had worked during the war who extended the invitation:

> When the Americans were handing us over to our troops, the director came to see us off.
>
> 'From now on, if you stay, we won't treat you differently from the German workers,' he said. 'You will all be equal, and you'll receive the same pay. [. . .] Everything in your country is in ruins, and you may well find that your families are no longer alive.'

While some were certainly reluctant to return home, for many the prospect of remaining in Germany, a country where they had suffered so much pain and humiliation, was far from inviting. Fedor Khmara said:

> All anyone wanted was for [the liberating troops] to arrive as soon as possible – for them to liberate us as soon as they could so that we could go back to our homeland. What was there for us in Germany? What good could we find there? [. . .] There weren't even any birds.

Tatiana Veselovskaya had been sent to work for a German family. Despite their entreaties for her to stay, as soon as she heard Russian voices she left in search of a transit camp from where she could journey home: 'Suddenly I met two Russian girls. When I heard them speaking Russian, I ran up to them, crying. I told them that I would travel with them.'

The majority of the *Ostarbeiter* were eager to get home. We heard how people sought out different modes of transport, or simply headed east on foot. Anna Gulyaeva:

> We deliberated for a while, but then we decided to leave – we thought we might get home faster. The Polish had already left for wherever they wanted to go. Everyone else had run off, but we Russians had been left behind – two thousand of us! We needed to cover a distance of twenty-six kilometres. We set off in our work brigade, waving a red flag that somebody had got hold of. There were thirteen carts ahead of us carrying the old, the sick and those too weak to walk. Anyone strong enough to walk was to do so. We were in a neutral zone, but we were granted permission to cross over into Russian territory.

Those who had been working on farms attempted to join up with larger groups or tried to find their own way to assembly camps from where they could cross into Soviet territory.

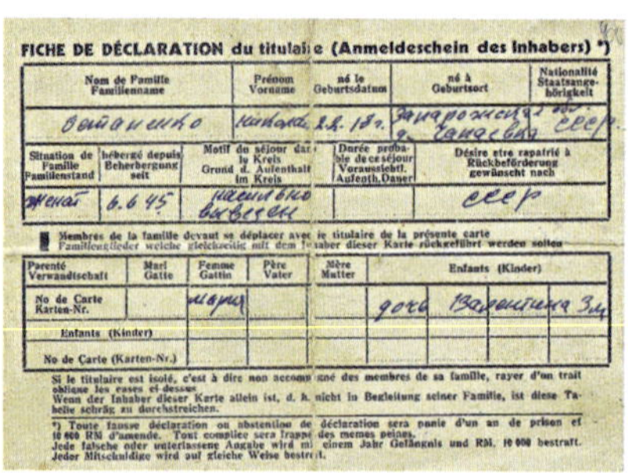

FICHE DE DÉCLARATION du titulaire (Anmeldeschein des Inhabers) *)

Nom de Famille / Familienname	Prénom / Vorname	né le / Geburtsdatum	né à / Geburtsort	Nationalité / Staatsangehörigkeit

Situation de Famille / Familienstand	hébergé depuis / Beherbergung seit	Motif du séjour dans le Kreis / Grund d. Aufenthalt im Kreis	Durée probable de ce séjour / Voraussichtl. Aufenth. Dauer	Désire être rapatrié à / Rückbeförderung gewünscht nach
	6.6 45			СССР

Membres de la famille devant se déplacer avec le titulaire de la présente carte
Familienglieder welche gleichzeitig mit dem Inhaber dieser Karte rückgeführt werden sollen

Parenté / Verwandtschaft	Mari / Gatte	Femme / Gattin	Père / Vater	Mère / Mutter	Enfants (Kinder)			
No de Carte / Karten-Nr.								
Enfants (Kinder)								
No de Carte (Karten-Nr.)								

Si le titulaire est isolé, c'est à dire non accompagné des membres de sa famille, rayer d'un trait oblique les cases ci-dessus.
Wenn der Inhaber dieser Karte allein ist, d. h. nicht in Begleitung seiner Familie, ist diese Tabelle schräg zu durchstreichen.

*) Toute fausse déclaration ou abstention de déclaration sera punie d'un an de prison et 10 000 RM d'amende. Tout complice sera frappé des mêmes peines.
Jede falsche oder unterlassene Angabe wird mit einem Jahr Gefängnis und RM. 10 000 bestraft. Jeder Mitschuldige wird auf gleiche Weise bestraft.

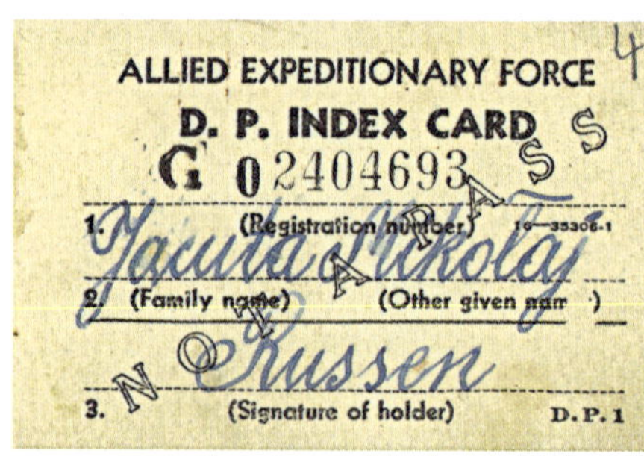

ALLIED EXPEDITIONARY FORCE

D. P. INDEX CARD

G 02404693

1. (Registration number)

2. (Family name) (Other given name)

Russen

3. (Signature of holder) D.P.1

Above: Registration card from the Allied-occupied zones.

Below: Assembly point for Soviet citizens awaiting transport home.
(Russian State Film and Photo Archive, Krasnogorsk, Opis'.3, Delo.902, Sn.94)

Raissa Pervina described the first days following her liberation:

> We crossed into English territory, but were given a very cool reception. They were polite, but cool. We decided to move on towards our Soviet zones. The English shut us up in a room once, and we feared that we were going to be taken to England to work there too. So we escaped.

Before long, the Allies began sending almost all Soviet citizens to assembly camps from where they could be handed over to the Soviet authorities. It was hoped that this might help to restore order and bring an end to the thieving and looting. Nikolai Kireev's story provides an insight into the disorder of the time. Having been freed from Mauthausen concentration camp he was, in effect, a vagrant, roaming Austria alongside others in the same position:

> Five days later we arrived in Linz. We went into a huge villa and found two barrels of rum in the cellar, and a couple of Belgian draught horses in the stables. We loaded up a cart and harnessed the horses to it. We decided to set off for home – it would be a long journey, but we would drink rum and eat chocolate on the way. We travelled as far as the Danube – the Russian side – where I spotted some sort of establishment from which people were emerging, looking rather wobbly. I must go in, I thought! It turned out to be a wine warehouse, and every barrel was the size of this room. Just as I was thinking that I might sample some, two Americans with automatic rifles arrived on the scene. In fright, I slipped and fell down into one of the barrels of cold wine. The Americans fished me out, cold and wet. By the time I left, a sign written in Russian had already been hung on the gate, instructing us to register in such and such a place.

Not all the *Ostarbeiter* we interviewed felt the same way about repatriation. Later in life, many came to recognise this post-liberation period as the first time in their lives that they had experienced freedom of will. Of course, this sense of freedom was often magnified with hindsight, but the awareness that life could have been different nevertheless did occasionally give rise to regrets about missed opportunities.

Some people we interviewed had harboured doubts about returning to the USSR. Many remembered the speeches made by Soviet officials who, keen to dispel such doubts, travelled around the assembly camps in Allied-occupied zones and stirred up enthusiasm for returning to the Soviet Union. They promised the *Ostarbeiter* that they would be met with a warm welcome back home and assured them that any 'transgressions' committed in Germany would be forgiven. Pavel Mikhailov, whose camp was in the American zone, remembers:

> Two Russians arrived at the camp – they had been sent to work their way round the camps with the express purpose of explaining the situation to the newly liberated inmates. [. . .] They talked about the Motherland and they told us what our lives there would be like from now on. They made no mention of anything negative, but we had our doubts nonetheless.

Reading the newspaper *Happy Journey*, published for Soviet citizens, at an assembly point in Germany, 1945. (State Archive of the Russian Federation Fond.9526, Opis'.4, Delo.62, List.4)

Soviet citizens at an assembly point. (State Archive of the Russian Federation Fond.9526, Opis'.4, Delo.43, List.8)

Artists painting at an assembly point for Soviet citizens, Germany, 1945. (State Archive of the Russian Federation Fond.9526, Opis'.4, Delo.62, List.11)

Victor Zhabsky remembered:

> Our Russian officer came to see us at the camp.
>
> 'Heavens! Life in Russia now . . .!' he began, before proceeding to paint a picture of the most wonderful life. Why? So that we would all return to the Motherland, of course.

Raissa Nefyodova recalled:

> A major general, I think he was called Dragunov, came to talk to us. He told us that we would soon be sent home.
>
> 'If any of you have done wrong,' he said, 'don't worry. Go back to the Motherland – everything will be OK.'

Victor Shuldeshov cast his mind back and told us:

> A government official came to see us. We were lined up and he delivered a speech about going home.
>
> 'America will likely invite you to go there,' he said. 'Don't even think about going! It's propaganda. The Motherland is waiting for you – she hasn't forgotten you.'

Thinking back to these gatherings, some of those we interviewed expressed their regret that they had been taken in by the promises, and deceived. Nikolai Kireev:

> Some of Stalin's dashing officers came round to sweet-talk us into returning. They told us that everything in the Motherland was wonderful.
>
> 'You've grown a little wild here,' they said. 'The Motherland has made a great leap forward and our future is bright.'
>
> They carried on in that vein for a while. We decided we should go. All I wanted was to go back home – I didn't really think about it. It was only later, when I was back here, that I began to wonder whether I had made the right decision – when I saw that I was being scuppered at every turn. I could have run away to any country I pleased. Others did – some went to Australia, some to Canada and America. They went every which way, with nothing to stop them.

Those who found themselves in the English or American zones had the best chance of avoiding repatriation to the USSR. However, the window of opportunity was small. In the face of sharp criticism, in the autumn of 1945 the British and American governments signed a document granting certain individuals the right to voluntary repatriation.* Many remembered the Allies coming to the camps and trying to persuade them not to return to the Soviet Union. Their argument was twofold. Firstly, they said, you will face repercussions back home and, secondly, life there will be difficult – there will be poverty and hardship. Valentina Gridchina had been sent to work in Germany alongside her mother:

> After the Americans had liberated us, my Mama drew a portrait of Stalin and a portrait of Lenin on bed sheets. A Canadian officer came over and picked up the portrait of Stalin. Laying it face down, he said to her, 'When you get home to Russia,

* According to information from the Department for Authorised Delegates of the Council of People's Commissars of the USSR on the subject of repatriation, after the war 2,654,100 Soviet citizens were repatriated from abroad. This same source states that, as of 1 January 1952, more than 450,000 displaced Soviet people, including prisoners of war and *Ostarbeiter*, were still living abroad. (The State Archive of the Russian Federation F-9526, Op. 4a, D.7, L.3, 4, 6)

> Stalin will pack you all off to Siberia. But we are offering you the chance to come and live in Canada, where you will have wonderful lives.'

Of course, those who had experienced political repression before the war had their doubts about returning home. Valentina Gridchina said:

> Many people from our large camp were enticed into going to Canada. Some really were frightened. The events of 1937, and all that had happened in general, had scared them, and they chose to sign up for emigration. As soon as they had done so, they were taken away to a different camp. My Mama refused to go. 'No,' she said. 'I won't go to Canada, I will only go back home – to Russia.'

Galina Agranovskaya remembers arguing with her parents about whether or not they should return:

> The Americans told us to write a list indicating who wanted to go where. Mama was wracked with doubts.
>
> 'Fedya,' she said to my father, 'what will happen to us there? They've been watching us since 1937.'
>
> My father, however, who had been arrested in 1937 and spent two years in prison, was adamant that he would go nowhere but home. When we reached the Soviet occupied zone of Kaliningrad, where the Americans unloaded us, the driver, who was a very nice man, held two fingers to his temple like this [she demonstrates] and said goodbye.

In many cases, the Allies' efforts to dissuade displaced Soviet citizens from returning to the Soviet Union, where they would probably face reprisals, fell on deaf ears. Very few believed what they were being told, and even if they did suspect that the warnings held some truth, any doubts were usually eclipsed by their desire to return home to their loved ones. Dina Stefanenko was one of those who decided to go home, in spite of all the warnings she had received:

> 'You're a fool,' I was told. 'You'll be sent straight to Solovki* as soon as you get home. You'll soon find out what kind of place your homeland is.'
>
> I brushed off their threats and told them that if my Motherland was calling and awaiting our return, then I had to go home. [. . .] I believed in the Soviet state, I believed that my family would be waiting for me.

'I wanted to go home,' Sergei Bogdanov told us when we asked why he decided against leaving for America. 'I wanted to find my mother and grandmother.'

Lidia Beketova gave a similar explanation: 'I could have chosen not to return – I could have gone anywhere. But I wanted to go home to my parents.'

Zinaida Komissarova said:

A propaganda poster. (The State Archive of the Russian Federation Fond.9526, Opis'.4, Delo.71, List.106)

> The people who left Germany for other countries were laid-back, but fickle characters. They wanted a better life.
>
> 'Why are you going home?' one girl asked me. 'What is there for you there? There's been a war, and even before the war we never clapped eyes on any bread.'
>
> 'Well, you don't have to come,' I told her. 'But I'm going home to my parents.'

* A notorious Russian prison camp on the remote Solovetsky archipelago in the White Sea.

Frida Palko felt similarly: 'I saw my hometown of Starodub in my dreams. All I needed was to get home.'

Some of the *Ostarbeiter* spoke of the people who had taken up emigration offers from the Allies. Sergei Bogdanov:

> The area of land around the little town of Halberstadt and the factory was due to become a Soviet zone. [. . .] When this information came to light, the majority of the camp population left with the Americans. Nobody could frighten us into going, but the majority – more than half of the camp – left for the West.

Ivan Krasnov told us: 'Lots of our people left. Scores of them! And I could have gone too. Do you see, we were being offered freedom on a plate.'

Maria Mudrak remembered that:

> A meeting was held. Many people signed up to leave. I didn't sign up straight away. I came back to the camp, changed my mind, and then decided to go back and put my name down for America. But one of the Ukrainian guys at the camp challenged me.
>
> 'Where do you want to go?' he asked. 'Don't you remember that when you were sent to Germany, they assured you then too that you'd be given milk. But you saw the reality for yourself - can you even remember the colour of milk any more? His words made me reconsider. I decided not to go.

Some of the Europeans living in the camps alongside the *Ostarbeiter* invited them home to their countries.

Victor Zhabsky said:

> There was a French chap in the camp – I called him Gabriel.
>
> 'Come and stay with me in France,' he said. 'You won't be a labourer, you'll be more like a brother. We live a comfortable life.'
>
> I didn't take him up on his offer.

A postcard, dated 1 November 1943. (State Archive of the Russian Federation Fond.10014, Opis'.1, Delo.14, List.6)

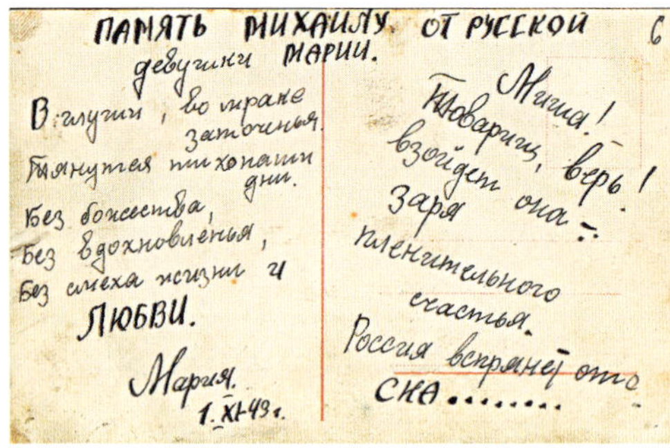

The stories we heard from *Ostarbeiter* do not provide a comprehensive picture of repatriation, nor do they indicate the extent to which it was voluntary or forced. We were told that many *Ostarbeiter* women did not return home to the Soviet Union, choosing instead to marry and follow their husbands home to France, Holland, Poland and elsewhere. Zinaida Komissarova: 'Many did not return to Russia. The girls married. [. . .] They were whisked off by their blokes – there was an exodus to Australia, and to France.'

Zinaida Valikhova described how she met her future husband and later decided to leave with him:

> He asked me to go to Holland with him. In truth, I had been so intent on getting home – I had yearned to go back to my family. But when you love a person so deeply, it's like nature's call – you go with them. When he asked me, I felt so ashamed that I turned and faced the wall as I replied, 'Yes.'
>
> I remember too that one of the American commandants said to him, 'If you take this girl with you, you must give your word that you really will marry her. Otherwise you'll take her away, have a little fun, and then . . .'
>
> The commandant was a smart man – he wrote out this pledge in German, Dutch, French and English, and then stamped it.

In some cases, however, neither stamps nor documents could

An assembly point for Soviet citizens in France. (State Archive of the Russian Federation Fond.9526, Opis'.4, Delo.16)

guard people against forcible repatriation. Officials from the Department for Repatriation were everywhere, and they hunted down many displaced Soviet citizens, and sent them home.

Antonina Serdyukova married the French prisoner of war Claude Strett and gave birth to their son, Michael, in November 1945. The young family were living in Paris when their life together was abruptly cut short:

> Suddenly, I heard a car pulling up outside. I looked out of the window and saw an army Jeep and people in Soviet uniforms. I couldn't understand what was going on. They had a few words with the landlady and then climbed the stairs towards me.
>
> 'Pack your things and come with us,' they said.
>
> I couldn't take anything, except little Michael, who I held in my arms. I couldn't understand what was going on.
>
> They took us to the Beauregard camp (Seine-et-Oise), just outside Paris, where all the Russians were being held.*

It wasn't until 1960 that Antonina told her son who his father was. Until then, she had led him to believe that he was dead, always referring to him with a fictitious name and surname.

Zinaida Valikhova managed to avoid falling into the hands of the Soviet consulate thanks to some decisive behaviour on the part of her husband:

* Antonina Serdyukova, together with many other *Ostarbeiter* women, was deported in accordance with an order from the Supreme Soviet of the USSR on 15 February 1947 entitled 'On the interdiction of marriages between Soviet citizens and foreigners'.

They sent a letter informing me that I was to go to such and such a place. It was 1945, and the Soviet soldiers were doing their utmost to ensure that we were all sent back to the Soviet Union. But my husband ripped up the paper.

'You are a Dutch citizen now,' he said.

An assembly point for Soviet citizens, Siegen, 1945.

Lidia Yerastova, who had fallen in love with a young German man (Rolf Uetze) and was living with his family, had no desire to return home to the Soviet Union. But she was to have no choice in the matter – she lived in a Soviet-occupied zone:

> It was night-time on the 18th of July. There was a bang on the door – the sound of boots on wood. The noise was so loud that it woke us all up. [. . .]
>
> 'Open the doors!' came the shout.
>
> We opened them. I had gone downstairs without a sweater. They grabbed me by the collar and dragged me out into the pouring rain. I was taken straight to the headquarters of the military police.

After liberation, Nadezhda Bulava worked in the secret police department of a filtration camp, writing out documentation on individuals being repatriated against their will. She remembers:

> Our work in the special department was mainly done at night. Anyone who had been caught the night before would be sent onwards the following morning. They were seized, and then sent to labour camps in Central Asia or Siberia. At night, we had to write up all the reports by hand [. . .] When we tired, our boss (the colonel) would say: 'Girls, go and hold your heads under the tap for a while – you can work longer yet. I don't

know why we had to write everything out by hand – it wasn't as if they didn't have typewriters.

'Sifted through the sieve'

One way or another, most of the *Ostarbeiter* were returned to the Soviet Union. But first, they had to pass through 'filtration', a process by which they were screened to establish their loyalty to the Soviet state. Once *Ostarbeiter*, they were now renamed 'repatriates'. Victor Zhabsky: 'We were assigned with a hitherto unknown label: "repatriate". It was the word everyone used to refer to us.'

Although every person returning to the Soviet Union was required to undergo screening at a filtration point or camp,* first they had to reach one, which sometimes necessitated a long journey on foot.

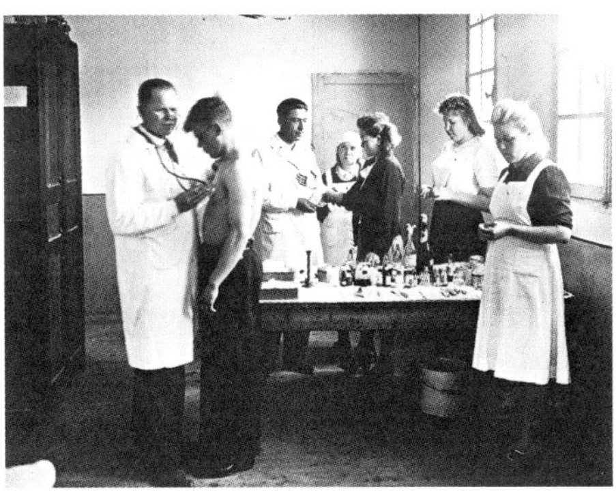

From an album depicting the lives of Soviet citizens at assembly points, following their liberation from Fascist captivity. The picture on the left depicts the medical centre at a filtration point, Senne, 1945. (State Archive of the Russian Federation Fond.9526, Opis'4, Delo.12, List.25/ Fond.9526, Opis'4, Delo.47, List.12)

Yevdokiya Verkholantseva remembered:

We were marched along in a column of a hundred people by our own soldiers. My feet were so sore – the work in Germany

* Approximately two hundred filtration camps and filtration points were established outside the borders of the USSR. The majority of repatriates were screened in army camps, sometimes along former front lines, but filtration was also conducted at the People's Commissariat for Defence Assembly and Transit Points, and NKVD filtration points.

> had caused them to swell. But we had to walk in line, marching in rows. Then they led us into a town where we were to receive our documents.

Nadezhda Izmalkova remembered that people were 'filtered' as soon as they arrived at a camp:

> They took us to Chemnitz! Lord, the things that went on at Chemnitz! Our people were taken there. The men were siphoned off straight away, and escorted away under guard. You could hear the cries of the women – some were already romantically involved with these chaps; a few had children. The men were taken away to be questioned, and then either sent to Donbass or Siberia, conscripted into the army, or given ten years in a labour camp.

Conditions at the filtration camps were sometimes little better than they had been in the German work camps. There was overcrowding, and many had been poorly constructed in haste. Nikolai Bogoslavets described one such camp:

> An assembly camp was established at Halberstadt – it had been constructed on the site of the bombed-out railway station. [. . .] We were given lodgings in discarded railway cars fitted with chimneys for heating. [. . .] We found eighteen vats of pure alcohol at the station, but no water. So we used this alcohol to wash both ourselves and our clothes, and to get drunk.

Nikolai told us that, as a result of these conditions, seventy people lost their sight and around fifty people died.

A strict regime was soon established at the filtration camps; days were timetabled and inmates were no longer free to leave the barbed-wire perimeter of the camp.

Olga Golovina was liberated from Ravensbrück concentration camp. She remembers:

> We were taken to one of the secret service units – I think it was called SMERSH,* or something of the sort. The upshot was that, once again, we found ourselves behind a barbed-wire fence. The first time we went out to use the toilets, we did so under guard. Of course, later, once our screening was complete, we were released. But they questioned us, and questioned us. It was a long process – we were screened for a month. And then, at last, we were given the go-ahead to return home.

Ostarbeiter who had been freed by the Allies compared the conditions they had experienced at the American assembly camps with those at the Soviet filtration camps. The comparison did not cast the Soviet camps in a particularly positive light. In a letter to Memorial, Mikhail Zerkal wrote:

> The Americans treated us very well. They gave us good food, and offered us cigarettes, sweets and crackers. [. . .] In July 1945, we were living in Soviet assembly camp No. 219. Life there was very different. There was strict discipline – we went everywhere in formation – and the food was very poor.

A Soviet singing and dance troupe at an assembly point in Denmark. (State Archive of the Russian Federation Fond.9526, Opis'.4, Delo.7)

* An acronym for the Russian slogan 'Death to Spies'. SMERSH encompassed a number of independent Red Army counter-intelligence agencies operating in the Soviet Union during the Second World War. It was formerly called the Main Administration of Counter-intelligence (GUKR).

Raissa Nefyodova says: 'The camp for Soviet citizens was run like a military barracks – there was a wake-up call, exercise period, and we walked to and from the canteen in formation.'

Some recalled participating in the so-called 'cultural work for the masses' projects that were organised within the camps. These involved drawing portraits of Stalin, writing slogans and articles for wall newspapers, and organising concerts. Anna Kirilenko:

> It was a large camp with lots of people – including activists. They organised activities and performances, and staged concerts. Soldiers from the military base would come to watch. [. . .] We put on concerts of a very high standard – we had singers and dancers and, if I remember correctly, we used to create human pyramids. I would stand in front of the red banner and read poetry to music while others formed these pyramids. There were about twenty-five or thirty of us, I think. We were a large group, and there were some very talented people among us – we even had a magician.

An official document confirming participation in a club at a filtration camp, dated 25 October 1945:

> An official document issued to Alexandra Yakovlena Belikh to attest that she participated in a club at camp No. 25 from 17 July until 15 September 1945, performing both as a soloist in the choir and as an actress in the drama circle. She approached her work in an honest and diligent manner and carried out all orders from her supervisors with care and attention. Her supervisors were grateful for the work she carried out in the club at camp No. 25.
>
> Club Supervisor Lieutenant Yermishin.

Though several *Ostarbeiter* recalled taking part in activities at the filtration camps, memories of the long and humiliating screening process through which they passed were etched far more deeply. The filtration process was carried out by a commission composed of

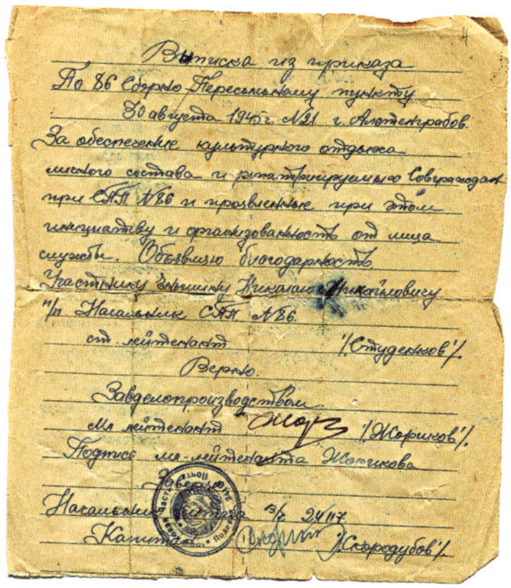

Выписка из приказа
По 86 Сборно-Пересыльному пункту
30 августа 1945 г. №21 г. Альтенграбов.
За обеспечение культурного отдыха личного состава и репатриируемых Советских граждан при СПП №86 и проявленные при этом инициативу и организованность от лица службы. Объявляю благодарность Участнику Еньшину Николаю Николаевичу
п/п Начальник СПП №86
ст. лейтенант /Студенков/
Верно.
Делопроизводитель
мл. лейтенант [illegible] /Жариков/
Подпись мл. лейтенанта Жарикова
Начальник [illegible] в/ч 24117
Капитан [illegible] /Стародубов/

A notice from the camp authorities at Assembly and Transit Point No. 86.

Altengrabow. 30 August 1945: . . . For arranging cultural activities for the community of Soviet citizens at Assembly and Transit Point camp No.86 and in doing so, putting his initiative and organisational skills to use. I wish to thank Nikolai Nikolaevich Yenshin on behalf of the camp staff.

Supervisor of Assembly and Transit Point No 86. Senior Lieutenant Studenkov

representatives from the NKVD, NKGB and SMERSH,* and their approach to each 'case' was determined by a number of different factors. Much depended upon who the *Ostarbeiter* had been liberated by – those liberated by the Allies (and this constituted the majority) were treated with marked suspicion. Zinaida Komissarova remembered: 'It was called "sifting" – we were told that we would be "sifted through the sieve".'

Vera Dergachova recalls:

> We were taken to some city where we were kept for a long time. I think we were there for about two weeks. Lord, we wrote absolutely everything down – where we had been, what we had done, whether we had agreed to collaborate with the Americans . . . I didn't meet a single person who was returning voluntarily. [. . .] They told us straight away that Stalin didn't even believe his own son. In other words, we were to be guiltless but guilty.

Being suspected of having betrayed their country was often one of the most hurtful and insulting aspects of the filtration process.

* V. N. Zemskov, 'Repatriation of Soviet Citizens and their Further Destiny (1944–1956)', *Journal of Social Research*, 1995, No.5, Article 6.

НКВД СССР

Проверочно-фильтрационный пункт

Город Франкфурт н/О

Видом на жительство служить не может

Действительно по «10» октября 1945 г.

УДОСТОВЕРЕНИЕ

Фото-карточ

Выдано
(фамилия, имя, отчество)

год рождения
место рождения

в том, что он по прибытии из Германия

с «25» июля м-ца по «5» августа

м-ца 1945 г. содержался в лагере проверочно-фильтрационном пункте НКВД СССР и следует к избранному месту жительства

(указать точный адрес)

Удостоверение по приезде к месту жительства должно быть сдано в местный орган НКВД для получения вида на жительство.

Начальник провероч[но-ф]ильтрационного пункта

(печать)

(подпись)

A card attesting that the bearer had passed through an NKVD filtration camp. Frankfurt an der Oder, 10 October 1945.

The country girls who had been deported to Germany at the age of just fifteen or sixteen often struggled to work out exactly what was wanted from them during the interrogations. According to Yevdokiya Verkholantseva:

> They began to call us in, one by one. There was a table inside the room, and our soldiers sat behind it. You would go in, and they would ask your surname.
>
> 'I'm Yevdokiya Panteleevna Petrova,' I told them.
>
> They already had documents on me in front of them.
>
> 'Did you help the Germans?'
>
> 'Yes,' I replied.
>
> 'You worked hard, really tried? Did you devote yourself to your work? And what if the Germans killed our soldiers?'
>
> 'I was frightened that they would beat me,' I told the panel. 'I thought that they would kill me if I didn't work for them.'
>
> 'Why didn't you join the Partisans?' they asked next.
>
> 'What Partisans?' I replied. 'There weren't any Partisans around us – only the Germans, who arrived in 1941. And in the early days of March 1942, I was taken away.'
>
> I was in there for a long time, sweating, red-faced. Oh, the questions that they asked me!

Those who had been released from concentration camps were treated with even greater suspicion. Surely, it was assumed, they had only managed to survive because they had cooperated with the Germans. Nikolai Bogoslavets said:

> The first interrogation was on 13 May – the very same day I arrived. [. . .] Of course, one of the first questions they asked me was, 'You're one of the lowlifes who worked for the Germans, are you?'
>
> The first 'touch' was in the teeth – I felt as though I had gone straight from one concentration camp to another. I began to explain my story – who I was and so on. One man sat, writing, while the other conducted the interrogation. I thought that they would hit me again. But no, they apparently deemed once to be sufficient. That was the ration you got for breakfast. Each time you were called in, you'd get one smack in the mouth. That was the bind we were in.

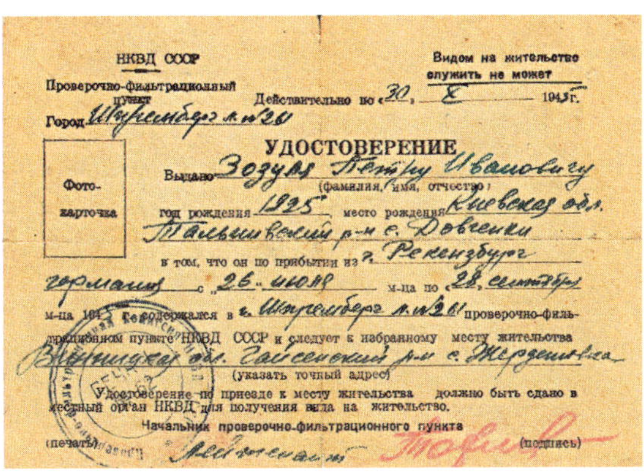

НКВД СССР
Проверочно-фильтрационный пункт
Видом на жительство служить не может
Действительно по «30» X 1945 г.
УДОСТОВЕРЕНИЕ
Выдано Зозуля Петру Ивановичу
(фамилия, имя, отчество)
год рождения 1925 место рождения Киевская обл.
в том, что он по прибытии из г. Регенсбург Германия с 26 июня м-ца по 28 сентября м-ца 1945 г. содержался в г. Шпремберг проверочно-фильтрационном пункте НКВД СССР и следует к избранному месту жительства Винницкая обл.
(указать точный адрес)
Удостоверение по приезде к месту жительства должно быть сдано в местный орган НКВД для получения вида на жительство.
Начальник проверочно-фильтрационного пункта
(печать) (подпись)

Left: Document attesting to the fact that the bearer had spent time at an NKVD filtration camp, Spremberg, 30 October 1945.

Below: Document stating that the bearer had passed filtration and been hired to work in a military unit, 2 October 1945.

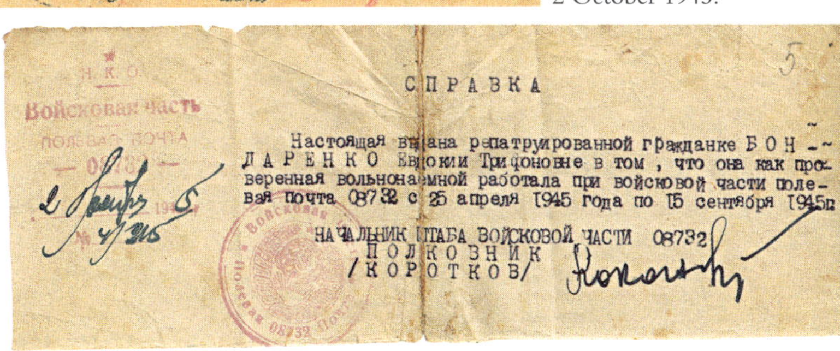

Н.К.О.
Войсковая часть
полевая почта 08732
2 октября 1945
№ 4/215

СПРАВКА

Настоящая выдана репатриированной гражданке БОНДАРЕНКО Евдокии Трифоновне в том, что она как проверенная вольнонаемной работала при войсковой части полевая почта 08732 с 25 апреля 1945 года по 15 сентября 1945 г.

НАЧАЛЬНИК ШТАБА ВОЙСКОВОЙ ЧАСТИ 08732
ПОЛКОВНИК
/КОРОТКОВ/

SMERSH were particularly suspicious of any Jews who, to escape repression in the Soviet Union in the pre-war years, had changed their surnames and hidden in Germany under new identities. For Nadezhda Izmalkova, the treatment of her Jewish friend Dora was incomprehensible: 'How did they think she had come to be in Germany in the first place? It was hardly as though she had wanted to collaborate with the Germans, was it?!'

Fear – first, of the Germans, and later, fear of their own authorities– drove many *Ostarbeiter* to adopt new names and nationalities and to pretend to be younger than they were. Nikolai Kireev was deported to Germany when he was sixteen years old. He lied about his age while in the filtration camp, claiming that he was younger in the hope that the interrogators would treat him with a lighter hand:

> SMERSH, or whoever they were, gave me a form to fill out. I had to write down who I was and where I had been born. To tell the truth, I managed to shave a couple of years off, and only corrected it just before I reached retirement age.

Aldona Volynskaya changed her name several times: 'We changed our surnames. To this day, I cannot remember when and where I used each particular name. I changed my surname from Volynskaya to Likhodievskaya, and my first name from Aldona to Nona.'

SMERSH also recruited informants in an effort to obtain compromising material – *kompromat* – on the repatriates. Lavrenty Novokhatko, who had been imprisoned in Gusen concentration camp, recalls being asked by a SMERSH officer to inform on his campmates:

> 'Report back to us with anything that you see. These are Soviet people – how were they taken prisoner?'
>
> 'All right,' I told him.
>
> 'But don't say a word to them,' he cautioned.
>
> 'OK,' I agreed.

> Of course, as soon as I returned to camp, I told them everything. 'I won't spy on you,' I said.
>
> 'Lavrik,' they said, using my nickname, 'do it. Otherwise someone else will.'
>
> They were very good people, a really wonderful bunch.

The process was easier for the 'youngsters' who had been deported to Germany before they turned eighteen (as was the case for Nikolai Kireev, who claimed to be two years younger than he was). However, even in these cases, much depended upon the individual conducting the filtration process. Lev Tokarev was deported to Germany at the age of fourteen. He told us:

> The filtration took place at the reserve battalion barracks, where a SMERSH task force had been established. The man in charge was a lieutenant colonel and a Leningrad man like us. He was a good shap, for the record. Everyone cursed the SMERSH guys, but he was a good man, a really great man. [. . .] He called us 'my boys'.
>
> 'Well now, my boys,' he would say, before asking us how we had ended up in Germany, where we had been, what we had done and so on. And that was all.
>
> 'Will you let us join the army?' we asked.
>
> 'No, boys, I won't. Enough of that – you've been here three years. It's time you went home. Some members of your family may still be alive. It's time to go home.'

Lev Tokarev was not conscripted into the army after filtration as he had not yet turned eighteen. As a rule, any men eligible for conscription were sent to the conscription centres near one of the former fronts or in the surrounding areas. Being enlisted into the army was, for many of the repatriates, the most unequivocal stamp of 'trustworthiness' they could receive.

A letter from a Red Army soldier and former *Ostarbeiter*, Rügen, 3 June 1945:

Greetings, my dear sister, Nastya!

I send my warm regards to you, Vasya, your son and elderly father-in-law. I am writing this letter from Germany. I have been here since the beginning of 1944. Until 28 April of this year I have lived as a civilian prisoner of Fascist Germany, having been sent there to work. As of 28/IV-45 I have been serving in the ranks of the Workers' and Peasants' Red Army in Germany and have been forced to leave the city of Kopys in the Orsha district, where my wife and son Gennady, who will be 4 years old now if he is still alive, are still living. I know absolutely nothing about their fate. [. . .] I have endured a great deal here in Germany. [. . .] I have had to suffer starvation and put up with every betrayal imaginable, both by the camp authorities and the foremen at the company where I worked. Eight times, we were subjected to the most terrible bombing raids by the Americans and British. More than once, I saw piles of human corpses, and aeroplanes mangled by high-explosive bombs. Twice, they blew the barracks where we lived to smithereens, but I managed to get out of these furnaces alive and unhurt.

Such is man's fate!

In both a moral and a material sense, life is now good. I am no longer a slave; now I have rights and am a member of Soviet society, a son of my Motherland. I am no longer poverty-stricken, as was the case before. Now I am clothed, shod and fed, not with some sort of gruel made from dirty potatoes – no, now I eat meals that are tasty and sufficiently nourishing.

Our commanders, although strict, treat their soldiers in a cordial and straightforward fashion. We are now stationed on a German island – it is a place with many holiday resorts and nature's beauty here is particularly striking.

I'll leave it at that. Your brother.
Write as many letters as you can – no stamps needed. My address: Field Post Office No. 97668 – Rügen.

Pavel Mikhailov recalled:

> Once the soldiers had questioned us and written down all the details, we were sorted: one group into one barn, the other into another. [. . .] We later learned through letters that those in the second barn were sent voluntarily-compulsorily to the mines in Karaganda or the oilfields in Baku. [. . .] I ended up in the army.

Sergei Bogdanov told us: 'I was enlisted into the army, and this saved me from being shipped off far far away, beyond the Ural mountains. [. . .] This time, the Soviet army saved me in every sense of the word.'

Even for those who were enlisted into military service, however, life was far from easy. Army clothing was poor in the immediate post-war period, and the new recruits were given little to no training. Many were required to serve for four years. Franz Marmurash remembered the clothing: 'I was enlisted into the army and sent to Hungary. We were given clothing: a German overcoat, Soviet trousers, boots and two-metre foot wraps.'

Fedor Apyonkin was posted to Yugoslavia without any prior military training. He told us:

> Nobody explained a thing. You went. And that was that. As it happened, I didn't even know how to shoot a gun, or how to

Transporting Soviet citizens back to the Soviet Union, Hemer, 1945. (State Archive of the Russian Federation Fond.9526, Opis'.4, Delo.62, List.30)

handle a weapon. I had never held an automatic rifle in my hands. I wasn't shown in school and I never saw one during my time with the Partisans either. That's a gun, I could say, and that was all. There was an active regiment in Yugoslavia at the time. We were combing the woods there.

Some of the less fortunate *Ostarbeiter* were conscripted into the Labour Army after filtration. They joined numerous prisoners of war and other *Ostarbeiter* repatriates from the western regions of Ukraine and the Baltic states. Some men claimed that they were married in an effort to avoid conscription. Vera Dergachova described the moment she was approached at a filtration camp by an unfamiliar man:

Справка
Дана сов. гражданке Панковской
Евдокии Константинов. в том, что она
работала при в/ч п/п 08617 х-ва 386
с мая 1945 года по 1947 года 27 мая
в должности официантки офицерской
столовой.
В настоящее время направляется на
Родину.

Confirmation of army service, 1947.

I remember that he asked me to say that he was my husband because the men were being separated from the women.

'You could at least tell me your name,' I said to him. 'I'll say that you're my husband, but I don't even know what to call you.'

But they didn't ask for either our names, or our surnames. All they asked was, 'Is this your wife?' to which he replied, 'Yes.'

'Yes, he's my husband,' I agreed.

And that was it. Since he was my husband, he was allowed to stay. I saved him.

Repatriates conscripted into the Labour Army were usually sent to rebuild the infrastructure that had been damaged or bombed during the war. Nikolai Zubkov worked in the Donbass region for almost two years: 'I was conscripted into the Labour Army and sent to Donbass, to rebuild mines. The mines there were flooded; they were frightening places.'

The Soviet military administration kept some of the *Ostarbeiter* behind to work as clerks in offices that had been occupied, or as translators, cooks, laundresses and in other such positions. Valentina Gridchina, who had been deported to Germany alongside her mother and grandmother, described her experience:

> A Soviet officer came over to us and asked, 'Which of you can do what?'
>
> My mother told him that she could sew, draw and use a typewriter. 'And my mother can work as a cook,' she said.
>
> 'And can she work in the fields?' the officer asked.
>
> 'Of course!' my grandmother replied. 'I can scythe, reap, cook and clean – I can do everything.'
>
> 'In that case, come and work for the military, you can help out at our army base.'
>
> He hired us to work there as civilian employees.

After liberation, Anna Gulyaeva was forced to do heavy manual labour at an army base:

> 'We want to go home,' we told the officer.
>
> 'You sluts!' said the officer. 'You'll work for the Germans, but you don't want to work for your own country.'
>
> They had amassed so many cattle there – about two thousand of them. People had just abandoned their livestock and left, you see . . . and these cows were left wandering about, mooing, their udders swollen.
>
> 'You're going to milk the cows,' the officer told us. 'I don't care if you know how to, or not. You are capable of tugging at a nipple. And you will learn to do so.'

It wasn't until December 1945 that Anna was granted permission to return home.

Aldona Volynskaya was sent to work for the subdivision of the NKVD responsible for rooting out Nazi criminals in occupied Germany. Her story illustrates how the Soviet secret police's 'prior experience' of repression was put to use in post-war Germany:

Confirmation of having worked for the military, 17 June 1945.

This statement has been issued to Lidia Ivanovna Krisyuk to confirm that she was taken into service by military unit 03102 to care for their livestock upon her release from Dresden concentration camp on 11 May 1945. This statement was issued for the purpose of travelling to her homeland in the USSR, in the Vinnytsia region.

Our task was this: we were to fill the camps.* In one case, the officer conducting an interrogation asked the German detainee, 'Are you a Nazi?'

'No,' he replied.

'Did you listen to the radio? Did you listen to Nazi propaganda?'

'Yes, I did.'

'Did you read newspapers?'

'Yes, I did.'

'Engaged in Nazi propaganda', we wrote. [. . .] We could see that these people were not Fascists in any shape or form, and once I even interrupted one of the senior officers as he questioned somebody.

He simply looked at me and said, 'Do not meddle in matters that do not concern you.'

Well, I understood then that it was none of my business. The atmosphere there was such that you came to understand things very clearly, very quickly.

Aldona Volynskaya also described the process by which the Soviets recruited informers:

---

* Translator's note: Aldona is probably referring here to the NKVD 'special camps' in Germany's Soviet-occupied zone, where non-military citizens considered hostile to the Soviet occupying forces, or those who had committed Nazi crimes, were imprisoned after the war. The prisoners, many of whom were entirely innocent, were denied contact with the outside world, which resulted in these camps being labelled 'silence camps' (*Schweigerlager*).

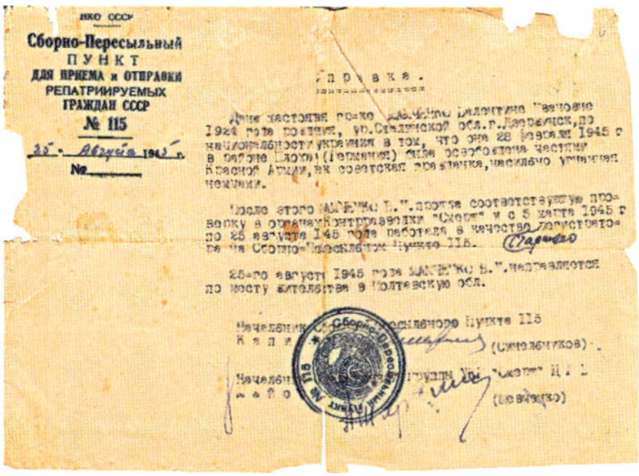
НКО СССР
Сборно-Пересыльный
ПУНКТ
ДЛЯ ПРИЕМА и ОТПРАВКИ
РЕПАТРИИРУЕМЫХ
ГРАЖДАН СССР
№ 115
25 Августа 1945 г.
№

A document stating that the bearer had worked as a clerk at an assembly and transit camp for the receipt and dispatch of citizens being repatriated to the USSR.

Statement issued to citizen V. I. Mamchenko. [. . .] to confirm that she, a Soviet citizen deported against her will by the Germans, was liberated by the Red Army in the Schlochau region of Germany on 28 February 1945. After this, V. I. Mamchenko passed through the corresponding screening procedure overseen by the SMERSH Counter-intelligence service and [. . .] worked as a clerk at Assembly and Transit Camp No.115. On 25 August 1945, V. I Mamchenko was sent to her place of residence in the Poltava region. [. . .]

> We recruited a school teacher. She was white-faced and frightened to death. They offered people like her a little money – around ten Reichsmarks per month, I think. She took it with a trembling hand. And in return, she had to inform upon people.
>
> 'You must help us,' the authorities told her.

All those approved by the filtration process were sent home to the Soviet Union. Conversely, any *Ostarbeiter*, prisoners of war or would-be repatriates who were considered to be in any way 'suspicious' were arrested and sent to the Gulag. Several of those we interviewed had suffered this fate, including Lev Mishchenko, who was sent to a labour camp in Pechora following his release from Buchenwald concentration camp. He explained that somebody had denounced him as a spy during a SMERSH interrogation, and though he insisted upon his innocence, he was charged – as a prisoner of war – with 'treason by military personnel' (Article 58-1b of the Russian Penal Code). This charge usually carried a death sentence, but Lev received ten years in the Gulag instead.

Anna Kirilenko was more fortunate. She recalled:

> The train cars would line up, and they would be filled according to their destination – i.e. who was going where. Some people were going to the Rostov region, others to Belarus. We were held at the camp until late November or early December I

> think. Then we were loaded into the train cars and dispatched. And off we went, home.

So began a new chapter in the lives of the *Ostarbeiter.* They had very little idea of what lay ahead of them back home in the Motherland.

A photograph from an album entitled 'Home to the Motherland', Brandenburg, 1945–7. (State Archive of the Russian Federation Fond.9526, Opis'.4, Delo.47)

PART 5

Back Home in the Motherland

'There was nothing to live on . . .'

The repatriates heading for home had little idea of what lay ahead. The propagandists sent to promote life in the Soviet Union and encourage the *Ostarbeiter* to return home had painted a picture of a good life back in the Motherland. Needless to say, there had been no mention of anything that might have evoked doubts about their return – the starvation and devastation went unmentioned. Vadim Novgorodov told us: 'Nobody had any idea what life was like in the [Soviet] Union. The officers didn't say a word about it – they had been given strict orders not to speak of how difficult it had been there.'

In any case, most of the *Ostarbeiter* told us that when making their decisions they hadn't even stopped to consider what life might be like for them when they returned – all they wanted was to get home as soon as possible. More often than not, their yearning to return to their families had supplanted memories of the hardships of their former lives. Only those who had managed to receive news via letters from home had any inkling of what they might be heading back to.

Anna Gulyaeva said:

> I remember the first letter that I received after I left – it had been folded into a little triangle. Oh, how I cried when Mama described the situation back home – the Germans had burned the house down and taken the cow, so my family were now living in a dugout. Papa had been wounded four times.

Vera Fedorchenko remembered her return:

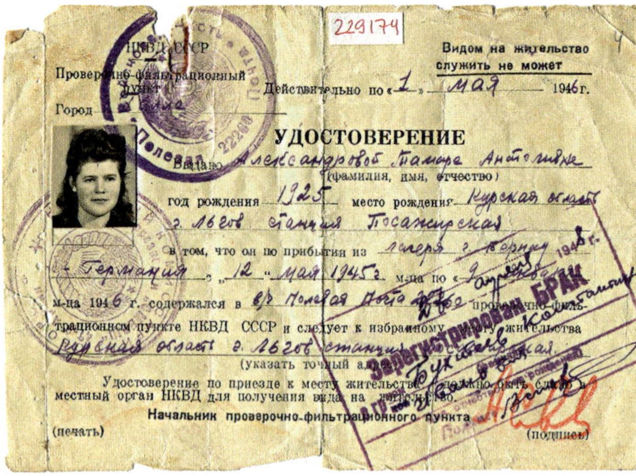
229174

НКВД СССР
Проверочно-фильтрационный пункт
Город
Видом на жительство служить не может
Действительно по «1» мая 1946 г.

УДОСТОВЕРЕНИЕ

Выдано Александровой Тамаре Анатольевне
(фамилия, имя, отчество)
год рождения 1925 место рождения Курская область
в том, что он по прибытии из
Германия « 12 » мая 1945 г.
м-ца 1946 г. содержался в проверочно-фильтрационном пункте НКВД СССР и следует к избранному месту жительства
Курская область г. Льгов
(указать точный адрес)
Удостоверение по приезде к месту жительства должно быть сдано в местный орган НКВД для получения вида на жительство.
Начальник проверочно-фильтрационного пункта
(печать)
(подпись)
Зарегистрирован БРАК

Identity record card from a filtration point, Halle, 1946.

We arrived home to find hell. Our hut had been burned to the ground – and it had only been a modest one in the first place. Lord above! My father was covered in wounds. He stood there, in a pair of homemade long johns. My mother looked completely exhausted. There was nothing to eat, nothing there at all. Lord, what suffering.

Zinaida Komissarova recalled:

> During the war my mother had hidden in anti-tank trenches with some other local people. Everything had been burned to the ground, everything looted. [. . .] When I arrived, there was nothing at home – not even potatoes. Even the horse had been taken. The women pulled the plough themselves, so that they could sow cereals for bread or plant potatoes. [. . .] There was one tractor, but it was constantly being sent for repairs at the machine tractor station.

Fedor Khmara returned to his home village of Buiskoye in the Poltava region on leave from the army. It was 1950, five years after the end of the war, but life there had become no easier. He remembers: 'I arrived in my village and, my God, what a sight. Just think – there were no schools, no clubs, and the church had been completely demolished. [. . .] The stables where we had kept the horses had been reduced to ruins too.'

Those whose relatives had survived remembered the moment they were reunited with their families. Vladimir Shchebetyuk's family had believed him dead. He described his return home:

> It was another twenty-five or thirty kilometres to Kamenets-Podolsk, but the train stopped, and wasn't going on any further. We walked along the railway line to Zhvantse, where I had some relatives. I went to see them and they told me that they had just returned from Isakovtsy, where my mother and family lived. They said that my family believed I was dead, gone for ever, having heard neither hide nor hair from me.
>
> 'We'll go quickly to Isakovtsy,' my relatives suggested, 'and bring your father back here to collect you.'
>
> I was absolutely exhausted and I'm not ashamed to say that there in Zhvantse with my relatives I cried and howled like a small child. I had never cried before. I was overcome with emotion – all the tears came at once.

Zinaida Komissarova described the unforgettable moment she arrived home:

> The train arrived at Dno station, where I got out. It was night, and there were no lights anywhere. I sat down near a little shed and waited.
>
> 'Have you come from Germany?' people asked as they walked by. 'Do you have any nylons?'

The question about nylons wasn't just a casual remark. It was expected that people arriving from Germany would bring with them items that could be sold or exchanged for a profit. However, very few of those we spoke to actually succeeded in bringing anything of any value back from Germany. It was predominantly the soldiers who managed to return bearing 'trophies'.

Anna Shtepa told us:

> Our officers took so much home with them! My God, they rifled through so many people's suitcases, and by the time we left we had nothing. [. . .] I arrived home to find both my mother and father waiting for me, but I can't tell you how their faces fell when they saw that I had arrived home 'empty-handed' so to speak.

Those who did manage to bring items home were frequently targeted by thieves. Victor Zhabsky said:

> We arrived in Novocherkassk. I didn't go home – it was late, and I wasn't carrying much. [. . .] I walked out of the railway station, which was in ruins, sat down on the steps, and dozed off. I had a pair of boots slung across my shoulders. They weren't mine – just spares. Well, when the sun came up and I came round, I saw that the boots were gone. Somebody had pinched them! I wondered then what kind of place I had come back to!

Victor Zhabsky was not the only *Ostarbeiter* to be robbed on his journey home. Galina Agranovskaya told us:

> After changing transport a number of times, we got to Mozhaisk with the few bundles we were carrying. Weak from the journey, we arrived at the little railway station and our whole family promptly went to sleep. We were robbed of everything. They cut through the sacks beneath us and pulled everything out.

Some repatriates simply had their belongings taken off them. Anna Miftakhutdinova recalls:

> The train stopped and a voice said, 'Open that suitcase and let's have a look inside.'
>
> They took all the good things.
>
> 'The rest you can keep,' they said.

Konstantin Tsibulkin, who had been in Mauthausen and Ebensee concentration camps, told us: 'Everything was taken from us – suitcases, and whatever else we had – it was all snatched away. It all went to the officers and soldiers. We were left with nothing – we arrived empty-handed.'

Lidia Beketova remembered: 'I arrived home crawling with lice. My family stripped off my clothes, built a fire in the middle of the courtyard and burned all my clothes to ash.'

Anastasia Arkhipenko managed to get hold of a winter coat: 'I arrived home, where I had my overcoat altered. I would wear this overcoat out to the community club.'

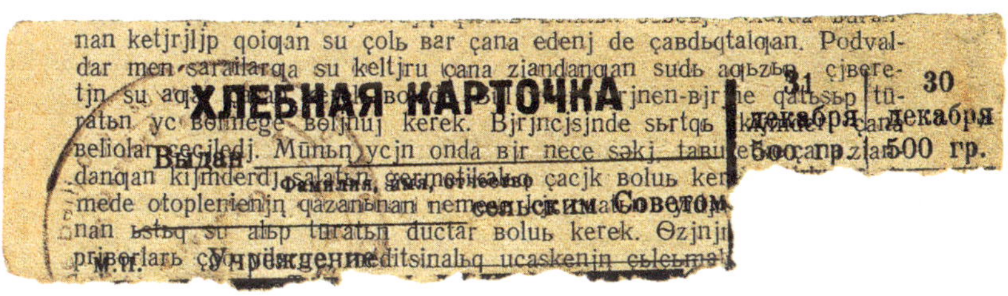

A bread coupon, December 1947. (From the collection of M. Poizner)

Occasionally, albeit rarely, an *Ostarbeiter* would succeed in bringing home something of value. Maria Ausheva brought back a sewing machine, a prize that proved very useful: 'I took it apart, folded it flat like a table and tied it together – that's how I got this sewing machine home with me. I knew how to sew, and you couldn't get these machines anywhere at home.'

Life was very hard for those who returned home in 1946 or 1947. Starvation, particularly in the southern regions of the Soviet Union, had gripped the country. Taissa Tolkachova had been deported from the small port city of Genichesk. She recalls her return:

> The famine was terrible in 1946. I returned home to a frightening scene. My father was swollen from hunger and Mama was the same. Her brother, Stepan, came to our house and his body too was distended. Mama didn't know what to feed them. My sister lay sick. [. . .] They were given one kilogram of cornflour

> per month. Nobody had any bread. People got hold of food any way they could – we mainly tried to source fish. But fish were scarce, and fishing was illegal. Wages were also very low and there was nothing in the shops. In short, the situation was truly desperate.

Pavel Kosushko, deported in August 1943, returned home to Dnepropetrovsk. He remembers:

> Everything was traded for coupons – you needed coupons for everything. There was nothing in the shops, and all the groceries were rationed. There was nothing. People were starving. [. . .] My wage was six hundred roubles, and a loaf of bread at the market cost six hundred roubles. That meant that my entire monthly wage went on one loaf of bread!

In 1946, Valentina Gridchina returned home to Taganrog with her mother and grandmother:

> The famine in Taganrog was terrible. Bread could be bought with ration coupons, but there weren't any. Mama didn't have a job – she couldn't get one anywhere. Who was going to give her a coupon? You had to buy one at the market – that was the only option. And then we would have to split however many grammes of bread we received with one coupon between the family. We drew rugs* and sold them at the market. You would sell something and then pray. 'Lord, just let us sell enough for a jar of wheat, just let us sell enough for a jar of wheat.' If we sold enough, we'd make porridge.

In the wake of the war, circumstances were so difficult that many of the *Ostarbeiter* were unable to pick up their studies where they had left off before their deportation. Tatiana Teplova explains:

---

* Translator's note: Most likely 'wall rugs', which were popular alternatives to paintings. Designs were drawn or painted onto linen and then hung on walls.

> There was nothing to live on. When I returned home, I immediately asked my mother whether I could go and study.
>
> 'Sweetheart, how can you study when I can't afford to buy you any exercise books? We have absolutely nothing.'

The *Ostarbeiter* were equally troubled by their reception back home. From the very moment they arrived, they were met with suspicion and open hostility. Ekaterina Kriklivets said:

> Our health – for those of us who had been in the concentration camps – had improved a little. But our legs were still swollen, as were our bodies. We arrived home, and as we walked we heard some old women who were selling sunflower seeds at the side of the road saying, 'Oh, clearly life wasn't bad in Germany – look at them, nice and plump!' But our bodies had just swollen; we were all puffy. Our health improved later, when we were back home. But never mind, I survived.

Tatiana Veselovskaya remembered:

Ration card for meat, cereals, fats and sugar, 1947.

> When I returned home, the first word I was met with was 'slut'. I didn't know what it meant, and yet there it was – the very first word I heard. I walked up to my Auntie and asked her what it meant.
>
> 'Shush! Don't listen to such words,' she said.

'Not everything in your profile is quite as it should be'

Ostarbeiter that we interviewed told us that, even once they had returned home, having passed through the rigorous screening processes in the filtration camps, the authorities often dragged their heels when it came to issuing them with passports. All repatriates were registered with the NKVD (previously MGB and KGB) upon their return, and although this same secret police service had granted them permission to return to the Soviet Union, it continued to treat them with suspicion; interrogating and investigating them at will. Screening procedures that had commenced abroad were continued back home. During the investigations conducted at the filtration camps, a file was compiled on each repatriate, and this was sent back to the NKVD branch local to their place of residence. Most of the former *Ostarbeiter* remained under the surveillance of the secret police until the mid-1950s.

Vera Dergachova described her return to the USSR:

> I arrived back in my village [. . .] and was given a registration document valid for three months. In three months' time I was to return to the passport office, where they would give me a document valid for six months. This would be followed by another six-month document. I couldn't go away to study because you needed a passport to do so, and I didn't have one. The policeman here would call me to visit him – he'd send a summons for me to 'present myself'. In Germany, I had lived with the military police on my back; I arrived home with the Soviet police trailing me instead.

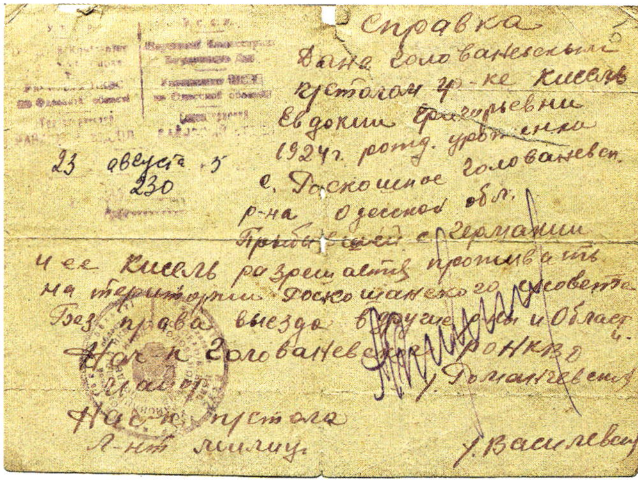

Справка
Дана Голованевским участком гр-ке Кисель Евдокии Григорьевны 1924 г. рожд. уроженке с. Розкошное Голованевск. р-на Одесской обл. Прибывшей с Германии и ее Кисель разрешается проживать на территории Розкошанского сельсовета. Без права выезда в другие р-ны и Области.
Нач-к Голованевского РОНКВД майор
Нач-к участка л-нт милиц.

Confirmation of registration at place of residence, Odessa region, dated 23 August 1945. The text reads:

Document issued by the Golovanevsk Passport Office regarding citizen Yevdokiya Grigorevna Kissel, year of birth 1924, born in the Rozkishne-Golovanevsk district in the Odessa region. On her return from Germany she is permitted to remain in the area under the Rozkishne Council. She does not have the right to travel to other districts and regions.

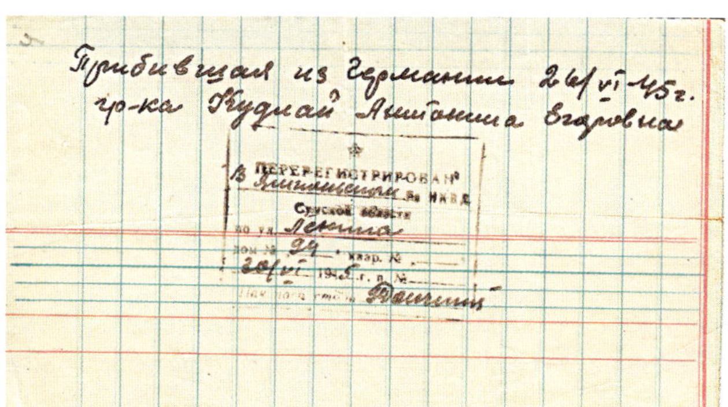

Прибывшая из Германии 26/VI-45 г. гр-ка Кудлай Антонина Егоровна
Перерегистрирован ... НКВД Сумской области по ул. Ленина дом № 24 кварт. № ... 30/VI 1945 г.

Confirmation of re-registration issued by the Sumy region NKVD branch, 30.06.1945

Zoya Yeliseeva said:

> We immediately understood that we were now outsiders; we were considered to be tainted and not to be trusted. We needed to be checked, checked, and checked again. Everybody began to scrutinise us, asking endless questions . . . 'When did you

leave? Where did you depart from? Who with? Who else went with you? Where did you go? What did you do there? When did you come back? Who liberated you?'

Neonila Rozhkova remembered:

> We were constantly being called to the NKVD headquarters – day and night. A car would arrive to take you away. At least when the Germans tortured you, you could tell yourself, 'He's a Fascist, he's a German.' But this NKVD interrogator was one of us! And when he looked me in the eyes and accused me of selling out to the Germans, I retorted, 'And why is that? I was sixteen years old. Who is to blame for the fact that the Germans took me? It wasn't as though we went there by choice.'

Anna Gulyaeva described her treatment at the hands of the Soviet authorities:

> The NKVD questioned us while we were still in the camp. And then they questioned us later, when we had returned home. Sometimes they would give us a knock with their fists, and accuse us of having gone to Germany voluntarily.
>
> 'You know we didn't go voluntarily,' we told them. 'I've even got a document here, stating that we were forcibly deported to Germany.'

The atmosphere of mistrust and suspicion that surrounded the men and women returning from Germany quickly spread to

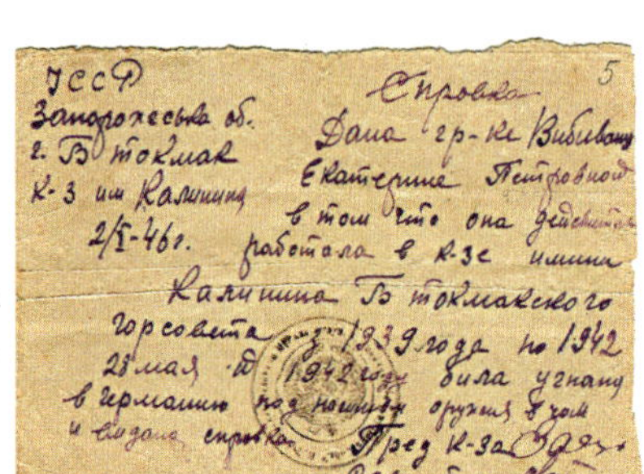

Document confirming forced deportation to Germany from the Kalinin kolkhoz, Zaporozhye region, dated 2 October 1946. The text reads:

Document issued to citizen Ekaterina Petrovna Vibivan to affirm that she truthfully worked in the Kalinin kolkhoz under the Tokmakovsky city soviet from 1939 until 1942. This document confirms that on 28 May 1942 she was deported, at gunpoint, to Germany.

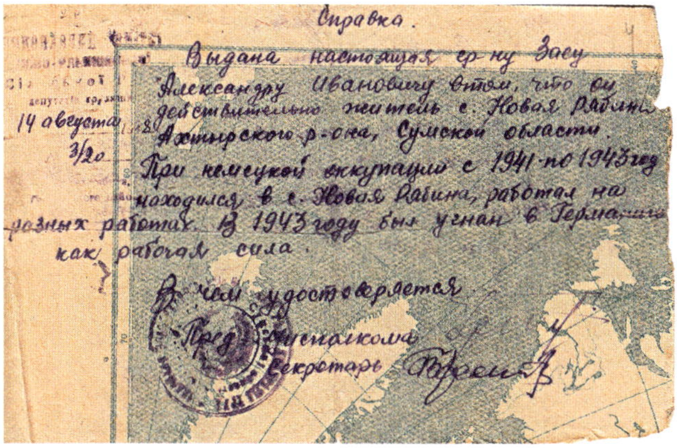

Справка.
Выдана настоящая гр-ну Заец Александру Ивановичу в том, что он действительно житель с. Новая Рябина Ахтырского р-она, Сумской области.
При немецкой оккупации с 1941 по 1943 год находился в с. Новая Рябина, работал на разных работах. В 1943 году был угнан в Германию как рабочая сила.
В чем удостоверяется
Пред. исполкома
Секретарь
14 августа
3/20

A document confirming deportation for forced labour in Germany, Sumy region, 14 August 1948. The text reads:

Document issued to citizen Alexander Ivanovich Zaets to affirm that he was truly a resident of Novaya Ryabina in the Okhtyrsky district of the Sumy region. From 1941 until 1943, he lived under Nazi occupation in Novaya Ryabina, carrying out various forms of work. In 1943, he was deported to Germany to work as a labourer. This has been verified.

envelop those nearest to them. The word 'repatriate' alone was enough to cause misgivings, not least because it failed to convey exactly why these people had ended up in Germany in the first place. In the minds of the majority of the population the word 'repatriate' fostered an image of traitors and collaborators; namely people who ought not to be trusted.

By stirring up this attitude towards all *Ostarbeiter*, the government was able to avoid shouldering the blame for their tragic fate. In this way, it rejected all responsibility for the fact that millions of people

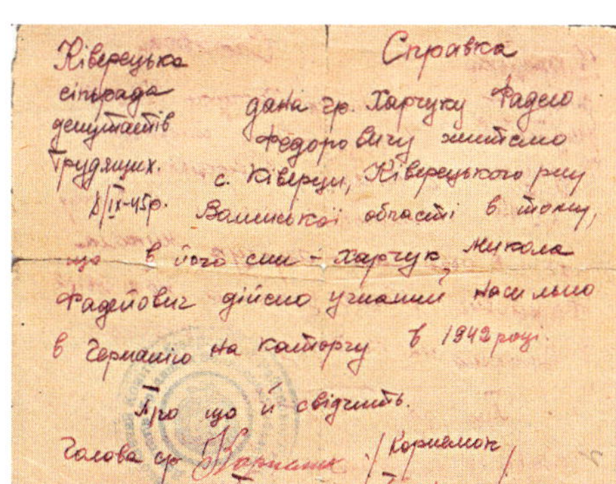

Ківерецька сільрада депутатів трудящих. 8/IX-45р.
Справка
дана гр. Харчуку Фадею Федоровичу жителю с. Ківерци, Ківерецького р-ну Волинської області в тому, що в його син - Харчук Микола Фадейович дійсно угнаний насильно в Германію на каторгу в 1943 році.
Що і свідчить.
Голова с/р Корнелюк
Секретар с/р

Document confirming deportation to Germany, 8 September 1945 (translated from Ukrainian). The text reads:

Document issued to Fadey Fyodorovich Kharchuk, resident of Kivertsi in the Kivertsi district of the Volyn region, to assert that his son Nikolai Fadeevich Kharchuk truly was deported against his will to carry out forced labour in Germany. This document confirms these facts.

had spent the first part of the war living in occupied territories, before being deported against their will to work in Germany.

Many encountered suspicion and hostility even as they made their way home from Germany. Galina Agranovskaya and her family were evicted from a train carriage by a drunk officer: 'There is no place in here for Fascist collaborators alongside defenders of the Motherland!' he told them.

Zinaida Komissarova had all her money and belongings stolen by drunken soldiers as they escorted her train home: 'They viewed us as enemies,' she explained. 'In their eyes, they had fought to defend the Motherland, and we had betrayed our country by leaving to live in Germany.'

Nikolai Kireev explained the dilemma for the *Ostarbeiter*:

> I was left in no doubt that in Stalin's eyes, those who had been abroad and had seen another world fell into one category alone – irrespective of whether they had been in a jail or a concentration camp. And if you survived . . . well, then you were asked why you were still alive. How could I answer that?
>
> They let the Germans penetrate almost as far as the Urals, and then ask, 'How did you end up in Germany?'!

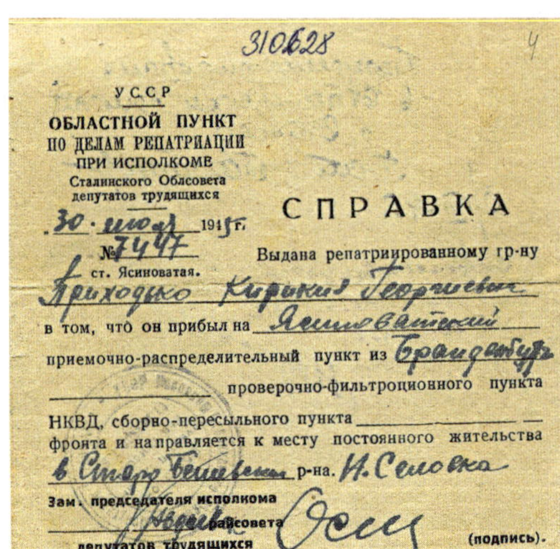

310628

УССР
ОБЛАСТНОЙ ПУНКТ
ПО ДЕЛАМ РЕПАТРИАЦИИ
ПРИ ИСПОЛКОМЕ
Сталинского Облсовета
депутатов трудящихся
30 · ____ 1945 г.
№ 7447
ст. Ясиноватая.

СПРАВКА

Выдана репатриированному гр-ну ____________________
в том, что он прибыл на ____________________
приемочно-распределительный пункт из ____________________
____________ проверочно-фильтроционного пункта
НКВД, сборно-пересыльного пункта ____________ —
фронта и направляется к месту постоянного жительства
____________ р-на. ____________
Зам. председателя исполкома
____________ райсовета
депутатов трудящихся (подпись).

A document authorising a repatriate's transportation to his place of residence, Stalingrad, 1945.

Vasily Voronin told us: 'They looked upon us with suspicion. As if we were guilty of the fact that they had abandoned us – children of fourteen, elderly people – while they fled to Stalingrad.'

Many of the memoirs written by former *Ostarbeiter* emphasise the ordeals that they faced after the war. They describe the pains to which they had to go to acquire documents, find a job or get a place at a vocational college or university. On top of this, the dawn of the Cold War brought a new wave of suspicion and spy-mania and any repatriates who had been liberated by the Allies were viewed with particular mistrust.

Oksana Kossakovskaya, a former prisoner of both Auschwitz and Ravensbrück concentration camps, was overjoyed when she passed through filtration and returned home to Lvov. She enrolled in both the Philology faculty of the university and the Musical Academy but was arrested just one year later, accused of 'colluding with the Fascists'. 'They asked me why the Germans hadn't shot me and how I had remained alive. I was sentenced to ten years in a Kolyma labour camp.'

Elizaveta Krestyantseva was also repressed after returning home. After liberation, she had been held in Germany for six months and put to work in the military supply store, mending soldiers' clothes. Later, after returning to her hometown of Kirovograd, this was to become the reason for her arrest. 'Why didn't you return immediately?' she was asked. 'Didn't you want to see your family?'; 'Why did you join the 5th Shock Army?' She was accused of having 'found herself a job' with the army so as to 'spy on our soldiers'.

She was threatened too – 'Now we'll put you up against the wall'; 'We'll press on your eyes, and blind you' were just two threats that she remembers – and ultimately forced to sign a confession. The court considered her case for just ten minutes before sentencing her to ten years in a labour camp 'for betraying her country'.

Raissa Pervina faced a similar fate. After returning from Germany, she spent two years studying at the Moscow Institute of Construction before the secret police came for her. Prior to this, she had been called in for questioning a number of times, and during these interrogations she was repeatedly asked why she had stayed with the army rather than returning with all the other repatriates. Raissa described the perpetual fear of being called in for questioning as 'more frightening than the arrest itself'. During the night of 1 June 1947 she was called to the Lubyanka. She remembers:

> They began to interrogate me. What made matters worse was that this interrogation was conducted overnight, and they wouldn't let me sleep at all. [. . .] First, they accused me of wanting to be an agent for the Gestapo. They accused me of informing on my own people, but then they dropped this line of questioning. They were left with one accusation: 'Voluntary departure to Germany', and I was sentenced to eight years in a labour camp.

Lidia Yerastova says:

> I was sentenced to six years. They accused me of working as an agent for the Gestapo, of betraying Soviet citizens and having connections with the American counter-intelligence agency. They said that I had pledged to work with the Americans and accused me of having entered into 'liaisons' with the Germans and the SS.

The majority of *Ostarbeiter* returning to the Soviet Union were spared the injustice of a sentence in a labour camp, but very few were able to avoid being fettered by restrictions and controls over their citizens' rights.

During filtration, every repatriate was required to complete a form. Ten of the twenty-nine questions on this form pertained to life under occupation and abroad. Moreover, even forty years later, information regarding the time an individual, or their family, spent in occupied territory was still included in a wide variety of standard forms, including employment forms, which Soviet citizens were required to complete. In the 1950s 'poor' questionnaires were often cited as reasons for unsuccessful job or university applications.

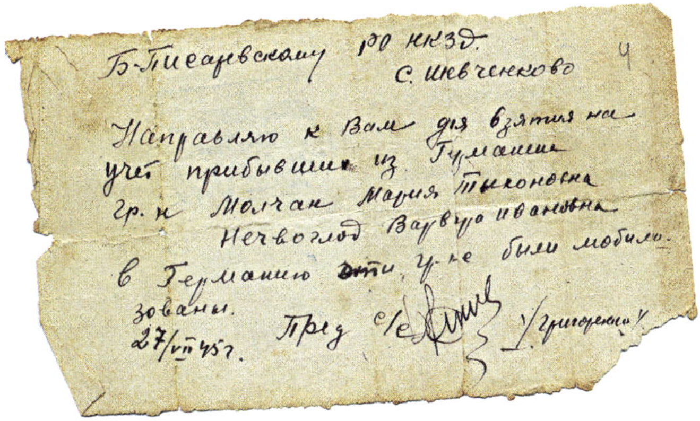

Б-Писаревскому РО НКВД.
с. Шевченково 4

Направляю к Вам для взятия на
учет прибывших из Германии
гр. н Молчан Мария Тихоновна
Нечвоглод Варвара Ивановна
в Германию ~~дети~~, и не были мобило-
зованы.
27/VII 45 г. Пред с/с /Григоренко/

Referral to a district branch of the NKVD, 27 July 1945.

Frida Palko told us: ‘When I first arrived home, nobody would even hire me as a cleaner. As soon as I wrote that I had been in Germany . . . that was it. Time and again I heard the response: “No, no, we don’t need anyone. We have found someone already.”’

Galina Sivoded also remembered how difficult it was to find employment:

> People didn’t like it. ‘Aaah. You were in Germany,’ they would say.
>
> I didn’t work for a year. I traded things at the flea market. I made some alterations to an old pair of long johns, sewing them into stirrup leggings and underwear, which I then dyed.

In an extract from a letter from Valentina Yanovskaya, she says:

> Countless times, I went to apply for a job and was asked, almost straight away, ‘Where were you during the war? Did you live in an occupied area, or were you evacuated?’
>
> You’d hear these words, and you’d just want to die. Oh, how many times I regretted having ever returned home.

It was particularly difficult to get a place to study at a university. After he was liberated, Sergei Bogdanov served in the army and then attended evening classes to complete his schooling before applying to enrol at the Leningrad Electrotechnical Institute. He described his experience:

> I showed them my documents, which established that I had been a gold medallist at school.* After a couple of minutes, I was taken aside and asked to pop in to see the Secretary of the Admissions Committee.
>
> 'Young man,' they began, gently. 'We wouldn't advise you to submit your documents. You will not be admitted – not everything in your profile is quite as it should be. [. . .] They informed me that the six letters of commendation from my former commanding officer would not alter their decision.

Galina Shalankova said: 'When I arrived home, I went to enrol at the Teacher Training College. But they wouldn't take me because I had been abroad.'

Some attempted to conceal the fact that they had been in Germany. Occasionally this proved successful.

Having experienced discrimination towards repatriates in Novocherkassk first hand in 1947, Victor Zhabsky managed to get hold of the form that he had filled out previously for employment purposes, and changed the words 'spent time in German territory' to 'spent time in occupied territory'. As a result, he lived with a fake profile for the rest of his life. He never mentioned his work in Germany to anybody – even his wife and children knew nothing of this chapter of his life until the early 1990s.

Vera Sherenkova told us:

> I was hired to work at 'Soyuzpushnina'.† If I had told them that I had been in Germany they wouldn't even have let me in the door. It was the first time in my life that I had been forced to

* Translator's note: Silver and gold medals were awarded to the students who obtained the highest marks across all of their subjects. Achieving a medal significantly improved a child's chances of being admitted into a competitive institute of higher education.

† Translator's note: Soyuzpushnina: a Russian fur-trading company that monopolised the fur market in the USSR for many years.

> lie. They gave me a form to complete. One of the questions was, 'Have you spent time abroad?'
>
> 'No, No, No, No,' I answered to this question and those that followed.
>
> I got away with it. I worked there for fourteen years.

Nikolai Kireev also managed to keep his past a secret:

> I understood that I needed to keep a low profile. I had been admitted into the vocational college and had never put anywhere in writing that I had been imprisoned at Mauthausen concentration camp. I had erased this chapter of my life entirely. I succeeded in graduating, but the Sword of Damocles was always hanging over my head. They ran checks on everybody back then.

Some of those we interviewed had achieved great success in their lives, completing PhDs and progressing up the ladder in their careers. Occasionally, former *Ostarbeiter* even rose to managerial positions, although often they did so reluctantly, tormented by a sense that they were second-class citizens. Almost all, however, were barred for many years from joining the Communist Party of the Soviet Union.

Nikolai Bogoslavets applied to join the Party while he was a student at Kharkov's Institute of Culture. At the meeting where his application was to be decided, he was asked to share his life story:

> When I reached the part where I described my time in the concentration camp, our teacher of Marxism-Leninism at the Institute, Ivan Andreevich Dudkin, got to his feet. Incidentally, he dropped down dead three years later after a bout of alcohol misuse. Anyway, he exclaimed to the room, 'He was in a concentration camp in Germany, and we're still going to accept him into the Party?'
>
> I turned on my heel and heard the doors slam shut behind me. Never again did I feel any desire at all to join the Party.

By the 1960s, attitudes towards former *Ostarbeiter* were slowly changing. But deep-seated fears still held many people back. Mikhail Daragan said:

> People had begun to suggest that I apply to join the Party. But I was always afraid to do so. If I tried, and they rejected me because I had been in Germany, I knew I would carry the bitterness in my soul with me for the rest of my life. So I didn't apply.

Vadim Novgorodov revealed: 'To me, it was clear as day that I was inferior – a leper in society. As a result, I never sought to be promoted to a managerial role.'

This sense that they were 'inferior' and 'lepers' sometimes destroyed relationships with families and friends, and prevented people from enjoying a traditional family life. Many of those we interviewed spoke bitterly of the impact of deportation on this aspect of their lives. They were most hurt by the reactions of those in their immediate circles – not the public officials and authorities, but their co-workers, neighbours, friends and relatives.

Nikolai Bogoslavets told us of his attachment to a girl he had met at night school. She was his first love, and they had intended to marry. But everything went wrong when he was in his third year at the Institute of Culture:

> As I later found out [. . .] her uncle was the vice secretary of the Gorkom.* And he had turned her mother against me, advising her not to let her daughter marry me.
>
> 'He's been in a concentration camp,' he told her. 'He won't have a path forward in life.'

Alexandra Mikhailova recalls that her future husband, a policeman, sought approval from his supervisors before marrying her. 'I am planning to marry her,' he told them. 'May I do so, or not? She was in a concentration camp.'

---

* Translator's note: City Committee of the Communist Party.

Nadezhda Izmalkova said:

> Before you were allowed to marry, you had to go to some place or other and tell them who your wife was. I know of one case involving a woman who had been in occupied territory and her fiancé, who was in the army. He was a teacher at the Military College but was thrown out of both the army and the Party when he married her without asking first. At one point I had been seeing the director of the south-western railway. [. . .] I thought that we would marry, but he never asked me. When I saw him again several years later, I asked him why he hadn't proposed.
>
> 'Why do you think, Nadya my dear?' he replied. 'It was for ideological reasons.'

Maria Pudyakova told us:

> I was seeing an Armenian soldier and fell pregnant fairly early on. When I gave him the news, he said that he couldn't marry me because I had been in Germany. It was a bitterly painful moment – I slowly gathered up my belongings and left. [. . .] I gave birth to a girl. I didn't have a home, and nobody would employ me. I wandered about, begging, spending the night wherever I could. [. . .] Finally, in utter despair, I went to the Executive Committee. They found me a job as a nanny in a kindergarten. By that time, my daughter was a year and a half old, but she was very malnourished. She couldn't even crawl – she just sat, pulling at my hand, and crying. It was too difficult to save her, and she soon died. I cannot begin to describe my grief and despair. [. . .] I was called to the police department several times and questioned about my time in Germany. Once, they kept me overnight. When they brought me in, I would freeze, retreating into myself so much that I was incapable of answering their questions.

In a letter to Memorial, Valentina Yanovskaya wrote:

> My husband, with whom I lived from 1954 until 1988, never let my past rest. He reproached me constantly, calling me a traitor and a sell-out because I had worked at a munitions factory in Germany. He threatened to have me locked up, and said that he would tell the secret police about me. [. . .] Not a day went by when he didn't remind me of my past. 'You know where you were,' he would say. 'You know what kind of person you are.'

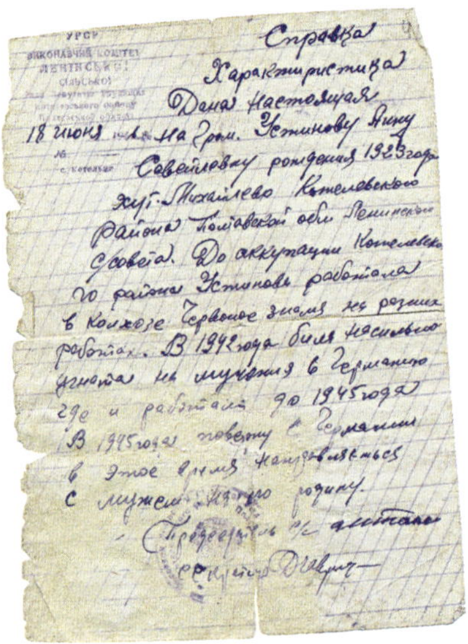

A document confirming deportation from the Poltava region to carry out forced labour in Germany, dated 18 June 1946. The text reads:

[. . .] Prior to occupation [. . .] she worked at the Chervon kolkhoz, where she had a range of responsibilities. In 1942 she was forcibly deported to suffer in Germany, where she worked until 1945. [. . .]

Lyubov Shkulyova remembers that when she asked the people she shared a *kommunalka** with not to hold drunken arguments in the corridors, or simply to turn down the radio a little, she would be met with the following response: 'You German bitch! This isn't Germany, you Fascist.'

Anna Shtepa said: 'One of my girl friends said to me: "My husband calls you a German shepherd."'

Women who returned from Germany were treated with particular suspicion. Accusations that they had had entered into 'liaisons' with Germans followed them everywhere they went. Lyubov Yerokhova remembered:

> We arrived back here and everyone held us in contempt.

* Translator's note: A communal apartment shared by several families.

Виконавчий Комітет

Справка

A document confirming deportation from the Stalin region to carry out forced labour in Germany, dated 8 December 1945. The text reads:

Document issued to citizen Maria Yevdokimovna Sosnilo to affirm that she was deported in May 1942 and forced into German slavery by the German invaders.

> 'Ah, you German sluts,' they said. 'You went there of your own accord.'
>
> I traipsed around everywhere looking for a job, but nobody would hire me because I had been in Germany.

Maria Ausheva was harassed by her neighbours:

> One woman went up to my mother in the village and called her a German whore. They began to call me awful names. My God! It was so bad that I went to the doctor and got a note to say that I was still a virgin. I wanted to take them to court over it, but my Mama wouldn't let me.
>
> 'Leave it,' she said. 'There's no need – we will move away. Let God be their judge.'

Unsurprisingly, many *Ostarbeiter* chose to conceal the fact that they had spent time in Germany from those around them, often keeping even their closest family members in the dark:

> I never said a single word to anybody. (Anna Yermilova)

> I never told anyone about it. Not even my husband. (Valentina Gridchina)

> Not even my husband knew. (Hanna Muzalyova)

For Varvara Khabarova, fear crept in the moment she returned home. In Germany, she had worked as a nanny for a family that had treated her very well. Her employer had gone to see her off when she left for the Soviet Union, and he had asked her to let him know when she had arrived home safely. Varvara duly wrote him a letter, and shortly afterwards she received a summons to the NKVD headquarters:

> I had written to tell him that I was alive and in good health and to thank him for his letter. I wanted to let him know that all was well with me and only told him the things he had asked to know.
>
> And were you frightened when you received the summons?
>
> Of course I was! I thought to myself, 'Well, here comes yet more sorrow.'
>
> Aren't you interested now in finding out how the children you worked with in Germany are doing?
>
> I am interested. But I'm frightened that this interest could land me in more trouble. I sit here, afraid to do anything.

Former Auschwitz prisoner Dina Stefanenko remembers receiving a letter from a former campmate in Poland, inviting her to visit. But her husband refused to let her go: ' "Not under any circumstances," he said. "And don't tell anyone about this letter either." [. . .] He was frightened for himself too.'

Fear, particularly in the early years after the war, drove people to destroy letters, postcards and photographs from Germany. They worried that such things could become examples of *kompromat* that might be used against them.

Valentina Yanovskaya explained: 'Keeping letters and photographs was risky for me – somebody could have seen them and informed on me to the police. They could have said that I supported the Germans because I had kept things that reminded me of my time there.'

Anna Kirilenko decided to write a memoir after returning home from Germany, so she got back in touch with the friends she had made in the concentration camp, and began to accrue quite a collection of letters. Shortly afterwards, however, she was arrested by the MGB and spent a month in prison while they attempted to extract information from her about another girl who had spent time at Ravensbrück concentration camp. When Anna was released and returned home, she could find no trace of the letters – her mother had burned every last one.

Several *Ostarbeiter* spoke with bitterness of the unshakeable sense of guilt that followed them for the rest of their lives. Yevgenia Savranskaya: 'Lord knows, I felt guilty nonetheless. Why hadn't I been able to find those Partisans? If I had found them, I would have stayed in Russia. But I didn't find them. Of course, I felt I was to blame.'

Alexander Fomenko wrote in a letter:

> Those three years that I spent in Germany felt like an eternity. I believe that life was harder for the unskilled Soviet workers like us than it was at the front. At least at the front, the soldiers were fighting and dying for their Motherland, for freedom, for victory. Whereas we felt ashamed and afraid, knowing that we were working for the enemy, even if we were doing so against our will.

Sergei Bogdanov saw matters differently:

> I understood my situation – I realised that I was working for Germany, a country that was fighting against my own Motherland. But I did not feel ashamed in the slightest. Our army, under the leadership of our Generalissimo Joseph Vissarionovich Stalin, had abandoned me. They never gave a damn about us.

Every one of the men and women we spoke to would have been justified in voicing a similar defence, but for many the scars left by the hurt and injustice simply ran too deep. In a letter to Memorial, Tatiana Savenko summed up the tragedy of their situation: 'In Germany we had been considered "the enemy" and in Russia we were "traitors to the Motherland".'

Afterword

The Burden of Silence

We began documenting the memories of *Ostarbeiter* in the early 1990s, travelling from Russia to Ukraine and Belarus to hear from anyone who was prepared to share their experiences. Not everyone was willing to open up to us immediately, and sometimes it was difficult to convince people that others really would be interested in hearing about their lives. But once they saw that we were interested in learning their *whole* story, rather than focusing solely on the two or three years that they had spent in Germany, most began to trust us. It quickly became apparent that these years in Germany had, in almost every case, come to define these people's futures.

Over the course of our conversations, we also came to appreciate just how difficult it was for *Ostarbeiter* to categorise people (not only the Germans, but also their campmates and liberators) as either 'good' or 'bad', for the realities of life blurred these lines and complicated traditional views. Harder still was the challenge of breaking out from under the shadow of their past and freeing themselves from the constraints that it placed on their lives.

For the majority of the former *Ostarbeiter* ours was to be the first open conversation they had about their past.

Victor Zhabsky served in the army after the war and later took evening classes to obtain the necessary qualifications for admission into a polytechnic institute. Having graduated, he worked as a factory foreman. During our interview I asked:

> 'Have you ever told anyone else your whole story like this?'
>
> 'No,' he replied. I have never told anyone. No, no no. Not a single soul. You are the first person I have confided in.'

After returning to the Soviet Union, the *Ostarbeiter* took different paths. However, even by the standards of post-war Soviet life, which was peppered with challenges, their lives were extremely difficult. It wasn't until the 1960s that light began to appear on the the horizon. Frida Palko told us that having never managed to complete her education she could only find work as an unskilled labourer following her return to the Soviet Union. She described the poverty of her living conditions: 'The kitchen was practically out in the street – the house was nothing but a rickety old shack. A corridor led along to a room at one end and we lived in this little corridor.'

Anna Odinokova worked as a forewoman at a clock factory: 'You cannot imagine how we lived. Three children, three beds and all of us packed together into one room. You weren't even allowed to fence yourself off from the other people. What kind of life was that?'

Antonina Vladimirova worked as a shopkeeper: 'It was a tough life, I tell you. Life only became more or less OK under Brezhnev. Well, it had begun to improve a little back when Khrushchev was in power.'

Vera Fedorchenko's life played out in a manner typical of many of the repatriated *Ostarbeiter.* In 1945 she married a man from the same work camp in Germany, but he was conscripted into the army a few months later and married again shortly afterwards. Vera, who returned to her village and lived with her mother, gave birth to their daughter in 1946. She was sent to work in the kolkhoz, where she was endlessly assigned all the tasks involving heavy manual labour. Her supervisor constantly threatened to 'write to the secret police' to ask them to check up on her. There were no opportunities for her to study. In time, she decided to leave the village, where everybody knew about her past, and she never again spoke of her time in Germany.

Even many years after their return to the Soviet Union, *Ostarbeiter* often attributed any hardships and calamities that befell them to their time in Germany. Many mentioned health problems, from which they had begun to suffer prematurely.

Lyudmila Stanyeva worked in a factory before finding a job as a bank cashier. She described her battle with poor health:

> I became very ill and was given type two invalid status. It was all connected with what I had gone through in Germany. The pain became severe and I was endlessly having to go to hospital. The ambulance was often called out to me at work and the doctors would tell me that I ought not to be working because my heart was very weak. But I kept going.

Many *Ostarbeiter* suffered from terrible nightmares and insomnia for years after their return. Nikolai Zubkov was liberated from Mauthausen concentration camp, but rather than being allowed to return home he was conscripted into the Labour Army and sent to the Donbass region to assist with rebuilding infrastructure. He attempted to run away, but was caught and sent to a correctional labour facility in Chukotka. He later worked as a carpenter, a furnace stoker and a metal worker. He told us about his nightmares:

> I had countless nightmares – they were so bad that I would jerk awake at night.
>
> 'What on earth's the matter?' my wife would ask. 'What are you shouting for?'
>
> You see, I would cry out alarmingly in my sleep.

Nadezhda Bulava returned to the Soviet Union and completed her education at a vocational college before taking a job as a stock manager. 'After the war,' she told us, 'I would often wake up with the feeling that I needed to run to roll call. It still happens now. It's all a consequence of the war.'

Looking back on their lives, some of those we spoke to expressed regret at having returned home after the war rather than seizing the opportunity to live in the West.

Valentina Sekhina never received an education. She worked as a record-keeper at a chemical plant:

> Many people left – I was invited to stay in Germany too. I desperately wanted to return home though. I really missed home. [. . .] But when I got home, I regretted – and I still

> regret now – not having stayed in Germany. I wouldn't have lived like this.

Zinaida Valikhova was one of those who did not return home. Following liberation, she married a Dutch man and moved to Holland with him. However, although she enjoyed a more comfortable life than most of the *Ostarbeiter* who returned to the Soviet Union, she found the separation from her loved ones very painful. It wasn't until Khrushchev came to power in 1953 that she began to hope that she might one day see them again. She remembers:

> If I sat down and let my mind wander, my thoughts would immediately turn to home. Each time, I imagined the moment I was reunited with my mother a little differently. Sometimes she wasn't in the house when I got there, and I went looking for her . . . And when my thoughts reached the moment when we met, my eyes would prick with tears. When finally, in 1958, I obtained a visa for the first time and made the journey home, I was able to return to Holland with a light heart and soul. Of course, I had lived in hope of returning to the Soviet Union some day, but I had feared that it would never happen.

Many of those we interviewed managed to overcome adversities and improve their lives by putting the skills that they had acquired in Germany to use back in the Soviet Union. However, despite such achievements, being classified as 'second-class citizens' never ceased to hurt.

Mikhail Chernenko graduated from university and became a writer and journalist. He told us:

> When life had settled down, a train route was re-established from Moscow to Berlin, via Belarus. I knew full well that this train was not for me. Some people travelled abroad or went to other countries for conferences, but it was implicit that such opportunities would not be extended to me.

Antonina Serdyukova graduated from a polytechnic institute and became a university teacher. She remembers:

> We were reassessed every five years. One day my superior told me that he wasn't going to allow me to teach at the department any more because he didn't like my past. Can you believe it!
>
> 'With a past like yours,' he told me, 'you don't have the right to teach young people.'
>
> I have never forgotten his words – they have stayed with me all my life.

Finally, the time came when former *Ostarbeiter* could speak openly about their past, without fear of retribution. But they felt that nobody, even those closest to them, would be interested in hearing their stories.

Anna Kirilenko graduated from an agricultural engineering institute before taking a job at a design-engineering bureau. Her grandson only recently found out that she had spent time in a concentration camp: 'I mentioned it in passing and it transpired that he didn't know. I hadn't even told my daughter – I didn't think that it would mean anything to them.'

In the eyes of many, the *Ostarbeiter* had neither contributed to the war effort, nor had they been victims of the war.

After graduating from art college, Nikolai Bogoslavets became the director of an art school. He remembers:

> When my grandson entered Year One at his school, I received an invitation to give a speech, as a veteran of the war, to the students on Victory Day. But when I told his teacher where I had spent the war years, she replied, 'Oh, there'll be no need for you to speak, no need at all.'

The *Ostarbeiter* were to endure further misfortune in old age as they struggled to understand and adapt to the sudden changes they witnessed within their countries. Many lost their savings in the financial crash that accompanied the collapse of the Soviet Union in the 1990s, and the devaluation of the currency left them with woefully inadequate pensions. Furthermore, although the German foundation Remembrance: Responsibility and Future later began to reimburse former 'eastern workers' for their forced labour in Germany, many died before receiving their compensation. 'So many people had died by then,' Nadezhda Bulava explained. 'They would have been thrilled to have received it.'

However, despite the financial hardships, the 1990s brought relief for many. It came in the form of dialogue – for the first time in their lives, many *Ostarbeiter* felt able to speak openly about their past.

When Memorial first began holding conversations with former *Ostarbeiter* some years ago, we knew only the broad brushstrokes of their experience, for their fate had been largely disregarded in the broader history of the Great Patriotic War. Our opinions too, had been influenced by stereotypes, and we had failed to comprehend quite how difficult it must have been to keep the book closed on this chapter of their lives – a completely blank page in the history of the Second World War – for so long. We had failed to appreciate the scale of this 'forgotten' episode in history and the consequences of the long years of silence endured by hundreds of thousands of people. There was no collective memory that *Ostarbeiter* could relate to, and since their accounts had been omitted from the war narrative, the magnitude of their trauma had been largely ignored. Little thought had been spared for the teenagers who had been forcibly taken from their homes, deported to the country of their enemy and condemned to servitude, hunger and humiliation.

In sharing their stories with us, the hundreds of people we interviewed were finally shaking off the burden of a prolonged period of silence and, though their stories only scratch the surface of the vast subject of Ostarbeiter experience, it was important to hear and record them. For the *Ostarbeiter*, despite their reservations, it was important to finally be heard.

Biographical List

The *Ostarbeiter* men and women whose memoirs, interviews, letters and diaries were used in the composition of this book. Further information is also available on the archive website (http://tastorona.su).

Abkovich, Josif Ivanovich, d.o.b. 1922. Imprisoned in the Grodno ghetto before being transported to Auschwitz concentration camp in June 1942. (Interview, Moscow, 2005)

Agafonova, Anastasia Alexeevna, d.o.b. 1922. Deported in March 1944 from the village of Pulovshchina, Vitebsk region. Prisoner at Ravensbrück concentration camp. (Memoir, St Petersburg, 1990)

Agranovskaya (née Kamanina), **Galina Fedorovna**, d.o.b. 1928. Deported with her parents in 1942 from Dyatkovo, Bryansk region, to Frankfurt. She worked in several places including a leather factory, as a domestic helper and in a munitions factory. (Interview, Moscow, 2005)

Apyonkin, Fedor Yevsevich, d.o.b. 1929. Deported August 1943 from Tolochyn, Vitebsk region. He worked on a farm and was sent to a concentration camp following an escape attempt. He was imprisoned in Natzweiler-Struthof concentration camp, followed by Mauthausen. (Interview, Kotovsk, Tambov region, 2002)

Arkhipenko, Anastasia Ivanovna, d.o.b. 1925. Born in Maryevka, Dnepropetrovsk region. Her family moved to Horlovka, Stalin region, from where she was deported to Neustadt am Rübenberge in May 1943. She worked as a domestic helper in a hotel. Accused of spreading anti-Hitler propaganda, she was sent first to Ravensbrück concentration camp and later to Mauthausen. (Interview, Maryevka, 2002)

Artemyeva, Maria Pavlovna, d.o.b. 1923. Deported from Luga, Leningrad region, to Mannheim in April 1942. She worked in the Daimler-Benz factory. (Memoir, St Petersburg, 1995)

Ausheva, Maria Maximovna, d.o.b. 1927. Deported in spring 1942 from the Velikomikhailov district, Belgarod region, to Göttingen. She worked in a munitions factory. (Interview, Moscow, 1991)

Basarab (née Palashchenko), **Anna Arsentevna**, d.o.b. 1924. Deported in May 1942 from the village of Nikolayevka, Sumy region, to Primkenau (now Przemków, Poland). She worked in a munitions factory but was sent to a concentration camp following an escape attempt. She was imprisoned in both Auschwitz and Mauthausen concentration camps. (Interview, Dachne, Crimea, 2002)

Beketova, Lidia Nikolaevna, d.o.b. 1928. Deported May 1942 from Taganrog. She first worked for a farmer in Soest before being transferred to a factory for optical instruments in Wedel. (Interview, Taganrog, 2005)

Bobrovskaya (née Tkach), **Vera Ivanovna**, d.o.b. 1926. Deported in August 1943 from Aleksandriya, Kirovograd region, to Gutenberg. She worked at a munitions factory before being accused of sabotage and was sent to a concentration camp. She was imprisoned in both Auschwitz and Mauthausen. (Interview, Aleksandriya, 2002)

Bogdanov, Sergei Nikolayevich, d.o.b. 1926. Deported June 1942 from Rzhev to Halberstadt. He worked at a Junkers aviation factory in Halberstadt. (Interview, St Petersburg, 2005)

Bogoslavets, Nikolai Ivanovich, d.o.b. 1925. Deported July 1943 from Zenkov, Poltava region, to Frankfurt an der Oder. He was sent to a concentration camp following a failed escape attempt and imprisoned in both Gross-Rosen and Mittelbau-Dora camps. (Interview, Taganrog, 2005)

Bulava (née Kislaya), **Nadezhda Filippovna**, d.o.b. 1923. Deported May 1942 from Stalino to Trier. She worked for a farmer but was sent to a concentration camp for a 'breach of discipline'. She was imprisoned in both Auschwitz and Mauthausen. (Interview, Donetsk, 2002)

Bulavin, Alexander Pavlovich, d.o.b. 1924. Deported March 1942 from Spasskoye, Dnepropetrovsk region, to Nuremberg. He worked in a factory but was sent to a concentration camp following an escape attempt. He was imprisoned in both Dachau and Mauthausen. (Interview, Zaporozhye, 2002)

Chernenko, Mikhail Borisovich, d.o.b. 1926. Deported from Kharkov in spring 1942. He worked in munitions factories in Fürstenberg and Berlin. (Interview, Moscow, 1991)

Dadzis, Lidia Yavnova, d.o.b. 1924. Deported alongside her mother from Gatchina, Leningrad region, to Welzheim in December 1943. She worked for a farmer. (Interview, St Petersburg, 2005)

Daragan, Mikhail Petrovich, d.o.b. 1924. Deported from Kharkov to Hanover in June 1942. He worked as a lathe operator in a factory. He was sent to a concentration camp following an escape attempt and imprisoned in both Dachau and Mauthausen. (Interview, Kharkov, 2002)

Demchuk, Vasily Vladimirovich, d.o.b 1923. Deported from Popelyukhi, Murovanokurylovetsky region, to Vienna. He was sent to Mauthausen concentration camp, and later Dachau following a failed attempt to escape three days after his arrival at a work camp. (Interview, Pavlograd, 2002)

Dergachova, Vera Semenova, d.o.b. 1923. Deported from the village of Skotovataya, Stalin region, to Wittenberg in August 1942. She worked in the Singer factory and for a farmer. (Interview, Astrakhan, 2006)

Dmitrash, Grigory Andreevich, d.o.b. 1925. Deported from Male Starosillya, Cherkassk region, to Ried im Innkreis in May 1942 for arguing with police. Imprisoned at Mauthausen concentration camp and conscripted into the Red Army upon his release. (Interview, Bila Tserkva, 2002)

Domoratsky, Vasily Maximovich, d.o.b. 1927. Deported from the Shklov region in February 1944. He was sent to Mauthausen concentration camp for having links with the Partisans. (Interview, Minsk, 2002)

Driga, Sergei Vasilyevich, d.o.b. 1916. Prisoner of war. Imprisoned in Mauthausen concentration camp. (Interview, Donetsk, 2003)

Dudko, Fedor Victorovich, d.o.b. 1925. Deported from Kryski, Chernigov region, in June 1942. He was sent to Auschwitz (1942 to 1944) and later Ebensee (Mauthausen) concentration camp from 1944 to 1945. (Interview, Volgograd, 1990)

Fedorchenko (née Bulaenko), **Vera Khotievna**, d.o.b. 1925. Deported from Romanovo, Zhytomyr region, to Nindorf in July 1942. She worked in a munitions factory. (Interview, Astrakhan, 2006)

Fomenko, Alexander Andreevich, d.o.b. 1924. Deported from Sumy to Bad Lauterberg in March 1942. He worked in a munitions factory. (Letter, Sumy, 1991)

Fursevich (née Bykoskaya), **Maria Rodionova**. Deported from the Minsk region to Eschwege in March 1942. She worked for a farmer. (Letter, Veseya village, Minsk region, 1991)

Fyodorova (née Brish), **Valeria Adamovna**, d.o.b. 1924. Deported from the village of Dashkovichy, Brest region to Tharau, Königsberg region, in March 1944. She worked in a brick factory and for a farmer. (Interview, St Petersburg, 2005)

Golovina, Olga Vasilyevna, d.o.b. 1923. Prisoner of war, imprisoned in Ravensbrück concentration camp. (Interview, Moscow, 2005)

Goryainov, Yevgeny Romanovich, d.o.b. 1925. Deported from Kursk to Vienna in spring 1942. He worked at an automotive manufacturing plant. Following a failed escape attempt, he was sent to Mauthausen concentration camp. (Interview, Kursk, 2002)

Gribovsky, Gennady Nikolaevich, d.o.b. 1931. Deported from the village of Smolnoye, Gomel region, in summer 1943. He was sent to a work camp in Dessau. (Interview, Penza, 2005)

Gridchina, Valentina Pavlovna, d.o.b. 1930. Deported alongside her mother and grandmother from Taganrog to Zwickau in summer 1943. She worked in an aviation factory. (Interview, Rostov-on-Don, 2005)

Gritsenko, Varvara Kalistratovna, d.o.b. 1923. Deported from Budy in the Kharkov region to Soldau (now Działdowo, Poland) in spring 1942. She worked for a farmer. She was sent to a concentration camp following a failed escape attempt. She was imprisoned in both Ravensbrück and Mauthausen. (Interview, Budy, 2003)

Gulyaev, Nikolai Alexandrovich, d.o.b. 1928. Deported from Taganrog in June 1942. He worked in factories in Magdeburg, Klein Wanzleben and Regensburg. He was mobilised into the Labour

Army, where he served from 1945 to 1946. (Interview, Taganrog, 2005)

Gulyaeva, Anna Konstantinova, d.o.b. 1926. Deported from Novoduginskaya, Smolensk region, to Schwerin in spring 1942. She worked in a potato factory. (Interview, Minsk, 2011)

Gumenny, Vadim Ilyich, d.o.b. 1923. Deported from Dunaivtsi, Kamenets-Podolsk region, to Vienna in autumn 1943. He worked in an automotive factory but was sent to Mauthausen concentration camp following a 'breach of discipline'. (Interview, Lvov, 2003)

Izmalkova, Nadezhda Ivanovna, d.o.b. 1923. Deported from Kiev to Erfurt in May 1942. She worked for a farmer. (Interview, Kiev, 1989)

Karvatovsky, Valentin Pavlovich, d.o.b. 1924. Deported from the village of Muksha Borishkovetskaya [Kamenets-Podolsk region] to Wiener Neudorf in the summer of 1942. He worked in a brick factory and an aviation factory. He was sent to a concentration camp following a failed escape attempt. He was imprisoned in both Gusen-I and Gusen-II. (Interview, Kamenka, Kamenets-Podolsk region, 2002)

Kepet, Nadezhda Victorovna, d.o.b. 1927. Deported from Pukhovichy, Gomel region, to Düsseldorf in March 1944. She worked in a factory making nylon stockings and later in a munitions factory. (Interview, Minsk, 2011)

Khabarova (née Morozova), **Varvara Antonovna**, d.o.b. 1926. Deported from Zolotonosha, Poltava region, to Bregenzerwald in September 1942. She worked for a farmer. (Interview, Bogoslovka, Penza region, 2005)

Khmara, Fedor Ivanovich, d.o.b. 1927. Deported from Buiskoye, Poltava region, to Zwickau in January 1943. He worked for a farmer. (Interview, Penza, 2005)

Kireev, Nikolai Pavlovich, d.o.b. 1926. Deported from Bolkhov, Bolkhov district, Oryol region, to Berlin in May 1942. He worked in a munitions factory but was sent to Mauthausen concentration camp following a failed attempt to escape. (Interview, Moscow, 2002 and 2005)

Kirilenko, Anna Ivanovna, d.o.b. 1926. Deported from Rostov-on-Don to Düsseldorf in September 1942. She worked in a textile factory but was sent to a concentration camp for 'participation in underground activity'. She was imprisoned in both Ravensbrück and Buchenwald concentration camps. (Interview, Rostov-on-Don, 2005)

Klintsov, Mikhail Sergeevich, d.o.b. 1925. Deported from Nikolayev to Baden bei Wien in May 1942. He worked in a munitions factory. He was sent to Mauthausen concentration camp following a failed escape attempt. (Interview, Nikopol, 2002)

Komissarova, Zinaida Dmitrievna, d.o.b. 1924. Deported from the village of Vyazhishche, Pskov region, to the outskirts of Mettenheim in April 1942. She worked for a farmer. (Memoirs, St Petersburg, 1990)

Kononenko, Vasily Antonovich, d.o.b. 1926. Deported from Nizhyn, Chernigov region, in March 1943. Arrested on suspicion of involvement with the Partisans and sent to Mauthausen concentration camp. (Interview, Moscow, 2002)

Kormakova (née Dikhtyareeva), **Olga Mikhailovna**, d.o.b. 1926. Deported from Markovka, Sumy region, to Remscheid in May 1943. She worked at a hardware factory. (Interview, Kiev, 1990)

Kosarevsky, Ivan Terentyevich, d.o.b. 1924. Deported from Rostov-on-Don to Wuppertal in September 1942. He worked for a farmer but was sent to Buchenwald concentration camp after a failed escape attempt. (Interview, Rostov-on-Don, 2005)

Kossakovskaya, Oksana Romanovna, d.o.b. 1923. She was arrested in 1943, accused of killing a German soldier, and deported from Lvov. She was imprisoned in both Auschwitz and Ravensbrück concentration camps. (Interview, St Petersburg, 2006)

Kosushko, Pavel Andreevich, d.o.b. 1925. Deported from Dnepropetrovsk to Bolzano in August 1943. (Interview, Tula, 2011)

Kozhaev, Arkady Filippovich. Deported from Stalino to Herten in 1942 (possibly February). He worked in a mine. (Interview, Moscow, 1990)

Kramarenkova, Varvara Grigoryevna, d.o.b. 1923. Deported from Sevastopol, Crimea, to Eisenach in September 1942. She worked in a BMW factory. (Memoir, Simferopol, 1990)

Krasnov, Ivan Fedorovich, d.o.b. 1924. Deported from Kmytov, Zhytomyr, to Danzig in March 1942 and worked for a farmer. He was accused of participation in underground activity and sent to Mauthausen concentration camp. (Interview, Zhytomyr, 2002)

Krestyantseva (née Guseva), **Elizaveta Afanasevna**, d.o.b. 1926. Deported from Kirovograd to Berlin in September 1943. She worked in a rubber factory. Upon her return to the Soviet Union, she was sent to the Karlag labour camp from 1946 to 1954. (Memoirs, St Petersburg, 2000)

Kriklivets (née Kutsenko), **Ekaterina Vasilyevna**, d.o.b. 1926. Deported from the village of Yulyevka, Zaporozhye region, to Wolfsburg in summer 1943. She worked in the Volkswagen factory but was sent to a concentration camp following a failed escape attempt. She was imprisoned in both Auschwitz and Hirtenberg (a subcamp of Mauthausen) concentration camps. (Interview, Zaporozhye, 2002)

Kulbaka, Grigory Nikonovich, d.o.b. 1925. Deported from the village of Kyslychuvatoye, Dnepropetrovsk region, to Kiel in October 1942. He worked in a camp in Wellendorf but was sent to Neuengamme concentration camp following a failed escape attempt. (Interview, Moscow, 2006)

Lavrovich (née Molokovich), **Regina Alexandrovna**, d.o.b. 1932. Deported from the village of Osovets, Gomel region, to Cherbourg and Stuttgart in June 1944. She worked in a gypsum mine. (Interview, Minsk, 2011)

Lilyeev, Nikolai Ivanovich, d.o.b. 1921. Prisoner of war. He worked for a farmer in Estonia, at a mine in Neukirchen and a metallurgical plant elsewhere in Germany. From 1945 to 1954 he was a prisoner at the Pechorlag (Gulag). (Interview, St Petersburg, 2006)

Malitsky, Igor Fedorovich, d.o.b. 1925. Deported from Kharkov in March 1942. After making several attempts to escape, he was sent to a number of different concentration camps: Terezín, Auschwitz and Mauthausen. (Interview, Kharkov, 2003)

Markova (née Ivanova), **Elena Vladimirovna**, d.o.b. 1923. Lived through occupation in the town of Krasnoarmeysk, Donetsk region. Arrested in the Soviet Union and sent to the Vorkutlag and the Rechlag (Gulag) from 1943 to 1953. (Interview, Moscow, 2008)

Marmurash, Franz Kazimirovich, d.o.b. 1926. Deported from the city of Kamenets-Podolsk to Wiener Neustadt in July 1942. He worked for a farmer. He was charged with sabotage and sent to Mauthausen concentration camp. (Interview, Kamenets-Podolsk, 2002)

Marunchak, Peter Petrovich, d.o.b 1926. Deported from Gumentsy, Kamenets-Podolsk region, to Vienna in July 1942. He was imprisoned in both Lanzendorf and Mauthausen following several failed escape attempts. (Interview, Gumentsy, 2002)

Maxina (née Bolotina), **Antonina Prokhorovna**, d.o.b. 1923. Deported from Rostov-on-Don to the outskirts of Cologne in September 1943. She worked in the Walzwerk factory. (Interview, Novocherkassk, 2005)

Miftakhutdinova (née Bagautdinova), **Anna**, d.o.b. 1926. Deported from Zaporozhye in February 1943. She worked for a farmer on the outskirts of Libá. (Interview, Perm, 2005)

Mikhailov, Pavel Mikhailovich, d.o.b. 1926. Deported from Lozovoy hamlet, Zaporozhye region, to Salzgitter in September 1943. He worked at a metallurgical plant. (Memoir, St Petersburg, 1990)

Mikhailova, Alexandra Ivanovna, d.o.b. 1924. Deported from the village of Belaya, Moscow region, to Bad Belzig in summer 1942. She worked in a munitions factory but was sent to concentration camps (both Auschwitz and Mauthausen) following a failed escape attempt. (Interview, Moscow region, 2002)

Mikhailova (née Naumova), **Elena Semyonova**, d.o.b. 1922. Deported January 1943 from the village of Pushkinskiye Gory, Pskov region, in January 1943. She worked in a mine in Thil and was later sent to Fürstenberg concentration camp. (Memoir, St Petersburg, 1990)

Mishchenko, Lev Glebovich, d.o.b. 1917. Prisoner of war. He worked in a munitions factory in Leipzig but was sent to Buchenwald concentration camp following a failed escape attempt. From 1945 to 1954 he was a prisoner at the Pechorlag (Gulag). (Interview, Moscow, 2006)

Mudrak (née Moskalenko), **Maria Serafimovna**, d.o.b. 1925. Deported from the village of Maryevka, Zaporozhye region, to Schönebeck in spring 1942. She worked in an ammunition factory but was sent to a concentration camp following a failed escape attempt. She was imprisoned in both Auschwitz and Mauthausen. (Interview, Zaporozhye, 2002)

Muzalyova (née Ped'ko), **Hanna Nikitichna**, d.o.b. 1924. Deported from Novosyolka, Kharkov region, to Bad Tölz in August 1943. She worked in a kitchen. (Memoir, Alupka, Crimea, 1990)

Nefyodova, Raissa Alexandrovna, d.o.b. 1928. Deported from the village of Ukrainka, Kirovograd region, to Strasbourg in June 1943. She worked in a food factory. (Interview, Astrakhan, 2006)

Novgorodov, Vadim Leonidovich, d.o.b. 1923. Deported from Taganrog to Bochum in May 1942. He worked in a number of mines and at a coke processing plant. (Interview, Taganrog, 2005)

Novokhatko, Lavrenty Afanasevich, d.o.b. 1925. Deported from Seletskoye, Dnepropetrovsk region, to Neudietendorf in June 1942. He worked on the railways. He was charged with sabotage and sent to a concentration camp – imprisoned in Linz, Gusen-I and Gusen-II. (Interview, Nikopol, 2002)

Odinokova (née Protiven'), **Anna Yefimovna**, d.o.b. 1925. She was deported from the village of Dubovichy, Chernigov region, to Żagań in June 1943. She worked for a farmer. (Interview, Penza, 2006)

Odolinskaya, Nina Fominichna, d.o.b. 1920. Departed from Odessa in April 1942. She lived in Töpchin, Potsdam and Fichtengrund. She worked in a chemical factory, in a hairdressing salon and as a domestic helper. Following her return to the Soviet Union, she was a prisoner at the Norillag, Rechlag and Gorlag camps (Gulag) from 1945 to 1955. (Memoir, Odessa, 1989)

Osipov, Leonid Pavlovich, d.o.b. 1930. Deported from Khuralevo, Gomel region, to Dessau in April 1944. He worked at a munitions factory. (Interview, Astrakhan, 2006)

Palko (née Berlina), **Frida Leibovna**, d.o.b. 1927. Imprisoned in the Starodub ghetto. She escaped and, after changing her surname, was deported from the village of Klintsy, Bryansk region, to Ludwigsdorf in April 1942. She worked at a chemical factory, on a farm, and as a domestic helper. (Interview, Perm, 2005)

Pervina, Raissa Iosifovna, d.o.b. 1921. Deported from Baranovichy, Brest region, to the outskirts of Bremen (via a distribution camp in Soltau) in spring 1942. She worked for a farmer and later at an aviation factory in Delmenhorst. Following her return to the Soviet Union, she was sent to a labour camp in the Komi Republic from 1947 to 1951. (Interview, Moscow, 1989)

Pudyakova, Maria. Deported from the Pskov region in May 1942.

Rozhkova (née Vanglinskaya), **Neonila Konstantinovna**, d.o.b. 1926. Deported from Korvinovka, Zhytomyr region, to Guttenberg in 1943. She worked in a potato factory and a munitions factory but was accused of subversive behaviour and sent to a concentration camp. She was imprisoned in both Auschwitz and Mauthausen. (Interview, Aleksandriya, Kirovograd region, 2002)

Savenko (née Protsenko), **Tatiana Vasilyevna**, d.o.b. 1924. Deported from the village of Bashmachka, Dnepropetrovsk region, to Gdynia. She worked on the railways, for a farmer and at a brick factory. (Letter, Bashmachka, 1991)

Savranskaya, Yevgenia Leonidovna, d.o.b. 1920. Deported from Krolevets, Sumy region, in summer 1942. She worked in factories in Falkensee and Berlin and also worked for a farmer in Świebodzin. (Interview, Moscow, 1991)

Sechkina (née Morozova), **Anna Ivanovna**, d.o.b. 1923. Deported from the village of Volodarskoye, Leningrad region, to Eastern Prussia. She worked for a farmer. (Memoir, St Petersburg, 1997)

Sekhina (née Svinukhova), **Valentina Romanovna**, d.o.b. 1925. Deported from Stalino to the outskirts of Breslau in August 1942. She worked for a farmer but was sent to a concentration camp following a failed escape attempt. She was imprisoned in both Ravensbrück and Mauthausen. (Interview, Donetsk, 2002)

Selivanova (née Soklokova), **Tamara Timofeevna**, d.o.b. 1925. Deported from Simferopol to Frankfurt am Main in 1942. She worked as a housemaid for the director of the Torpedo-Werk enterprise. (Memoir, Alupka, 1990)

Serdyukova, Antonina Mikhailovna, d.o.b. 1925. Deported from Stalingrad to Lauta in September 1942. She worked in the Lautawerk aluminium-vanadium factory. (Interview, Perm, 2005)

Shalankova, Galina Vasilyevna, d.o.b 1924. Born in the Ordzhonikidze region. Deported from Seredyna-Buda to Berlin in March 1942. She worked at a coal-processing plant near Wittenberg. (Interview, 2005)

Shchebetyuk, Vladimir Vasilyevich, d.o.b. 1926. Deported from Isakovtsy, Kamenets-Podolsk region, to Austria in March 1942. He worked for a farmer but was sent to Mauthausen concentration camp following a failed escape attempt. (Interview, Khotyn, Chernovitsy region, 2002)

Sherenkova (née Nagornaya), **Vera Antonovna**, d.o.b. 1922. Deported from the Northern Caucasus to Kalsdorf bei Graz in summer 1942. She worked for a farmer. (Interview, St Petersburg, 2005)

Shkulyova (née Sedova), **Lyubov Mikhailovna**, d.o.b. 1926. Deported from Kirovograd to Osterfeld in September 1942. She worked on a crane at the Krupp factory but was sent to Dachau concentration camp having been accused of spreading anti-Hitler propaganda. (Memoir, St Petersburg, 1993 and interview, St Petersburg, 2002)

Shpakova (née Fomichova), **Yadviga Georgievna**. Deported from Vitebsk to Bad Rappenau in 1944. She worked on the railways. (Letter, Vitebsk, 1990)

Shtepa, Anna Petrovna, d.o.b. 1923. Deported from Rostov-on-Don to Meschede in October 1942. She worked in a munitions factory. (Interview, Rostov-on-Don, 2005)

Shuldeshov, Victor Vasilyevich, d.o.b. 1929. Deported from Kryukovo, Kursk region, to Leipzig in spring 1942. He worked in the smelting workshop at the Marion factory. (Interview, Perm, 2005)

Shvidchenko (née Samokhvalova), **Larisa Mikhailovna**, d.o.b. 1926. Deported from Rostov-on-Don to Düsseldorf in September 1942. She worked in munitions production. (Interview, Astrakhan, 2006)

Sivoded, Galina Karpovna, d.o.b. 1917. Arrested in March 1943 on suspicion of having involvement with the Partisans. Deported from the village of Tsarkud, Zaporozhye region, to Mauthausen concentration camp. (Interview, Zaporozhye, 2002)

Sizova (née Pavlova), **Antonina Alexandrovna**, d.o.b. 1924. Deported alongside her mother and brother from Gdov, Pskov region, to Leipzig in summer 1943. (Memoir, St Petersburg, 1997)

Skiba (née Shagan), **Domnikiya Karpovna**, d.o.b. 1919. Deported from the village of Zasluchnoe, Kamenets-Podolsk region, to

Innsbruck in April 1942. She worked as a domestic helper, at an aviation factory, and at a post office. She was sent to a concentration camp for a breach of discipline. She was imprisoned in both Ravensbrück and Mauthausen. (Interview, Krasilov, Khmelnitsky region, 2002)

Smirnova, Olga Ippolitovna, d.o.b. 1923. Deported from Lyuban, Leningrad region, to Stuttgart in 1942. She worked in the Siemens factory but was sent to Ravensbrück concentration camp following a failed escape attempt. (Interview, St Petersburg, 2005)

Sokolova, Irina Nikolaevna, d.o.b. 1923. Deported from the village of Perevolochna, Chernigov region, to Freising in June 1942. She worked for several different families as a domestic helper. (Interview, Moscow, 1992)

Stanyeva, Lyudmila Dmitrievna, d.o.b. 1926. Deported from Haichur station, Zaporozhye region, in July 1943. She was charged with affiliation to the Partisans and sent to a concentration camp. She was imprisoned in both Auschwitz and Mauthausen. (Interview, Zaporozhye, 2002)

Stefanenko, Dina Yevstafyevna, d.o.b. 1920. Deported from Zaporozhye to Frankfurt am Main in 1942. She worked in an automotive factory but was sent to a concentration camp for a breach of discipline. She was imprisoned in both Auschwitz and Ravensbrück. (Interview, St Petersburg, 2005)

Teplova, Tatiana Arkhipovna, d.o.b. 1927. Deported alongside her mother and sister from the village of Griva, Kalinin region, in February 1943. She worked on the railways. (Interview, Moscow, 2006)

Tkachov, Georgiy Gavrilovich, d.o.b. 1928. Deported from Novocherkassk in October 1942. He worked on a farm, and in factories in Stettin and Berlin. (Interview, Novocherkassk, 2005)

Tokarev, Lev Petrovich, d.o.b. 1928. Deported from Peterhof, Leningrad region, to Reichenbach in 1942. He worked for a farmer and at a munitions factory. He was arrested in 1947 and sentenced to six years in a corrective labour camp in Russia. (Memoir, St Petersburg, 2000, and interview, St Petersburg, 2005)

Tolkachova, Taissa Vasilyevna, d.o.b. 1924. Deported from Genichesk to Seebach in May 1942. She worked in a munitions factory. (Interview, Penza, 2005)

Tsibulkin, Konstantin Konstantinovich, d.o.b. 1925. Arrested in Dnepropetrovsk in September 1943 for spreading anti-Hitler propaganda. He was sent to Mauthausen and Ebensee concentration camps. (Interview, Nikopol, 2002)

Ulanovskaya, Antonina Emelyanovna, d.o.b. 1927. Deported from Shterovka station, Voroshilovgrad region, to Weener in October 1942. She worked in a munitions factory. (Diary, Weener, Lower Saxony, 1942–4)

Vaindel, Albert Alexandrovich, d.o.b. 1927. Deported from Kerch to Weiz in late 1943. He worked at an electrical factory. (Interview, Kerch, 2012)

Valikhova, Zinaida, d.o.b. 1924. Deported September 1942 from Saky to Gladbeck. She worked in a glass factory. (Interview, Amsterdam, 1990)

Vasilkovskaya, Lyudmila Dmitrevna, d.o.b. 1923. Lived through occupation in the Poltava region, before being sent to the Minlag labour camp in Inta from 1948 to 1954. (Interview, Odessa, 2011)

Vatman, Irina Yakovlevna, d.o.b. 1934. Imprisoned in the Odessa ghetto. (Interview, Moscow, 2005)

Verkholantseva (née Petrova), **Yevdokiya Panteleevna**, d.o.b. 1926. Deported from the village of Kuzhaevo, Pskov region, to the outskirts of Stuttgart in March 1942. She worked for a farmer. (Interview, Perm, 2005)

Veselovskaya, Tatiana, d.o.b. 1928. Deported from Novo-Troitskoye, Zaporozhye region, in summer 1942. She worked in a rubber factory in Düsseldorf and then a photography factory in Leverkusen. (Interview, Moscow, 1990)

Vishnevskiy, Vladimir Grigorievich, d.o.b. 1924. Deported from Petlyuvka, Kamenets-Podolsk region, to Enns in April 1942. He worked for a farmer but was sent to Mauthausen concentration camp following an escape attempt. (Interview, Kamenets-Podolsk, 2002)

Vitkevich (née Drozdova), **Maria Ivanovna**, d.o.b. 1924. Deported from Krasnoye Selo, Leningrad district, to Berlin in January 1944. Worked as a domestic helper. She was sentenced to ten years in a labour camp on her return, which she spent in the Norillag labour camp (1945–55). (Interview, St Petersburg, 2005, 2012)

Vladimirova (née Il'yachova), **Antonina Nikolaevna**, d.o.b. 1921. Deported from Cherkessk to Munich in December 1942. She worked at a warehouse and a tank factory. (Memoir, St Petersburg, 2000 and interview, St Petersburg, 2005)

Volobueva, Maria Ivanovna, d.o.b. 1924. Deported from Dnepropetrovsk to Rothensee in June 1943. She worked on the railways. (Letter, Dnepropetrovsk, 1991)

Volynskaya, Aldona Vladimirovna, d.o.b. 1926. Deported from the village of Novoukrainka, Kirovograd region, in autumn 1942. She worked at an aerodrome in Cologne and then as a domestic helper in Wernigerode and Magdeburg. She was arrested by the

Soviet SMERSH and imprisoned from May until August 1947. (Memoirs, Moscow, 1990)

Voronin, Vasily Gavrilovich, d.o.b. 1927. Deported from Kamenka, Voronezh region, to Bremen in December 1942. He worked in the Focke-Wulf aviation factory. (Interview, Synel'nykove, Dnepropetrovsk region, 2002)

Yakovleva, Galina Arkadyevna, d.o.b. 1925. Arrested in Staraya Russa and sent to Ravensbrück concentration camp. (Memoir, St Petersburg, 1998)

Yanovskaya (née Krainyaya), **Valentina Stepanovna**. Deported from Krasnodar Krai to Berlin. She worked in a munitions factory. (Letter, Novocherkassk, 1990)

Yeliseeva (née Tsigurova), **Zoya Petrovna**, d.o.b. 1926. Deported from Dzhankoy in June 1942. She worked in textile factories in both Kassel and Netzschkau. (Memoirs, Alupka, Crimea, 1990)

Yerastova (née Balyuta), **Lidia Ivanovna**, d.o.b. 1927. Deported from Merefa, Kharkov region, to Artern in summer 1943. She worked on the railways. From 1947 to 1952 she was a prisoner at the Sevzheldorlag (Northern Railway Labour Camp). (Memoirs, St Petersburg, 2000, and interview, St Petersburg, 2012)

Yermilova (née Morozova), **Anna Matveevna**, d.o.b. 1927. She was deported in November 1943 from the Minsk region to a work camp in Hamburg. (Interview, Astrakhan, 2006)

Yerokhova (née Polivodova), **Lyubov Nikolaevna**, d.o.b. 1924. Deported from Pustoshka, Pskov region, in November 1941. She worked for a farmer in the village of Gardeja in Eastern Prussia. (Memoirs, Pustoshka village, Pskov region, 1990)

Zapirin, Ivan Dmitrievich, d.o.b. 1924. Deported from the Novozlatopil district, Zaporozhye region, to Magdeburg in August 1942. He worked in a factory recycling raw materials. He was sent to a concentration camp after a failed escape attempt and imprisoned in both Sachsenhausen and Mauthausen. (Interview, Volgograd, 2002)

Zerkal, Mikhail Alexeevich, d.o.b. 1925. Deported from Mezhova, Dnepropetrovsk region, to Essen in June 1943. He worked in several mines. (Letter, Vesyoloye, Dnepropetrovsk region, 1991)

Zhabsky, Victor Stepanovich, d.o.b. 1928. Deported from Novocherkassk to Allendorf in October 1942. He worked in a munitions factory and a tobacco factory in Koblenz. He also worked as a field engineer in Trier and Leipzig. (Interview, Novocherkassk, 2005)

Zhelamskaya (née Skarina), **Tatiana Andreevna**, d.o.b. 1922. Deported from the village of Ruda, Pskov region, to Danzig in March 1942. She worked on a farm and as a domestic helper. (Memoir, Pustoshka, Pskov region, 1990)

Zhukova, Iraida Fedorovna, d.o.b. 1932. Deported with her mother from Krasnoye Selo, Leningrad region, to Lithuania in August 1942, and later sent to Austria. She worked for a farmer. (Interview, Krasnoye Selo, 2003)

Zimnitskaya (née Khudobkina), **Olga Timofeevna**, d.o.b. 1932. Deported from the Smolensk region in 1942 alongside her mother and brother. She was imprisoned at Auschwitz concentration camp before being sent to a children's camp in Lodz in 1944. (Interview, St Petersburg, 2005)

Zubkov, Nikolai Ivanovich, d.o.b. 1925. Deported from Stalingrad to Linz in the summer of 1942. He was sent to a concentration camp following a failed escape attempt. He was imprisoned at Gusen concentration camp, Linz and Mauthausen. Following liberation he was mobilised into the Labour Army. (Interview, Volzhskiy, Volgograd region, 2002)

Interviews conducted by employees of International Memorial:

Moscow: Tatiana Askeri, Kirill Vasilenko, Lyudmila Kabanova, Alyona Kozlova, Irina Ostrovskaya, Grigory Shvedov, Irina Scherbakova.

Memorial Scientific Information Centre of St Petersburg: Yulia Belozerova, Yulia Karpenko, Nadezhda Kiselyova, Tatiana Morgachova, Anna Rezinkova.

Acknowledgements

The Memorial International (Международный Мемориал) publishing programme.

Edited by Alexander Daniel, Larisa Yeryomina, Elena Zhemkova, Tatiana Kasatkina, Nikita Okhotin, Yan Rachinsky and Arseny Roginsky.

Thanks to the following for their help in the production of this book: Elena Bagdasarova, Marina Golubovskaya, Elena Zhemkova, Galina Iordanskaya, Nikita Lomakin, Marina Rodionova, Ilya Saratovsky, Tatiana Safronova, Svetlana Tsibulskaya and Maria Shilova.

Special thanks to Natalya Korneeva and the Agey Tomesh publishing house, Maria Polyakova and Individuum Publishing, and Arseny Roginsky for reading the manuscripts and making many valuable observations.

Our thanks to Dimitry Zimina and the Heinrich Böll Foundation for their constant support of Memorial's archive.

This book* was published with the support of the Heinrich Böll Foundation.

* Translator's note: The original Russian edition.

Memorial: Retaining Our Memory of History

Memorial is an international historical and educational charity, set up in 1988 on a groundswell of public opinion from different generations. Its supporters had very varied biographies, and sometimes divergent political outlooks. They were not only former political prisoners and their families, but young people and others in favour of establishing a democratic state under the rule of law.

Memorial's first chairman was Academician Andrey Sakharov. Today, Memorial is a network of dozens of organisations in Russia, Germany, Italy, France, the Czech Republic and Ukraine who conduct research and educational work and defend human rights. In 1991, on Memorial's initiative and with the society's participation, a law was passed on the rehabilitation of victims of political repression. It declared 30 October a Day of Remembrance of Victims of Political Repression.

From the outset, Memorial has considered one of its principal tasks to be the creation of a tradition of informed remembrance of political repression in the USSR. An essential part of this work has been collecting and preserving the testimony of over 12 million people persecuted during the Stalin era. In the course of thirty years, Memorial has established the only systematic public archive of its kind in Russia: museum holdings, collections of documents, and a specialised library.

Another aspect of the work is restoring and making publicly available the identities and biographies of victims. A Book of Remembrance provides the foundation for an electronic database of more than three million victims of political repression.

Memorial organises discussions directly related to remembrance and analysis of current policy towards history.

The charity is constantly studying not only the means of transmitting historical memory from generation to generation, but actively encouraging this by organising a nationwide history essay competition for older school students on the topic of 'Man in History: Russia in the Twentieth Century'.

Memorial sees scholarly and research work as an integral part of its mission. Among its main projects are:

> – creating maps of the Gulag and a definitive work describing the Gulag system;
>
> – creating reference works giving the biographies of the organisers and perpetrators of the Terror;
>
> – studying the role and significance of social-democratic opposition to the Stalin regime;
>
> – researching the administrative structure and statistics of the Terror;
>
> – studying sites associated with the topography of the Terror;
>
> – studying family memories of the Terror;
>
> – monitoring museum collections relevant to the history of the Gulag;
>
> – studying the fate of different national and religious groups of victims of political repression.

Memorial's archival and museum collections

Memorial's archive began acquiring materials from the very inception of the society in 1988, when victims of repression, their relatives and friends began passing documents, photographs and manuscript memoirs from their family archives to the movement's activists. The archive consists of several themed collections.

Archive of the History of Political Repression in the USSR, 1917–56

The backbone of this collection is personal files of people who were persecuted: shot, sentenced to prison camp terms, exiled, or 'dekulakised' in the case of more prosperous peasants. The collection contains in excess of 60,000 personal archives. These consist of such materials directly related to the persecution as originals and copies of official arrest warrants, records of searches; pages from archival, criminal, prison camp or surveillance files; notifications of sentence, death certificates, certificates of release and rehabilitation; and such personal documents as lists of parcels sent to prisons and camps, and appeals by prisoners and relatives for a review of their case. There are also documents from the period of detention: character references, poetry, posters for camp amateur performances, certificates of good behaviour, home-made cards, sheet music, and personal notes.

Correspondence between prisoners and their families is of particular interest. This includes not only officially authorised correspondence, read and often with deletions by the censor, but also letters passed to the outside world illegally: snatches of news from prison trains in transit, notes scrawled on fabric or cigarette paper and hidden in the seams of clothing or in buttons. The personal files also contain documents from before arrest: birth certificates, school-leaving and degree certificates, membership cards of various organisations, service records, diplomas and award certificates, letters, family and work photographs, and the like.

Memoir and Literary Works Collection

The Memoir and Literary Works Collection contains over 1,000 files and represents a unique source of personal testimony about life in the USSR in the twentieth century, about arrests, investigations, camps, and exiles (the latter reflecting the entire history and geography of the Gulag). In addition to memoirs, the archive includes collections of letters, diaries, sketches and articles, and literary and journalistic works. Most of these texts have never been published.

Archive of the 'Victims of Two Dictatorships' Programme

This archive of materials, on the fate of Soviet people deported to perform forced labour in Germany during the Second World War, contains some 400,000 case files. Many of these people were subjected to harassment and persecution when they returned to the USSR. The files contain biographical information, letters and memoirs, documents issued by the German administration;

documentation of their passage through 'filtration' when they were repatriated; data from Soviet state and ministry archives, as well as from the International Tracing Service of the Red Cross; personal papers (photographs, letters and postcards from Germany and filtration camps).

A database on individuals has been compiled, drawing on the archive's holdings, which, among other things, gives information on where *Ostarbeiter*, slave labourers from the East, lived and worked in Nazi Germany.

Archive of the History of Dissidence in the USSR, 1953–87

Memorial's collection of documents on the history of dissidence in the post-Stalin era is the largest in Russia and one of the most extensive in the world. It comprises 125 holdings and collections, as well as archives of photos and collections of rare publications which appeared in very limited editions.

The holding comprises some 400,000 sheets. These include a collection of Samizdat works assembled by Memorial International. Personal collections and archives include letters, diaries, memoirs, drafts of articles, and other working materials of prominent dissidents, totalling about 100 personal files. The archive contains photocopies of around 13,000 index cards of prisoners sentenced in the 1950s to 1980s for political and dissident activities. The collection is an important source for research into oppositional social and political activity and the repressive policies of the USSR during this period. Samizdat and other materials connected with dissidence come in a variety of shapes and forms: typescripts, photocopies, home-made albums with illustrations. Some are truly unique: a letter from exile typed on cloth, a tape recording made secretly in the camp, and so on. The collection also contains some 5,000 photographs.

The Centre for Oral History and Biography

The Centre has ongoing projects on Women's Memories of the Gulag and Children of 'Algeria' [the Akmolinsk Camp for Wives of Traitors to the Fatherland, opened in January 1938], which have recordings of some 300 interviews, as well as thousands of documents, photographs, memoirs, letters and diaries, depicting the fate of wives of 'traitors to the fatherland', who were sent off to the camps, and of their children, who were placed in 'orphanages'. The collected materials and, in particular, the oral evidence, enable us to trace how the history of mothers dispatched to the Gulag affected the biography and destiny of their children, and to reassess the traumatic experience of families under the Soviet system.

In the course of the projects Survivors of Mauthausen, and Forced Labour in National Socialist Germany, about 300 audio and video interviews were recorded with former prisoners of concentration camps and *Ostarbeiter*, which portray the tragic vicissitudes of these people during the war and their long experience of discrimination in the post-war era.

The Memorial Museum Collection

The Memorial Museum Collection began to be formed as early as 1988. Along with documents, relatives of the persecuted brought memorabilia, drawings and photographs for safekeeping by Memorial, and in 1990 a museum was set up. The main source of acquisitions was families of the persecuted, which had kept relics, paintings and drawings; some of the exhibits were acquired on expeditions to the sites of former camps. The museum currently houses some 6,000 items. With 1,500 exhibits, this is the world's largest collection of works created in captivity. The greater part of the collection is paintings and drawings by imprisoned artists: genre drawings, portraits, interiors, landscapes, and sketches for scenery and costumes for productions in the camp theatres. Some of them are by famous artists who ended up in the camps and in exile.

Closely related to the museum collection are some 12,000 works in the photograph archive. These are originals or copies of documentary photographs depicting the history of political repression in the USSR from the 1920s to the 1980s, the life and labour of the prisoners of the Gulag, the everyday life of the USSR, and Soviet propaganda.

ADDRESS:

Memorial International
5/10 Karetny Ryad,
Moscow 127006
Russia
tel. (+7 495) 650 7883
e-mail: nipc@memo.ru
websites: www.memo.ru;
www.urokiistorii.ru